PREACHERS AND PEOPLE IN THE REFORMATIONS
AND EARLY MODERN PERIOD

PREACHERS AND PEOPLE IN THE REFORMATIONS AND EARLY MODERN PERIOD

EDITED BY

LARISSA TAYLOR

BRILL
LEIDEN · BOSTON · KÖLN
2001

Illustration on the cover: Painting of an early seventeenth-century church service (1624) by Pieter de Bloot. © Copyright: Museum Catharijneconvent, Utrecht, The Netherlands.

BV
4208
.E85
P74
2001

This book is printed on acid-free paper.

Library of Congress Cataloging-in-Publication Data

The Library of Congress Cataloging-in-Publication data is also available.

Die Deutsche Bibliothek - CIP-Einheitsaufnahme

Preachers and people in the reformations and early modern period / ed. by Larissa Taylor. – Leiden ; Boston ; Köln : Brill, 2001.
ISBN 90-04-11564-1

ISBN   90 04 11564 1

To my mother and father:
Taffy and Paul Steiner

TABLE OF CONTENTS

PART THREE

PREACHING AND THE GEOGRAPHY OF
THE REFORMATIONS

PREFACE

Larissa Taylor
(Colby College)

> For as the rain and the snow come
>   down from heaven,
> and do not return there until
>   they have watered
>   the earth,
> making it bring forth and sprout,
>   giving seed to the sower and
>   bread to the eater,
> So shall my word be that goes out
>   from my mouth;
> it shall not return to me empty
> but it shall accomplish that which
>   I purpose
> and succeed in the thing for which I sent it.
> *(Isaiah 55:10-11)*

Neither this book, nor many like it, could have been written two decades ago. Although sermons have proven an invaluable source for our knowledge of religious history and sociology, anthropology, and social prescription, they were until recently either ignored entirely or studied solely for their literary merits (or lack thereof). Happily, so much has changed in the field of sermon studies that not only is there an entire society dedicated to it – The International Medieval Sermon Studies Society – but books, monographs, and articles are now so plentiful that it is impossible even to provide a short overview of the most important works.

What has changed? The simple answer is that history has changed. What was started half a century ago by Marc Bloch and Lucien Febvre – history as a discipline that combined the study of all disciplines in a time and place – has been taken much further than even they would have anticipated. Religious sociology, pioneered by Gabriel LeBras in his *Etudies de sociologie religieuse* and *Sociologie et religion*, has been taken further by historians of *mentalités* such as Jean Delumeau. In like manner, religious anthropologists such as William Christian and Jean-Claude Schmitt have profoundly altered our understanding of the mental landscape of the medieval and early modern man and woman. They have provided us with detailed knowledge of religious inquiries, visitation reports, criminal and inquisitorial proceedings, and folk practices. It was only natural in a climate that fostered the use of non-traditional sources in non-traditional ways that historians and religious scholars would begin to mine sermons for the information they can provide about what was taught and to some degree practiced by the people of pre-modern Europe. With monographs on individuals or groups of preachers, works of religious anthropology/ sociology and regional studies, used alongside more conventional sources such as memoirs, chronicles, and letters, we are now in a position to at least begin to understand the social history of preaching in the past. There are questions we will never be able to answer – how did an individual process the preached message from the pulpit? How exactly do written sermons duplicate the preached Word? Do they at all? Many different answers have been given to these questions, but the simple fact that they are being asked tells us a great deal about how our knowledge of religious history has changed.

This volume will attempt to provide some answers and will, I hope, lead to more questions. Because of space limitations, it is impossible to do an all-encompassing study of preaching in the Reformations and early modern period in Europe. The focus is on Catholic, Lutheran, and Reformed preaching. Geographically, it has been limited to western and central Europe. Discussions with colleagues in recent years have also convinced me that what was true for one region at a given time was by no means the case for another region at the same time. So this volume will not set forth sweeping generalizations about the social history of preaching in pre-modern Europe. Nor have the chapters followed a "set" format. Because of differences due to time and place, each of the leading scholars who has contributed to this book has approached the material and covered an appropriate time frame in his or her own way.

Part One deals with "The Sermon as Genre." Because there have been many studies of the changing nature of homiletics in the period, I wanted to allow each contributor who was studying the social history of a given country to be able to focus on the aspects of it that interest them most. Therefore, the three chapters that comprise Part One concentrate on the changes in sermon structure, style and content in Christian sermons.

In Chapter One, Thomas Worcester, S.J., provides an overview of how the Catholic sermon changed from the late medieval period to the Renaissance and as a result of the Catholic Reform and Tridentine preaching aims. The thematic sermon so typical of the Middle Ages, exemplified in the preaching of Bernardino of Siena, gave way in the sixteenth century (and earlier in some areas) to a wide variety of preaching styles that attempted to embody the goals of humanist eloquence alongside the Augustinian ideal of preaching to move, persuade, and delight. Yet Trent also emphasized the need for plain speaking. What was new was an emphasis on the bishop's role as a preacher – he was no longer to be the distant, indeed sometimes unknown appointee to a profitable diocese, but a model for priests and parishioners alike. Through preaching, he could set forth his goals for the diocese and ensure that they were carried out. But as Worcester demonstrates persuasively, Catholic preaching after Trent was not monolithic; rather than being uniform and intolerant, it was a hybrid of forms past and present, interpreted as needed to particular situations. Along with diversification of the genre came diversity of content.

In her study of "Lutheran Sermons," Beth Kreitzer argues that the sermon is "…the most significant genre of literature stemming from the Lutheran Reformation." This might seem self-evident to generalists but in the past, treatises, broadsheets, and pamphlets have received as much, if not more, attention. Kreitzer's point is well taken: for European culture, despite the changes wrought by the printing press, remained overwhelmingly oral. Yet the sermon was transformed by the printing press, as Luther and his followers used the new medium to help spread the message of the gospel to as wide an audience as possible. Lutheran preachers of the first generation were concerned to clarify doctrine in simple language and offer comfort and hope, while helping "…their audience…interpret and properly value the world around them." This was a significant change, as pre-Reformation preachers, however prominent, published their sermons for use by other members of the clergy, not to be read by (or to) the public at large. Beginning with Luther and tracing developments through Melanchthon, Kreitzer shows how homiletic theory developed. Melanchthon divided the classical *genus deliberativum*, the hortatory model, into 1) exhortations to faith and 2) how to lead the proper moral life. Melanchthon's homiletic treatises would become the standard for Lutheran preachers in the early modern period. Yet in the process a new orthodoxy, sometimes rigid, developed that unwittingly encouraged pietistic preaching. But for most of the early modern era, Lutheran sermons were intended to transform the worship service based on the exegesis of Scripture through a new form and method.

James Ford examines the "Reformed Tradition" in Chapter Three. As the centerpiece of Reformed worship, the expository sermon, often given on a daily basis with a continuing exegesis, was designed to communicate the tenets of the faith in terms that the laity could understand. More so perhaps than their Lutheran counterparts, Reformed sermons were embedded not only in the context of daily life, but became an integral part of society and culture. Favoring a literal/historical method, preachers often improvised, which may well account for the paucity of extant Reformed sermons, aside from those of Calvin. The style that resulted was simple, based on practical exposition, although it was not unstructured. The "plain style" thus dominated, for Reformed preachers did not want to dazzle their congregations but to change them. Still, it was not long before such preachers realized the need for "color," and began to see oratory as the means to that end. Homiletic handbooks increasingly appeared, the most famous of which was Hyperius's *De formandis concionibus sacris* of 1553 and Hemmingsen's *Evangelie Postil* of 1561.

Part Two is concerned with the social history of preaching in many countries or regions of Europe. Limitations of space and vast differences in content made it impossible to cover all of Europe in this period. There is, however, one outstanding *lacuna*–Spain. Unfortunately, the contributor who was scheduled to write the chapter on the Iberian Peninsula was unable to complete it, and we were not able to find a suitable replacement. The contributor's chapter would have covered the entire Iberian peninsula, for it is an anachronism to speak of "Spain" as a single entity in this period. The author had hoped to trace the transition from the *ars praedicandi* style of preaching through the revival of classical rhetoric and that of the Jesuit *ratio studiorum*, in the process demonstrating how a change in method influenced a change in content and response. He had hoped to tie sermons to "related spiritual trends" in Iberia such as spiritual Franciscanism, Erasmianism, and illuminism. Preaching was the means both to spread and control the faith as well as a vehicle for propaganda and demonstration of civic, political, and religious power. The author had also planned to look at how the civil wars of the late medieval period influenced preaching in political, geographical, and religious directions–turning the mission outward to the world at large. We are very disappointed not to have such an important chapter in this book, but at least some of the material is covered in the chapter on "The Catholic Sermon" and in chapters on regions which remained predominantly Catholic.

My chapter, "Dangerous Vocations," covers the country that was most deeply divided over religious issues in the sixteenth century–France. I have limited my coverage to the period of greatest drama, to that in which the social history of preaching is most obviously on display–from the late Middle Ages to the assassination of Henri IV in 1610. Preaching was indeed dangerous for both Catholics and Calvinists. In the period before the Religious Wars, it was often the preacher himself who was at greatest risk of palpable harm at the hands of kings and social elites angry at the message, or after the "Reformed" faith spread, by members of the other confession. After the beginning of the Religious Wars, however, and especially in the last years of Henri III and the period of intense civil war from 1589-1594, it was most typically the preachers–Protestant and Calvinist alike–who incited, or at the very least suggested, violence to their hearers. The violence usually took one of two forms–the first was perpetrated on human beings, and while no confession had a monopoly on death, the evidence has shown that Catholics in France were more likely to kill people. By contrast, Calvinists were more likely to attack holy objects, smash statues, and destroy altars, as Natalie Zemon Davis has shown. Yet we must understand that to sixteenth-century people, each faith saw the other as the cause of dangerous pollution that threatened the body social and religious. Trampling on the eucharistic host was, for a Catholic, as blasphemous or more so than the killing of a person. It is only within this context that the fanatical preachers of the League and their somewhat less zealous predecessors can be understood. Nor should we generalize–there were, even in the worst of times, preachers who called for conciliation, and men and women who protected those of the other faith. As the century wore on, the calls became more urgent, leading to the success of the once reviled *politique* movement and ultimately to the growth of absolutism with one king, one law, and one faith.

In Chapter Five, Corrie Norman examines the social history of preaching in the Italian peninsula. Norman shows that in the late medieval period, preaching involved "everyone," with its goal an expression of the divine and sacred power. This was at the heart of the power to transform. Norman invokes an important point – the degree to which Italian preaching was a "home-grown" product. Indeed, it is hard to find much in common in the social history of preaching in France and Italy during this period. This was partly due to the differences between northern and southern attitudes; partly it was due to the influence of civic life and Renaissance ideals. Preaching was thus a form of cultural representation described best by the maxim "continuity with change." Using accounts and itineraries of preaching, diaries, and devotional manuals to supplement her study, Norman looks at how the preacher went about his task of changing people's lives – or trying to. After a study of every aspect of the preaching of numerous men, she sums up her chapter with a quotation that exemplifies the degree to which preaching was the product of a given social milieu, and hence collective rather than singular. Sermons were both representative and not.

Susan Karant-Nunn explores "Preaching the Word in Early Modern Germany" in Chapter Six. She points to the revival of late medieval piety as a major reason for the later passion for direct access to the Word. This, according to Karant-Nunn, and fitting well with representations in art and ritual, was a manifestation of self-confidence. As the Lutheran Reformation made headway, there was an increasing call for a certain uniformity of practice, a practical necessity in view of the coexistence of Catholic, Lutheran, and radical beliefs in the Empire. Karant-Nunn traces the actual schedule assigned by Saxon visitors in 1529 that was intended to ensure adequate and correct preaching. Orthodoxy – both Lutheran and non-Lutheran – became more rather than less important as doctrinal strife increased. The preacher was to persuade his audience, but also to serve as its moral guardian. Karant-Nunn explores here and elsewhere how this could affect the most intimate aspects of daily life – in wedding and funeral sermons. She also looks at Catholic preachers in Germany, including the new orders, and how their work both differed from and yet resembled Lutheran preaching, especially in those given for Easter Week. In the age of the Reformations, preaching became a more prominent mode of communication than ever before; it influenced, if it never fully formed, the convictions people held. Sermons also aided communities faced with war and disease, informing people of current events.

In her chapter on preaching in Switzerland, Lee Palmer Wandel discusses the interaction that undoubtedly existed between preachers and active recipients of the Word, people whose reactions were part of their daily experience and innermost feelings and beliefs. She argues that while countless printed and manuscript sermons still exist, they bear "…at best an oblique and indefinite relation to the event of preaching [for] words were and are not fixed entities; an audience brought to a sermon a plethora of experiences, associations, [and] resonances from their individual and collective lives." That being said, Wandel explores preaching in the unique political context that was "Switzerland," a confederation unlike any found elsewhere in Europe. She closely examines Zwingli, who taught his congregation how to hear, and preaching in Zurich. For as the Word was preached, it "acquired sound" – hopefully to be lived out in the community. Other Swiss preachers who followed Zwingli sought, as he had, to bring religious practice, conduct, and government into line with Biblical teaching. It was to be a lived Christianity. Exploring as well preaching in Bern, Geneva, and Anabaptist communities, it becomes clear what Wandel emphasizes from the beginning – that Switzerland *was* different – politically, linguistically, religiously. Preaching took place above all in those communities in which politics promoted a new vision of Christian life and community. Ironically, as divided as Switzerland was in many ways, that vision extended far and wide, in its time and in the centuries that have come after.

In "The Boring of the Ear," Eric Carlson examines how the pastoral vision of preaching was shaped in the century from 1540-1640 in England. Carlson argues that while simplistic notions about medieval preaching must be dismissed, there was major change in practice in the century after the Reformation. Preachers now became the "indispensable agents of salvation," and preaching occupied a more central place in pastoral life than it had before. For men such as Richard Greenham, preaching was part of a "great cosmic drama," which not surprisingly put an awesome burden on the shoulders of the men who carried it out. Preachers had to be

vigilant in calling men and women from lives of sin, a delicate bal-
ancing act to say the least; they also had to recognize that some
would refuse to hear. While reading the Bible was important, it was
not sufficient unto itself – its meaning had to be drawn out as a
sword from its scabbard, the task of the preacher. Yet this was not
the only veriety of preaching. As previous studies from other countries have shown, the best efforts of the reformers often met with
varied success, or a lack of it, in the face of inadequately prepared
clergy and recalcitrant congregations. Some preachers insisted that
preaching was only part of understanding the Word: the church
must also be a house of prayer. Carlson maintains, however, that
while it is a commonplace that the role and prestige of the minister
was diminished in the Elizabethan and Jacobean period, this is simply not true. He suggests that it may have been the Laudians rather
than the first century of Anglicans who reduced the status of the
minister.

    In his study of Scandinavian preaching, Jens Chr. V. Johansen
looks at how the Lutheran Reformation both did and did not
change preaching. Prior to the Reformation, towns had easy access
to the preached Word, but rural areas were not well served; thus
the people of more urbanized Denmark had significantly more opportunities to hear preaching than did their counterparts in Sweden, Finland, and Norway. Seldom do the sermons engage in polemic or deal with church politics; interestingly, however, sorcery
occupies a significant place. In the years after the Reformation,
which was politically sponsored in Scandinavia, sermons were to
have a clear didactic aim. King Gustavus Vasa insisted that preaching should include injunctions about obedience to the authorities,
obviously important in an era of state-building; it is evident that
preachers had few problems with this notion and even solidified it
in their sermons. While German sermons provided examples,
preachers and leaders in the different countries expanded upon the
Lutheran basics that were to be covered in preaching. This largely
exegetical style of preaching concentrated essentially on the themes
of a call for penance and personal reform, the role of the sacraments, and catechesis during childhood. Yet in the end, Johansen
finds that it remained as difficult after the Reformation as before to
capture and retain the attention of the congregation. Still, there
was a definite shift toward the role of the congregation in the act of
worship during the early modern period.

In his study of preaching in the Low Countries, Jelle Bosma begins with medieval preaching, with a focus on Jan Brugman, a man
who had such an impact that the Dutch still have a saying "talking
like Brugman." But Protestantism had a strong and lasting impact
in the Low Countries, and Bosma traces this transition. The church
service itself became more highly regulated and hierarchical. Specific to the Dutch situation was its great variety—numerous denominations, all with their own churches and particular practices in
terms of preaching. Yet central to reform in the Low Countries was
an attack on the monopoly of worship by churchmen, for "any
Christian is as close to God as an ordained priest…" The sermon
thus became an effective weapon in the war of "old" versus "new."
Political differences in the Low Countries produced a remarkably
widespread set of beliefs, and clandestine gatherings of Anabaptists
and radical Protestants with apocalyptic dreams gathered wherever
they could to spread their message. By the 1560s, the situation had
changed dramatically, as international politics impinged directly on
religious practice in the northern Low Countries. Iconoclasm and
hedge-preaching was the signal for Protestants to show their sympa-
thies openly, leading to overt acts of resistance, both political and
religious. With the taking of the town of Brill by the Sea Beggars,
the tide turned definitely in favor of the reformers, at least in the
north. Ultimately this led to Catholicism going underground and
the stripping of the churches in the north; yet as in so many other
areas, Reformed ministers faced serious challenges of their own,
not the least of which were tiny congregations. Preaching had become more important than ever, Bosma asserts, yet fewer people
attended church services. But the chaos that characterized the early
reformed church was replaced in the seventeenth century with increasingly organized forms of worship along with greater participation by the citizenry.

Part Three consists of one very important chapter by Anne
Thayer on "Ramifications of Late Medieval Preaching: Varied
Receptivity to the Protestant Reformation." It may seem peculiar
to end a book on the social history of preaching in the Reformations and early modern period with a chapter that looks at the influence of late medieval preaching, yet I can think of no better
place to end. Thayer has studied countless sermons which she has
broken down into categories that ultimately help us understand the
importance of preaching, its influence on behavior, and the mes-

sage it attempted to inculcate. Most importantly, her study offers one of the few explanations that truly makes sense of why some areas remained Catholic, some became reformed or Lutheran, and others battled over matters of faith and belief. Through her study of model sermon collections, used by most preachers especially after the advent of the printing press, she shows that a diversity of emphasis on how the practice of penance was preached (and received) very likely affected the appeal (or not) of the Lutheran/Reformed message in a given country. Where medieval sermons stressed a rigorist approach, countries were more likely to prove receptive to the Protestant message; where they were absolutionist or mixed, they were more likely to produce either a country that remained largely Catholic or one with a mixed population in terms of belief. If this sounds simplistic, it is not. Having read large numbers of sermons myself, and having pondered the question of how, say, France could be so very different from Germany, I have come to the conclusion that Anne Thayer may have found a very large key, albeit not the only one, to the religious and social appeal of Protestantism in certain parts of Europe.

I owe a great debt to numerous individuals for the production of this volume. First and foremost, credit must go to the senior editor, Julian Deahl, who proposed this project as part of a continuing series and has been a great source of support whenever difficulties arose. Special thanks must go to the individual contributors, without whom this book could never have been produced. It is in the diversity of their approaches and their answers that we can begin to come to an understanding of the social history of preaching. I would like to add my personal thanks to Colby College, which not only gave me a Social Sciences Research Grant to support work on my chapter, but provided library, student support, and other essential services.

PART ONE

THE SERMON AS GENRE

CHAPTER ONE

CATHOLIC SERMONS

Thomas Worcester, S.J.

Introduction

The Franciscan preacher Bernardino of Siena was canonized as a saint in 1450, a mere six years after his death. Bernardino had gained much attention throughout Italy in the first half of the fifteenth century, as he traveled from town to town preaching conversion from vice to virtue to large crowds of people from every class and rank of society. His canonization took place in the same era as the invention of the printing press. If Bernardino's recognition as a saint points to the high regard in which such a preacher could be held, the new technology later gave renewed life to his sermons; printed editions of them circulated in Italy and beyond.

With particular attention to questions of genre and form, this essay will offer an overview of Catholic preaching in the two centuries following the invention of the printing press. It is based on selected primary texts from the early modern era and the abundant scholarship on the history of preaching that has appeared in recent decades. In so doing, I shall focus on ways in which the medieval "thematic" sermon was rivaled, but not altogether eclipsed, by alternate genres of preaching in the era of the Renaissance and Reformation. Other essays in this book will treat Protestant sermons; my concern is with Catholic preaching, already an enormous topic. To keep such a large field of enquiry manageable, I divide it into four parts: Late medieval thematic sermons; Humanism in the pulpit; The Council of Trent on preaching; and Sermons after Trent.

1. *Late Medieval Thematic Sermons*

The "thematic" sermon used a verse of Scripture as a point of departure for amplification of a moral or doctrinal question, topic or theme. Associated with the scholastic method of logic and disputation, this type of discourse was not primarily an explication of a biblical text but a presentation of a theme. Bernardino of Siena (1380-1444) and his generation of preachers inherited this genre of pulpit oratory, a genre that predated them by at least two centuries. In the generation just ahead of Bernardino's, Jean Gerson (1363-1429) stands out.

A theologian and secular priest, Gerson was also Chancellor of the University of Paris. Though at times modified, the basic structure of the thematic sermon is evident in Gerson's many extant sermons: a Scriptural verse as theme, normally from the liturgical texts of the day; a related "protheme," perhaps a prayer or second Scriptural text; then an introduction to the theme and what the preacher is going to do with it; announcement of division of the theme into parts, usually three or four; amplification of the parts, including subdivisions of each; a summary or peroration; and a final exhortation to the congregation.[1] D. Catherine Brown, who includes in her book *Pastor and Laity in the Theology of Jean Gerson* an excellent chapter on Gerson's preaching, stresses his ethical goal: they draw some moral lesson. For Gerson, preachers should seek to move "hearts and affections to love, desire and accomplish the good."[2] Though an academic figure, Gerson was never "dry, pedantic, or abstruse" in his sermons.[3] Brown also asserts that Gerson was "following the medieval tradition in insisting that sermons aim above all at the moral reform of the audience, a tradition brought to a climax by the popular itinerant preachers of the fifteenth century."[4]

While Brown includes Bernardino on her short list of such itinerant preachers, Franco Mormando has recently demonstrated the intolerant, fanatical tenor of this friar's preaching. Pointing out that Bernardino's sermons "faithfully reproduce" the form of the medieval, thematic sermon, Mormando devotes most of his study to showing how themes such as fear of hell and damnation dominate.[5]

---

[1]   D. Catherine Brown, *Pastor and Laity in the Theology of Jean Gerson* (Cambridge: Cambridge University Press, 1987), pp. 12-14.
[2]   Ibid., p. 18.
[3]   Ibid., p. 34.
[4]   Ibid., p. 21.
[5]   Franco Mormando, *The Preacher's Demons: Bernardino of Siena and the Social Underworld of Early Renaissance Italy* (Chicago: University of Chicago Press, 1999), pp. 8-9, 150.

For Bernardino, most especially worthy of hell were witches and sodomites, with Jews not far behind. Bernardino's preaching was a fear-inducing, scapegoating, persecuting discourse, in which plague, famine, and other woes were blamed on the Other.[6] Commenting on the pessimistic tone of Bernardino's preaching, Mormando asserts that his sermons contribute to the "already crumbling portrait of the Italian Renaissance as an optimistic period of intellectual-religious illumination and cultural-scientific progress."[7]

If Bernardino was one of the best-known Franciscan preachers in fifteenth-century Italy, Girolamo Savonarola (1452-98) was surely one of the most famous, or infamous, of Dominican preachers. With an apocalyptic fervor far more intense than that of a Bernardino, Savonarola exhorted the Florentines of the mid-1490s to repent lest the wrath of God strike them down. In his collection of primary texts entitled *The Catholic Reformation: Savonarola to Ignatius Loyola,* John Olin includes a sermon preached by the Dominican friar on January 13, 1495, in the Duomo in Florence; it was first published, in pamphlet form, shortly after. Preaching in a time of war and political upheaval – the French invasions of Italy – Savonarola explains these events as God's "flagellation" of sinners.[8]

This sermon begins with a summary and reminder of the preacher's earlier sermons on the same themes; he had warned his hearers of what was to come if they did not mend their ways, and now those things have come to pass.[9] Savonarola goes on to "demonstrate" ten "reasons" how and why the Church must be renewed, assigning particular urgency to reform of the church in Rome; "see if in Rome the wicked are not always multiplying!"[10] The preacher then turns to Scripture and cites "examples" from the Old and New Testament that show the flagellation to come and the need to renew the Church. To these Savonarola adds an account of his own "visions" of the divine wrath: he had seen a black cross "above the Babylon that is Rome," and upon which was written *Ira Domini* (wrath of the Lord); on this cross "there rained

---

   6   Ibid., pp. 230-31.
   7   Ibid., p. 232.
   8   Girolamo Savonarola, "On the Renovation of the Church," in *The Catholic Reformation: Savonarola to Ignatius Loyola,* ed. John Olin (New York: Fordham University Press, 1992), pp. 1-15.
   9   Ibid., pp. 4-5.
   10   Ibid., p. 6.

swords, knives, lances and every kind of weapon, and a tempest of hailstones and rocks, and awesome and very great flashes of lightning."[11] In another vision, he had seen a quivering sword poised above Italy; dwelling on this threatening image, Savonarola completes the sermon with an ever more urgent appeal for repentance, before it is too late. Shifting to alimentary metaphors, Savonarola declares, "I say to you in conclusion that God has prepared a great dinner for all Italy, but all the foods will be bitter."[12] Yet the image of the sword is the image with which Savonarola leaves his hearers/readers:

> O Italy, O princes of Italy, O prelates of the Church, the wrath of God is over you, and you will not have any cure unless you mend your ways....O noblemen, O powerful ones, O common people.... Do penance while the sword is not out of its sheath, and while it is not stained with blood! Flee from Rome! O Florence! Flee from Florence, that is, flee in order to do penance for your sins, and flee from wicked men![13]

While Florentines of the 1490s were repeatedly exhorted to repent at once lest the imminent, divine wrath strike them down, one may wonder how common such preaching was elsewhere. Was Savonarola a singular fanatic, without peers? Was he, as it were, a Bernardino in a particularly bad mood, but nevertheless atypical of Catholic preachers on the eve of the sixteenth century? What about preaching north of the Alps?

Ian Siggins has studied the question of the kind of preaching Martin Luther (1483-1546) would have heard in his youth, especially in the 1490s.[14] Using volumes of printed, model sermons that enjoyed a wide circulation among parish clergy in Germany c. 1500, Siggins examines the kind of religious culture with which the young Luther was imbued. Siggins relies heavily on the sermons of a Dominican, Johannes Herolt, and of two Franciscans, Johannes Werden and Johannes Gritsch. Their printed sermons were composed in a simple Latin, ready for translation and adaptation to the vernacular. Their "style" was either a didactic and explanatory one,

---

[11] Ibid., p. 9.

[12] Ibid., p. 14.

[13] Ibid., pp. 14-15. For two examples of how Savonarola's preaching was received by his audiences, see Roberto Rusconi, *Predicazione e vita religiosa nella società italiana da Carlo Magno alla Controriforma* (Turin: Loescher, 1981), pp. 217-20.

[14] Ian Siggins, *Luther and his Mother* (Philadelphia: Fortress, 1981), pp. 53-70.

using Scripture passages, other texts, and exemplary stories, to prove a point, or a more persuasive style, in which the practical, moral sense of Scripture (the tropological meaning) was featured, and illustrated with "allusive visual imagery, drawn from nature, the bestiaries, legend, or iconographical tradition."[15]

Siggins argues that two themes dominate these sermons: the salutary awareness of death, and the need for contrition. Such preaching offered its audiences "a catena of warnings on the inevitability and unpredictability of death . . . the ensuing examination in judgment, and the accompanying temptation by demons."[16] Preachers relentlessly exhorted their hearers to "true" contrition, to "utter sincerity and constant, searching sorrow for sin."[17] Siggins argues that such discourses would have produced and encouraged unrelieved anxiety about salvation, and fear of a demanding God; such anxiety is what led Luther, in the midst of a thunderstorm, to make a vow to St. Anne to enter a monastery, if his life were spared.[18]

Though some friars on both sides of the Alps may have preached in this manner, and may have encouraged other preachers to follow suit, was this kind of pulpit terrorism the sole genre of Catholic preaching on the eve of what would become the Protestant Reformation? Were no other themes developed in the "thematic" sermons of the period?

Pelbart of Temesvar (d. 1504) offers an example of a different agenda. A Hungarian Observant Franciscan, Pelbart published several volumes of sermons in Latin in Germany, France, and elsewhere.[19] Receiving a bachelor's degree in 1463 at the University of Cracow, Pelbart was later a professor of theology at the Franciscan house of studies in Buda. In addition to collections of sermons for Lent, for Sundays, and on the saints, Pelbart published a corpus of sermons on the Virgin Mary, in fulfillment of a vow he had made to her when struck down by the plague. He had recovered from the plague, he believed, thanks to her intercession.[20]

---

[15]   Ibid., p. 59.
[16]   Ibid., p. 65.
[17]   Ibid., p. 70.
[18]   Ibid., p. 67.
[19]   See Anscar Zawart, *The History of Franciscan Preaching and of Franciscan Preachers (1209-1927): A Bio-Bibliographical Study* (New York: Wagner, 1928), pp. 333-34.
[20]   See Z.J. Kosztolnyik, "Some Hungarian Theologians in the Late Renaissance," *Church History* 57 (1988): 8-12.

The work offered in fulfillment of this vow, *Stellarium coronae benedictae Mariae Virginis in Laudem eius pro singulis praedicationibus elegantissime coaptatum*, was published in several editions, including in Strasbourg in 1496 and in Hagenau in 1498.[21] Harvard University possesses a 1502 edition, published in Augsburg; it includes a woodcut frontispiece showing the Virgin standing on a crescent moon, and holding the infant Jesus, both figures surrounded by the rays of the sun, with two angels about to crown the Virgin with a star-studded crown. This edition includes a prologue in which Pelbart explains that his purpose is praise of the "most glorious" Virgin Mother of God, through whom the "grave illness" from which he suffered was made empty.[22] Yet this is not his sole announced goal: he seeks to provide "material for more simple preachers," with the Virgin's help. Already in the prologue Pelbart explains that the book's title refers to the woman crowned with twelve stars, in chapter 12 of the Apocalypse (Book of Revelation). Thus the book is divided into twelve books on her mysteries: 1) Annunciation and Incarnation; 2) Visitation; 3) Purification; 4) Immaculate Conception; 5) Nativity; 6) Name; 7) Virtuous life; 8) Virginity; 9) Charity; 10) Assumption; 11) Multiple privilege and dignity; and 12) the Cult of devotion to be offered to her.

Though Pelbart states that he wishes to provide material for more simple preachers, he brings to this task the language and methods of a scholastic theologian, especially a penchant for multiple subdivision of themes. These are some examples: In Book 8, part I, three "mysteries" of her virginity are examined: congruity, dignity, attestability. Under "congruity" Pelbart first discourses on four "presuppositions" and then presents five reasons why it was "fitting" for Mary to be a virgin. Book 12 consists of three parts: these are divided into articles, and the articles into questions. Book 12, part I, article 1, question 4 asks about the sorts of veneration owed to the Blessed Virgin. Pelbart distinguishes three types of veneration (*latria, dulia, hyperdulia*), and goes on to give reasons why *hyperdulia* is owed to the Mother of God. Yet Pelbart does not indulge in scholastic distinctions solely for their own sake; he remains,

---

[21] Zawart, *The History of Franciscan Preaching*, p. 333.
[22] Pelbart of Temesvar, *Stellarium coronae benedictae Mariae Virginis...*(Augsburg, 1502), prologue. The pagination in this volume is unclear; I shall refer to the books, parts, and other divisions of the work.

ultimately, focused on piety and how the preacher may promote it. In his discussion of question 4, he concludes with a prayer : "O truly glorious Lady exalted above the stars, rightly man ought to serve you with the greatest affection, and every creature should do so...."

What Pelbart of Temesvar offered to his clerical readers in the *Stellarium coronae benedictae Mariae Virginis* was not so much ready-made sermons as material to use in constructing sermons, especially for Marian feast days. This late medieval Franciscan seems to have promoted a religion not of fear and pessimism, but themes of hope, praise, and thanksgiving. If Martin Luther's vow in the midst of stormy weather led him into a monastery where his fear and anxiety grew worse, Pelbart of Temesvar's vow in time of plague had quite a different outcome. Preachers informed by Pelbart's optimism – a literally starry, sunny optimism – would have been unlikely to deliver sermons in which hellfire and damnation were the main attractions. Pelbart sought to both teach and clarify doctrine, and to move audiences to greater devotion. Devotion to the Virgin Mary meant love: "with loving affection" one ought to praise her, since after God she is "above all creatures: above all angels, holy apostles, prophets, martyrs, confessors, virgins. Rightly she is called the most blessed Queen of the World."[23]

2. *Humanism in the Pulpit*

If Pelbart of Temesvar's themes of loving affection, praise, and glory, were quite different from the themes preached by Mormando's Bernardino, or by the friars studied by Siggins, these preachers all shared the tradition of the thematic sermon. This genre of preaching did not, however, go unchallenged during the Renaissance. In their zeal for recovery of ancient texts, Renaissance humanists focused new attention on both "pagan" sources and on the Bible. Their study of Greek and Roman antiquity included rhetorical theory and practice; works of Quintilian and Cicero became

---

[23]   Ibid., Book 12, part I, article 1, question 4.

textbooks for those who would take up public speaking.[24] Preaching was by no means immune from these new priorities.

As John O'Malley has shown, sermons at the papal court in the late fifteenth and early sixteenth centuries frequently adopted the "epideictic" genre of classical rhetoric.[25] This *genus demonstrativum* was an art of praise and blame, designed to delight and move its audiences. Compared to medieval "thematic" sermons, with their complex division of parts and questions, these discourses were less structured; they also gave relatively little attention to teaching doctrine or to resolving disputed points. Rather, "demonstrative" oratory celebrated God's grace and power, God's generosity, God's harmonious government of the universe. Sermons of this genre sought to move their hearers to admiration and praise of these divine qualities, and indeed to imitation of them.[26]

O'Malley points out that the sermons he has studied did not focus on a call to repentance.[27] Given that the sermons at issue were preached before the pope, this does not seem too surprising. Savonarola had paid with his life for over-zealous penitential jeremiads that excoriated and irritated Alexander VI;[28] most preachers, even before Savonarola's 1498 execution, may well have been far more cautious in pointing out any papal sins. Yet if the preachers of the papal court did not dwell on the need for penance, they did articulate an ideal Christian life that was one of love of neighbor. Forgiveness of enemies, aid for the needy, and charity in attitude and action were extolled.[29]

Love of neighbor, forgiveness of enemies: such ideals had biblical foundations. But what role did Scripture play in epideictic sermons? O'Malley points out that in panegyrics of the saints, the preacher might use a biblical text to "justify" his sermon.[30] Though O'Malley

---

[24]   Charles Nauert, *Humanism and the Culture of Renaissance Europe* (Cambridge: Cambridge University Press, 1995), pp. 12-13, 35, 208.

[25]   John O'Malley, *Praise and Blame in Renaissance Rome: Rhetoric, Doctrine, and Reform in the Sacred Orators of the Papal Court, c. 1450-1521* (Durham: Duke University Press, 1979).

[26]   Ibid., pp. 36-76.

[27]   Ibid., p. 124.

[28]   Many works have been published in connection with the fifth centenary of his death; see Konrad Eisenbichler, "Savonarola Studies in Italy on the 500th Anniversary of the Friar's Death," *Renaissance Quarterly* 52 (1999): 487-95.

[29]   O'Malley, *Praise and Blame*, 165-75.

[30]   Ibid., p. 176.

does not say so, such a "use" of Scripture seems very much like, if not identical to, that favored by the medieval thematic preachers. A verse of Scripture is a kind of proof text, or perhaps a point of departure for a discourse; explanation or exegesis of biblical texts is not seriously attempted.

By the early sixteenth century there were, however, Renaissance scholars concerned to make preaching more exegetical, that is, more explanatory of biblical passages. Such a reform of preaching was not necessarily Italian.[31] In the English context, John Fisher (1469-1535) was an outstanding example of a humanist scholar and orator. Founder of St. John's College, Cambridge, Chancellor of Cambridge University, Bishop of Rochester, theologian and preacher, Fisher would eventually be condemned to death for his opposition to Henry VIII's assertion of supremacy over the English Church.[32]

Richard Rex's study of Fisher's theology includes a chapter on Fisher and the pulpit. For Fisher, preaching was the objective to which all other concerns were subordinated.[33] In his statutes for St. John's College, a preacher was to expound the Scripture readings of the day every day.[34] From Fisher himself, seventeen sermons have survived: ten on the seven penitential psalms, probably delivered in the presence of Lady Margaret Beaufort and her household;[35] two sermons delivered at St. Paul's Cathedral, London, on the falsity of Lutheran doctrine; a Good Friday sermon on the crucifix; two that formed an introduction to a series of sermons – now lost – on the Ten Commandments; and two funeral orations, one for Henry VII, and the other for his mother, Lady Margaret.[36]

The sermons on the penitential psalms were first published in London in 1508; several other editions appeared in sixteenth-cen-

---

[31] On the development of Renaissance ideals and practices outside Italy, see especially Peter Burke, *The European Renaissance: Centres and Peripheries* (Oxford: Blackwell, 1998).

[32] For a biography of Fisher, see, e.g., Michael Macklem, *God Have Mercy: The Life of John Fisher of Rochester* (Ottawa: Oberon Press, 1968).

[33] Richard Rex, *The Theology of John Fisher* (Cambridge: Cambridge University Press, 1991), p. 31.

[34] Ibid., p. 31.

[35] The mother of Henry VII, Lady Margaret Beaufort, was instrumental as a patron in the founding of St. John's College.

[36] Rex, *The Theology of John Fisher*, pp. 31-33.

tury England as late as 1559.[37] Rex points out that Fisher's sermons were among the first to be published anywhere in English, and took "the unusual form of a continuous exposition of scripture, with the relevant texts consistently (though loosely) translated into English."[38]

If one examines, as an example, Fisher's sermon on Psalm 6, one finds both a division of parts very much in the tradition of thematic sermons, *and* a close attention to explanation of the biblical text. Fisher declares that the psalm itself is divided into three parts: 1) the mercy of God is asked; 2) reasons are given whereby the goodness of God may be moved to mercy; and 3) great gladness is showed for the undoubted obtaining of forgiveness.[39] This tripartite division structures the sermon, and further subdivisions or parts appear, such as three ways in which God deals with sinners. Scholastic language and distinctions play a role, with assertions such as this: although God in Himself and of His nature is without mutability, "diverse properties" are attributed to him.[40] At the same time, Fisher dwells at great length on showing how the psalm, like St. Paul, teaches that where sin is abundant, grace is superabundant.[41]

As Rex notes, Fisher's sermons mention hell and damnation but in passing. Indeed, the joys of heaven receive more detailed consideration than the pains of purgatory or hell; the "most striking feature" of Fisher's sermons on the psalms is their emphasis on God's mercy.[42] Defending God's righteousness, Fisher insists that there is "no blame" in God for the suffering in purgatory and hell; such blame rests solely with sinners.[43] Sinners need but repent to receive God's mercy. Expounding Psalm 6:6, "I have laboured in my groanings; every night I will wash my bed: I will water my couch with my tears," Fisher asserts that for one weeping from the heart of a sinner the Lord forgives. Weeping does for the soul what "rubbing and fretting" do for iron: rubbing takes away rust from iron,

---

[37] See John Fisher, *Sermons on the Seven Penitential Psalms*, ed. Kenelm Vaughan (London: Burnes and Oates, 1888), p. viii.

[38] Rex, *The Theology of John Fisher*, p. 48.

[39] Fisher, *Sermons*, p. 10.

[40] Ibid., pp. 10-11.

[41] Ibid., p. 19.

[42] Rex, *The Theology of John Fisher*, p. 35.

[43] Fisher, *Sermons*, p. 15.

and weeping puts away from the soul the "infection" of sin; the iron, with rubbing, will shine brightly; so the soul, with weeping, is made fair and white. By the "bed" is to be "understood the heap and multitude of sins, wherein all are heaped and gathered upon a rock." With a "great shower or flood" of weeping tears, "the whole mass of sins shall be washed away."[44]

Humanists such as Fisher, whose devotion to ancient texts included devotion to the Bible, sought both to recover and disseminate Scripture in its original Hebrew and Greek versions, and also in vernacular translation. Even in his own time, Erasmus (c.1466-1536) was the most famous of such humanist scholars. Dutch by birth, Erasmus became an itinerant scholar in several European countries, and gained an international reputation sustained by abundant publishing: editions of ancient texts, including a Greek New Testament, as well as a broad range of commentaries, treatises, colloquies, and other works.[45] John Fisher was a friend of Erasmus, who spent several years in Cambridge.[46]

The importance of Erasmus for the history of preaching goes beyond his seminal role in promoting biblical studies. One of Erasmus' publishers was Johann Froben, of Basel. In 1535 Froben printed the first edition of *Ecclesiastes, sive De Ratione Concionandi*, Erasmus's last major work and the longest of all.[47] Erasmus wrote it at the urging of Fisher.[48] John O'Malley has argued that this treatise on preaching, which went through some ten editions after 1535, "was the great watershed in the history of sacred rhetoric." Thereafter, the thematic sermon ceased to be advocated in theory (in treatises on pulpit oratory), even if some elements of thematic preaching would persist in practice. After 1535, treatises on how to

---

[44] Ibid., pp. 22-24.

[45] Lisa Jardine has examined his deliberate creation of an international persona; see her *Erasmus, Man of Letters: The Construction of Charisma in Print* (Princeton: Princeton University Press, 1993).

[46] Some letters of these two humanists have been preserved; see *Erasmus and Fisher, Their Correspondence 1511-1524*, ed. Jean Rouschausse (Paris: Vrin, 1968).

[47] John O'Malley, "Erasmus and the History of Sacred Rhetoric: the *Ecclesiastes* of 1535," *Erasmus of Rotterdam Society Yearbook* 5 (1985): 1.

[48] Germain Marc'Hardour, "Erasmus as Priest: Holy Orders in His Vision and Practice," in *Erasmus' Vision of the Church*, ed. Hilmar Pabel and Erika Rummel (Kirksville: Sixteenth Century Journal Publishers, 1995), p. 142.

preach were "indebted directly or indirectly to Erasmus' great work."[49]

Yet O'Malley makes clear that Erasmus' *Ecclesiastes* was not without its difficulties. On the one hand, Erasmus enthusiastically championed use of the axioms of pagan, classical rhetoric. On the other hand, "the more closely Christian preaching attached itself to the text of Scripture, a goal Erasmus surely promoted, the more difficult it became to adopt the principles of classical oratory." Classical oratory did not envision "dealing with a text but with an event, a situation, a person, a practical decision."[50]

While O'Malley found the demonstrative genre to dominate preaching before the papal court in the late fifteenth and early sixteenth centuries, in the *Ecclesiastes* he finds Erasmus advocating the "deliberative" genre. In his approach to preaching, "Erasmus was more concerned with inculcating and persuading to good morals and ethically correct behavior than he was to any other end."[51] The *genus deliberativum* suited such a goal, for its aim was to help audiences make good decisions, to deliberate correctly about possible courses of action.

Though the *Ecclesiastes* may be the most important text of Erasmus on preaching, there are many other references to preaching in his *opera omnia*. For example, in a treatise on the Christian widow, Erasmus declares:

> There is no eloquence more powerful or more helpful than that which persuades to good by the authority of the speaker . . . .If you read Exodus, Numbers, Leviticus, Chronicles, and Deuteronomy, you will see that Moses, the prince of such a great multitude, was nothing but a preacher, and that he exercised his power almost entirely by his eloquence, even pleading the case of his people from time to time before God.[52]

---

[49] Ibid., pp. 2, 13.

[50] Ibid., pp. 19-20. On this tension, see also O'Malley, "Content and Rhetorical Forms in Sixteenth-Century Treatises on Preaching," in *Renaissance Eloquence*, ed. James Murphy (Berkeley: University of California Press, 1983), p. 247. On rhetoric, see also Lee Sonnino, *A Handbook to Sixteenth-Century Rhetoric* (London: Routledge & Kegan Paul, 1968).

[51] Ibid., p. 24.

[52] Erasmus, "On the Christian Widow," trans. Jennifer Roberts, in *Collected Works of Erasmus*, vol. 66, ed. John O'Malley (Toronto: University of Toronto Press, 1988), pp. 196-97.

Like Fisher, Erasmus imagined God as a God of mercy. In 1524 Froben published Erasmus' *Concio de immensa Dei misericordia*.[53] In an introduction to his recent translation of the "sermon" – probably never actually preached by Erasmus – Michael Heath states that this discourse "mingles the free homiletic style of the Fathers, based on copious scriptural quotation and exegesis, with elements of the classical demonstrative and deliberative rhetoric."[54] Yet if the genre is a mixture or hybrid, the religious content is more uniform in putting aside fear in favor of trust in God. Fisher lauded human tears of repentance; Erasmus recalls the tears of Jesus for those who would not repent:

> The Lord does all he can to save us; why, then, do we wilfully abandon hope of salvation? In the Gospel he even sheds tears for Jerusalem, who was bringing ruin upon herself by persisting in her sin. 'How often,' he says, 'have I wished to gather you to me, as a hen gathers her chicks under her wings, but you would not' (Matthew 23:37). Our most merciful Lord laments that he is not allowed to save those wretched creatures; how can we distrust and pretend that he would not save us?[55]

Erasmus had studied at the University of Paris in the 1490s. It would not seem to be there that he experienced mercy, divine or otherwise; Roland Bainton's biography of Erasmus recalls a scholastic curriculum that interested him little, a curriculum accompanied by rotten food, frequent floggings, and malaria.[56] Perhaps this helps explain why Paris was not a city Erasmus favored much in his later years as an itinerant scholar.

Yet the mature Erasmus had considerable influence in France. Larissa Taylor has shown how the "Christian humanism espoused by Erasmus" had a "critical effect", in particular on preaching.[57] By the 1530s, the thematic sermon "had been replaced almost completely by a much freer and more expressive rendering of theological and Biblical material."[58] In an overview of Catholic preach-

---

[53] Erasmus, "A Sermon on the Immense Mercy of God," trans. Michael J. Heath, in *Collected Works of Erasmus: Spiritualia and Pastoralia*, vol. 70, ed. John O'Malley (Toronto: University of Toronto Press, 1998), pp. 69-139.

[54] Ibid., p. 71.

[55] Ibid., p. 120.

[56] Roland Bainton, *Erasmus of Christendom* (New York: Crossroad, 1982), pp. 35-37.

[57] Larissa Taylor, "The Influence of Humanism on Post-Reformation Catholic Preachers in France," *Renaissance Quarterly* 50 (1997): 120.

[58] Ibid., p. 119.

ing in late medieval and Reformation France, Taylor has also examined how a focus on human beings as sinful was, in most sermons, "balanced by an optimistic soteriology in which, thanks to God, everything was possible for the repentant sinner."[59] Thus, even before the spread of Erasmus' influence and that of humanism, French preachers seem to have offered a positive vision of God's dealings with humanity.

It would be a mistake, however, to imagine that the 1530s saw a definitive triumph of humanist preaching in the Catholic context. Anti-Protestant polemics were gaining in intensity, including in the pulpit and in printed sermons. Humanism itself was suspect in the eyes of many Catholics, as a seedbed for heresy. Also, even if preachers adopted in some ways a humanist genre of pulpit oratory, they may have, at the same time, made denunciation of heresy and heretics their main goal.

An excellent example of this, from the German context, is Johan Eck (1486-1543). A secular priest, Catholic apologist and virulent opponent of Luther,[60] his published works include *Homiliarum sive Sermonum (I. Eck) adversum quoscunqz nostri temporis haereticos, super evangelia de tempore*, in two volumes.[61] Eck calls these discourses "homilies or sermons," and they are at the same time both expositions of the gospel text of each day, and "sermons" on various themes, especially the excellence of Catholic beliefs and practices, and the errors of the heretics. A very detailed index of topics and page numbers completes each volume. Volume I includes *Fides sola inutilis* (Faith alone useless); *Heretici canes* (Heretics are dogs); *Heretici seditiosi* (Heretics are seditious); *Luther precursor Antichr* (Luther precursor of AntiChrist); and *Maria intercedit pro nobis* (Mary intercedes for us). Volume II includes *Ecclesie magnitudo contra Lutherum* (The magnitude of the Church against Luther); *Heretici sunt leprosi* (Heretics are lepers); *Opera bona merentur* (Good works are meritorious); *Sacerdotalis dignitas* (Priestly dignity); and *Scripturam iudicat Ecclesia* (The Church judges Scripture).

---

[59]   Larissa Taylor, *Soldiers of Christ: Preaching in Late Medieval and Reformation France* (Oxford : Oxford University Press, 1992), p. 86.

[60]   On Eck, see Walter Moore, "Eck, Johann," *Oxford Encyclopedia of the Reformation*, 4 vols. (Oxford : Oxford University Press, 1996): 2, pp. 17-19.

[61]   Johan Eck, *Homiliarum sive Sermonum adversum quoscunqz nostri temporis haereticos, super evangelia de tempore*, 2 vols. (Ingolstadt, 1533).

3. *The Council of Trent*

Eck died in 1543, and Luther in 1546. Also in the mid-1540s, Pope
Paul III succeeded in calling a general council, to meet at Trent.[62]
In the event, this council of bishops would meet intermittently from
1545 to 1563. It produced a series of decrees and canons that, on
the one hand, condemned heresy and affirmed Catholic doctrine
(in a manner like that of Eck), and, on the other hand, ordered an
institutional and moral reform of the Catholic Church, starting
with the clergy.[63] The task of preaching did not go unnoticed in
these "reform" decrees.

Bishops were not necessarily theologians—indeed many had very
little theological training—but they frequently brought along expert
advisors. These *periti* included Franciscans and Dominicans, members of other, older religious orders, as well as some Jesuits.[64]
Founded by Ignatius of Loyola, and approved by Paul III in 1540,
the Society of Jesus gave preaching a prominent place in its ministries.[65] The 1540 Bull of Institution declared that the Society of
Jesus is

> principally instituted to work for the advancement of souls in Christian
> life and doctrine, and for the propagation of the faith by public preach-
> ing and the ministry of God's Word, by spiritual exercises and works of
> charity, more particularly by grounding in Christianity boys and unlet-
> tered persons, and by hearing the confessions of the faithful, aiming in
> all things at their spiritual consolation.[66]

A Basque Spaniard, Ignatius received much of his education at the
University of Paris, indeed living for a time in the same college
where Erasmus had lived and suffered.[67] The extant writings of

---

[62]   On Trent, see especially Hubert Jedin, *A History of the Council of Trent*, trans.
Ernest Graf, 2 vols. (London: Nelson, 1957-61).

[63]   On the distinction between "Catholic Reformation" and "Counter Reformation," see Hubert Jedin, "Katholische Reformation oder Gegenreformation?," in *Gegenreformation*, ed. Ernst Walter Zeeden (Darmstadt: Wissenschaftliche Buchgesellschaft,
1973), pp. 46-81.

[64]   Jesuits at Trent did not necessarily find a favorable reception for their views; see
John O'Malley, *The First Jesuits* (Cambridge: Harvard University Press, 1993), p. 303.

[65]   On the early Jesuits and preaching, see O'Malley, *The First Jesuits*, pp. 91-104.

[66]   Paul III, "Bull of Institution," in *The Catholic Reformation: Savonarola to Ignatius
Loyola*, ed. John Olin (New York: Fordham University Press, 1992), p. 204.

[67]   On Ignatius in Paris, see O'Malley, *The First Jesuits*, pp. 28-32.

Ignatius include no sermons;[68] yet in the Jesuit Constitutions, written in large part by Ignatius in the 1540s and 1550s, the importance of preaching is very strongly affirmed. The "Word of God" is to be "constantly proposed to the people by means of sermons, lectures, and the teaching of Christian doctrine"; this may be done in the Society's own churches, or in "other churches, squares, or places of the region, when the one in charge judges it expedient for God's greater glory."[69]

Both the Bull of Institution and the Constitutions suggest a strong affinity of preaching with the teaching of Christian doctrine. Did such an affinity or association mean that Jesuit preaching would put more emphasis on teaching audiences rather than on moving or delighting them? Did the Council of Trent, in its efforts to promote preaching, stress that the preacher's goal should be especially to teach (*docere*) more than to move (*movere*) or to delight (*delectare*)? Was the humanist effort to revive and integrate classical genres of oratory validated or rejected? Was homiletic exposition of Scripture endorsed? Was medieval, thematic preaching reaffirmed?

I shall examine later, as a case study of post-Tridentine preaching, a French Jesuit preacher of the early seventeenth century; regarding Trent, however, it is important to notice what the Council addressed and what it did not.

In its "reform" decrees, Trent was concerned above all else with making certain that bishops and parish priests take seriously the care of souls (*cura animarum*). No longer were pastoral duties to be abandoned to the friars and other religious, as had so often been the case in the late medieval period. In its decrees of 17 June 1546, the council declared preaching to be the "chief duty" of bishops; bishops and parish clergy were ordered to

> feed the people committed to them with wholesome words in proportion to their own and their people's mental capacity, by teaching them those things that are necessary for all to know in order to be saved and by impressing upon them with briefness and plainness of speech the vices that they must avoid and the virtues that they must cultivate, in order

---

[68] Ibid., p. 95.
[69] *Constitutions of the Society of Jesus*, ed. John Padberg (St. Louis: Institute of Jesuit Sources, 1996), ##645, 647.

that they may escape eternal punishment and obtain the glory of heaven.[70]

With this emphasis on plain speech and the modest intellectual capabilities of most preachers and their audiences, the council implicitly warned against a scholastic preaching that dwelt on subtle philosophical and theological distinctions. Stress on vices and virtues, as the proper content of preaching, also implied exclusion, or at least marginalization, of other content. The council's reference to preaching on vices and virtues was a paraphrase from the Rule of St. Francis;[71] the Capuchins, a reformed branch of the Franciscans, were founded shortly before Trent. In the Capuchin Constitutions of 1536, the friars were exhorted to follow the example of St. John the Baptist, and the Rule of St. Francis, in preaching penance: "let them discourse of vices and virtues, of punishment and glory, in few words, not desiring or seeking anything but the glory of God." [72]

Yet what most concerned the council about preaching was renewal of the episcopal role in it. Who was to preach was far more the issue than were the various "genres" of preaching, or the content. The bishops at Trent delineated two roles for themselves in the task of preaching. First, bishops were ordered to preach personally or, if "hindered by a legitimate impediment," to appoint others competent to do so. Second, bishops were to oversee and control all preaching done in their dioceses. In a direct attack on the principle of a religious order's exemption from episcopal jurisdiction, Trent decreed that any religious clergy who preached outside the churches of their own order would henceforth need the bishop's permission. Such permission could, moreover, be revoked, "if, which heaven avert, a preacher should spread errors or scandals among the people."[73]

In 1563, in the last weeks of the council, these two points were again underscored. Recalling its 1547 decree on preaching, the council declared that bishops themselves, in their own churches, unless "lawfully hindered," are to "announce the Sacred Scriptures

---

[70] Trent, Session V, Decree on reform, ch. 2.
[71] John O'Malley, "Erasmus and the History of Sacred Rhetoric," p. 25.
[72] "Capuchin Constitutions of 1536," in *The Catholic Reformation: Savonarola to Ignatius Loyola*, ed. John Olin (New York: Fordham University Press, 1992), p. 174.
[73] Trent, Session V, Decree on reform, ch. 2.

and the divine law." If so hindered, they must appoint others. The permission required in order to preach pertained henceforth even to religious clergy preaching in their order's own pulpits. "But no one, whether secular or regular, shall presume to preach, even in churches of his own order, in opposition to the will of the bishop."[74]

At Trent, therefore, questions about episcopal oversight of preaching received far more attention than questions about genre, form, or even content of sermons. In effect, individual bishops were left with the task of judging what was and what was not appropriate in the pulpits of their dioceses. Such latitude meant, at least in theory, that one bishop might promote classical genres of oratory, while his colleague in the neighboring diocese might condemn them. One bishop might favor thematic sermons while another sought to eliminate them in order to make way for exposition of Scripture. Trent put no limits on episcopal discretion in these matters. Trent did decree that the bishops create seminaries – an innovation at the time – to train a diocesan clergy suited for *cura animarum*; among the topics to be studied in such schools were the "homilies of the saints."[75] Religious orders had a long tradition of training their men in their own houses of study or in the universities. By ordering establishment of seminaries by the bishops and for the bishops in their task of training the secular clergy, Trent took a step in the direction of closing the intellectual gap between religious and secular clergy. Yet one must not overstate the differences between these two groups. For one thing, a good number of the bishops at Trent were themselves also members of religious orders.[76]

One such bishop was Girolamo Seripando (1493-1563), superior general of the Augustinian friars from 1539 to 1551, and archbishop of Salerno from 1554 until his death. In 1561 Seripando was also made a cardinal and a papal legate to Trent.[77] Francesco Cesareo has shown how Seripando's sermons anticipated the Tridentine legislation on frequent episcopal preaching. Many of his

---

[74] Trent, Session XXIV, Decree on reform, ch. 4.

[75] Trent, Session XXIII, Decree on reform, ch. 18. On Trent and seminaries, see James O'Donohoe, *Tridentine Seminary Legislation: Its sources and its Formation* (Louvain: Publications Universitaires, 1957).

[76] On bishops at the council, see Jedin, *A History of the Council of Trent*.

[77] See Hubert Jedin, *Papal Legate at the Council of Trent: Cardinal Seripando*, trans. Frederic Eckhoff (St. Louis and London: Herder, 1947).

sermons had a "moralistic quality and persuasive character;" seeking to avoid "elaborate theological discussions," Seripando "sought to move his listeners to cultivate their religious and spiritual life by presenting them with simple explanations of the elements of the faith."[78] In Seripando's sermons on the Lord's Prayer, Cesareo finds a certain emphasis on sin, but concludes that the archbishop's purpose was "not to admonish but to build up the Christian way of life in his listeners."[79]

Cornelio Musso (1511-74) was a Franciscan bishop and preacher; he delivered the inaugural oration at Trent. Corrie Norman has sought to demonstrate how Musso's vernacular preaching was at least as important as this one Latin discourse; bishop of Bitonto from 1544, Musso left some 150 Italian sermons.[80] On questions of genre, Norman points out how Musso sometimes explicated a Scriptural text phrase by phrase, but more often "mixed" this homiletic form with elements of thematic and classical sermons. Musso's discourses were "florid" rather than plain; the shorter sermons would have lasted at least an hour.[81]

4. *Catholic Preaching after Trent*

Frederick McGinness has examined the ways in which the decades after Trent were a kind of golden age of preaching in Rome itself. Though post-Tridentine popes did not normally ascend the pulpit in person, they fostered a rich proliferation of sermons at the papal court and throughout the city of Rome. By the end of the sixteenth century, Rome itself as the holy city, as the light to the nations, became a prominent theme in Roman preaching. The classical *genus demonstrativum*, or epideictic genre of oratory, enjoyed a renewed season of favor as it served well discourses devoted to praise of Roman and papal virtue.[82] Progress in virtue was the principal goal

---

[78] Francesco Cesareo, "Penitential Sermons in Renaissance Italy: Girolamo Seripando and the Pater Noster," *Catholic Historical Review* 83 (1997): 3.

[79] Ibid., p. 19.

[80] Corrie Norman, *Humanist Taste and Franciscan Values: Cornelio Musso and Catholic Preaching in Sixteenth-Century Italy* (New York: Peter Lang, 1998), pp. 3, 10.

[81] Ibid., pp. 64-66.

[82] Frederick McGinness, *Right Thinking and Sacred Oratory in Counter-Reformation Rome* (Princeton: Princeton University Press, 1995), pp. 170-90.

of preaching in Rome after Trent; "sermons aimed at touching the heart and moving sinners to compunction – the prelude to sacramental confession, communion, and a reordered life."[83]

Most of the sermons studied by McGinness were the work of Franciscans, Dominicans, Jesuits, and other religious orders. Outside Rome, however, diocesan bishops did begin to take seriously Trent's injunction to make preaching their principal task. By ca.1600 many bishops were themselves frequently preaching, or at least making provision for other, qualified orators to preach on their behalf. Carlo Borromeo (1538-84), archbishop of Milan, was one of the most prominent bishops to make implementation of a Tridentine model of the episcopate his priority.[84] He was canonized as a saint in 1610, scarcely more than a quarter century after his death.[85]

Borromeo's reputation as an austere holy man, as a cardinal, and as a pastorally-active bishop was not restricted to Italy. An example of his growing cult among the French clergy is evident in the sermons of Jean-Pierre Camus (1584-1652), the bishop of Belley.[86] Among the many volumes of sermons he published is a collection of eight "panegyric homilies" on St. Charles.[87] Most of these were preached in Paris between 1616 and 1621; they praise at great length the virtues of this episcopal saint.

Though Bishop Camus calls these discourses "homilies" they are not expositions of biblical texts. He begins each with a verse of Scripture, but it functions more as an entry into some theme or themes than as a sustained focus. Yet "panegyric" does indicate more clearly what these discourses are. The principal focus throughout is praise of St. Charles, St. Charles as model for imitation.

One of the eight "homilies" treats at length the oratorical virtues

---

[83]　Ibid., p. 44.

[84]　On Borromeo's implementation of Trent, see Hubert Jedin and Giuseppe Alberigo, *Il tipo ideale di vescovo secondo la Riforma Cattolica* (Brescia: Morcelliana, 1985), pp. 69-77.

[85]　See Niels Rasmussen, "Liturgy and Iconography at the Canonization of Carlo Borromeo, 1 November 1610," in *San Carlo Borromeo*, eds. John Headley and John Tomaro (London: Associated University Presses, 1988), pp. 264-76.

[86]　On Camus as preacher, see my *Seventeenth-Century Cultural Discourse: France and the Preaching of Bishop Camus* (Berlin: Mouton de Gruyter, 1997).

[87]　Jean-Pierre Camus, *Homélies panégyriques de Sainct Charles Borromée* (Paris: Chappelet, 1623).

of the archbishop of Milan.[88] Camus begins by citing chapter 24 of
the gospel of Matthew on the faithful servant who feeds the master's family; he then praises the eloquence of both Plato and St.
Ambrose, one of the "glorious" predecessors of Borromeo in the
see of Milan. Compared to these two, St. Charles was greater, even
though he knew less philosophy than Plato and spoke less eloquently than Ambrose; Charles spoke an efficacious word with such energy that one may term his remonstrances against sin the sword of
God (*le glaive de Dieu*).[89]

After an *Ave Maria*, seeking the "light of grace" for his own
words, Camus devotes the body of this discourse to demonstrating
how St. Charles was a "poor" preacher according to the world's
judgment, but a perfect one according to the school of Jesus Christ.
Camus asserts that the world "hates" the cross of Christ; St.
Charles was an evangelical trumpet, preaching the gospel of Christ
in season and out. Every word from the mouth of God is the wheat,
wine, and oil that are better than the heady wine (*vin fumeux*) of profane discourses, and more fragrant than the perfumes of the words
of human rhetoric.[90] St. Charles "distributed" the word of God to
a wide variety of people: milk to some, solid food to others, adapting his discourse (*proportionant son discours*) to the level of his audience. He knew that just as animals live on different fodder, so too
it was necessary to change terms, style, and material (*changer de
termes, de stile, et de matiere*), according to the "qualities" of those to
whom he spoke.[91]

Camus is quick to clarify: even in this variety, the sermons of St.
Charles always promoted penance and compunction, not vanity
and curiosity. He knew that sublime conceits (*sublimes conceptions*) do
not make a person holy, but rather that virtue makes one agreeable
to God. Horrified by the pompous ornaments of oratorical artifices
(*les ornemens pompeux des artifices oratoires*), "our saint" did not amuse
himself with sublimity of language, but rather gave himself to the
efficacy of virtue and truth. Like St. Francis of Assisi, St. Charles
was not well endowed with acquired learning, but he was a great

---

88   Ibid., pp. 139-66.
89   Ibid., p. 140.
90   Ibid., pp. 140-46.
91   Ibid., pp. 147-48.

preacher.[92] Stripped of all other interest than the glory of Christ crucified, St. Charles took care to speak with brevity. Not seeking worldly applause, he sought progress in virtue. He knew that just as the sound travelling through the narrow channel of a trumpet strikes the ear powerfully, so too a remonstrance made with brevity penetrates the spirit further.[93]

Camus makes a number of other allusions to continuity between the preaching of St. Francis (or of the Franciscan and Dominican friars) and that of St. Charles. Such allusions or comparisons suggest that in the post-Tridentine era, when diocesan bishops took up seriously the task of preaching, a primary model and example of a preacher continued to be that of a friar.

Yet the example that Camus followed most closely in his own pastoral ministry was neither Francis of Assisi nor Carlo Borromeo, but rather François de Sales (1567-1622). Bishop of Geneva from 1602, and resident in the *savoyard* town of Annecy, François was friend and mentor to Camus, whose diocese of Belley was adjacent. Indeed it was François de Sales who consecrated Camus bishop in 1609. The bishop of Belley would eventually publish a six-volume life of his senior colleague, a life written to promote the latter's chances for beatification.[94] In the event, François de Sales was beatified in 1661 and canonized in 1665.[95]

One of the differences, however, between these two bishops was in publication of sermons. While both preached frequently throughout their respective dioceses and in many other places as well, the bishop of Geneva published only one sermon (a funeral oration) during his lifetime, while the bishop of Belley published more than 400. What were later published as the sermons of François de Sales are in part the work of disciples composing what they thought the preacher had said or ought to have said.[96] A more reliable source

---

[92]   Ibid., pp. 152, 155-58.
[93]   Ibid., pp. 164-65. For an interesting discussion of how Charles Borromeo both denounced and promoted use of 'pagan' rhetoric, see Peter Bayley, "Accommodating Rhetoric," *Seventeenth-Century French Studies* 19 (1997): 43.
[94]   Jean-Pierre Camus, *L'esprit du Bienheureux François de Sales, évêque de Genève*, 6 vols. (Paris: Alliot, 1639-41).
[95]   For a good overview of his life, see André Ravier, *Un sage et un saint François de Sales* (Paris: Nouvelle Cité, 1985).
[96]   On the paucity of published or otherwise reliably authentic sermons of François de Sales, see Peter Bayley, *French Pulpit Oratory 1598-1650: A Study in Themes and Styles* (Cambridge: Cambridge University Press, 1980), p. 246.

for gaining access to François de Sales in his approach to preaching is a lengthy letter he wrote in 1604 to André Frémyot (1573-1641), archbishop of Bourges from 1603 and the brother of St. Jeanne de Chantal (1572-1641).[97]

The bishop of Geneva explains to Frémyot that he will treat four questions in this letter: who should preach; for what purpose one should preach; what one should preach; the manner (*la façon*) in which one should preach.[98] Citing Trent on preaching as the principal duty of a bishop, de Sales asserts that episcopal consecration confers a "special grace" for preaching; therefore the preaching of a bishop has a greater "power" than that of other preachers, even if he is not learned. Developing this latter point further, the bishop of Geneva cites both Francis of Assisi and Carlo Borromeo. St. Francis was not learned and nevertheless was a great preacher, and "in our age," the blessed Cardinal Borromeo had but mediocre learning and yet accomplished marvels.[99]

As for what one preaches, François de Sales insists that virtues and vices should be taught, and the will moved and "warmed" to flee vice and embrace virtue. The preacher should also delight his audiences, at the same time as he teaches and moves them without, however, relying on worldly and profane elegance, with its curiosities and artifice. Such worldly orators make themselves the content of preaching, but what one preaches should be Jesus Christ crucified.[100]

François de Sales insists that Scripture is what one should preach in order to preach on virtue and vice, heaven and hell. Asking whether other texts are necessary or helpful, he subordinates them to Scripture. What is the doctrine of the Church Fathers but the gospel explained, but Holy Scripture exposed (*que l'Evangile expliqué, que l'Escriture Sainte exposée*)?[101] In expounding Scripture, one may rely on the various senses: literal, allegorical, anagogical, and

---

[97] François de Sales, "A Monseigneur André Frémyot," in *Oeuvres de Saint François de Sales*, 26 vols. (Annecy: Niérat, 1892-1932): 12, pp. 299-325. See also Bayley, *French Pulpit Oratory*, pp. 63-66.

[98] François de Sales, "A Monseigneur André Frémyot," p. 300.

[99] Ibid., p. 301.

[100] Ibid., pp. 304-05.

[101] Ibid., p. 305.

tropological.[102] As for the lives of the saints, they may be used in the pulpit, for what is the life of a saint but the gospel in action (*mis en oeuvre*)? Secular histories may also be used, but in small quantities, and only to awaken the appetite. Natural history may be more useful, for the earth, made by the word of God, sings in all its parts the praise of its creator. But the preacher should avoid recounting false miracles, ridiculous stories, and "indecent" things.[103]

Though François de Sales exhorts Frémyot to expound Scripture when he preaches, he also warns him against continuous exposition of long passages. Treating an entire text from the gospel is less "fruitful" than treating a single sentence, for when the preacher is able to pause but briefly on each phrase he can neither explain it well nor inculcate what he wants in his audience.[104] Yet brevity of the entire sermon is recommended to Frémyot; it is better for preaching to be short rather than long; provided it lasts a half hour, it is not too short.[105] Then, in evident continuity with the tradition of thematic sermons, de Sales offers his colleague detailed advice on how to organize a sermon on humility, with a "disposition" of four points.[106] No doubt keenly aware of Protestant insistence on Scripture alone as the content of preaching, Bishop de Sales thus exhorted his colleague to expound the Bible in the pulpit. Yet François de Sales was also eager to retain what he saw as the advantages of the thematic sermon tradition, advantages he considered absent in verse-by-verse exegetical homilies. Such a hybrid approach may well have been adopted by many Catholic preachers after Trent, as they both drew on the legacy of late medieval preaching and attempted to respond to new challenges and needs.

In the late sixteenth-century Wars of Religion, anti-Protestant polemic in French Catholic pulpits had even included fervent appeals for extermination of the "heretics" as wild boars and wolves, as a gangrene or a cancer eating away at the body of Christ.[107] With the era of François de Sales and the decades of relative peace

---

[102] Ibid., pp. 308-11. On the history of these four senses, see Henri de Lubac, *Exégèse médiévale: Les quatre sens de l'écriture*, 4 vols. (Paris: Aubier, 1959-64).

[103] François de Sales, "A Monseigneur André Frémyot," pp. 306-07.

[104] Ibid., p. 318.

[105] Ibid., p. 323.

[106] Ibid., p. 319.

[107] See Barbara Diefendorf, *Beneath the Cross: Catholics and Huguenots in Sixteenth-Century Paris* (Oxford: Oxford University Press, 1991), pp. 147-58.

that began ca. 1600, such overheated rhetoric cooled somewhat but did not disappear entirely. Actual military conflict was at times succeeded by militant, verbal warfare. For example, Bishop Camus, in a series of sermons on the eucharist, never tired of denouncing Protestant "error." While not urging violence against the heretics, he warned his audiences to avoid all contact with them.[108]

Another well-known French preacher of the first half of the seventeenth century was Nicolas Caussin (1583-1651). In his *Rhetoric and Truth in France: Descartes to Diderot*, Peter France states that "it was the Jesuit colleges above all which established a regular pattern of linguistic studies," encompassing Latin grammar and literature, and a year of rhetoric proper.[109] Caussin represents this milieu. A Jesuit, spiritual director, preacher, and confessor to King Louis XIII, he published many works, among them *De eloquentia sacra et humana*, first printed in 1619. A tome of more than a thousand pages, it went through many editions, and included especially lengthy sections on epideictic rhetoric and on the emotions.[110]

Another of Caussin's publications was a series of Advent and Christmas discourses (*entretiens*), published in 1644.[111] Though probably not delivered from any pulpit by Caussin, these sermon-like texts were clearly designed for use by other preachers in preparing their own sermons. Providing an *entretien* for each of the Sundays of Advent, for Christmas, the Circumcision, and the Epiphany, as well as for several saints whose feasts occur in these weeks, Caussin begins with a verse of Scripture, but quickly turns to divide his discourse into two main parts: *moralitez* and *aspiration*. The *moralitez* he often divides into several points, points devoted principally to practical, moral application of the Scripture verse. For the first Sunday of Advent, Caussin lauds the Last Judgement as a "magnificent

---

[108]   Jean-Pierre Camus, *Premières homélies eucharistiques* (Paris: Chappelet, 1618).

[109]   Peter France, *Rhetoric and Truth in France: Descartes to Diderot* (Oxford: Clarendon Press, 1972), p. 4.

[110]   See Thomas Conley, *Rhetoric in the European Tradition* (Chicago: University of Chicago Press, 1990), pp. 155-57. Marc Fumaroli frequently cites Caussin in his *L'Age de l'éloquence* (Geneva: Droz, 1980). For a full list of Caussin's works, see Carlos Sommervogel, *Bibliothèque de la Compagnie de Jésus*, 9 vols. (Brussels: Schepens, 1890-1900): 2, pp. 902-27. On Caussin as a hagiographer, see my "Neither Married nor Cloistered: Blessed Isabelle in Catholic Reformation France," *Sixteenth Century Journal* 30 (1999): 457-72.

[111]   Nicolas Caussin, *La sagesse évangélique pour les sacrez entretiens de l'advent* (Paris: Taupinart, 1644).

theater" of the providence and the glory of God, in which three
things shine forth: the visible marks of God's power; the punishment of vice; and the recompense of virtue.[112] The *aspiration* in each
entretien is a prayer that brings it to a conclusion.

Like Camus, however, Caussin is keen to teach Catholic doctrine, especially on points contested by the Protestants. Luther and
Calvin had insisted on grace alone as necessary for salvation; they
had also attacked the cult of the saints. The relationship of divine
grace and human free will is a theme to which Caussin returns several times. In examining the call of St. Andrew, he emphasizes the
gratuity of God's grace, but also adds the necessity of the liberty of
our free will (*la liberté de notre franc arbitre*).[113] On the feast of St. Nicholas, Caussin insists that while our talents are God's graces given to
us, we need to contribute our free will and make a good use of
them. St. Nicholas provides an illustrious example of such a use;
the excellence of his virtue was heroic.[114] Fulsome in his praise of
the Virgin for the feast of the Immaculate Conception (8 Decem-
ber), Caussin asserts that this conception was more sacred than the
creation of the world; the Virgin's conception was the beginning of
the happiness of the universe.[115]

The happiness of France, and praise of its monarchy, were also
prominent themes in early seventeenth-century French preaching.
The cult of St. Louis (King Louis IX) also grew considerably in this
period, and many new churches were dedicated to him, such as the
Jesuit church in Paris. In Rome, at the French national church of
San Luigi, panegyric sermons were delivered on the feast (25
August) of St. Louis. For example, on 25 August 1640, Jean-
Jacques Bouchard, a secular priest and doctor of theology, preached a sermon published later that year.[116] Bouchard explains, in his
dedication of the printed version to King Louis XIII, that most of
his audience was not French, and that he sought to persuade them
of the advantages of the French nation.[117] The text of the sermon
goes well beyond a panegyric of St. Louis to an unrestrained cele-

---

[112]   Ibid., p. 4.
[113]   Ibid., p. 24.
[114]   Ibid., pp. 56-57.
[115]   Ibid., p. 87.
[116]   Jean-Jacques Bouchard, *Sermon panégyrique sur Saint Louis Roy de France* (Rome:
Joseph Lune, 1640).
[117]   Ibid., pp. 3-4.

bration of the superiority of France, and especially of its capital. Thus Paris is what Rome and Athens once were: the throne of grandeur and power, the treasure of riches and delights, the academy of arts and the school of sciences.[118] This French inclination to letters has "always" been accompanied by wise laws and by a civility (*politesse*) and courtesy that have been the admiration and the model of other peoples. The French monarchy, was "predestined by the eternal Father," and the beautiful kingdom of France is the first of all kingdoms of the earth.[119] The political sermon was not new in the seventeenth century,[120] but the Thirty Years' War (1618-48) helped to promote national consciousness and national rivalry, including rivalry between Catholic nations.[121] Catholic sermons were by no means insulated from such developments, indeed they may have helped to produce them. Bouchard's 1640 panegyric of St. Louis and of France is an excellent example of preaching in the epideictic genre of classical oratory, in service of a political and religious agenda.

Conclusion

In the time of Bernardino of Siena, the thematic sermon was the dominant genre of Catholic sermons; the two centuries following his death (1444) saw other genres of preaching challenge and rival this dominance. Humanist veneration of antiquity included both a new emphasis on exegesis of biblical texts and a revival of classical genres of public speaking, including the *genus demonstrativum* and the *genus deliberativum*. In the Reformation era, some Catholic preachers continued to structure their discourses in the thematic tradition, while other preachers delivered homilies that were humanist expositions of Scripture, and still other pulpit orators adopted the classical genres.

Catholicism after the Council of Trent has often been portrayed

---

[118] Ibid., p. 13.

[119] Ibid., pp. 14-16.

[120] On the monarchy in sixteenth-century French sermons, see Larissa Taylor, "Comme un chien mort: Images of Kingship in French Preaching," *Proceedings of the Western Society for French History* 22 (1995): 157-70.

[121] On this war and religion, see, e.g., Stephen Lee, *The Thirty Years War* (London: Routledge, 1991), pp. 36-39.

as monolithic and intolerant of diversity.[122] Perhaps true in some ways, such a portrayal is surely inaccurate for the *genera* of Catholic sermons. Growing variety and hybridization, not uniformity, is what characterizes the genres of post-Tridentine Catholic preaching. Fear of hellfire and damnation may have been the most prominent theme in Bernardino's thematic preaching. Yet, diversification of sermon genres over the following two centuries appears to have accompanied diversification of sermon content. Neither Trent, nor post-Tridentine preachers such as Camus, Caussin, or Bouchard made fear of divine punishment the sole theme of preaching. The God of Catholic preachers was more catholic than that.[123]

Bibliography

Bainton, Roland, *Erasmus of Christendom* (New York: Crossroad, 1982).

Bayley, Peter, "Accommodating Rhetoric," *Seventeenth-Century French Studies* 19 (1997): 37-47.

— *French Pulpit Oratory 1598-1650: A Study in Themes and Styles* (Cambridge: Cambridge University Press, 1980).

Bouchard, Jean-Jacques, *Panégyrique sur Saint Louis Roy de France* (Rome: Ioseph Lune, 1640).

Brown, D. Catherine, *Pastor and Laity in the Theology of Jean Gerson* (Cambridge: Cambridge University Press, 1987).

Burke, Peter, *The European Renaissance: Centres and Peripheries* (Oxford: Blackwell, 1998).

Camus, Jean-Pierre, *L'esprit du Bienheureux François de Sales, évêque de Genève*, 6 vols. (Paris: Alliot, 1639-41).

— *Homélies panégyriques de Sainct Charles Borromée*, (Paris: Chappelet, 1623).

The Canons and Decrees of the Council of Trent, ed. H.J. Schroeder (St. Louis: Herder, 1941).

Caussin, Nicolas, *La sagesse évangélique pour les sacrez entretiens de l'advent* (Paris: Taupinart, 1644).

---

[122] For an excellent example of such a perspective, see Steven Ozment, *The Age of Reform* (New Haven: Yale University Press, 1980), pp. 397-418.

[123] On post-Tridentine preaching beyond Italy, Savoy, or France, see, e.g., Hilary Dansey Smith, *Preaching in the Spanish Golden Age: A study of some preachers of the reign of Philip III* (Oxford: Oxford University Press, 1978); Urs Herzog, *Geistliche Wohlredenheit: Die katholische Barockpredigt* (Munich: Beck, 1992).

Cesareo, Francesco, "Penitential Sermons in Renaissance Italy: Girolamo Seripando and the Pater Noster," *Catholic Historical Review* 83 (1997): 1-19.

Conley, Thomas, *Rhetoric in the European Tradition* (Chicago: University of Chicago Press, 1990).

Constitutions of the Society of Jesus, ed. John Padberg (St. Louis: Institute of Jesuit Sources, 1996).

Diefendorf, Barbara, *Beneath the Cross: Catholics and Huguenots in Sixteenth-Century Paris* (Oxford : Oxford University Press, 1991).

Eck, Johann, *Homiliarum sive Sermonum [J. Eck] adversum quoscunqz nostri temporis haereticos, super evangelia de tempore*, 2 vols. (Inglostadt, 1533).

Eisenbichler, Konrad, "Savonarola Studies in Italy on the 500th Anniversary of the Friar's Death," *Renaissance Quarterly* 52 (1999): 487-95.

Erasmus, Desiderius, *Collected Works* (Toronto: University of Toronto Press, 1974-).

Erasmus, Desiderius and Fisher, John, *Erasmus and Fisher, Their Correspondence, 1511-1524*, ed. Jean Rouschausse (Paris: Vrin, 1968).

Fisher, John, *Sermons on the Seven Penitential Psalms*, ed. Kenelm Vaughan (London: Burnes and Oates, 1888).

France, Peter, *Rhetoric and Truth in France: Descartes to Diderot* (Oxford: Clarendon Press, 1972).

Fumaroli, Marc, *L'Age de l'éloquence* (Geneva: Droz, 1980).

Herzog, Urs, *Geistliche Wohlredenheit: Die katholische Barockpredigt* (Munich: Beck, 1992).

Jardine, Lisa, *Erasmus, Man of Letters: The Construction of Charisma in Print* (Princeton: Princeton University Press, 1993).

Jedin, Hubert, *A History of the Council of Trent*, trans. Ernest Graf, 2 vols. (London: Nelson, 1957-61).

—— "Katholische Reformation oder Gegenreformation?" in *Gegenreformation*, ed. Ernst Walter Zeeden (Darmstadt: Wissenschaftliche Buchgesellschaft, 1973), pp. 46-81.

—— *Papal Legate at the Council of Trent: Cardinal Seripando*, transl. Frederic Eckhoff (St. Louis and London, Herder, 1947).

Jedin, Hubert and Alberigo, Giuseppe, *Il tipo ideale di vescovo secondo la Riforma Cattolica* (Brescia: Morcelliana, 1985).

Kosztolnyik, Z.J., "Some Hungarian Theologians in the Late Renaissance," *Church History* 57 (1988): 5-18.

Lee, Stephen, *The Thirty Years War* (London: Routledge, 1991).

Lubac, Henri de, *Exégèse médiévale: Les quatre sens del'écriture*, 4 vols. (Paris: Aubier, 1959-64).

Macklem, Michael, *God have Mercy: The Life of John Fisher of Rochester* (Ottawa: Oberon Press, 1968).

Marc'Hardour, Germain, "Erasmus as Priest: Holy Orders in his Vision and Practice," in *Erasmus' Vision of the Church*, eds. Hilmar Pabel and Erika Rummel, pp. 115-49 (Kirksville: Sixteenth Century Journal Publishers, 1995).

McGinness, Frederick, *Right Thinking and Sacred Oratory in Counter-Reformation Rome* (Princeton: Princeton University Press, 1995).

Mormando, Franco, *The Preacher's Demons: Bernardino of Siena and the Social Underworld of Early Renaissance Italy* (Chicago: University of Chicago Press, 1999).

Nauert, Charles, *Humanism and the Culture of Renaissance Europe* (Cambridge: Cambridge University Press, 1995).

Norman, Corrie, *Humanist Taste and Franciscan Values: Cornelio Musso and Catholic Preaching in Sixteenth-Century Italy* (New York: Peter Lang, 1998).

O'Donohoe, James. *Tridentine Seminary Legislation: Its Sources and its Foundations* (Louvain: Publications Universitaires, 1957).

Olin, John, ed., *The Catholic Reformation: Savonarola to Ignatius Loyola* (New York: Fordham University Press, 1992).

O'Malley, John, "Content and Rhetorical Forms in Sixteenth-Century Treatises on Preaching," in *Renaissance Eloquence*, ed. James Murphy, pp. 238-52 (Berkeley: University of California Press, 1983).

— "Erasmus and the History of Sacred Rhetoric: the *Ecclesiastes* of 1535," *Erasmus of Rotterdam Society Yearbook* 5 (1985): 1-29.

— *The First Jesuits* (Cambridge: Harvard University Press, 1993).

— *Praise and Blame in Renaissance Rome: Rhetoric, Doctrine, and Reform in the Sacred Orators of the Papal Court, ca. 1450-1521* (Durham: Duke University Press, 1979).

Oxford Encyclopedia of the Reformation, 4 vols. (Oxford: Oxford University Press, 1996).

Ozment, Steven, *The Age of Reform, 1250-1550* (New Haven: Yale University Press, 1980).

Rasmussen, Niels, "Liturgy and Iconography at the Canonization of Carlo Borromeo, 1 November 1610," in *San Carlo Borromeo*, ed. John Headley and John Tomaro, pp. 264-76 (London: Associated University Presses, 1988).

Ravier, André, *Un sage et un saint François de Sales* (Paris: Nouvelle Cité, 1985).

Rex, Richard, *The Theology of John Fisher* (Cambridge: Cambridge University Press, 1991).

Rusconi, Roberto, *Predicazione e vita religiosa nella società italiana da Carlo Magno alla Controriforma*. (Turin: Loescher, 1981).

Sales, François de, *Oeuvres*, 26 vols. (Annecy: Niérat, 1892-1932).

Siggins, Ian, *Luther and his Mother* (Philadelphia: Fortress, 1981).

Smith, Hilary Dansey, *Preaching in the Spanish Golden Age: A Study of Some Preachers in the Reign of Philip III* (Oxford: Oxford University Press, 1978).

Sommervogel, Carlos, *Bibliothèque de la Compagnie de Jésus*, 9 vols. (Brussels: Schepens, 1890-1900).

Sonnino, Lee, *A Handbook to Sixteenth-Century Rhetoric* (London: Routledge & Kegan Paul, 1968).

Taylor, Larissa, "Comme un chien mort: Images of Kingship in French Preaching," *Proceedings of the Western Society for French History* 22 (1995): 157-70.

— "The Influence of Humanism on Post-Reformation Catholic Preachers in France," *Renaissance Quarterly* 50 (1997): 119-35.

— *Soldiers of Christ: Preaching in Late Medieval and Reformation France* (Oxford: Oxford University Press, 1992).

Temesvar, Pelbart of, *Stellarium coronae benedictae Mariae Virginis* (Augsburg, 1502).

Worcester, Thomas, "Neither Married nor Cloistered: Blessed Isabelle in Catholic Reformation France," *Sixteenth Century Journal* 30 (1999): 457-72.

— *Seventeenth-Century Cultural Discourse: France and the Preaching of Bishop Camus* (Berlin: Mouton de Gruyter, 1997).

Zawart, Ansgar, *The History of Franciscan Preaching and of Franciscan Preachers (1209-1927): A Biographical Study* (New York: Wagner, 1928).

CHAPTER TWO

THE LUTHERAN SERMON

Beth Kreitzer
(Saint Vincent College)

The sermon, despite often being ignored in earlier scholarship, is perhaps the most significant genre of literature stemming from the Lutheran Reformation. While sermons were not invented by Luther or his colleagues, they were given a new status in religious life and liturgy, and served a primary function in transferring the new ideas and reforms to audiences far and wide. The reason for this is two-fold: in the largely oral culture of early modern Europe, the spoken word was the vehicle through which the majority of the population received information. The sermon was dominant in print culture, so much so that Luther's sermons appeared in mass quantities in the first decade of the reform movement. Thus Luther and his followers seized upon a pre-existing form, the sermon, transforming it into a teaching tool of great significance. They built upon developments in the late medieval period, but placed their own distinctive stamp upon the terms, forms, and uses of the sermon in the sixteenth and early seventeenth centuries.

Historical Background

Many scholars have noted that popular preaching in vernacular languages had been in vogue for at least a generation before the Reformation.[1] In the later medieval period, sermons were not

---

[1]　See, for example, R. W. Scribner, "Oral Culture and the Transmission of Reformation Ideas," in *The Transmission of Ideas in the Lutheran Reformation*, ed. Helga Robinson-Hammerstein (Dublin: Irish Academic Press, 1989), p. 84. The literature on preaching in the Middle Ages is quite large; a few examples in English include: G. R. Owst, *Preaching in Medieval England: An Introduction to Sermon Manuscripts of the Period c. 1350-1450* (Cambridge: Cambridge University Press, 1926); idem, *Literature and Pulpit in Medieval England* (Cambridge: Cambridge University Press, 1933); R. Petry, *No Uncertain Sound: Sermons*

always (and in places not often) part of the mass, but were commonly reserved for special occasions and days of penance and fasting (such as the Lenten seasons), festivals, revivals (often penitential), and days of indulgence.[2] In cities and larger towns in the fifteenth century, however, preaching could occur quite often, while in smaller towns or villages it was much less frequent. Mendicant friars, especially Dominicans, Franciscans, and Augustinians, specifically trained their members for preaching, and the traveling preachers were often quite popular and could attract large crowds. Diocesan priests spent less and less of their time preaching, often delegating this duty to assistant priests and chaplains.

Increasing dissatisfaction with the quality of preaching in the fifteenth century led many cities, lay groups, or even individual leaders or princes (particularly in southern Germany) to found preaching posts, which often paid quite well, in order to attract a skilled preacher. Steven Ozment points out that such preacherships were a joint venture of laity and clergy: "a decision was taken by local laity and clergy to improve a local situation, with distant episcopal authority playing a very secondary if nonetheless indispensable role."[3] Ozment documents that many of the men who held preaching posts in the early sixteenth century became involved in the reform movement; in Württemberg, more than half of the towns with active preacherships became Protestant, and in other regions (such as Thüringia) many of the leaders of reform had served in such posts.[4]

The most well-known of these late medieval preacherships is probably the post created for Johann Geiler of Keisersberg (d. 1510) in Strasbourg's cathedral church in 1479. Before settling in Strasbourg, Geiler had served in several positions at the university in Basel, where he received his doctorate in 1475, and taught theol-

---

that Shaped the Pulpit Tradition (Philadephia: Westminster Press, 1948); D. L. D'Avray, "The Transformation of the Medieval Sermon" (D.Phil. diss., University of Oxford, 1977); Thomas L. Amos, *De ore Domini: Preacher and Word in the Middle Ages* (Kalamazoo, Mich.: Medieval Institute Publications, 1989); H. Leith Spencer, *English Preaching in the Late Middle Ages* (Oxford: Clarendon Press, 1993).

   [2] Yngve Brilioth, *A Brief History of Preaching*, trans. Karl E. Mattson (Philadelphia: Fortress Press, 1965), p. 87.

   [3] Steven E. Ozment, *The Reformation in the Cities: The Appeal of Protestantism to Sixteenth-Century Germany and Switzerland* (New Haven and London: Yale University Press, 1975), p. 41.

   [4] Ibid., p. 39.

ogy and served as rector of the university in Freiburg am Breisgau.[5] A scholastically-trained doctor of theology, he was also part of a large circle of humanists and intellectuals. It was Geiler's duty in Strasbourg to preach every Sunday during the year, daily during Lent, and also on special holidays, and he may have influenced the model sermon structure presented by Ulrich Surgant (d. 1503) in his famous preaching manual, the *Manuale curatorum*.[6]

In his published sermon collections, intended as model sermons for other preachers, Geiler stressed that sermons must be tailored to the audience: the common people needed training in the basics of the Christian faith, not in the technical terms of the scholastics. Geiler felt that theological disputations should be reserved for the schools, not for sermons.[7] He defended his use of metaphors and parables in the service of the simplicity and comprehensibility needed for his listeners. The form of preaching most commonly used by Geiler was the thematic sermon, in which the preacher would choose a specific theme from a biblical passage to develop. This was the type of sermon recommended and taught in many of the preaching manuals, or *artes praedicandi*, of the later medieval period. Preaching on a theme was a departure from the homiletic style, or the *explication de texte*, practiced in the patristic period. The manuals sketched the structure of such sermons: the *antethema* (a biblical passage related to the theme), a prayer, the theme itself, the divisions of the theme (including scriptural proof texts, selections from the Fathers, and illustrations), and also suggested that a preacher develop appropriate gestures and humor to accompany his sermon.[8]

While thematic sermons had to be based upon a biblical passage

---

[5] E. Jane Dempsey Douglass, *Justification in Late Medieval Preaching: A Study of John Geiler of Keisersberg*, Studies in Medieval and Reformation Thought, vol. I, ed. H. A. Oberman (Leiden: E. J. Brill, 1966), p. 6.

[6] Ibid., p. 31. See also Dorothea Roth, *Die mittelalterliche Predigttheorie und das Manuale Curatorum des Johann Ulrich Surgant* (Basel: Helbing & Lichtenhahn, 1956).

[7] Douglass points out that not all Geiler's contemporaries felt this way: the Frenchmen Michel Menot and Olivier Maillard often introduced theological questions in the style of *Sentences* commentaries into their sermons. See Douglass, p. 33. For late medieval French preaching, see Larissa J. Taylor, *Soldiers of Christ: Preaching in Late Medieval and Early Modern France* (New York: Oxford University Press, 1992).

[8] Brilioth, pp. 80-81. The major study of the *artes praedicandi* is T. M. Charland, *Artes Praedicandi, Contribution à l'histoire de la rhétorique au moyen âge* (Ottawa: Publications de l'institut d'études médiévales d'Ottawa, 1936).

or, at the very least, word, the medieval methods of biblical interpretation allowed a very wide latitude in the actual subject of such
sermons. The "fourfold sense" of scriptural interpretation common
in the Middle Ages is quite well known: the literal sense (following
Augustine, considered to be the basis of all biblical interpretation),
the moral or tropological sense, the allegorical sense, and finally the
anagogical sense were commonly used to interpret biblical texts.
For example, the city of Jerusalem, the capital of Judea in the literal sense, signified tropologically an orderly state and community
life, allegorically the church, and anagogically the holy city, or eternal life.[9] The fourfold sense of scripture, or "quadriga," was often
explained in couplet form: *Littera gesta docet, quid credas allegoria,
Moralis quid agas, quo tendas anagogia* ("The letter teaches what has
happened, allegory what one believes, the moral meaning what one
does, and anagoge where one is going.")[10] However, the fourfold
model, which appeared in such writers as Gregory the Great, John
Cassian, Thomas Aquinas, Hugh of St. Cher, and Nicholas of
Lyra, was not the only possibility in medieval exegesis. Thomas
himself, along with Albert the Great, tended to promote the literal
meaning of the biblical text (although they did not reject spiritual
interpretations.)[11]

Along with the various senses of the biblical text which allowed
preachers to range far afield from their pericopes, the practice of
preaching thematic sermons, both on Sundays and on special occasions, led to a large body of sermonic material that was clearly addressed to present concerns and problems. While many sermons

---

[9]   The fourfold sense of scriptural interpretation has been highly criticized by nine-
teenth- and twentieth-century Protestant scholars. For example, Brilioth suggests that
this "misuse" of the Bible led even the best preachers to ignore the biblical content in
favor of prooftexting: "the possibility for real exegetical preaching was destroyed by the
method of exegesis itself." (pp. 90-91)

[10]   Richard A. Muller, "Biblical Interpretation in the Era of the Reformation: The
View from the Middle Ages," in *Biblical Interpretation in the Era of the Reformation: Essays
Presented to David C. Steinmetz in Honor of His Sixtieth Birthday*, eds. Richard A. Muller and
John L. Thompson (Grand Rapids, Mich. and Cambridge: William B. Eerdmans Pub-
lishing Company, 1996), p. 9. See also Harry Caplan, "The Four Senses of Scriptural
Interpretation and the Medieval Theology of Preaching," *Speculum* 4 (1929): 282-90.

[11]   Some of the most important works in the area of medieval exegesis are Beryl
Smalley, *The Study of the Bible in the Middle Ages* (Notre Dame: Notre Dame University
Press, 1964); Ceslaus Spicq, *Esquisse d'une histoire de l'exégèse latine au moyen âge* (Paris: J.
Vrin, 1944); Henri de Lubac, *Exégèse mediaevale: les quatre sens de l'Ecriture*, 4 vols. (Paris:
Aubier, 1959-64).

took allegorical flight, presenting an even mystical quality to their listeners in tune with popular pious and devotional literature and movements (the Dominican mystic and spiritual writer John Tauler [d. 1361] had also been a preacher in Strasbourg), at least as many took the opportunity to provide moral instruction and preach repentance. The *"Bußpredigten"* of an earlier time turned into social criticism, occasionally severe, of many areas of both secular and religious life.[12] The critiques of prelates and the lesser clergy became especially common in the fifteenth and early sixteenth centuries.

Martin Luther and his Preaching

In order to gain an understanding of the development of the genre of sermons in Lutheranism, what continuities and discontinuities it had with the preceding medieval tradition, one must take into account both the theory and the practice of preaching, both the form and the content. Martin Luther, the founder of the Lutheran movement, and an active and able preacher, provides the natural beginning of such a study. The main difficulty with such an endeavor is that Luther left behind no treatise on preaching, and very few theoretical statements about it. More practical examples of his preaching "theory," that is, examples of his sermons composed and collected for a clerical audience and their edification, are available in his two early postils, the "Wartburg Postil" published in 1522, and the "Lent Postil" published in 1525. Of the remainder of his more than two thousand extant sermons, the majority were edited and published by his contemporaries, often in condensed or partial-Latin versions.

Luther was commissioned to preach by Johann von Staupitz (d. 1524), the Vicar General of his order, the observant Augustinians, and from 1514 until the appointment of Johannes Bugenhagen (d. 1558) in 1522 he preached in the city church in Wittenberg, while

---

12 Alfred Niebergall, "Die Geschichte der christlichen Predigt," in *Leiturgia: Handbuch des Evangelischen Gottesdienstes*, Bd. II, ed. K. F. Müller and W. Blankenburg (Kassel: Johannes Stauda-Verlag, 1955), p. 255. On penitential preaching on the eve of the Reformation, see Anne T. Thayer, "Penitence and Preaching on the Eve of the Reformation: a Comparative Overview from Frequently Printed Model Sermon Collections, 1450-1520" (Ph.D. diss., Harvard University, 1996).

also maintaining his teaching position at the university. His early sermons followed scholastic technique, while in the period 1515-1517 he exhibited the influence of German mysticism and especially Tauler's *Theologia Germanica*. In this period before his conflict and eventual break with Rome, Luther preached a message of reform common in the early sixteenth-century context, that of a reform of morals and life, both of the clergy and the laity. He preached catechetical sermons on the Ten Commandments, attacking common superstitions and the empty performance of religious duties.[13] He began preaching against the indulgence traffic in 1515, which led him into several of his early conflicts, most notably the reaction to his *Ninety-Five Theses* of 1517 and the more widely published *Sermon on Indulgences and Grace*.

In the years after the publication of his *Sermon on Indulgences and Grace*, his first "best-seller," Luther's sermon production and their publication increased. In the years from 1518 to 1525, Luther published over 200 works in the vernacular, reprinted numerous times, so that over 1800 editions of works by Luther had come out of presses in the Empire by the end of 1525.[14] And, as Mark Edwards notes, two out of every five printings through this period were sermons, and one in every three until 1530. These handy, cheap publications, which flooded the German-speaking market, focused on devotional and pastoral issues, stressing that Christians should "acknowledge their own sinfulness and surrender all reliance on their own works, and, second, that they should trust God and God's promise in Christ as their only source of salvation."[15] While they rejected good works and were critical of the clergy and their assumed powers, Luther's popular publications rarely mentioned his problems with the papacy, at least until late in 1520 when Luther published several important treatises attacking the Roman religious authorities.

---

[13] Harold J. Grimm, *Martin Luther as a Preacher* (Columbus, Oh.: Lutheran Book Concern, 1929), pp. 66-67. This book carries Luther hagiography to an extreme, but conveniently gathers together a number of disparate comments and quotations relating to Luther's preaching.

[14] Mark U. Edwards, Jr., *Printing, Propaganda, and Martin Luther* (Berkeley: University of California Press, 1994), pp. 26-27.

[15] Ibid., p. 164.

Luther's Theology of the Word

Despite his quarrel with and definitive break from Rome, Luther continued to publish successfully. Most notable were his translation of the New Testament, and eventually the entire Bible, his postils (comprising sermons for the entire church year), and catechisms. In reflecting upon his conflict with Rome over indulgences, Luther remarked in one of the famous *Invocavit* sermons preached in 1522 upon his return to Wittenberg from the Wartburg:

> I opposed indulgences and all the papists, but never with force. I simply taught, preached, and wrote God's word; otherwise I did nothing. And while I slept, or drank Wittenberg beer with my friends Philipp [Melanchthon] and [Nikolaus von] Amsdorf, the word so greatly weakened the papacy that no prince or emperor ever inflicted such losses upon it. I did nothing; the word did everything.[16]

In light of this statement, an investigation of what Luther means by "word" would be helpful, especially in this context of a study of his preaching.

For Luther, the "Word," in its most basic form, is Christ. Luther reads the prologue of John's gospel, "In the beginning was the Word, and the Word was with God, and the Word was God" to mean that the Word is Christ, the revelation of God to the world. Luther also often speaks of both scripture and preaching as "the Word," but that does not mean that for Luther every literal word in the Bible is "the Word." Rather, the center and meaning of scripture is Christ, and thus the Bible can only be understood insofar as it is interpreted through Christ. This interpretive scheme includes both Old and New Testaments, for to Luther the Old Testament foreshadows and prepares the way for Christ, while the New Testament opens and reveals the prophetic nature of the Old.[17] In scripture, the Word can be found in two forms: law and gospel. The law serves to show the perfect will of God, but also to prove to human beings that they are sinful and unable to do God's will. The gospel, on the other hand, first calls Christians to repentance (through the law), then provides forgiveness and grace through Christ.

---

[16]   Luther, *Invocavit* sermon no. 2, in *Luther's Works* [hereafter cited as LW], vol. 51, *Sermons I*, ed. John W. Doberstein (Philadelphia: Fortress Press, 1959), p. 77.

[17]   Philip S. Watson, *Let God Be God! An Interpretation of the Theology of Martin Luther* (Philadelphia: Fortress Press, 1947), pp. 149-151.

The "Word" is found in scripture, but most accurately it is the spoken rather than the written word; the New Testament was only recorded to help combat heresy. Because the Word is a living word, however, Luther felt it must be preached in order for it to be effective. In a similar way that Christ is present in the sacraments, Christ is present in the spoken word of preaching: "for Luther, wherever there is a manifestation or utterance of the Divine will of love, there is the living Word of God."[18] Luther insisted, against the spiritualists, that the Spirit works through the external word to awaken repentance and faith in people's hearts, for "where the Word is proclaimed, Christ is present; where it is not, he is not."[19] This does not mean that the preacher controls God's word or power – the preacher is the instrument or medium through whom God works to change his listeners: "It is easy enough for someone to preach the word to me, but only God can enter it into my heart. He must speak it in my heart, or nothing at all will come of it."[20]

Interpreting the Bible correctly is also a concern of Luther's: although it is God's power and the Spirit that work through the preacher's words to move his auditors, he still must struggle to understand and speak God's word correctly. A preacher must meet certain moral and spiritual preconditions in order to interpret the Bible rightly, and he must particularly possess the virtue of humility.[21] The interpretation of scripture must also take place under the authority and witness of the church: Luther calls the church the "gate of salvation" and insists that "outside of the church there is no true knowledge of God."[22] The interpretation of scripture is a public event under the jurisdiction of the church's magisterium.

Theoretical Issues in Luther's Preaching
Because Luther, unlike a number of his contemporaries (most notably Melanchthon and Erasmus), did not write a specific treatise on

---

[18]   Ibid., p. 152.
[19]   Ibid., p. 162.
[20]   Martin Luther, *D. Martin Luthers Werke. Kritische Gesamtausgabe.* 62 vols. Weimar: Böhlaus, 1883-. (Hereafter cited as WA). This citation is from WA 10^{III}, p. 260. See also WA 17^{II}, p. 174.
[21]   David C. Steinmetz, *Luther and Staupitz: An Essay in the Intellectual Origins of the Protestant Reformation*, Duke Monographs in Medieval and Renaissance Studies, no. 4 (Durham, N.C.: Duke University Press, 1980), p. 51. See Luther, WA 3, p. 515.
[22]   Ibid. See Luther, WA 4, p. 25 and 3, p. 268: "*Extra enim Ecclesiam non est cognitio vera Dei.*"

how to preach, any study of his mode of preaching must look to other materials for information. A number of his early sermons follow scholastic models, especially the "thematic" model recommended in the medieval *artes praedicandi*. Even after turning away from this style, scholastic elements can still be found in some sermons: a *thema* or scriptural quotation is often present at the beginning; biblical proof-texts often play an important role; a definitive conclusion is often missing.[23] Yet the style of sermon that Luther came to prefer is quite different from that recommended by medieval authors, and has more in common with the patristic homily, or verse-by-verse exegesis of the text. He, along with many of his contemporaries, was often highly critical of allegorical modes of exegesis found in many medieval commentaries and sermons, and usually preferred a more literal and/or prophetic mode of interpretation (also found in Nicholas of Lyra). But although Luther rejected the allegorical flights of fancy and criticized the disinterest in the "plain sense" of scripture in much medieval exegesis, he was not opposed to finding a spiritual sense in biblical texts. His interpretive key remained focused upon Christ, which also determined the goal of his preaching: the Christ-centered truths hidden in the text – law and gospel, grace and faith over works – often made up the content of his sermons.

Luther's use of the homiletic form was not unique in the early sixteenth century: along with the continued use of verse-by-verse exegesis, John O'Malley has documented a number of earlier innovations from the scholastic forms recommended in the *artes*. Humanists, particularly in Italy, had attempted to apply the rules of classical rhetoric to the art of preaching and other sacred discourse, and helped to transform the style of sermons in the sixteenth century.[24] Already at the end of the fourteenth century, Italian humanists began to abandon the traditional medieval thematic sermon form, and adapt the classical *genus demonstrativum*, what O'Malley calls the "art of praise and blame," to doctrinal sermons and ser-

---

[23] John W. O'Malley, "Luther the Preacher," *Michigan Germanic Studies* 10 (1984): 4.

[24] Ibid., pp. 5-6. See also his article "Content and Rhetorical Forms in Sixteenth-Century Treatises on Preaching," in *Renaissance Eloquence: Studies in the Theory and Practice of Renaissance Rhetoric*, ed. James J. Murphy, pp. 238-252 (Berkeley: University of California Press, 1983).

mons relating to the life of Christ and the saints.[25] This adaptation
of classical rhetoric influenced both a change in terminology, with
the substitution of classical terms for their medieval equivalents,
and in content, with sermons focusing more on God's deeds and
actions and less on abstract doctrines: "the very purpose of the sermon was transformed from an exercise in proof and dialectical argumentation to an exercise in praise."[26] Luther, of course, would
not have been familiar with this movement, as the majority of sermon manuals written and published even in Italy continued to rec-
ommend traditional medieval forms. He may have known
Reuchlin's 1504 treatise *Liber congestorum de arte praedicandi*, a brief
and transitional work that allowed the preacher to use all three of
the classical *genera*, the judicial, the deliberative, and the demonstrative.[27]

Luther, according to O'Malley, can more accurately be described
as fitting into the tradition of the "Christian grammarian," who had
both philological concerns and a "poetic" interest in the meaning
of texts.[28] Luther occasionally presented philological points to his
audience, discussing the translation or mistranslation of terms, and
how this might affect their meanings. One good example of this
focus on terms is Luther's critique (taken up by many of his followers) of the Latin term *gratia plena*, in the angel's annunciation to
Mary (Luke 1:28). In his translation of the New Testament, Luther
rendered the Greek term *kecharitomene* as *holdselige* ("gracious," or
"lovely," with a passive sense), rather than *voll gnade* (a translation of
the Vulgate's *gratia plena*). While he argued in his treatise on translation that, apart from the theological problems with this term, *voll
gnade* is simply bad German, in his House-postil sermon he reiterates
that Mary, like all Christians, needs God's grace for her salvation.[29]
She is not "full of grace" of herself, nor does she dispense grace to
others, which he felt could be implied by *gratia plena*.

---

[25] O'Malley, "Content and Rhetorical Forms," p. 239.
[26] Ibid., p. 240. O'Malley argues that this focus on praise, and a positive apprecia-
tion of God and all his creation, was highly influential in developing the "peculiarly
Renaissance theme of the 'dignity of man.'"
[27] Ibid., p. 241.
[28] O'Malley, "Luther the Preacher," p. 8.
[29] Luther, WA 52, p. 626: "'*Gegrüsset (spricht er) seist du holdselige' oder begnadete, 'der
Herr ist mit dir, du Hochgelobte unter den weybern.'*" WA 52, p. 633: "*Und durch solchen glauben
allein ist [Maria] auch selig unnd von sünden ledig worden, unnd nicht durch das werck, das sie den
Son Gottes hat an die welt gebracht.*" Luther's *Sendbrief am Dolmetschen* is in WA 30[II].

Although Luther often disdained methodology and rules, he was not ignorant of classical rhetoric, and was even willing to allow the use of Aristotle's manuals on logic, rhetoric, and poetics if they would serve the church by helping to produce good preachers.[30] In his recommendations to other preachers, Luther usually contented himself with suggesting a simple faithfulness to the text or the subject of the sermon. This stress on simplicity and freedom from the traditional rules, and his rejection of the quadriga and allegorical methods of interpretation, has led some scholars to suggest that Luther rejected all forms and conventions, instead preaching "spontaneously and freely."[31] More recent scholars, however, notably Ulrich Nembach, have shown that the humanistic emphasis on classical rhetorical forms also influenced Luther's preaching.[32] Nembach suggests that Luther relied significantly on the ancient author Quintillian, and adopted the mode of speech "in exhortation of the people," or the *genus deliberativum* for his sermons.[33] Luther himself said that preaching is both teaching and exhortation – *doctrina et exhortatio*.[34] Thus the goal of his sermons was both to instruct (hence the doctrinal content) and to move his audience to improvement. A good example of Luther's use of the classical *contio*, that is, a "speech of the *genus deliberativum*... addressed to popular audiences," is his "Sermon on Keeping Children in School" (1530).[35] This sermon, addressed to parents, not only strongly encourages them to send their children to school, but also establishes Luther's views on the necessity of education and training for the ministry, and especially for the office of preaching. A preacher, he

---

[30] Luther, "Appeal to the German Nobility (1520)," WA 6, p. 458.

[31] Grimm, *Martin Luther as a Preacher*, p. 78: "True genius never allows itself to be shackled by form." Brilioth, who criticizes others of "uncritical hero worship," suggests that Luther's homiletic faults included "the neglect of form and the lack of discipline in the arrangement," but insists that only such a lack of form was consistent with Luther's sermons' "spontaneous impetuosity" and their "epochal significance." Brilioth, *Brief History of Preaching*, p. 112.

[32] Ulrich Nembach, *Predigt des Evangeliums: Luther als Prediger, Pädagoge und Rhetor* (Neukirch: Neukirchener Verlag, 1972).

[33] Ibid., pp. 147-152, 156. Quintilian (ca. 35-95), was author of the *Institutio oratoria*, which Luther highly valued.

[34] Luther, WA, *Tischreden*, 2, 359, 18-21, no. 2199. See Nembach, *Predigt des Evangeliums*, 25-26; also Birgit Stolt, "Docere, delectare und movere bei Luther," *Deutsche Vierteljahresschrift für Literaturwissenschaft und Geistesgeschichte* (1970): 433-474.

[35] O'Malley, "Luther as Preacher," p. 9. This sermon is found in LW 46, pp. 209-258, and in WA 30[II], pp. 517-588.

writes, who must be an educated man, confirms, strengthens, and helps to sustain authority of every kind, and temporal peace generally. He checks the rebellious; teaches obedience, morals, discipline, and honor; instructs fathers, mothers, children, and servants in their duties; in a word, he gives direction to all the temporal estates and offices.[36] Luther stresses and praises the importance of the preacher to his audience in order both to instruct them in what God's word can accomplish, and to encourage and admonish them to provide an education for their sons.

While the hortatory aspect of Luther's sermons is derived from the classical *genus deliberativum* – the *genus* that became the central form for preaching in the sixteenth century, both in Protestant and Catholic circles – the doctrinal or teaching aspect is more closely related to a *genus* of Melanchthon's invention, the *genus didascalicum* or *didacticum*, which will be discussed in a later section.[37] Luther's pedagogic or doctrinal message was constantly repeated: "the message of works-faith, law-gospel, wrath-grace recurs implicitly or explicitly in practically everything he wrote."[38] He was also quick to point out the enemies of the gospel: papists, spiritualists, and *Schwärmer* (fanatics). What might in other forms be abstract doctrine became in Luther's sermons a righteous program of life and belief: he insisted the faithful should live their lives in Christian freedom, and provided practical directions for how this could be accomplished.

Preaching and Practical Matters

For Luther, any theoretical concerns having to do with preaching were in the service of his practical concerns: they related to the correct proclamation and transmission of the gospel. As we have seen, he did not write a preaching manual to instruct others in the proper manner of preaching. He did, however, write and publish a number of works relating to the proper context of preaching, that is, the worship service. In his earliest essay on divine worship in 1523, Luther expressed concern over the place (or lack thereof) of

---

[36]   LW 46, p. 226.
[37]   O'Malley, "Luther as Preacher," p. 10.
[38]   Ibid., p. 12.

the sermon in the Roman mass.[39] Along with critiquing the content of the sermons of his contemporaries, complaining that they were full of lies, fables, and legends rather than God's word, he also accused the "papists" of suppressing the proclamation of the word in their services.[40] Every worship service, including the daily services, should include expository preaching: in the morning, an Old Testament lesson should be preached, while in the afternoons the New Testament should be expounded. For Sunday services, in the mornings the gospel should be read and explained, while at vespers either the epistle should be the chosen text, or the preacher had the option of treating a book of the Bible consecutively. In spite of much criticism, Luther maintained the traditional pericopic division of the biblical text for Sunday worship.[41]

Although his "purified" Latin mass was published in 1523, Luther did not introduce his new German mass in Wittenberg until Christmas, 1525.[42] This service was intended for the simple folk, and particularly young people, and thus had a catechetical focus. Preaching was, of course, a main element of the service: a sermon was held on the epistle at matins (6:00 a.m.) and on the gospel at the morning mass (8:00 or 9:00 a.m.). At the afternoon service, Old Testament texts were read and explained.[43] The sermons that were read were in fact usually a portion of Luther's own postil sermons: thus in areas where this service was instituted, Luther became the authoritative preacher.[44] He also instituted programs of preaching for the weekday services: Mondays and Tuesdays had sermons based on the catechism; Wednesday sermons treated the gospel of

---

[39]   The 1523 tract "Concerning the Order of Public Worship" is found in WA 12, pp. 31-37 and LW 52, pp. 7-14.

[40]   Alfred Niebergall, "Luthers Auffassung von der Predigt nach 'De Servo Arbitrio,'" in *Reformation und Gegenwart*, eds. H. Graß and W. G. Kümmel, Marburger Theologische Studien 6 (Marburg: N. G. Elwert Verlag, 1968), p. 84.

[41]   Brilioth, *Brief History of Preaching*, p. 117. Brilioth remarks that Luther's preservation of the church year and traditional pericopes had "a far-reaching significance since it gave later Lutheran preaching the unique pattern by which it differentiates itself to a great extent from practically all other Christian preaching." (p. 118)

[42]   The "Deutsche Messe (1526)" can be found in WA 19, pp. 44-113, and LW 53, pp. 51-90.

[43]   Martin Brecht, *Martin Luther: Shaping and Defining the Reformation, 1521-1532*, trans. James L. Schaaf (Minneapolis: Fortress Press, 1990), pp. 255-6.

[44]   Brecht indicates that, at least in Electoral Saxony, the use of Luther's mass was mandated, although after 1528 another service developed by Bugenhagen and Justas Jonas began to replace it. See Brecht, *Martin Luther*, pp. 256-7.

Matthew; on Thursdays and Fridays other New Testament books
were to be preached; and on Saturdays the text was from the gospel
of John.

Luther himself preached constantly, both in Wittenberg and
while traveling. On Sundays and festivals he preached on the appointed gospels, while in the afternoons he gave continuous sermons on the books of 1 Peter (beginning in May 1522), 2 Peter and
Jude (from the beginning of 1523), and Genesis (from March 1523
until the fall of 1524), among others.[45] In the Lenten season it was
not unusual for Luther to preach a series of sermons around a
theme, such as catechetical sermons, or the *Invocavit* sermons he
preached upon his return from the Wartburg in 1522. Most of
these sermons were published, either with or without Luther's permission. He was also involved in these years in the preparation of
his postils: the "Wartburg" postil of Advent and Christmas sermons
was prepared by Luther specifically as a book of model sermons to
help other preachers. He extended these sermons through the
pericopes for Easter (published in 1525), and several later collections were edited and published by his students and colleagues.[46] In
the "Brief Introduction" which he included with his Christmas
postil (and throughout the postil itself), Luther again stressed the
centrality of the preached word for the Christian faith.[47] The gospel
rightly preached, he felt, would produce the proper fruit (i.e. right
living, good works). That this transformation did not often occur
was one of Luther's major disappointments: there was even a period in 1529 when he refused to preach in Wittenberg. He told his
audience at one point, "I do not want to be the shepherd of such
pigs."[48] He, like many other reform-minded pastors, was dismayed
by the continued ignorance of the parishioners and the stubborn
maintenance of Catholic or superstitious beliefs. While the quality
of the education and training of Lutheran pastors improved after
the first generation, their effectiveness and catechetical influence
usually did not.[49]

---

[45]   Ibid., p. 58.
[46]   Ibid., pp. 15-16, 285-7.
[47]   WA 10[1,1], pp. 8-18; LW 35, pp. 117-24.
[48]   Brecht, *Martin Luther*, p. 288, citing WA 29, p. 83, a sermon of February 1529.
[49]   See especially Susan C. Karant-Nunn, *Luther's Pastors: The Reformation in the Ernestine Countryside*, Transactions of the American Philosophical Society, v. 69, pt. 8 (Philadelphia: American Philosophical Society, 1979), p. 53; Lorna Jane Abray, "The

Melanchthon and the Development of Theory

While Philipp Melanchthon, a distant relative of the famous Hebraïst and humanist Reuchlin, was not himself a preacher, he exercised a wide influence upon preaching in the sixteenth century through his several treatises on the art of speaking. He published the *De officiis concionatoris* in 1529, and the *Elementa rhetorices* in 1532 – and although he expressed his views in other texts, and may have changed some elements originally presented in these two treatises, they remained the most well-known and influential of his works on preaching.[50]

In the *De officiis*, Melanchthon adapts the classical *genus deliberativum*, the exhortation to preaching, dividing it into two forms: the *epitrepticum*, which exhorts to faith, and the *paraeneticum*, which exhorts to good morals.[51] These two *genera*, along with the previously mentioned new *genus didascalicum* (which teaches), constituted the essence of the sermon for Melanchthon. In fact, he felt that the *genera* related to teaching (*didascalicum, epitrepticum*) were far more important than that which dealt with action. The content of the sermon should be drawn from scripture, and should always include both law and gospel.[52] The rules of rhetoric were to be followed in preaching (and thus must be part of education in preparation for the ministry) in order to insure that the message of sin and grace was properly and effectively conveyed to the people. Melanchthon also recommended the "loci" method of preaching, that is, preaching by the topics in the text, rather than a straightforward verse-by-verse exegesis.[53] Promoting the "loci" method, a focus on proposi-

---

Laity's Religion: Lutheranism in Sixteenth-Century Strasbourg," in *The German People and the Reformation*, ed. R. Po-Chia Hsia (Ithaca: Cornell University Press, 1988), pp. 216-33.

50 He also published *De Rhetorica Libri Tres* (1519), *Quomodo concionator novitius concionem suam informare debeat* (1531/36?), and *De modo et arte concionandi* (1537-1539). See Uwe Schnell, *Die homiletische Theorie Philipp Melanchthons* (Berlin and Hamburg: Lutherisches Verlagshaus, 1968), part 2.

51 O'Malley, "Content and Rhetorical Forms," p. 242. The *De officiis* can be found in the *Supplementa Melanchthoniana*, ed. Paul Drews and Ferdinand Cohrs, vol. 5, pt. 2 (Leipzig: R. Haupt, 1929).

52 Schnell, *Die homiletische Theorie*, p. 171.

53 Ibid., pp. 46-51. Also see Quirinus Breen, "The terms 'Loci Communes' and 'Loci' in Melanchthon," in his *Christianity and Humanism: Studies in the History of Ideas*, ed. Nelson Peter Ross, pp. 93-105 (Grand Rapids, Mich.: W. B. Eerdmans Publishing Co., 1968). Brilioth terms the *loci* method the "articulated" method, and notes it is consid-

tional and dialectically-arranged doctrine, may have unintention-ally led to a reemergence of scholastic forms and models in later sixteenth- and seventeenth-century preaching. But it was Melanch-thon's new *genus didascalicum* that was particularly influential: along with his overwhelming influence among Protestants, O'Malley re-cords how Melanchthon's preaching theories were drawn wholesale into Catholic circles, and were particularly welcomed by those who were dissatisfied with Erasmus's theories.[54]

Erasmus's *Ecclesiastes, sive Concionator evangelicus*, published in 1535 and his last major work, was according to O'Malley, "the single most important treatise on the theory of sacred oratory since Au-gustine's *De Doctrina Christiana*," a work that greatly influenced Eras-mus.[55] Erasmus understood all of scripture to be a form of "wis-dom literature," and thus defined preaching as principally teaching: the preacher's main role is to teach and explain the "philosophy of Christ."[56] He tended to promote the *genus deliberativum* (also known as the *genus suasorium*) as the main mode of preaching; the sermon should consist largely of persuasion to live a godly life. So, as for Lutherans (Melanchthon, we have seen, placed the *genus deliberativum* second only to the *genus didascalicum* in preaching), for sixteenth-cen-tury Catholics the persuasive or hortatory genre was considered highly appropriate and necessary to preaching.[57]

Melanchthon's Influence on Lutheran Homiletics

Melanchthon's treatises, particularly the *Elementa*, were immediately influential among Lutherans. Already in the 1530s other authors such as Georg Major and Arsacius Seehofer incorporated Me-lanchthon's adaptation of the classical rules of rhetoric. Major ap-propriated Melanchthon's ideas, and in 1535 published his *Quaestio-*

---

ered one of the earliest methods in Lutheran homiletics; see Brilioth, *Brief History of Preaching*, pp. 124-5.

[54] O'Malley, "Content and Rhetorical Forms," pp. 244-245.

[55] Ibid., p. 243. Erasmus's treatise can be found in his *Opera omnia*, ed. J. Clericus, 10 vols. (Leiden: P. Van der Aa, 1703-1706), 5.769-1100. See also James Michael Weiss, "*Ecclesiastes* and Erasmus: The Mirror and the Image," *Archiv für Reformationsgeschichte* 65 (1974): 83-108.

[56] O'Malley, "Content and Rhetorical Forms," p. 244.

[57] O'Malley treats sixteenth- and seventeenth-century Catholic developments in rhetoric and preaching in the remainder of his essay.

nes Rhetoricae die Predigt in a question-and-answer format.[58] Seehofer's *Enarrationes Evangeliorum Dominicalium* (first published in 1538), a postil directed toward students, praised Melanchthon's contributions to homiletics, and applied the *genera* to specific scriptural pericopes.[59] In his preface, Seehofer maps out the "types" of holy speaking: the *genera* include the *"didascalico,"* in which both simple ("law, gospel, faith, etc.") and composite ("The law does not justify. Faith justifies. etc.") themes are treated in various divisions; the hortatory (or *"de liberatiuo"*), in which the audience is exhorted to practice faith, charity, piety, and good works, and to avoid drunkenness, pride, impiety, and other sins; and finally the *"demonstratiuo,"* in which the subject (i.e. justice, temperance, or a person) is praised.[60] Other Lutheran theoretical treatises on rhetoric and preaching owed a great debt to Melanchthon, such as Weller's *De modo et ratione concionandi pro studiosi Theologiæ* (1558), Pankratius's *Methodus Concionandi* (1571), Lucas Osiander's *De ratione concionandi* (1584), Andreae's *Methodus concionandi* (1595), and Hunnius's *Methodus concionandi* (1595), all published in Wittenberg.[61]

The first actual Protestant homiletic textbook was composed by the Dutchman Andreas Gerhard of Ypres (1511-1564), called Hyperius, who was a professor at Marburg. His manual appeared in 1533, then in an enlarged edition in 1562. Like Melanchthon, he applied the terms and categories of classical rhetoric to preaching, while asserting that the basic element and content of preaching is always scriptural exegesis.[62] Hyperius felt that while the goal of preaching was always to further the reconciliation between God

---

58   Schnell, *Die homiletische Theorie*, p. 173.

59   Seehofer, *Enarrationes Evangeliorum Dominicalium, ad dialecticam Methodum, & Rhetoricam dispositionem accommodatæ* (Augustae Vind.: Heinrich Steiner, 1539). Herzog August Bibliothek [hereafter HAB Yv 1309.8° Helmst. (2)].

60   Seehofer, *Enarrationes*, preface, a iiij v.

61   Schnell, *Die homiletische Theorie*, pp. 174-5. See also Martin Schian, "Die lutherische Homiletik in der zweiten Hälfte des 16. Jahrhunderts," *Theologische Studien und Kritiken* 72 (1899): 62-94.

62   Niebergall, who critiques Melanchthon by suggesting that it is through him that the "preponderance of rhetoric" enters Lutheran homiletics, suggests that although Hyperius used the rules of the rhetoricians, he tried to "free homiletics from the chains of classical rhetoric," making clear the distinction between an evangelical sermon and "the forensic speech of antiquity." This championing of Hyperius seems to rest as much upon a traditional distrust of Melanchthon and unfamiliarity with all his writings on rhetoric, as it does upon an ingrained dislike of rhetorical categories. See Niebergall, "Die Geschichte der christlichen Predigt," pp. 278-9.

and humankind, the formal characteristics of the sermon were *docere, delectare, flectere* – to teach, to delight, and to influence.[63] He divided the sermon into the following parts, which became the standard: reading of the biblical text (*lectio scripturae sacrae*), invocation (*invocatio*), introduction (*exordium*), announcement of the subject and divisions (*propositio sive divisio*), treatment of the subject (*confirmatio*), argumentation (*confutatio*), conclusion (*conclusio*).[64] From several biblical passages (II Tim. 3:16 and Romans 15:4), Hyperius deduced five categories through which to analyze the scriptural text (in Lutheran homiletics known as the *usus quintuplex*): teaching, rebuttal, training, correction, and comfort.[65]

Lutheran Orthodoxy and Early Pietism

In the later years of the sixteenth and into the seventeenth centuries, the homiletical methods found in Melanchthon's treatises and the preaching manual of Hyperius became standard, and preaching in this period (usually known as "Orthodoxy" or the "age of confessionalization") is usually characterized as increasingly formal, rule-bound, and focused on law. The Lutheran retention of the pericope (where the scriptural texts for each Sunday and holiday were the same year after year) and the doctrine of the verbal inspiration of scripture have been blamed for some of the excesses found in orthodox preaching: for example, the preacher Georg Strigenitz (d. 1603) preached four different sermons on the words "to Jonah, son of Amittai" (Jonah 1:1b).[66] Preachers in the period of orthodoxy felt the need to provide Christian instruction and training consistently and repeatedly, witnessed by the regular appearance of polemic against various opponents, both within and without Lutheranism. Lutheran preaching at the end of the sixteenth century was also affected by the reintroduction of Aristotelian metaphysics, which increasingly came to dominate the terms

---

[63]   Ibid., p. 279. See also Martin Schian, "Die Homiletik des Andreas Hyperius, ihre wissenschaftliche Bedeutung und ihr praktischer Wert," *Zeitschrift für praktische Theologie* (1896): 289ff.
[64]   Brilioth, *Brief History of Preaching*, p. 126.
[65]   Ibid.
[66]   Niebergall, "Die Geschichte der christlichen Predigt," p. 293.

of homiletics.[67] Orthodox preaching, as Bodo Nischan remarks, "became less concerned with the discovery of truth and more devoted to its defense."[68] In other words, both the style and the content of sermons were adjusted to meet the perceived needs of church leaders and educators.

Not surprisingly, new forms soon began to appear to challenge the standard sermons of orthodoxy. The movement called Pietism began with some of the early challengers to the dominance of the legalistic, formal sermons of orthodoxy. Johann Arndt (1555-1621), the popular author of books such as *True Christianity* and *The Garden of Paradise*, was highly influenced by medieval authors such as Thomas à Kempis, and the German mystics such as Tauler. Arndt's postil *True Christianity* (first published in 1606) was designed to provide an alternative to the "too argumentative and quarrelsome theology," which he felt had become a "new *theologia scholastica*."[69] Other preachers, including Valerius Herberger (1562-1627), Joachim Lütkemann (1608-1655), and Heinrich Müller (1631-1675), published devotional literature that grew out of their more pietistic preaching. These preachers, according to Niebergall, "prepared the age for the pietistic sermon."[70] The movement of pietism, however, belongs to a later era.

It may also be a mistake to paint all orthodox Lutheran preaching with such a wide brush: recent scholars have noted a great deal of variety in preaching in this period. In his study on sermons in Augsburg in the age of confessionalization, Hans-Christoph Rublack has noted that orthodox sermons were neither one-dimensional, exclusively didactic, nor purely argumentative.[71] Rather, the Augsburg preachers in the confessional era were concerned to clar-

---

[67] Bodo Nischan, "Demarcating Boundaries: Lutheran Pericopic Sermons in the Age of Confessionalization," *Archiv für Reformationsgeschichte* 88 (1997): 200-1. See also Janis Kreslins, *Dominus narrabit in scriptura populorum: A Study of Early Seventeenth-Century Lutheran Teaching on Preaching and the 'Lettische lang-gewünschte Postill' of Georgius Mancelius* (Wiesbaden: O. Harrassowitz, 1992), pp. 78-83; Norbert Haag, *Predigt und Gesellschaft: Die lutherische Orthodoxie in Ulm 1640-1740* (Mainz: Verlag P. von Zabern, 1992).

[68] Nischan, "Demarcating Boundaries," p. 201.

[69] Niebergall, "Die Geschichte der christlichen Predigt," p. 293. Arndt's treatise can be found in *Arndts Hausbuch vom wahren Christentum*, ed. K. Kelber (Neuffen/Württemberg: Sonnenweg-Verlag, 1951).

[70] Ibid.

[71] Rublack, "Augsburger Predigt im Zeitalter der lutherischen Orthodoxie," in *Die Augsburger Kirchenordnung von 1537 und ihr Umfeld*, ed. Reinhard Schwarz, Schriften des Vereins für Reformationsgeschichte, Bd. 196 (Gütersloh: Gerd Mohn, 1988), p. 155.

ify doctrine in simple language, to speak to the situations in people's lives, and to offer comfort and hope to their listeners. Both doctrine and polemic remained important in these sermons, for "proper belief was necessary for salvation," and clear demarcation from rival groups was vital for Lutheran self-preservation.[72] But these sermons also helped their audiences to interpret and properly value the world around them. Other research has shown that while complicated dogmatic ideas were often contained in orthodox sermons, and confessional conflicts often pushed preachers to present controverted theological issues to their audiences, preachers were usually conscious of the need to make such issues more simple and accessible to their listeners.[73]

Lutheran Sermons after Luther

Luther's sermon collections, or postils, were widely influential among his contemporaries and followers. In some territories, including Saxony, parishes were required to own copies of Luther's postils, as well as postil books by other Lutheran authors. Inventories of pastors' libraries indicate that they often owned more postils than were required.[74] Numerous Lutheran preachers published their sermon collections in the sixteenth and early seventeenth centuries: a new Lutheran postil or reprint edition appeared almost every year at the great book fair in Frankfurt.[75] Several of the earliest postils inaugurated a new literary genre called *summaria*, or brief homiletic instructions and pastoral helps. Such *summaria* were published by Johannes Bugenhagen and Veit Dietrich. Bugenhagen's *Indices* (or his similar *Postillatio... in Evangelia*) of 1524 provides short summaries of the most important *loci* of each Sunday's text, espe-

---

[72] Ibid., pp. 155-6.

[73] See Patrick T. Ferry, "Confessionalization and Popular Preaching: Sermons against Synergism in Reformation Saxony," *Sixteenth Century Journal* 28 (1997): 1143-66; idem, *Preachers of Grace and Confessionalization in the Later Lutheran Reformation* (Ph.D. diss., University of Colorado, 1996).

[74] Gerald Strauss, "The Mental World of a Saxon Pastor," in *Reformation Principle and Practice: Essays in Honour of Arthur Geoffrey Dickens*, ed. P. N. Brooks (London: Scolar Press, 1980), p. 161.

[75] Hans-Christoph Rublack, "Lutherische Predigt und gesellschaftliche Wirklichkeiten," in *Die Lutherische Konfessionalisierung in Deutschland*, ed. H.-C. Rublack (Gütersloh: Gerd Mohn, 1988), pp. 347-8.

cially pointing to what the text exemplifies and teaches. For the second Sunday after Epiphany, Bugenhagen finds these important points in the traditional gospel of the wedding at Cana [John 2]: 1. Christ confirms marriage by his presence. 2. Mary gives an example of prayer, for although she was "repulsed" by Christ, she did not give up hoping for his help—"see the faith of the little woman." 3. This gospel is a sign that Christ is present to help us in our need, both bodily and spiritually.[76] The three points should help a preacher focus on the proper aspects in his sermon.

Postils of various kinds were also published in great number by Luther's friends and followers. Some of the Latin postils, such as the *Evangelicae Conciones Dominicarum* (1537) and later *Postilla* (1550) of Peter Artopoeus and the *Enarratio Brevis et Orthodoxa Evangeliorum Dominicalium et Festorum* of Daniel Greser (1567), were intended for student use. The majority of the postils, both in Latin and German, were designed both as pastoral aids and as pious reading for educated laypeople. Some of these texts may have been written strictly as models and were never preached, but many of the postils were actually collections of preached sermons. Occasionally these sermons were collected and published after a preacher had died, such as the postils of Joachim Mörlin (published in 1587, although he died in 1571) and Johann Spangenberg (whose *Postilla Evangelia* was published in 1553, shortly after his death in 1550). Spangenberg, a pastor and school principal, composed a postil in question-and-answer format intended for young people (similar to Luther's *Small Catechism*), and his later *Auslegung der Episteln und Evangelien* (1584), edited by his son Cyriacus, was also published in this popular style.[77] Another postil

---

[76]   Johannes Bugenhagen, *INDI//CES QVIDAM IOANNIS// BVGENHAGII PO-MERA=//ni in Euangelia (ut uocant) Do=//minicalia, Insuper usui tempo//rum et Sanctorum totius// anni seruientia. AB IPSO AVTORE IAM// primum emissi et locupletati.* (VVIT-TEMBERGÆ: Ioannem Lufft, 1524), n.p.: "*1. Christus sua præsentia confirmat nuptias. 2. Exemplum est hic orandi, Maria quanquam repulsa, tamen non desistit fidere, sed iubet fieri quicquid præcepturus eßet Christus. Vide fidem mulierculæ. 3. Signu[m], confirmatio Euangelij. Christus præsto est nostræ necessitati et corporali et spirituali.*" HAB [919.135 Th. (2)].

[77]   Joachim Mörlin, *POSTILLA:// Oder// Summarische// Erinnerung bey den Son=//teglichen Jahrs Euangelien vnd// Catechism* (Erffurd: Esaiam Mechlem, 1587) HAB [365 Th. 2°]; Johann Spangenberg, *POSTILLA.//Euangelia, & E-//PISTOLAE, QVAE DOMINICIS//& Festis diebus per totum Annum in// Ecclesia proponuntur, per Quæstio-//nes piè ac synceriter explicata,// & imaginibus exornata.// Item eadem// EVANGELIA, ET PRECATIO-//nes, quas Collectas uocant, quibus utitur Ec-//clesia, Carmine Elegiaco reddita* (Francofortum: Chr. Egenolphum, 1553). HAB [C 779-780.8° Helmst].

written specifically for children was Veit Dietrich's *Kinderpredig* of
1546.[78]

Other Lutheran preachers who published important postils include Johannes Brenz, whose erudite and biblically competent sermons were still being published in the nineteenth century; Anton
Corvinus, whose postils were addressed to "poor pastors and house-
fathers," and contained practical advice for heads of households;[79]
the Wittenberg pastor Paul Eber; Niels Hemmingsen, active in
Denmark; the *gnesio*-Lutheran Tilemann Hesshusen; Caspar
Huberinus, who published more than two hundred writings in his
lifetime; and Georg Major, the dean of the theology faculty at
Wittenberg.

Other Forms of Sermon Literature

Along with postils, many sermons were published individually as
pamphlets, or bound into books with other sermons and treatises.
The variety of these sermons expose a difference in the kinds of
sermons preached that might not be expected considering the pericopic nature of Sunday and festival sermons. However, as in the
late medieval period, occasional sermons remained very common
in the sixteenth century. During the Lenten season, it remained
common for pastors to preach series of sermons on topics such as
the catechism, specific themes from scripture, or even the lives of
martyrs or "saints" such as Luther. While catechetical sermons
were extremely common (and in fact, most pericopic preaching had
a catechetical element)[80], examples of the second and third kinds of
sermons can be seen in the postils of Johannes Mathesius [1504-
1565], a prolific preacher and author who spent most of his active
years in the silver-mining town of Joachimsthal in Bohemia.
Mathesius's *Sarepta*, or "mountain postil," contains homilies that

---

[78]   Dietrich, *Kinder=//predig/ von für//nembsten Festen durch// das gantze Jar/ ge=//stelt
durch// Vitum Dietrich* (Nürnberg: Johann vom Berg vnd Vlrich Neuber, M.D.XLVI).
HAB [C 565 Helmst. 8° (2)].

[79]   One example is Corvinus, *Kurtze vnd ain//feltige Außlegung der Epi=//stolen vnd
Euangelien/ So auff die// Sonntage vnd fürnemesten Feste/// durch das gantz Jar in der// Kirchen
gelesen// werden.// Für die arme Pfarrherren vnd// Haußuätter gestellet/ Durch// M. ANTO-
NIVM CORVINVM* (Augspurg: Valentin Othmar, M.D.XLV). HAB [434.9 Th.2° (1)].

[80]   Mary Jane Haemig, "The Living Voice of the Catechism: German Lutheran
Catechetical Preaching 1530-1580" (Th.D. diss., Harvard University, 1996).

explain stories, sayings, and examples from the Bible relating to mining, while his *Diluuium Mathesij* contains fifty-four sermons on Noah and the flood delivered in 1557 and 1558.[81] He also preached a series of sermons on the life of Luther, which correspond to the medieval sermons upon saints' lives, and were highly influential in developing the traditional picture of Luther.[82]

Preaching on the saints' days or festivals continued in many Lutheran areas – ecclesiastical constitutions regulated which days would be observed and which would be abolished.[83] While Lutheran preachers in general avoided polemic against the veneration of the saints in the festival sermons, they did attempt to redirect interest toward Christ as sole mediator, and use the saints as models for human piety and imitation.[84] Another medieval type of sermon that retained its place in Lutheran preaching was the funeral sermon – in fact, the number of such sermons increased in the sixteenth century, in part because preaching services replaced masses for the dead.[85] While medieval funeral sermons tended to follow the *genus demonstrativum*, providing mostly *laudatio* or praise of the departed, Lutheran and other Protestant funeral sermons maintained a more pedagogical tone.[86] Many pastors took the opportunity provided by funeral sermons to promote the married life (over celibacy), and virtues necessary for such a life, as well as the responsibilities of the *Hausvater* and *Hausmutter*. These sermons supported

[81] Brilioth, *Brief History of Preaching*, p. 121.

[82] M. Johann Mathesius, *D. Martin Luthers Leben in siebzehn Predigten*, ed. Georg Buchwald (Leipzig: Philip Reclamjun., n.d.). Also see Susan Boettcher, "Martin Luther seliger gedechnis: The Memory of Martin Luther, 1546-1566" (Ph.D. diss., University of Wisconsin-Madison, 1998).

[83] For Protestant ecclesiastical constitutions (*Kirchenordnungen*), see *Die Evangelischen Kirchenordnungen des XVI. Jahrhunderts*, ed. Emil Sehling (Leipzig: O. R. Reisland, 1902-1913).

[84] Robert Kolb, "Festivals of the Saints in Late Reformation Lutheran Preaching," *The Historian* 52 (August 1990): 613-615. See also idem, *For All the Saints: Changing Perceptions of Martyrdom and Sainthood in the Lutheran Reformation* (Macon, Ga.: Mercer University Press, 1987). For presentations of the Virgin Mary in Lutheran sermons of this period, see my dissertation, "Reforming Mary: Changing Images of the Virgin Mary in Lutheran Sermons of the Sixteenth Century" (Ph.D. diss., Duke University, 2000).

[85] See Eberhard Winckler, *Die Leichenpredigt im deutschen Luthertum bis Spener*, Forschungen zur Geschichte und Lehre des Protestantismus, ed. Ernst Wolf, 10th series, v. 34 (Munich: Chr. Kaiser Verlag, 1967).

[86] Eileen Theresa Dugan, "Images of Marriage and Family Life in Nördlingen: Moral Preaching and Devotional Literature, 1589-1712" (Ph.D. diss., The Ohio State University, 1987), p. 14.

public peace and the social order: listeners were encouraged to marry within their class, to maintain the proper social standards in their dress and activities, and to send their children to school.[87]

Along with funeral sermons, the wedding sermon became an important subgenre of Lutheran literature: in the medieval period, sermons on women and marriage were sometimes given, but not on the occasion of weddings.[88] Lutheran weddings normally took place before the entire congregation, and gave the pastor the opportunity to preach on issues of marriage, family, and the nature of women. The *Ehespiegel*, or collections of wedding sermons, became a common form of publication – authors of these collections include Mathesius and Cyriacus Spangenberg, among others. Both the funeral and wedding sermons are related to the increasingly popular *Hausväterliteratur*. Books and treatises intended to help the *Hausvater* govern his home were often based on sermons, and many of the viewpoints presented in such literature come from the same sources: writings of famous theologians (such as Luther and Brenz), the Small Catechism, the Bible, and the *Haustafel*.[89]

While published sermons were often focused upon the moral improvement of their audience, devotional sermons were also quite common. In another form derived from the medieval period, meditations upon Christ's passion were a common and quite popular type of sermon literature. Luther published a *Passional*, and Bugenhagen's *Historia des Leidens Jesu Christi* can be found in numerous reprints and translations.[90] Other Lutherans who published sermons on Christ's passion include the Tübingen professor Jacob Andreae, who helped formulate the Lutheran Concord; the future

---

[87] Ibid., p. 168.

[88] Susan Karant-Nunn, "*Kinder, Küche, Kirche*: Social Ideology in the Sermons of Johannes Mathesius," in *Germania Illustrata: Essays on Early Modern Germany Presented to Gerald Strauss*, eds. Andrew C. Fix and Susan C. Karant-Nunn, Sixteenth Century Essays & Studies, ed. Charles G. Nauert, Jr., volume XVIII (Ann Arbor: Edwards Brothers, 1992), p. 122.

[89] See Julius Hoffmann, *Die "Hausväterliteratur" und die "Predigten über den christlichen Hausstand." Lehre vom Hause und Bildung für das häusliche Leben im 16., 17. und 18. Jahrhundert*, Göttinger Studien zur Pädagogik, ed. Herman Nohl, v. 37 (Weinheim a. d. B. and Berlin: Verlag Julius Beltz, 1959).

[90] Bugenhagen's passion sermons appeared in low German as *Historia des Li=//dendes vnde der// Vpstandinge vnses Heren// Jhesu Christi/ vth den// veer Euangeli=//sten/ dorch// D. Johan. Bugenhagen// Pamern uppet nye vlitigen// thosamende gebracht.// Ock de Vorstöringe Je=//rusalem vnde der Jöden/ up// dat körteste begrepen* (Magdeborch: Christian Rödinger, 1546). HAB [G 331.8° Helmst. (1)].

bishop Johannes Drach; Johannes Heune, pastor in Silesia who also published several postils; the Nördlingen pastor and author Kaspar Kantz; Cyriacus Spangenberg, son of Lutheran preacher Johannes; and the pastor and superintendent Christoph Vischer, also author of an extensive postil.[91]

Summary

The significance of the sermon for the Lutheran Reformation is indisputable – Luther and his followers transformed the entire worship service into a vehicle for the proclamation of the gospel. From its roots in the late medieval preaching revival, the Reformation's messages were spread through the largely illiterate population of the early modern Empire as much by actual preaching as by the written word, and many of the early books and pamphlets were sermons. In their explicit rejection of much of medieval preaching theory and practice, Luther and his followers helped to create new forms and styles of sermons and preaching manuals that were highly influential among succeeding generations of both Protestants and Catholics. Philipp Melanchthon, whose reputation often languishes in the shadow of the more forceful Luther, was second to none in the sixteenth century (even Erasmus) in the importance of his treatises on preaching. Lutheran authors virtually created the genre of the postil, collections of sermons covering the Sundays and/or festivals of the church year, as well as other popular forms of homiletic material. Besides insisting that, above all, the sermon must be exegesis of scripture, the most significant contribution of Luther and other Lutheran preachers was their focus on doctrine and the pedagogical content of sermons: Melanchthon's new *genus didascalicum* allowed and encouraged (perhaps even occasionally required) pastors to use the sermon as the primary vehicle for instructing their audience in the true faith and the Christian way of life.

---

[91] For biographical and bibliographical information on these texts, refer to the bibliography and appendix of my dissertation, "Reforming Mary," pp. 284-302, 273-283.

60   BETH KREITZER

Bibliography

Abray, Lorna Jane, "The Laity's Religion: Lutheranism in Sixteenth-Century Strasbourg," in *The German People and the Reformation*, ed. R. Po-Chia Hsia (Ithaca: Cornell University Press, 1988), pp. 216-233.

Brecht, Martin, *Martin Luther: Shaping and Defining the Reformation, 1521-1532*, trans. James L. Schaaf (Minneapolis: Fortress Press, 1990).

Breen, Quirinus, "The terms 'Loci Communes' and 'Loci' in Melanchthon," in his *Christianity and Humanism: Studies in the History of Ideas*, ed. Nelson Peter Ross (Grand Rapids, Mich.: W. B. Eerdmans Publishing Co., 1968), pp. 93-105.

Brilioth, Yngve, *A Brief History of Preaching*, trans. Karl E. Mattson (Philadelphia: Fortress Press, 1965).

Bugenhagen, Johannes, *INDI//CES QVIDAM IOANNIS// BVGENHAGII POMERA=//ni in Euangelia (ut uocant) Do=//minicalia, Insuper usui tempo//rum et Sanctorum totius// anni seruientia. AB IPSO AVTORE IAM// primum emissi et locupletati* (VVITTEMBERGÆ: Ioannem Lufft, 1524).

Charland, T. M., *Artes Praedicandi, Contribution à l'histoire de la rhétorique au moyen âge* (Ottawa: Publications de l'institut d'etudes médiévales d'Ottawa, 1936).

Douglass, E. Jane Dempsey, *Justification in Late Medieval Preaching: A Study of John Geiler of Keisersberg*, Studies in Medieval and Reformation Thought, vol. I, ed. H. A. Oberman (Leiden: E. J. Brill, 1966).

Dugan, Eileen Theresa, "Images of Marriage and Family Life in Nördlingen: Moral Preaching and Devotional Literature, 1589-1712," Ph.D. diss., The Ohio State University, 1987.

Edwards, Jr., Mark U., *Printing, Propaganda, and Martin Luther* (Berkeley: University of California Press, 1994).

Erasmus, Desiderius, *Opera omnia*, ed. J. Clericus, 10 vols. (Leiden: P. Van der Aa, 1703-1706).

Ferry, Patrick T., *Preachers of Grace and Confessionalization in the Later Lutheran Reformation*, Ph.D. diss., University of Colorado, 1996.

— "Confessionalization and Popular Preaching: Sermons against Synergism in Reformation Saxony," *Sixteenth Century Journal* 28 (1997): 1143-66.

Grimm, Harold J., *Martin Luther as a Preacher* (Columbus, Oh.: Lutheran Book Concern, 1929).

— "The Human Element in Luther's Sermons," *Archiv für Reformationsgeschichte* 49 (1958): 50-60.

Haag, Norbert, *Predigt und Gesellschaft: Die lutherische Orthodoxie in Ulm 1640-1740* (Mainz: Verlag P. von Zabern, 1992).

Haemig, Mary Jane, "The Living Voice of the Catechism: German Lutheran Catechetical Preaching 1530-1580," Th.D. diss., Harvard University, 1996.

Hoffmann, Julius, *Die "Hausväterliteratur" und die "Predigten über den christlichen
Hausstand." Lehre vom Hause und Bildung für das häusliche Leben im 16., 17.
und 18. Jahrhundert*, Göttinger Studien zur Pädagogik, ed. Herman
Nohl, v. 37 (Weinheim a. d. B. and Berlin: Verlag Julius Beltz, 1959).

Karant-Nunn, Susan C., *Luther's Pastors: The Reformation in the Ernestine Countryside*, Transactions of the American Philosophical Society, v. 69, pt. 8
(Philadelphia: American Philosophical Society, 1979).

— "*Kinder, Küche, Kirche*: Social Ideology in the Sermons of Johannes
Mathesius," in *Germania Illustrata: Essays on Early Modern Germany Presented
to Gerald Strauss*, eds. Andrew C. Fix and Susan C. Karant-Nunn, Sixteenth Century Essays & Studies, ed. Charles G. Nauert, Jr., volume
XVIII (Ann Arbor: Edwards Brothers, 1992), pp. 121-140.

Kolb, Robert, "Festivals of the Saints in Late Reformation Lutheran
Preaching," *The Historian* 52 (August 1990): 613-626.

Kreitzer, Beth, "Reforming Mary: Changing Images of the Virgin Mary
in Lutheran Sermons of the Sixteenth Century," Ph.D. diss., Duke
University, 2000.

Kreslins, Janis, *Dominus narrabit in scriptura populorum: A Study of Early Seventeenth-Century Lutheran Teaching on Preaching and the 'Lettische lang-gewünschte
Postill' of Georgius Mancelius* (Wiesbaden: O. Harrassowitz, 1992).

Luther, Martin, *D. Martin Luthers Werke. Kritische Gesamtausgabe*, 62 vols.
(Weimar: Böhlaus, 1883-).

— *Luther's Works. American Edition*, 55 vols. (Philadelphia: Fortress Press,
and St. Louis: Concordia Publishing House, 1955-).

Melanchthon, Philipp, *Corpus Reformatorum*, vols. 1-28, ed. C. G. Bret-
schneider (Halle, 1834-60).

— *Supplementa Melanchthoniana* (Leipzig: R. Haupt, 1910-29).

Muller, Richard A., "Biblical Interpretation in the Era of the Reformation: The View from the Middle Ages," in *Biblical Interpretation in the Era
of the Reformation: Essays Presented to David C. Steinmetz in Honor of His Sixtieth Birthday*, eds. Richard A. Muller and John L. Thompson (Grand
Rapids, Mich. and Cambridge: William B. Eerdmans Publishing Company, 1996), pp. 3-22.

Nembach, Ulrich, *Predigt des Evangeliums: Luther als Prediger, Pädagoge und
Rhetor* (Neukirch: Neukirchener Verlag, 1972).

Niebergall, Alfred, "Die Geschichte der christlichen Predigt," in *Leiturgia:
Handbuch des Evangelischen Gottesdienstes*, Bd. II, eds. K. F. Müller and W.
Blankenburg (Kassel: Johannes Stauda-Verlag, 1955), pp. 181-352.

— "Luthers Auffassung von der Predigt nach 'De Servo Arbitrio'," in *Reformation und Gegenwart*, ed. H. Graß and W. G. Kümmel, Marburger Theologische Studien 6 (Marburg: N. G. Elwert Verlag, 1968), pp. 83-109.

Nischan, Bodo, "Demarcating Boundaries: Lutheran Pericopic Sermons in the Age of Confessionalization," *Archiv für Reformationsgeschichte* 88 (1997): 199-216.

O'Malley, John W., "Content and Rhetorical Forms in Sixteenth-Century Treatises on Preaching," in *Renaissance Eloquence: Studies in the Theory and Practice of Renaissance Rhetoric*, ed. James J. Murphy (Berkeley: University of California Press, 1983), pp. 238-252.

— "Luther the Preacher," *Michigan Germanic Studies* 10 (1984): 3-16.

Ozment, Steven E., *The Reformation in the Cities: The Appeal of Protestantism to Sixteenth-Century Germany and Switzerland* (New Haven and London: Yale University Press, 1975).

Roth, Dorothea, *Die mittelalterliche Predigttheorie und das Manuale Curatorum des Johann Ulrich Surgant* (Basel: Helbing & Lichtenhahn, 1956).

Rublack, Hans-Christoph, "Augsburger Predigt im Zeitalter der lutherischen Orthodoxie," in *Die Augsburger Kirchenordnung von 1537 und ihr Umfeld*, ed. Reinhard Schwarz, Schriften des Vereins für Reformationsgeschichte, ed. Gustav Adolf Benrath, Bd. 196 (Gütersloh: Gerd Mohn, 1988), pp. 123-158.

— "Lutherische Predigt und gesellschaftliche Wirklichkeiten," in *Die Lutherische Konfessionalisierung in Deutschland*, ed. H.-C. Rublack, Schriften des Vereins für Reformationsgeschichte, ed. Gustav Adolf Benrath, Bd. 197 (Gütersloh: Gerd Mohn, 1988), pp. 344-395.

Schian, Martin, "Die lutherische Homiletik in der zweiten Hälfte des 16. Jahrhunderts," *Theologische Studien und Kritiken* 72 (1899): 62-94.

Schnell, Uwe, *Die homiletische Theorie Philipp Melanchthons* (Berlin and Hamburg: Lutherisches Verlagshaus, 1968).

Scribner, Robert W., "Oral Culture and the Transmission of Reformation Ideas," in *The Transmission of Ideas in the Lutheran Reformation*, ed. Helga Robinson-Hammerstein (Dublin: Irish Academic Press, 1989), pp. 83-104.

Seehofer, Arsacius, *Enarrationes Evangeliorum Dominicalium, ad dialecticam Methodum, & Rhetoricam dispositionem accommodatæ* (Augustae Vind.: Heinrich Steiner, 1539).

Steinmetz, David C., *Luther and Staupitz: An Essay in the Intellectual Origins of the Protestant Reformation*, Duke Monographs in Medieval and Renaissance Studies, no. 4 (Durham, N.C.: Duke University Press, 1980).

Stolt, Birgit, "Docere, delectare und movere bei Luther," *Deutsche Vierteljahresschrift für Literaturwissenschaft und Geistesgeschichte* (1970): 433-474.

Strauss, Gerald, "The Mental World of a Saxon Pastor," in *Reformation Principle and Practice: Essays in Honour of Arthur Geoffrey Dickens*, ed. P. N. Brooks (London: Scolar Press, 1980), pp. 155-170.

Thayer, Anne T., "Penitence and Preaching on the Eve of the Reformation: A Comparative Overview from Frequently Printed Model Sermon Collections, 1450-1520," Ph.D. diss., Harvard University, 1996.

Watson, Philip S., *Let God Be God! An Interpretation of the Theology of Martin Luther* (Philadelphia: Fortress Press, 1947).

Wengert, Timothy J., *Philip Melanchthon's "Annotationes in Johannem" in Relation to Its Predecessors and Contemporaries*, Travaux d'Humanisme et Renaissance (Geneva: Librarie Droz, 1987), p. 220.

Winckler, Eberhard, *Die Leichenpredigt im deutschen Luthertum bis Spener*, Forschungen zur Geschichte und Lehre des Protestantismus, ed. Ernst Wolf, 10th series, v. 34 (Munich: Chr. Kaiser Verlag, 1967).

CHAPTER THREE

PREACHING IN THE REFORMED TRADITION

James Thomas Ford
(Marian College of Fond du Lac)

Preaching in the Reformed tradition began on 1 January 1519 when Huldrych Zwingli began to expound the Gospel of Matthew verse by verse as the people's priest at the Grossmünster in Zurich.[1] His introduction of the expository sermon replaced the custom of preaching through selected pericopes of the liturgical calendar. Seven years later, Zwingli made a more audacious move in distilling from the mass liturgy a service of the Word and a communion service on Easter Sunday, a momentous liturgical step for the Reformed tradition and the culmination of a trend among mendicant preachers in the late medieval period.[2] The consequences of Zwingli's homiletic and liturgical changes would be developed and re-worked in the course of the Reformation.

This chapter will focus rather selectively on preaching in the Swiss Reformed and English Puritan tradition in the sixteenth century, exploring particular themes and devoting particular attention to the luminaries Huldrych Zwingli (1484-1531), John Calvin (1509-64), Heinrich Bullinger (1504-75), and William Perkins (1558-1602). While the early Reformed tradition produced important preachers and homilists in other countries and regions, the limits that I have placed upon this discussion are based upon my knowledge and the view that developments in Zurich, Geneva and Puritan England gave the distinctive shape to preaching found *mutatis mutandis* in the other Reformed enclaves of Europe. These studies can reveal the depth and richness of preaching in the Reformed tradition as a whole.

---

[1] On the significance of this event, see Oskar Farner, *Huldrych Zwingli*, vol. 3: *Seine Verkündigung und Ihre ersten Früchte 1520-1525* (Zurich: Zwingli Verlag, 1954), pp. 29-35.

[2] See Nicholas Wolterstorff, "The Reformed Liturgy," in Donald K. McKim, ed., *Major Themes in the Reformed Tradition* (Louisville: William B. Eerdsman Publishing Company, 1992), p. 294.

Preaching the Word of God

Since the sermon became the centerpiece of Reformed worship, we lack a proper understanding of the tradition without a consideration of the importance and purpose of preaching. The lives of the reformers were rooted in a homiletic and pastoral context. They were preoccupied on a daily basis with shepherding their parishioners and instructing the flock in the Scriptures. In his will, Calvin expressed his life-long commitment to preaching and expositing on the Bible faithfully.[3] The reformers were confident that the transforming power of the Word of God could bring sinners to repentance and lead them to a life of godliness. Zwingli wrote that the "Word of God is so sure and strong that if God wills all things are done the moment that he speaks his Word."[4] The *Belgic Confession* attests that the Bible "contains the will of God completely" and teaches the good news of salvation sufficiently.[5] The preacher then was the mouthpiece of God who opened "the mystery of Christ," exhorting his listeners to live a life pleasing to God.

Preachers had a pedagogical responsibility to communicate the tenets of the faith. Trained in the interpretation of the Bible, they took great pains to teach the commonplaces of Christianity – original sin, faith and good works, divine providence, the resurrection and ascension of Christ – to the laity in terms they could understand. Yet, Reformed preachers expected a great deal from their listeners and would introduce theological problems and controversies that a biblical passage might impose. One can find more extensive discussion of sanctification in Calvin's sermons than in his other writings.[6] The sermon fits into the other pedagogical literature of the period such as the commentary, catechism, lecture and creed, in that it was a vehicle toward inculcating sixteenth-century

---

[3] "Je proteste...que j'ai tâche, selon la mesure de grâce que Dieu m'avait donnée, d'enseigner purement sa parole, tant en sermons que par écrit, et d'exposer fidèlement l'Ecriture sainte." Cited in Richard Stauffer, "Un Calvin méconnu: le prédicateur de Genève," *Bulletin de la société de l'histoire du protestantisme français* 123 (1977): 187.

[4] See G. W. Bromiley, ed., *Zwingli and Bullinger* (Philadelphia: Westminster John Knox Press, 1958), p. 68.

[5] Philip Schaff, *The Creeds of Christendom with a History and Critical Notes*, vol. 3 (Ada, Mich.: Baker Books, 1990), pp. 387-8.

[6] See Max Engammare, "Le Paradis à Genève: Comment Calvin prêchait-il la Chute aux Genevois," *Études théologiques et religieuses* (1994): 339-40.

townsmen and villagers in Biblical doctrine and giving them the tools they needed to resist the Roman church.

There was a strong "pastoral impulse" in preaching.[7] According to the Berne Synod of 1532, the sermon was intended for the improvement and edification of flock.[8] Calvin believed that the preacher spoke in two voices: one that exhorts the godly and sets them on the right path, and the other that wards off the wolves from the flock.[9] He encouraged ministers to follow the example of the prophet Micah who did not refrain from condemning rulers for misleading the people.[10] The preacher must exhort believers and apply the Scripture, because doctrine without such exhortations is "cold." The minister of the Word, according to Calvin, should not only give a clear understanding of Scripture, but must also add *véhémence* so that the message will penetrate the heart.[11] Zwingli deemed any sermon useless if it did not call people to repentance of their sins. The preachers must be willing to condemn the vices of their listeners even if such admonishments did not endear them to the people. Reformed ministers accordingly used the term "prophesying" with reference to their preaching ministries. The term referred not only to the exposition of Scripture, but also conjured up the image of the Hebrew prophet. Like Jeremiah and Ezekiel, the preacher of the Word of God condemned the vices of his people and warned them of God's displeasure and wrath. Calvin saw himself as such a prophet of God, rightly expounding Scripture and protecting his flock from false doctrine.[12]

Preaching became a regular part of urban and communal life. As the Reformation began to take hold in Swiss cities like Berne, Zu-

---

[7]   See Thomas H. L. Parker, *Calvin's Preaching* (Philadelphia: Westminster John Knox Press, 1992), p. 8.

[8]   Cited in Bruce Gordon, "Preaching and the Reform of the Clergy in the Swiss Reformation," in Andrew Pettegree, ed., *The Reformation of the Parishes: The Ministry and the Reformation in Town and Country* (Manchester: Manchester University Press, 1993), p. 78.

[9]   Erwin Mülhaupt, *Die Predigt Calvins, Ihre Geschichte, Ihre Form und Ihre Religiösen Grundgedanken* (Berlin and Leipzig: Walter de Gruyter & Co., 1931), p. 30.

[10]   See Jean Daniel Bonoît, ed., *Sermons sur le Livre de Michée* (Neukirchen: Neukirchen-Vluyn, 1964), p. 213.

[11]   For a citation and discussion of this passage, see Stauffer, "Un Calvin méconnu," p. 193.

[12]   On Calvin as prophet, see Rodolphe Peter, "Genève dans la prédication de Calvin," in W. H. Neuser, ed., *Calvinus Ecclesiae Genevensis Custos* (Bern, 1984), p. 40; Max Engammare, "Calvin: A Prophet without a Prophecy," *Church History* 67 (1998): 651.

rich and Geneva, city governments responded by issuing preaching mandates that favored evangelical sermons and funding lecture-ships that attracted prominent evangelical preachers.[13] The Ecclesiastical Ordinances of Geneva called for preaching throughout the week, though its injunctions were not always followed.[14] Ministers took on an exhausting preaching schedule. Between 1519 and 1522 Zwingli managed to deliver expository sermons that covered the Gospel of Matthew, the Book of Acts, and a number of Pauline and Catholic epistles.[15] The output of Zwingli's successor, Heinrich Bullinger, is staggering. In the course of his forty-four year ministry as the *antistes* (pastor) of the Zurich church, he preached between 7000 and 7500 sermons, covering every book of the Old and New Testaments. From 1531 to 1537, Bullinger preached six to eight times weekly until Caspar Megander relieved some of his preaching duties.[16]

Calvin's homiletic agenda is atypical but nonetheless indicative of the importance of preaching. Generally, the Genevan reformer preached two Sunday services on a Gospel or the Psalms, and every morning Monday through Saturday every other week, starting at 6:00 a.m. or 7:00 a.m., depending on the time of year. Calvin's sermons lasted about three-quarters of an hour, a relatively short time compared to those of his colleagues Guillaume Farel (1489-1565) and Pierre Viret (1511-71). Theodore Beza (1519-1605) estimated that Calvin preached about 286 sermons a year.[17] During his entire ministry at Geneva, he preached almost 4000 sermons.[18]

---

[13] See, e.g., Steven E. Ozment, *Reformation in the Cities: The Appeal of Protestantism to Sixteenth-Century Germany and Switzerland* (New Haven: Yale University Press, 1975), pp. 38-42.

[14] Thomas Lambert "Preaching, Praying and Policing the Reform in Sixteenth-Century Geneva" (Ph.D. dissertation, University of Wisconsin, Madison, 1998), p. 288). Lambert advises caution in using this source to gauge preaching in Geneva.

[15] Zwingli gives an account of his expository preaching in these years to the bishop of Constance in his *Apologeticus Archeteles*. See Emil Egli et al., eds., *Huldreich Zwinglis Werke*, vol. 1 (Berlin, 1905), p. 285.

[16] See Fritz Büsser, *Wurzeln der Reformation in Zurich: Zum 500. Geburtstag des Reformators Huldrych Zwingli* (Leiden: E. J. Brill, 1985), pp. 143-4.

[17] Mülhaupt, *Die Predigt Calvins*, p. 16.

[18] See Rodolphe Peter, "Genève dans la prédication de Calvin," pp. 23-4. To the 2500 sermons that Calvin delivered between 1549 and 1564, Peter calculated another 1500 sermons preached between 1537 and 1549. Of these 4000 sermons, 1500 (roughly 39%) have been preserved, an astounding number in comparison with other preachers. The editors of the *Opera Calvini* included 873 sermons, while the editors of the *Supplementa Calviniana*, a project that began in the late 1950s, will eventually provide editions

The Exegetical Foundations of Preaching

The prominence of preaching in the Reformation went hand in hand with developments in biblical exegesis. Instrumental in the development of biblical hermeneutics and homiletics was the *Prophezei* of Zurich, founded in 1525, which provided a training ground in biblical exposition. The institution was established in other Reformed communities such as Strasbourg and Geneva and spread in Puritan England via the Marian exiles.[19] Pastors and advanced students of the Latin school gathered in the early morning to give exegetical lessons from passages in the Old Testament. Such scholarly gatherings had a direct impact on preaching, since a passage expounded in the *Prophezei* in the morning would later that day be delivered to the congregation in the form of a sermon.[20]

Reformed expositors displayed the same basic hermeneutic principles in their sermons as in their commentaries and lectures, generally avoiding the use of allegory unless the text absolutely merited it and favoring the literal historical method. They rejected the medieval four-fold theory of interpretation and affirmed only one literal meaning in the text. To understand a passage one should know historical conditions existing during the composition of the biblical book. Perkins, giving exegetical advice in his preaching handbook, explains that interpreting a verse one should ask "who? to whom? upon what occasion? at what time? in what place? for what end? what goeth before? what followeth?"[21] Since the best way to interpret difficult passages was with Scripture itself, preachers continually make cross-references to other verses in the course of a sermon. For the expository sermon, preachers had to acquire the same

---

of almost 700 additional unpublished sermons. To date, the volumes include vol. 1: Hanns Rückert, ed., *Predigten über das 2. Buch Samuelis* (1961), vol. 2: Georges A. Barrois, ed., *Sermons sur le Livre d'Esaïe: chapitres 13-29* (1961), vol. 4: F. Higman, Parker and Thorpe, eds., *Sermons sur le Livre d'Esaïe: chapitres 30-41* (1995), vol. 5: Bonoît, ed., *Sermons sur le Livre de Michée* (1964), vol. 6: Rodolphe Peter, ed., *Sermons sur les Livres de Jérémie et des Lamentations* (1971), vol. 7: Erwin Mülhaupt, ed., *Psalmpredigten, Passion-, Oster-, und Pfingstpredigten* (1981), and vol. 8: Willem Balke and Wilhelmus H. Th. Moehn, eds., *Sermons on the Acts of the Apostles* (1994).

[19] For a brief comparative study, see Philippe Denis, "La prophétie dans les églises de la réforme au XVIe siècle," *Revue d'histoire ecclésiastique* 72 (1977): 289-316.

[20] See Farner, *Huldrych Zwingli*, pp. 84-5, 41.

[21] See Ian Breward, ed., *The Work of William Perkins* (Appelford, 1970), p. 338.

exegetical skills requisite in the commentary literature. The consecutive explication of a book, or *praedicatio continua*, could be more challenging than the pericope method in that the preacher had to offer a sustained exposition over a continuous text, covering different contexts that the text might impose, including difficult passages.[22]

Although sermons evince the same exegetical methods of commentaries and lectures, the difference in their intended audiences bring out important distinctions. The sermon was not refined at the scholar's desk but was improvised in a live setting before common folk with little exposure to theological doctrines. Calvin avoided the use of technical theological terms like "Trinity" and "person," not wanting to confuse his audience with theological jargon.[23] Preachers devoted more energy to the practical applications of a text in the course of a sermon that often reflected the events of the day. In a sermon delivered only days after the Amboise Conspiracy, when French nobles plotted to seize the king, Calvin severely criticized the abuse of royal power and justified active resistance to tyrants.[24]

Emergence of Reformed Homiletics:
Sermon Structure and Style

Generally, Reformed preachers, ever guided by both pastoral and pedagogical concerns, followed homiletic models of the early church and the Renaissance. In the celebrated homilies of John Chrysostom (ca. 349-407) they found a concise, simple exposition

---

[22] While expository preaching involved a verse-by-verse treatment of Scripture, this did not necessarily mean thorough coverage of every aspect of a verse. Calvin, for example, might give a disproportionate amount of attention to a part of a verse or passage and omit others; or he might draw out the general sense of the text and forego an analysis of each verse in the passage. On Calvin's selective exposition of a verse, see Stauffer, "Un Calvin méconnu," p. 189; and Parker, *Calvin's Preaching*, pp. 136-8. Similarly, Andreas Hyperius, in his handbook on preaching, advised preachers not to preach on all the doctrines that one could draw from a text, but to concentrate on only a only a few. This passage from Hyperius is cited in Joseph Pipa, Jr., "William Perkins and the Development of Puritan Preaching" (Ph.D. dissertation, Westminster Theological Seminary, 1985), p. 143.

[23] See Stauffer, "Un Calvin méconnu," p. 202.

[24] See Max Engammare, "Calvin monarchomaque? Du soupçon à l'argument," *Archiv für Reformationsgeschichte* 89 (1998): 207-25.

of Scripture *secundum ordinem textus*, while in the sermons and *De doctrina christiana* of Augustine (354-430) on John, they learned to place eloquence and learning at the disposal of clear and practical exposition.[25] They avoided the elaborate schemata of the "modern method" of sermon construction that had developed in the universities,[26] since they were difficult to follow and not intended for a lay audience. Reformers also turned to classical oratory as advocated by humanists such as Erasmus 1466-1536) and Johannes Reuchlin (1455-1522). The reformers did not adhere strictly to the parts of a classical oration – Exordium, Narration, Division, Confirmation, Confutation and Conclusion – but developed some and omitted others.[27] The reformer's pastoral concern to preach the Gospel merged with the Renaissance ideal, and the dictum of Petrarch (1304-74) that it is better to will the good than to know the truth.[28] Above all, the reformers, interested in communicating the Word of God to a spiritually malnourished laity of the sixteenth century, favored a simple and direct approach. They frowned upon the conspicuous use of eloquence and the display of learning.

The emerging "Reformed method" involved a triple schema whereby the preacher derived doctrinal lessons from the text, defend these doctrines with argument and counterarguments, and finally drew moral applications from them.[29] This hermeneutic approach was used by Chrysostom and Augustine and is found in the biblical commentaries of Reformed exegetes. According to the Puritan historian Thomas Fuller (1608-1661), the commentaries of Wolfgang Musculus (1497-1563) ushered in the preaching "by Use and Doctrine." Likewise, Andreas Gerardus Hyperius (1511-64)

---

[25] Bullinger showed that Zwingli's expository preaching was not a novelty, but rooted in the tradition of the church fathers Chrysostom and Augustine. See J. J. Hottinger and H. H. Vögeli., eds., *Heinrich Bullingers Reformationsgeschichte*, vol. 1 (Frauenfeld, 1838-40), p. 12.

[26] See J. W. Blench, *Preaching in England in the Late Fifteenth and Sixteenth Centuries* (New York: Barnes and Noble, 1964), pp. 70-1. The modern style divides the sermon into the exordium; the prayer; the introduction of the theme; the division; and the discussion. Blench's distinction between the "ancient" and "modern" sermon structures is useful and has been followed by other historians of Puritan preaching. But these categorizations tend to oversimplify the eclectic uses of schemata by individual preachers.

[27] See Blench, *Preaching in England*, pp. 85-6.

[28] Calvin expressed this view and other homiletic principles in a sermon on 1 Timothy. Cited in Richard Stauffer, *Interprètes de la Bible: Études sur les réformateurs du XVIe siècle* (Paris: Éditions Beauchesne, 1980), p. 174.

[29] See Blench, *Preaching in England*, p. 101; and Pipa, "William Perkins," p. 34.

wrote that the preacher, after careful reading of a biblical passage, should draw out *loci communes*, basic doctrines of the faith, and thereupon encourage, admonish, or console the audience on the basis of these doctrines.[30] John Hooper (d. 1555), in his sermons on Jonah, was the first English Puritan to employ this twofold approach to Scripture in his preaching.[31]

While Reformed preachers generally did not adhere closely to any schemata[32], the basic form of a sermon included an introduction or exordium, the body of the sermon, and a concluding prayer. At the outset of a sermon, the preacher might introduce the topic or passage of the sermon in general terms in a kind of exordium. The preacher or a *praelector* would recite or paraphrase the passage to be expounded. According to one observer, Zwingli sometimes would give an outline of the sermon at the outset and then invoke God in a prayer for illumination: "Gib, O Herr Got, Verstentnus."[33] Bullinger introduced each sermon in his *Decades* with prefatory comments about the doctrine or "commonplace" to be discussed.[34] In the first sermon of a series, Calvin would usually give a synopsis of the book's content.[35] As befitting expository preaching, which emphasized the continuum of Scriptural passages, preachers often recapitulated the sermon of the previous day or week in order to refresh the minds of the parishioners and maintain the flow of the biblical narrative.

The structure of the sermon in part depended upon the manner in which a preacher explicated the doctrines derived from the text. When drawing out a theological principle from a verse, a preacher, such as Thomas Cartwright (1535-1603) in his sermons on Colossians, might pose a series of questions and seek to answer them

---

[30] See Pipa, "William Perkins," pp. 141-2. This work, translated into English as *The Practis of Preaching* (1577), seems to have exercised more influence on the Puritans than on the continent.

[31] See Blench, *Preaching in England*, p. 94.

[32] There were of course exceptions to the rule, such as the popular and famous Puritan preacher, Henry Smith. See Horton Davies, *Worship and Theology in England*, Book I: *From Cranmer to Baxter and Fox, 1534-1690* (Grand Rapids: William B. Eerdmans Publishing Co., 1996), p. 311.

[33] "O Lord God, give us understanding!" See Farner, *Huldrych Zwingli*, p. 100.

[34] See Walter Hollweg, *Heinrich Bullingers Hausbuch: Eine Untersuchung über die Anfänge der reformierten Predigtliteratur* (Neukirchen: Kreis Moers, 1956), 231.

[35] See Rodolphe Peter, "Rhétorique et prédication selon Calvin," 257-60.

in the main body of the sermon.[36] Musculus, in both his commentaries and sermons, had in scholastic fashion divided a verse into various questions and objections.[37] Generally, construction of the sermon could consist of the doctrines, anticipated arguments against those doctrines, counterarguments in support of those doctrines, and finally their concomitant moral applications. Calvin was enslaved to no particular method or form but developed his sermon as the biblical narrative proceeded. He constructed each sermon brick by brick, engaging the text and drawing applications from it.[38] In expounding a passage, Calvin might explain the historical context, examine key words, make cross-references to other verses, or paraphrase a verse. Throughout his exploration of a text, Calvin evinced a desire to make even difficult passages and theological principles easy for the laity to understand. Likewise, the Puritans structured their sermons to be practical and simple and expended great energy on adapting the "Uses" of Scripture to their congregations.[39]

The concluding prayer served to signal the end of the sermon and reflect upon its basic insights. Zwingli was masterful in bringing the sermon to a conclusion in a brief prayer or exhortation.[40] Jean Budé, one of Calvin's editors, expressed the importance of these prayers in reinforcing the message in the hearts of the faithful listeners (or readers) and demonstrating the way to inform one's own prayer life with Scripture.[41]

The reformers' aim of being understood clearly led them to avoid ornamentation and to use common and plain speech. Consequently, a defining characteristic of Reformed preaching was the "plain style." While an authoritative exposition of Scripture required a high level of training in the biblical languages and exegesis, Reformed preachers did not want to dazzle the congregation

---

[36] See Pipa, "William Perkins," p. 154.

[37] Preaching on John 15:19, Musculus posed various objections to Christ's statement that his disciples are not of the world, and then sought to resolve these problems. See Wolrad von Waldeck, *Tagebuch während des Reichstages zu Augsburg 1548* (Hildesheim, 1980), p. 167.

[38] For informative analyses of structure in Calvin's sermons, see Parker, *Calvin's Preaching*, pp. 132-6; Mülhaupt, *Die Predigt Calvins*, pp. 36-8; and Rodolphe Peter, "Rhétorique et prédication selon Calvin," pp. 257-60.

[39] See Davies, *Worship and Theology in England*, pp. 304-8.

[40] See Farner, *Huldrych Zwingli*, pp. 102-3.

[41] Cited in Bonoît, ed., *Sermons sur le Livre de Michée*, p. xiii.

with their learning and thereby deflect listeners from the Word of
God. Zwingli was critical of those who sought to adorn their sermons with literary tropes and to amaze the audience with a display
of erudition.[42] William Perkins wrote that a "strange word" can
"draw the mind away from the purpose to some other matter."[43]
The use of human wisdom hinders the voice of God from speaking
through Scripture. All the preaching handbooks dealt with this
problem and advised preachers to hide their learning.[44]

Notwithstanding the pastoral concern for simplicity, preachers
who advocated and practiced the "plain style" recognized the need
to color their sermons with some rhetorical tropes. They saw the
use of oratory as a means to an end. While Zwingli rejected the
principles of classical oratory, he was not averse to using them or
making classical allusions. Calvin believed that eloquence was a gift
from God and, following Augustine, thought it could be used in the
service of the Gospel.[45] The Genevan reformer sought to model his
own style after the Scriptural model of simple eloquence and avoid
theological terms that were not found in the Bible.[46] Zwingli and
Calvin used many images from everyday life to enliven their sermons and make biblical principles more palatable to the lay listener.[47] For instance, while Zwingli often referred to Christ as a
captain[48], Calvin likened God to a schoolteacher and the Church
as *l'escole de Dieu*.[49] Calvin was particularly gifted in the use of fic-
tional speeches or dialogues to illustrate a point. In a sermon on
Micah 7:1, Calvin, to make the congregation identify with the

---

[42]   See Farner, *Huldrych Zwingli*, p. 98.
[43]   See Ian Breward, ed., *The Work of William Perkins*, p. 346.
[44]   Andreas Hyperius states that "it is a notable poynt of cunnynge to dissemble
Arte." Cited in Pipa, "William Perkins," p. 130. Following Hyperius, Perkins writes that
the preacher "ought in public to conceal all these [arts] from the people and not to
make the least ostentation. Artis etiam cleare artem: it is also a point of art to conceal
art." See Breward, ed., *The Work of William Perkins*, p. 345.
[45]   Calvin distinguished and condemned three groups of orators: the *maquignons*,
who disguised the truth under the pretense of preaching the Gospel; the *coquards*, who
prided themselves on their sagacity and thought the Gospel was not for them; and the
sophistes, who exchanged the simplicity of Scripture for their jargon and foolish specula-
tions. See Peter, "Rhétorique et prédication selon Calvin," pp. 252-3.
[46]   See Peter, "Rhétorique et prédication selon Calvin," pp. 254-5.
[47]   On Calvin's use of metaphors, see Mülhaupt, *Die Predigt Calvins*, pp. 39-63; on
Zwingli, see Farner, *Huldrych Zwingli*, pp. 112-6.
[48]   See Gottfried W. Locher, *Zwingli's Thought: New Perspectives* (Leiden: E. J. Brill,
1981), pp. 72-86.
[49]   See Mülhaupt, *Die Predigt Calvins*, pp. 57-9.

prophet's discouragement in his own day, had the "papists" present their derogatory view of Protestant reform.[50] While Puritan preachers were noted for their use of the "plain style," some opted for the relatively austere style of Zwingli and Calvin, but others made a more use of rhetorical tropes and schemata.[51]

As the century progressed, a number of Reformed preachers published their own homiletic handbooks, expressing elements of the new Reformed method and the plain style of preaching. Andreas Hyperius's *De formandis Concionibus Sacris* (1553) and Niels Hemmingsen's *Evangelie Postil* (1561) treated matters of exegesis, structure, and style. While neither Zwingli nor Calvin wrote a handbook on preaching, their published sermons could provide guides and exemplars of preaching. Zwingli encouraged priests throughout the canton of Zurich to preach like him in the *praedicatio continua* method, using the same sequence of biblical books.[52] Ministers in France also requested manuscripts of Calvin's sermons to help them in their ministry.[53]

Among the homiletic works written by Reformed authors, Heinrich Bullinger's *Decades* and William Perkins's *Arte of Prophesying* were the most influential. The *Decades*, consisting of ten sets of ten sermons originally delivered as lessons in the *Prophezei*, provided an authoritative treatment of Scripture in sermon form. The sermons are topical rather than expository, covering the commonplaces of

---

[50] "Et cependant les papistes prennent occasion de là de calumpnier nostre doctrine. 'Et quoy? disent ilz. Ces gentz font semblant de voulloir reformer tout le monde, et quelle reformation voit on entre eulx? En quoy se sont ilz amendez? Mais au contraire ilz empirent.' Voilà donc comme ilz mesdisent de la parolle de Dieu à nostre occasion. Et ainsi il ne nous fault point perdre courage, mais avoir ce regard icy, ascavoir que nostre Seigneur veult que son Evangile soit presché, combien qu'elle soit mal receue de plusieurs, et mesmes, comme desja nous avons dict, qu'elle leur soit occasion de mal, et qu'ilz en empirent au lieu d'amender." See Bonoît, ed., *Sermons sur le Livre de Michée*, p. 209.

[51] Blench, *Preaching in England*, p. 168, has distinguished three forms of the plain style: (1) "an extremely bare and austere form"; (2) a less colorless form, employing tropes but not schemata"; and (3) "a moderately decorated form, employing tropes, and occasionally schemata also." Like Pipa, "William Perkins," p. 37, I prefer to avoid such categories and see these stylistic differences, based upon the background and personality of the preacher, as slight variances on one style.

[52] See Farner, *Huldrych Zwingli*, pp. 44-5.

[53] See Jean-Français Gilmont, "Les sermons de Calvin: de l'oral à l'imprimé," *Bulletin de la société de l'histoire du protestantisme français* 141 (1995): 156-7.

Christian theology.[54] The *Decades* present as much a compendium of dogma, divided into theological *topoi*, as a collection of sermons. First published in Latin and intended for young ministers, the work eventually was translated into many languages and became a "family book" enabling the paterfamilias to instruct their families in the articles of the faith.

William Perkins's *Arte of Prophesying*, published in Latin in 1592 and translated into English in 1606, offered the first preaching handbook by an English Protestant. Based upon his reading of earlier homilists from Chrysostom to Theodore Beza, he provided a homiletic treatise that influenced Puritan preaching in the seventeenth century. In it, he discussed the importance and aim of preaching, basic hermeneutic principles, the delivery and application of Scripture, and the minister's preparation.[55] Most significantly he articulated the new Reformed method and the "plain style" in a concise fashion, bringing together the fruits of homiletic principles developed earlier in the century in England and on the continent. In his discussion of articulation and gesture, Perkins echoed Calvin in stating that the preacher must be "fervent and vehement" in exhortation.[56]

Preparation, Transmission and Redaction of Sermons

The sermon first took shape in the pastor's study as a product of reflection upon the biblical text. The reformers knew the importance of solid preparation. Once, during a sermon on Deuteronomy, Calvin admonished spiritualist-minded individuals who refused to apply themselves to Scripture under the foolish belief that God could work through them directly.[57] Bullinger did not intend his "model" sermons to be read *verbatim* in the way that Anglican ministers were to recite from the *Book of Homilies*; rather, he hoped to provide raw homiletic material that young ministers

---

[54]   In a letter to Oswald Myconius, Bullinger expressed his hope that the *Decades* would in fact supplant the *loci communes* method. See Hollweg, *Heinrich Bullingers Hausbuch*, p. 24.

[55]   For a good synopsis of the work, see Pipa, "William Perkins and the Development of Puritan Preaching," pp. 86-104.

[56]   See Breward, ed., *The Work of William Perkins*, p. 348.

[57]   See Stauffer, "Un Calvin méconnu," p. 188.

could rework and adapt to the needs of their particular congregation.[58]

But such preparatory study did not prevent a degree of spontaneity and flexibility in delivery. To the contrary, both Zwingli and Calvin preached extemporaneously with the original Greek and Hebrew texts of the Bible lying open on the pulpit or in hand.[59] Calvin, having lectured on the Bible throughout the week and publishing a number of commentaries, possessed a familiarity with Scripture that allowed him to deliver his sermons from memory. Zwingli did not preach from a manuscript or notes because he did not want to rely on human wisdom.[60] Perkins addressed the custom of delivering sermons by heart, advising young preachers to avoid the hazards involved in memorizing the entire sermon, and suggested helpful mnemonic techniques that would allow for a smoother and more natural delivery.[61] Because preachers, following the example of Zwingli and Calvin, generally did not write out their sermons or use notes (and the notes of listeners were usually discarded when a sermon went to press), we rarely get to view a sermon in its original form.

With the notable exception of Calvin, we have few opportunities to inspect sermons in manuscript form. Consequently, our knowledge of preaching in the early modern period has been based largely on published sermons. As historians turn to archival records and continue to edit the relatively few manuscript sermons, we can began to hear the sermon from the mouth of the preacher and gain a more accurate account of homiletic activity in the Reformation. The publication of sermons by Zwingli, Perkins, and Calvin demonstrate how the form and content of sermons could undergo alteration during its transmission from an oral delivery and transcript to a revision ready for printing.

None of Zwingli's sermons have been preserved in their original form. Some fragments of his sermons remain hidden in his exegetical *Nachlaß*, but it is difficult to determine which writings stem from a lecture given in the *Prophezei* and which served as sermon outlines. Matters are complicated because Zwingli might

---

[58]   See Hollweg, *Heinrich Bullingers Hausbuch*, pp. 41-2.
[59]   See Farner, *Huldrych Zwingli*, p. 99; Parker, *Calvin's Preaching*, p. 81.
[60]   See Farner, *Huldrych Zwingli*, p. 98.
[61]   See Breward, ed., *The Work of William Perkins*, p. 344.

preach a sermon on a passage exposited in the *Prophezei* early that morning. Consequently, Leo Jud, when editing the exegetical writings for publication, mixed in material from sermons and translated it into Latin to produce a bible commentary.

Upon request, Zwingli wrote down some of his sermons later from memory, but he usually reworked them into theological treatises. Zwingli's famous discourse on divine providence, *De providentia dei anamnema*, for instance, was originally a sermon delivered at the colloquy of Marburg before Philip of Hesse (1504-67). When Philip requested a copy of the sermon, Zwingli reworked and expanded it, explaining in a prefatory letter that, since his memory could not recall the arrangement of the sermon, he has opted to set down a summary and divide it into chapters. "When you examine them I think you will admit that you have received, if not the sermon itself, at least the same material and line of argument."[62] Zwingli's sermon to Dominican nuns at the convent of the Oetenbach, delivered in the summer of 1522, served as the basis for his seminal work, *Von Clarheit und Gewüsse.*[63] When he revised the sermon, Zwingli added an introductory section on the image of God which has little connection to the rest of the work. His reluctance to transcribe his sermons and to preserve their original form have led historians to extrapolate his homiletic method and style on the basis of his publications.

Perkins took more interest in the revision of his sermons for the press.[64] None of his sermons were published as sermons but were altered into other genres, such as topical or expository treatises, commentaries, or lectures.[65] His series of sermons on Galatians, for instance, became in the editorial process a commentary on the New Testament epistle. Redaction involved the removal of the introduc-

---

[62]   See Emil Egli et al., eds., *Huldreich Zwinglis Werke*, vol. 6, p. 69. English translation from Samuel M. Jackson and William J. Hinke, eds., *Zwingli: On Providence and Other Essays* (Ada, Mich.: Baker Books, 1983), p. 130.

[63]   Other sermon-based works, besides those already mentioned, include: *Marienpredigt, Von Erkiesen und Unterschied der Speisen*, the two *Berner Predigten, Wider die Pensionen, De providentia dei anamnema, Von göttlicher und menschlicher Gerechtigkeit*, and *Der Hirt.* These writings are published in Melchior Schuler and Johann Schulthess, eds., *Huldreich Zwinglis Werke* (Zurich: 1828-42).

[64]   For an informative discussion on the redaction of Perkins's sermons, see Pipa, "William Perkins," pp. 104-9.

[65]   Alan F. Herr, *The Elizabethan Sermon: A Survey and a Bibliography* (New York: Octagon Books, 1969), p. 9.

tory comments and conclusions of sermons, and the addition of chapter divisions. This transformed the sermon into a continuous exposition easy for the reader to follow. After Perkins's death, publishers reissued the publication of his expositions on Revelations 1-3 and Matthew 4 because the editors, limited to a hodgepodge of incomplete notes, made some errors. Often publishers shortened the content of sermons out of preference or because they lacked sufficient manuscripts. As is to be expected, the posthumously published treatises that most closely resemble their earlier incarnations as sermons were revised by an editor who heard Perkins's preaching and took notes.

Although Calvin hardly participated in the editorial process of the sermons, their transmission and redaction, thanks to some committed individuals, are sufficiently documented. Printers had difficulty in getting Calvin's permission to publish his sermons.[66] The only edition of sermons that he had a hand in editing (and to which he contributed a preface) was his *Quatre Sermons*. Calvin at the time intended the publication as a response to an earlier attack upon from the "Nicodemites." In this instance, Calvin may have reworked his sermon from notes taken by his auditors.[67] Calvin was reticent to have his sermons published because he felt they were rooted in a particular time and place and this could not be conveyed to a generic audience.[68] Moreover, a sermon, which is improvised and repetitive, lacks the "lucid brevity" that Calvin aimed for in his commentaries and *Institutes*. Nonetheless, Calvin's sermons, diligently recorded in manuscripts, moved speedily off the press.

The preservation of Calvin's unpublished sermons can largely be attributed to one man, Denis Raguenier, a French refugee whose precision and diligence as a stenographer was recognized by the Genevan government. The *Diacres administrateurs des biens aumosnez aus povres estragners*, or *Bourse française*, paid Raguenier to transcribe Calvin's sermons from 1549 until his death about eleven

---

[66]   For an excellent examination of Calvin and his editors, see Gilmont, "Les sermons de Calvin," pp. 145-62. Gilmont uses publishers' prefaces to printed editions of Calvin's works to reveal information on the exact circumstances of publication and Calvin's attitude toward it.

[67]   See Rodolphe Peter and Jean-François Gilmont, *Bibliotheca calviniana: Les oeuvres de Jean Calvin publiées au XVIe siècles*, vol. 1 (Geneva: Librairie Droz S.A., 1991), p. 465.

[68]   Gilmont, "Les sermons de Calvin," pp. 154-5.

years later.[69] From 1554, his notes served as the basis for the publications. He was the first to record Calvin's sermons systematically, professionally, and with remarkable accuracy. Raguenier wrote down the first page of each sermon from his shorthand memos, dictating the rest to scribes who then used the first page as a guide for their own transcription.[70] The proceeds from the published sermons went to refugees. Unfortunately, when editors redacted a sermon, the manuscript was discarded or used for the paper. But many manuscript originals and copies have been preserved and Raguenier's catalogue of over 200 manuscripts, drawn up in 1560, allows historians to assess Calvin's preaching activity.[71]

All specialists on Calvin's preaching wince with pain when they retell the "unbelievable story" of Calvin's unpublished sermons.[72] The deacons of the *Bourse française* preserved the manuscript sermons until they were deposited in the municipal library of Geneva in 1613. Library catalogues of the sermons in 1697 and 1702 reveal that some of the sermons in the original Raguenier catalogue were no longer in the collection, probably because they were discarded after their publication, and some post-Raguenier sermons were added. A catalogue drawn up in 1779 showed discrepancies with Raguenier's original catalogue and lists sermons that had been published and no longer existed in manuscript. Then, in 1806, "une année néfaste,"[73] the unthinkable happened. Not considering that the sermons were of much value since they were difficult to read and not in Calvin's own hand, the library sold all the existing vol-

---

[69]   See Erwin Mülhaupt, "Calvins 'Sermons inédits: Vorgeschichte, Überlieferung und gegenwärtiger Stand der Edition," in Karl Halaski, ed., *Der Prediger Johannes Calvin: Beiträge und Nachrichten zur Ausgabe der Supplementa Calviniana* (Neukirchen: Kreis Mors, 1966), pp. 14-5.

[70]   See Bernard Gagnebin, "L'histoire des manuscrits des sermons de Calvin," in Georges A. Barrois, ed., *Sermons sur le Livre d'Esaïe: chapitres 13-29* (Neukirchen: Kreis Mors, 1961), pp. xvii-xix.

[71]   See Gagnebin, "L'histoire des manuscrits," pp. xvi-xvii. The catalogue lists sermons on Genesis, Deuteronomy, Psalms, Jeremiah, Lamentations, Micah, Zephaniah, Hosea, Joel, Amos, Obadiah, Jonah, Daniel, Ezekiel, Acts, Galatians, Ephesians, 1 and 2 Thessalonians, 1 and 2 Timothy, Titus, 1 and 2 Corinthians. After the completion of the catalogue Calvin preached also on the synoptic Gospels, 2 Samuel, 1 Kings, and Hebrews.

[72]   Bernard Gagnebin, "L'incroyable histoire des sermons de Calvin," *Bulletin de la société d'histoire et d'archéologie de Genève* (1955): 311-34. Former librarian of the University library in Geneva, he gives the first complete account of the strange history behind the manuscripts.

[73]   Stauffer, "Un Calvin méconnu," p. 190.

umes of Calvin's unpublished sermons, except one that was kept as a sample. Scholars managed to recover only fourteen volumes of the original forty-four volumes. In the mid-twentieth century, presentation copies of sermons on Genesis emerged at the Bodleian library at Oxford University and the library of Lambeth Palace.[74] These manuscript sermons, despite the losses, provide a homiletic gold mine from the towering figure of the Reformed tradition.

Interaction between Audience and Preacher

While the literature on preachers and homiletics is vast, scholars have had a more difficult time in assessing the reception of sermons. This lacuna in the study of preaching is surprising in that preaching was intended to move auditors and provoke some kind of response. Nonetheless, information on popular responses to preaching is few and far between. Rare is the external source that allows us to see how a lay audience understood the message of a sermon.[75] What ideas and meaning did the laity draw from the preacher's message? How did they appropriate it and make it sensible within their social and intellectual milieu? These questions have been asked increasingly by historians who in recent years are interested in moving beyond the theological content of preaching and examining the social dimension of preaching. Understanding the sermon as "social event," involves knowing something about the style and personality of the preacher, the context of the sermon, the social makeup of the audience, and the events or issues of the day.

Heretofore scholars have relied primarily on internal evidence; they have tried to determine the audience's response based upon a sermon text. But this approach, replete with potential pitfalls, requires a degree of speculation. Scholars have been more successful in gleaning popular reception of sermons from archival records.

---

[74] For a thorough description of these findings, see Stauffer, "Les sermons inédits," pp. 26-36.

[75] One such document, for instance, is a report drawn up the civic officials of Nuremberg listing the reactions of eighteen laymen, primarily from the artisan class, regarding the sermons of a Franciscan preacher. See Gunter Zimmerman, "Die Rezeption der reformatorischen Botschaft: Laienaussagen zu Predigten des Franziskanerpaters Jeremias Mülich in der Fastenzeit 1524," *Zeitschrift für bayerische Kirchengeschichte* 58 (1989):51-70.

Most of the lay responses that have been documented, however, appear in the form of complaints about the moral or intellectual caliber of the preacher or about certain controversial statements made in the sermons. They do not yield detailed information on an auditor's understanding of a sermon.

We have little information on sermon reception in German-speaking Switzerland. Unfortunately, our knowledge of audience response to Zwingli is rather general. We know that he was quite forceful and persuasive as a preacher and his sermons had dramatic consequences. Bullinger says of Zwingli's auditors merely that his sermons could divide a congregation.[76] Parishioners remarked upon the reformer's hard-hitting attack on heresy, superstition, and apostasy, and upon his adamant calls to repentance and godly living. Indeed, the Zurich minister's unbridled attack upon the Roman church from the pulpit kindled the nascent flames of iconoclasm and anticlericalism. But the pastor's vision of reform was a double-edged sword that could not only incite parishioners to hasten the Reformation in the city but also offend them as well. When the preacher Johannes Ammann referred to some parishioners as criminals, they became incensed and sought legal redress.[77] When one zealous Zwinglian preacher, Johannes Schlegel, oriented his sermon against sectarian preachers, a cantankerous Anabaptist in the audience challenged Schlegel's own credentials as a preacher.[78] While the sectarians aggressively criticized Zwinglian preachers, others were more passively resistant. When called before the magistrates on account of an attendance problem, one Marti Weber responded that there was no point in attending since the sermon message was always the same.[79]

Since there is more information on the preaching activity of Calvin and the Genevans than in other Reformed communities, it is natural to find in Geneva relatively more documentation on popular and magisterial response. To ascertain the reception to Calvin's preaching, some historians have utilized not only Calvin's sermons,

---

[76]   See J. J. Hottinger and H. H. Vögeli., eds., *Heinrich Bullingers Reformationsgeschichte*, vol. 1, p. 13.

[77]   See Gordon, "Preaching and the Reform," p. 75.

[78]   This led to an exchange about the value of ordination until the disgruntled man departed the service. See Bruce Gordon, "Preaching and the reform of the clergy in the Swiss Reformation," pp. 73-4.

[79]   See Gordon, "Preaching and the Reform," p. 75.

but also the Registers of the Company of Pastors and the Records of the City Council.[80] Again, these references are always in the form of complaints. Calvin himself mentions in a sermon delivered on September of 1554 – a difficult period for Calvin – that his preaching had come under criticism after he had condemned the Genevans' dissolute behavior.[81] Earlier, in the 1540s, Calvin's sermons had been the source of public disturbances. A Genevan magistrate protested after a sermon in which Calvin voiced the need for strong measures against the *enfants de Genève*, a faction opposed to Calvin. A few years later, Calvin's sharp words directed at ill-disciplined Genevans provoked auditors to disrupt the service.[82] But Calvin was not alone in his vituperative condemnation of the vices of the Genevans. Other preachers were rebuked before the magistracy and even arrested for attacking the magistrates and offending parishioners.[83] Some Genevans objected to the preacher's straying from the text, while others, such as the wife of Pierre Biolley in a discussion with her servant about the Genevan pastors, dismissed the preachers outright in derogatory terms.[84] The few parishioners who managed to remember the sermon content demonstrated a rather simplistic if not wrong understanding of the message. Thus a certain communicative impasse existed between the preacher's intent and the popular reception.[85]

A sermon could elicit a response when it touched upon political issues of the day. Zwingli's sermon on the trafficking of Swiss mercenary soldiers, a controversial topic among the Swiss cantons, occasioned a clandestine Catholic auditor to take notes with the hope of demonstrating the reformer's disloyalty to the Swiss Federation.[86] The sermons during election time always seem to provoke reaction of one sort or another. Calvin specifically condemned candidates as *ennemis de Dieu* and objected that voters, who hardly frequented

---

[80] See, for example, William G. Naphy, *Calvin and the Consolidation of the Genevan Reformation* (Manchester: Manchester University Press, 1994); Lambert, "Preaching, Praying and Policing.'

[81] The occasion for this is the favorable treatment given to an imprisoned prostitute. See Peter, "Genève dans la prédication de Calvin," p. 36.

[82] See Naphy, *Calvin and the Consolidation of the Genevan Reformation*, p. 159.

[83] Ibid, pp. 159-60. In fact, according to Lambert, "Preaching, Praying," p. 368, all pastors "were denounced to the council at one time or another."

[84] See Lambert, "Preaching, Praying," pp. 387-8.

[85] Lambert, "Preaching, Praying," p. 364.

[86] For a reprint of the notes, see Farner, *Huldrych Zwingli*, pp. 58-65.

sermons, did not invoke God in the elections.[87] When Wolfgang
Musculus sought to dissuade Augsburgers from voting Catholics
into office because they were treacherous and two-faced, the audience, according to a Lutheran observer, thought that this charac-
terization of "papists" went a bit too far.[88]

The preacher might make obvious references to particular individuals. Zwingli was not afraid to single out wicked political leaders
from the pulpit.[89] Benedict Landenberg, the pastor at Bärentswyl,
was fined because he directed a sermon against an auditor.[90] Calvin
was asked to point his finger toward the reprobates whom he was
castigating but, as he stated in a sermon in the elections of 1555, he
did not have to since it was clear who they were. The expressions
that Calvin used in his sermons would lead one to believe that he
in fact pointed to those whom he was castigating.[91] But auditors
often believed they were being addressed even if they were not sin-
gled out by name. Pierre Ameaux, who led opposition to Calvin
throughout the 1550s, felt during a sermon as if he had been
"slapped on the nose." The Genevan parishioner Benoît Perrotel,
smarting from Calvin's general admonishments, believed that Calvin had clairvoyance, knew his hidden desire for a woman, and
even tailored his sermons from Perrotel's sinful thoughts.[92] The
Puritan preacher Richard Fletcher, a practitioner of the "personal
preaching" style in England, provoked parishioners when he sin-
gled out individuals from the pulpit.[93]

The creative use of published and manuscript sources in recent
years have allowed historians to explore more authoritatively the
impact of preaching. Our knowledge of lay reception in the sixteenth century, however, still rests on scraps and fragments. Historians continue to confront the paucity of sources, ever searching for
those zealous, indifferent, and hostile responses to a sermon to let

---

[87]   See Peter, "Genève dans la prédication de Calvin," p. 39.
[88]   See Wilhelm Germann, *D. Johann Forster der Hennebergishe Reformator: Ein Mitarbeiter und Mitstreiter D. Martin Luthers* (n. p., 1893), pp. 239-40.
[89]   See Farner, *Huldrych Zwingli*, p. 118.
[90]   See Emil Egli, ed., *Aktensammlung zur Geschichte der Zürcher Reformation* (Nieuwkoop, 1973), p. 518. The auditor, Jakob Meier, was also fined because of words he spoke and the actions he took against Landenberg.
[91]   See Peter, "Genève dans la prédication de Calvin," p. 39.
[92]   See Lambert, "Preaching, Praying," pp. 372-3.
[93]   See Patrick Collinson, *Godly People: Essays on English Protestantism and Puritanism* (Rio Grande, Oh.: Hambledon Press, 1983), pp. 409, 418.

them speak out once again. We are fortunate to hear them in those instances when a preacher directly addresses individuals in his congregation or when a recalcitrant parishioner speaks his mind before authorities. But the ways in which ministers of the Word present their material, the demands they make on their listeners, and the pedagogical methods they employ can reveal an unspoken exchange between those on each side of the pulpit. Presently, the anecdotal evidence that the sparse records provide do not allow us to make sweeping statements about the interaction between preacher and audience. We can only imagine what those Zurich parishioners thought when they heard for the first time their *Leutpriester* preach consecutively through an entire biblical book, delving into each verse and drawing out its importance for their daily lives.

Bibliography

Barrois, Georges, "Calvin and the Genevans," *Theology Today* 21 (1964/5): 458-65.

Blench, J. W., *Preaching in England in the Late Fifteenth and Sixteenth Centuries* (New York: Barnes and Noble, 1964).

Bullinger, Heinrich, *Heinrich Bullingers Reformationsgeschichte*, 3 vols., ed. J.J. Hottinger and H.H. Vögeli (Frauenfeld: Verlag von Ch. Beyel, 1838-40).

— *The Decades of Henry Bullinger*, 4 vols., ed. Thomas Harding (Cambridge: Cambridge University Press, 1949-52).

Büsser, Fritz, *Wurzeln der Reformation in Zürich: Zum 500. Geburtstag des Reformators Huldrych Zwingli* (Leiden: E. J. Brill, 1985).

Collinson, Patrick, *The Elizabethan Puritan Movement* (Oxford: Clarendon Press, 1967).

— *The Religion of Protestants: The Church in English Society, 1559-1625* (Oxford: Clarendon Press, 1982).

Davies, Horton, *Worship and Theology in England*, Book I: *From Cranmer to Baxter and Fox, 1534-1690* (Grand Rapids: Wm. B. Eerdmans Publishing Co., 1996, reprint).

Engammare, Max, "Calvin: A Prophet without a Prophecy," *Church History* 67 (1998): 643-61.

— "Calvin, connaissait-il la Bible? Les citations de l'Écriture dans ses sermons sur la Genèse," *Bulletin de la société de l'histoire du protestantisme français* 141 (1995): 163-84.

— "Calvin monarchomaque? Du soupçon à l'argument," *Archiv für Reformationsgeschichte* 89 (1998): 207-25.

— "Le Paradis à Genève: Comment Calvin prêchait-il la chute aux Genevois," *Études théologiques et religieuses* (1994): 329-47.

Farner, Oskar, *Huldrych Zwingli*, vol. 3: *Seine Verkündigung und ihre ersten Früchte 1520-1525* (Zurich: Zwingli Verlag, 1954).

Fischer, Danièle, "L'Element historique dans la prédication de Calvin: Un aspect original de l'homilétique du réformateur," *Revue d'histoire et philosophie religieuses* 64 (1984): 365-86.

Gagnebin, Bernard, "L'Histoire des manuscrits des sermons de Calvin," in Georges A. Barrois, *Sermons sur le Livre d'Esaïe: chapitres 13-29* (1961) (Neukirchen, Kreis Moers: Neukirchener Verlag, 1961), pp. xiv-xxviii.

Gilmont, Jean-François, "Les sermons de Calvin: De l'oral à l'imprimé," *Bulletin de la société de l'histoire du protestantisme français* 141 (1995): 145-62.

Gordon, Bruce, "Preaching and the Reform of the Clergy in the Swiss Reformation," in Andrew Pettegree, ed., *The Reformation of the Parishes: The Ministry and the Reformation in Town and Country* (Manchester: Manchester University Press, 1993), pp. 63-84.

Herr, Alan F., *The Elizabethan Sermon: A Survey and a Bibliography* (New York: Octagon Books, 1969).

Hollweg, Walter, *Heinrich Bullingers Hausbuch: Eine Untersuchung über die Anfänge der reformierten Predigtliteratur* (Neukirchen, Kreis Moers: Verlag des Buchhandlung des Erziehungsvereins, 1956).

Kelly, Douglas, "Varied Themes in Calvin's 2 Samuel Sermons and the Development of His Thought," in Wilhelm H. Neuser and Brian G. Armstrong, eds., *Calvinus Sincerioris Religionis Vindex: Calvin as Protector of the Pure Religion* (Kirksville: Sixteenth Century Journal Publishers, 1997), pp. 209-23.

Lambert, Thomas A., "Preaching, Praying and Policing the Reform in Sixteenth-Century Geneva," Ph.D. diss., University of Wisconsin, Madison, 1998.

Locher, Gottfried W., *Zwingli's Thought: New Perspectives* (Leiden: E. J. Brill, 1981).

Lutz, Samuel, "Was ist eine evangelische Predigt? Die Homiletik des Berner Synodus," in *Der Berner Synodus von 1532: Edition und Abhandlungen zum Jubiläumsjahr 1982*, vol. 2 (Neukirchen-Vluyn: Neukirchener Verlag, 1988), pp. 235-47.

Meyer, Walter E., "Die Entstehung von Huldrych Zwinglis neutestamentlichen Kommentaren und Predigtnachschriften," *Zwingliana* 14 (1976): 285-94.

Mülhaupt, Erwin, "Calvins 'Sermons inédits': Vorgeschichte, Überlieferung und gegenwärtiger Stand der Edition," in Karl Halaski, ed., *Der Prediger Johannes Calvin: Beiträge und Nachrichten zur Ausgabe der Supplementa Calviniana* (Neukirchen-Vluyn: Neukirchener Verlag, 1966), pp. 9-24.
— *Die Predigt Calvins, ihre Geschichte, ihre Form und ihre religiösen Grundgedanken* (Berlin and Leipzig: Walter de Gruyter & Co., 1931).
Naphy, William G., *Calvin and the Consolidation of the Genevan Reformation* (Manchester: Manchester University Press, 1994).
Old, Hughes O., "History of Preaching," in Donald K. McKim, ed., *Encyclopedia of the Reformed Tradition* (Louisville: Westminster John Knox Press, 1992), pp. 286-9.
Parker, Thomas H. L., *Calvin's Preaching* (Louisville: Westminster/John Knox Press, 1992).
Perkins, William, *The Work of William Perkins*, ed. Ian Breward (Appelford: The Sutton Courtenay Press, 1970).
Peter, Rodolphe, "Genève dans la prédication de Calvin," in W. H. Neuser, ed., *Calvinus Ecclesiae Genevensis Custos* (Bern: Peter Lang, 1984), pp. 23-47.
— "Jean Calvin prédicateur," *Revue d'histoire et de philosophie religieuses* 52 (1972): 111-7.
— "Rhétorique et prédication selon Calvin," *Revue d'histoire et de philosophie religieuses* (1975): 249-72.
Peter, Rodolphe and Jean-François Gilmont, *Bibliotheca calviniana: Les oeuvres de Jean Calvin publiées au XVIe siècles*, 2 vols. (Geneva: Librairie Droz S. A., 1991-4).
Pipa, Joseph A., Jr., "William Perkins and the Development of Puritan Preaching," Ph.D. dissertation, Westminster Theological Seminary, 1985.
Schreiner, Susan E., "'Through a Mirror Dimly': Calvin's Sermons on Job," *Calvin Theological Journal* 21 (1986): 175-93.
Seaver, Paul S., *The Puritan Lectureships: The Politics of Religious Dissent, 1560-1662* (Stanford: Stanford University Press, 1970).
Snavely, Iren L., "Huldrych Zwingli and the Preaching Office in German Switzerland," *Fides et Historia* 25 (1993): 33-45.
Stauffer, Richard, *Dieu, la création et la providence dans la prédication de Calvin*, Basler und Berner Studien zur historischen und systematischen Theolgie 33 (Bern: Peter Lang, 1978).
— *Interprètes de La Bible: Études sur les réformateurs du XVIe siècle* (Paris: Éditions Beauchesne, 1980).
— "Les sermons inédits de Calvin sur le livre de la Genèse," *Revue de théologie et de philosophie* 98 (1965): 26-36.

— "L'exégèse de Genése 1/1-3 chez Luther et Calvin," in *In Principio: Interprétations des premiers versets de la Genèse* (Paris: Études Augustiniennes, 1973), pp. 245-66.

— "Un Calvin méconnu: Le prédicateur de Genève," *Bulletin de la Société de l'histoire du protestantisme français* 123 (1977): 184-203.

Supplementa Calviniana. Sermon inédits, 8 vols. to date (Neukirchen-Vluyn: Neukrichener Verlag des Erziehungsvereins, 1936 to present).

Thiel, Albrecht, *In der Schule Gottes: die Ethik Calvins im Spiegel seiner Predigten über das Deuteronomium* (Neukirchen-Vluyn: Neukirchener Verlag, 1999).

PART TWO

THE SOCIAL HISTORY OF PREACHING

CHAPTER FOUR

DANGEROUS VOCATIONS:
PREACHING IN FRANCE IN THE LATE MIDDLE AGES
AND REFORMATIONS

Larissa Taylor
(Colby College)

See, I am sending you out like sheep into the midst of wolves; so be
wise as serpents and innocent as doves. Beware of them, for they will
hand you over to councils and flog you in their synagogues; and you
will be dragged before governors and kings because of me, as a testimony to them and the Gentiles. When they hand you over, do not
worry about how you are to speak or what you are to say; for what
you are to say will be given to you at that time; for it is not you who
speak, but the Spirit of your Father speaking through you…and you
will be hated by all because of my name. (Matthew 10:16-20,22)

Now who will harm you if you are eager to do what is good? But
even if you do suffer for doing what is right, you are blessed. Do not
fear what they fear, and do not be intimidated, but in your hearts
sanctify Christ as Lord. …Yet if any of you suffer as a Christian, do
not consider it a disgrace, but glorify God because you bear this
name. (I Peter 3:13-15, 4:16)

Modern news organizations and statisticians frequently print lists
of the most dangerous or hazardous occupations. Few today would
think of preaching in this context, but in fifteenth- and sixteenth-
century France, the role of preacher could be very dangerous indeed. Murder, attempted strangulation, imprisonment, exile and
other threats were common even in the period before the Religious
Wars, but were exacerbated as religious, political, and social tensions heightened. While many have argued that it is difficult or impossible to know how hearers responded to preaching, this chapter
will provide examples of behaviors that demonstrated responses to
preachers as individuals, and almost certainly to their sermons as
well. Of course, violence was not limited to the preachers – as war,

violence, and assassination became the norm after 1560, Catholic
and Huguenot preachers in some cases used the pulpit to incite
their listeners to violence against the enemies in their midst. While
I believe sermons *can* provide us with significant information on
social history, I will concentrate here on reactions provoked *by*
Catholic and Calvinist preachers, and crowd behavior directed *at*
them. I have chosen to combine the preachers' words, as they have
come down to us, with actions and behaviors recorded in memoirs,
chronicles, letters, and criminal proceedings so that we may more
easily understand the responses of the people in attendance. What
we find in a study of the period from the late Middle Ages to the
death of Henri IV (d. 1610) is a curious reversal of roles. While
prior to the Religious Wars preachers were frequently subjected to
persecution at the hands of kings or their ministers, after 1560 it
was kings, their supporters, and in some cases ordinary people who
were as often the victims of outspoken preachers, whether Catholic
or Calvinist.[1]

Medieval Antecedents

In 1878, Antony Méray published an important book entitled *La vie
au temps des libres prêcheurs*, the title of which alone alerts the reader
that this is not the "standard" interpretation of late medieval mendicant preaching. Méray sees the itinerant preachers of the fourteenth and fifteenth centuries, whom he calls "...masters of word
and thought, so free, so righteous, and so passionately in search of
the truth..."[2] as inherently subversive to the social order of the day.
"They did more to challenge royal despotism, feudal rapacity, and
Roman supremacy than any of the classes of society to whom they

---

[1] "For Catholic zealots, the extermination of the heretical 'vermin' promised the
restoration of unity to the body social and the reinforcement of some of its traditional
boundaries....For Protestant zealots, the purging of the priestly 'vermin' promised the
creation of a new kind of unity within the body social, all the tighter because false gods
and monkish sects would be purer, too..." Natalie Zemon Davis, "The Rites of Violence," in *Society and Culture in Early Modern France* (Stanford: Stanford University Press,
1976), p. 160.
[2] Antony Méray, *La vie au temps des libres prêcheurs ou les devanciers de Luther et de Rabelais: Croyances, usages et moeurs intimes des XIVe, XVe, et XVIe siècles* (Paris: Claudin, 1878),
vol. 2, p. 285.

preached."[3] Méray's assumption of a direct correlation between outspoken late medieval preachers and sixteenth-century Protestants is highly doubtful, but his contention that they often verged on sedition is indisputable.

While there was an implicit assumption that both rich and poor played necessary and complementary roles in the kingdom of this world and the next,[4] late medieval French preachers denounced the lack of charity exhibited toward the poor. Michel Menot (d. 1518) exclaims "...that the blood of Christ cries out for compassion toward the poor, despoiled and unjustly afflicted, and for punishment, for the very cloaks you wear were bought with the blood of the poorest people."[5] Guillaume Pepin (d. 1533) lashes out at those who "...rob the poor...of their earthly goods...making them go hungry and die of starvation...for the lack of life's necessities of which you have deprived them."[6] Yet the well-to-do had no trouble taking care of their animals: "...you will find neither cat nor dog, hen nor rooster, that does not have its place, but of the poor there is no mention."[7] Preachers also denounced women (and men) whose wearing of finery came directly at the expense of the lowest classes. "'You pompous lady,'" claims Menot, "' ...you have six or seven mantles in your chests that you might wear three times a year.' I don't know what excuse this lady will come up with when she finds a poor man, nearly naked, crying out from the cold."[8] For many late medieval preachers, the commandment to love one's neighbor as oneself was all too often ignored.

Challenges were not limited to the aristocracy and growing merchant classes. Kings and queens were, after all, at the pinnacle of the City of this World. Their frequent lack of example set the tone for those beneath them on the social ladder. Pepin preached: "Today there are many exalted and proud kings and princes who hate those who preach things they don't like, for example, that certain

---

[3] Ibid., vol. 1, p. 2.

[4] Larissa Taylor, *Soldiers of Christ: Preaching in Late Medieval and Reformation France* (New York: Oxford University Press, 1992), pp. 149-152.

[5] Joseph Nève, *Sermons choisis de Michel Menot* (Paris: Honoré Champion, 1924), p. 116.

[6] Guillaume Pepin, *Sermones quadraginta de destructione Ninive* (Paris: Claude Chevallon, 1527), fol. 60.

[7] Ibid., p. 210.

[8] Ibid., p. 362

bad things will come to pass if they don't change their ways from the oppression and tyranny they exercise over their people. Many of them are insolent and impious."[9] Using an inflammatory Biblical allusion, Pepin rails that "…there are so few who want to hear and fill themselves with the divine word, such as tyrannical princes waging unjust wars, despoiling their subjects, and ravaging churches. So we hear that King Ahab did not want to listen to the prophet Micaiah."[10] Earlier, in the days when France was at its low point during the Hundred Years' War, preachers such as Jacques LeGrand latched on to Queen Isabeau of Bavaria for her scandalous clothing and behavior. In 1405, even before she had disinherited the dauphin in favor of the English king Henry VI, LeGrand was incensed at her appearance in church and associated her clothing with her supposed promiscuity: "'Oh foolish queen,'" he cried, "'lower the horns of your headdresses, cover up your provocative flesh, give up for a moment your royal ornaments, and wearing normal garb mix with the good citizens of Paris, and you will hear what they say about the Court. You will hear what they say about you.'"[11]

LeGrand was hardly alone in his criticisms, and preachers did not restrict themselves to criticizing other important people. Several cases from Amiens in the late fifteenth century are detailed in the communal records. Jean Masselin, a Dominican preacher, was dragged off to the *hôtel de ville* after he denounced several married women of Amiens, about whose behavior he had apparently been briefed. Masselin got off relatively lightly, being banned from preaching in the city for three to four years.[12] In 1497, an unnamed Franciscan lashed out in the church of St-Frémin-en-Castillon against those who paid few taxes, allowing the burden to fall on those who could least afford it. After being brought before the magistrates' court after commotion and "sedition" resulted, the Franciscan claimed that he had only been trying to help the poor, and "had certainly not intended to cause riots."[13] Both preachers were relatively lucky compared with an Augustinian who had preached

⁹ Pepin, *Destructione Ninive*, fol. 29.
¹⁰ Guillaume Pepin, *Concionum dominicalium ex epistolis et evangeliis totius anni, pars hiemalis* (Antwerp: Guillelmus Lesteenius & Engelbertus Gymnicus, repr. 1656), p. 204.
¹¹ Quoted in Méray, *La vie*, p. 65.
¹² Archives communales d'Amiens, BB17, fol. 47.
¹³ Ibid., BB18, fol. 76.

in 1485 against discord between civic and ecclesiastical officials. After questioning, he was imprisoned.[14] The relatively complete records of remuneration for preachers in Amiens do not mention any of these preachers in the years involved, so it is quite likely that not only the preachers, but their orders, were punished.[15]

Exile, temporary or permanent, was a common punishment for preachers who fulminated in their sermons against those in high places, and was especially likely when kings were targeted. Antoine Farinier was sent into permanent exile in 1478 by Louis XI, and died in Rhodes during a Muslim siege. The possibility of sedition was extremely high, as can be seen in the reaction of the people who had loyally attended his sermons: "…[T]hey could be heard to say this was great folly, for the king knew nothing of these matters and should stay out of them."[16] The famous preacher Olivier Maillard (d. 1502) managed to incur the wrath of three kings, Louis XI, Charles VIII, and Louis XII, although he often served as part of the royal entourage on diplomatic missions and preached at court. Yet there is little evidence in Maillard's numerous extant sermons of overtly anti-royalist sentiment. In one sermon, he says, "in another sermon I said that those who provoke or incite others against the kingdom of the Father or to rebel against their prince is worthy of death."[17] Still, Louis XI threatened to have him tied up in a sack and thrown into the river, a threat that seems to have been a commonplace,[18] although before the Reformation and even after it was seldom actually carried out.[19] It appears the "Spider King" took Maillard's words in stride,[20] but late in his life, Maillard was exiled

---

[14]   Ibid., BB14, fol. 190.

[15]   See Taylor, *Soldiers of Christ*, pp. 24-25.

[16]   Bernard Mandrot, ed., *Journal de Jean de Roye connu sous le nom de chronique scandaleuse, 1460-1483* (Paris: Renouard, 1896), vol. 2, pp. 72-73.

[17]   Olivier Maillard, *Sermones de stipendio peccati* (Lyon: Stephan Gueygnardi, 1503), fol. 331.

[18]   "Being thrown into the river" threats can be traced at least as far back as the trial of Joan of Arc in 1431, for nullification trial testimony suggests that attempted coercion of this sort was used against four judges or assessors, Nicolas de Houppeville, Jean Beaupère, Nicolas Midy, and Jean Louhier in order to force them to attend the trial. Similar threats were made against Marguerite of Navarre and the famous Italian preacher Panigarole when he delivered sermons in Paris in the late sixteenth century.

[19]   Alexandre Samouillan, *Olivier Maillard: Sa prédication et son temps* (Toulouse: Privat, 1891), p. 26.

[20]   It is interesting that a century later, Boucher would use Louis as the epitome of royal tyranny in his anger at Henri III: "If it had not been for the fact that this rule was

briefly for his opposition to Louis XII's divorce from Jeanne de France. Before heresy, war, and assassinations became the norm, threats were often either simply that or were transmuted into relatively light punishments; afterwards, especially once the Religious Wars had begun, threats of punishment and death were more likely to become reality.[21]

Catholic Responses to "Protestantism" before 1572

Jacques Merlin (d. ca. 1541), an important Parisian prelate and preacher, was imprisoned in the Louvre from 1527 to 1529, and was forced into exile in Brittany for another year as a result of his opposition to the plans of the queen mother, Louise of Savoy, to tax the Parisian populace as well as her alleged inactivity in response to military threats to France.[22] Even more dramatic, in view of the spread of Reformation ideas, was the arrest and exile of several Paris bachelors of theology in 1533-1534 , including François Le Picart (d. 1556). Le Picart apparently accused the King of Navarre of heresy[23] and was incensed at the preaching of Gérard Roussel. Pierre Siderander reported that "Le Picart and others...in their preaching attacked and insulted the king...confident of the

---

diminished by the perfidy of Louis XI, who was quite evidently the first architect of tyranny in France (for the flatterers of kings say that kings should be defended from servitude and that royal liberty should be unfettered) and if it had not been for his [assumed] devotion for the Virgin, just as Henry [III] used deception by the pretence and mask of his ascetic and flagellant order, then we should perhaps have been preserved this role in its entirety and not be tortured by the wound of an oppressed public liberty." Adrianna Bakos, "The Historical Reputation of Louis XI in Political Theory and Polemic During the French Religious Wars," *Sixteenth Century Journal* 21 (1990):16n.

[21] However, on 26 April 1536 the minister Gonin, of the valley of Angrogne in Piedmont, returned from a mission to Geneva to his own church when, passing through Gap he was taken for a spy, arrested by the gentleman Georges Martin de Champoléon, and put into prison in Grenoble. They were going to let him go but then found several letters from Genevan reformers, so he was condemned as a Lutheran. The authorities, fearing a public burning would not go over well, threw him into the Isère at nine o'clock in the evening, his legs bound by rope." Eugène Arnaud, *Histoire des protestants du Dauphiné aux XVIe, XVIIe, et XVIIIe siècles*, vol. 1: 1522-98 (Geneva: Slatkine Reprints, 1970), p. 21.

[22] James K. Farge, *Biographical Register of Paris Doctors of Theology, 1500-1536* (Toronto: Pontifical Institute, 1980), pp. 327-326.

[23] A.-J. Herminjard, *Correspondance des réformateurs dans les pays de langue français* (Geneva and Paris, 1886-1887), vol. 3, p. 161.

authority of the Sorbonne. Next they tried to create a riot, and rouse the people so they would not put up with heresy."[24] First imprisoned in the monastery of Sainte-Magloire, Le Picart was exiled along with others to a distance of thirty leagues from Paris.[25] As evidence of the powerful reactions produced by preaching even in the early decades in sixteenth-century France, the impending exile of Le Picart and the others set off a war of placards and broadsheets.[26] Francis I believed both Catholics and reformers were trying to stir people to sedition,[27] yet ironically his relative tolerance may have fueled what would become the worst religious wars in sixteenth-century Europe. Like Farinier almost fifty years earlier, Le Picart's departure for Reims brought forth large, weeping crowds. His return was greeted with rejoicing, "…because a good man had been taken back from his enemies…"[28] Although he was imprisoned again in 1534,[29] Le Picart would become the most popular preacher in Paris until his death in 1556. He spent the final two decades of his career preaching for church reform[30] and as a "powerful lion"[31] using the pulpit as a weapon in the fight against heresy.[32] His accurate perception of the threat posed by "heretics," and quite possibly anger at the authorities who had not only imposed imprisonment and exile upon him but had allowed the situation to spin out of control, led Le Picart to attack the king, his sister, and the courtiers who favored new ideas. "Oh! Saint John [the Baptist] is not discreet. A person mustn't speak like that to kings and princes."[33] But Le Picart's polemic was not limited to kings and

---

[24]   Ibid, vol. 4, p. 446.
[25]   Ibid., p. 445; see also Larissa Juliet Taylor, *Heresy and Orthodoxy in Sixteenth-Century Paris: François Le Picart and the Beginnings of the Catholic Reformation* (Leiden: Brill, 1999), ch. 3.
[26]   Herminjard, *Correspondance*, vol. 3, p. 58
[27]   Ibid., vol. 4, p. 445.
[28]   Jean de Launoy, *Regii Navarrae Gymnasii Parisiensis Historia* (Paris, 1677), p. 412.
[29]   Taylor, *Heresy and Orthodoxy*, p. 59.
[30]   Ibid., chs. 5-6.
[31]   Artus Désiré, *Les regretz et complainctes de Passe partout et Bruitquicourt, sur la mémoire renouvellées de trespas et bout de l'an de feu tres noble et venerable personne Maistre Françoys Picart, docteur en théologie et grand doyen de Sainct Germain de l'Aucerroys* (Paris: Pierre Gaultier, 1557), fol. Aii.
[32]   Taylor, *Heresy and Orthodoxy*, ch. 4.
[33]   François Le Picart, *Les sermons et instructions chrestiennes, pour tous les Dimenches, & toutes les festes des saincts, depuis la Trinité iusques à l'Advent*, 2 parts (Paris: Nicolas Chesneau, 1566), part II, fol. 74; see also Taylor, *Heresy and Orthodoxy*, pp. 64-69.

courtiers. His sermons against heresy provoked a man "…who seemed dazed and impatient in his rage…[to try to] strangle the venerable doctor and excellent preacher, Master François Le Picart, while he was preaching in the church of St.-Jacques-de-la-Boucherie in Paris. After trying to put his enterprise into effect, [the man] was stopped by the people gathered around the pulpit, who threw him out of the church and killed him in their anger."[34] As Calvinism spread through France, its leaders, John Calvin and Théodore de Bèze attacked Le Picart in their writings. Calvin called him "…completely devoid of brains, [belonging] to a class of fanatics…little better than a madman"[35] and a "crazy man out of his mind."[36] Bèze, although admitting Le Picart was one of the main pillars of the Catholic Church in France, referred to him as a "choleric rabid dog."[37] Yet Le Picart was widely credited with keeping Paris Catholic.[38] His funeral was compared to that of a king, allegedly attracting 20,000 mourners, a crowd so great that the doors to Saint-Germain l'Auxerrois were broken down.[39]

Aside from Le Picart's approximately 300 sermons, published posthumously, few Catholic sermons have survived for the period from 1535-1565,[40] so with a few exceptions, much of our evidence must be drawn from non-sermon sources. Still, as the situation de-

---

[34] Jean de la Vacquerie, *Remonstrance adressé au roy, au princes catholiques, et à tous Magistrats & Gouverneurs de Republiques, touchant l'abolition des troubles & emotions qui se sont aujourd'huy en France, causez par les heresies qui y regnent & par la Chrestienté* (Paris: Jean Poupy, 1574), fols. 36-37.

[35] John Calvin, *Tracts and Treatises in Defense of the Reformed Faith*, trans. Henry Beveridge (Grand Rapids: W. B. Eerdman, 1958), vol. 3, p. 33.

[36] John Calvin, *Des scandales qui empeschent auiourdhuy beaucoup de gens de venir à la pure doctrine de l'Evangile, & en desbauchent d'autres* (Geneva: Jean Crespin, 1550), p. 110.

[37] Théodore de Bèze, *Le passavant de Théodore de Bèze, Epître de Maître Benoît passavant à Messire Pierre Lizet* (Paris: Isidore Liseux, 1875), p. 188.

[38] Emile Doumergue, *Jean Calvin: Les hommes et les choses de son temps* (Lausanne: Georges Bridel, 1899), vol. 1, pp. 240-241.

[39] F. Hilarion de Coste, *Le parfait ecclesiastique ou l'histoire de la vie et de la mort de François Le Picart, Seigneur d'Atilly & de Villeron, Docteur en Théologie de la Faculte de Paris & Doyen de Saint Germain de l'Auxerrois* (Paris: Sebastian Cramoisy, 1658), pp. 225-226.

[40] This is a rather perplexing issue in view of the tens of thousands of Catholic sermons printed in the seventy years before Reformation. Although a glut on the market may explain part of the decline of the printed sermon in the years between 1530-1560, the more likely answer may be found in the need to respond to constantly changing circumstances. See Larissa Taylor, "Out of Print: The Decline of Catholic Printed Sermons in France,1530-1560," in Robin Barnes et al, eds., *Books Have Their Own Destiny: Essays in Honor of Robert V. Schnucker.* (Kirksville, Mo.: Thomas Jefferson University Press, 1998), pp. 121-129.

teriorated dramatically between 1557 and 1562,[41] we can follow the outlines of response to pulpit rhetoric.

The growth of Calvinist churches throughout France, including the first assembly in Paris in 1555, increasing iconoclasm, rumor, and response in the form of religious riots, and the death of the adult king Henri II in a freak accident in 1559 all set the stage for a complete breakdown of the social order. This is evident in the preaching of the Dominican Pierre d'Ivollé (d. 1568) of Auxerre. According to the Catholic memoirist Claude Haton, when d'Ivollé was called to Provins to preach in 1560 during the minority of Francis II, he warned that if Calvinists took over, they would "...exterminate the king and his estate."[42] Ivollé was well aware "...that there are those present who will testify against me. If they would like to meet with me afterwards, I will sign with my hand and my blood the statements that I have made: That cursed is the land that has a young child for its king, and whose princes are disloyal, companions of thieves. Is this to speak ill of the king?"[43] Although Ivollé would become more outspoken as time went on, his statements appeared dangerously seditious and inflammatory. In a volume of extant sermons on the mass given at Chartres in 1558, Ivollé invokes the language of war: "There are two wars going on: one spiritual and one temporal. The spiritual war is carried on by the heretics and infidels who struggle to corrupt the faith. And also by invisible enemies, who are the Devils who [do so] through their suggestions and beguiling temptations..."[44] He begs God to defend his church from both types of enemies: "Because all the legions of the Devil push for war, to achieve victory over Christians by their ruses and finesse. Satan now reigns, and holds the world in blindness. This is a Great Dragon, spoken of in the Book of Revela-

---

[41]   See Barbara Diefendorf, *Beneath the Cross: Catholics and Huguenots in Sixteenth-Century Paris* (New York: Oxford University Press, 1991), ch. 3; Barbara Diefendorf, "Prologue to a Massacre: Popular Unrest in Paris, 1557-1572," *American Historical Review* 90 (1985), 1069; Nancy Lyman Roelker, *One King, One Faith: The Parlement of Paris and the Religious Reformations of the Sixteenth Century* (Berkeley: University of California Press, 1996), p. 184; Taylor, *Heresy and Orthodoxy*, pp. xiii, 210.

[42]   Félix Bourquélot, ed., *Mémoires de Claude Haton* (Paris: Imprimérie Impériale, 1857), vol. 1, p. 138.

[43]   Ibid., vol. 1, p. 140.

[44]   Pierre Dyvolé, *Dix sermons de la Saincte Messe et de ceremonies d'icelle* (Paris: Nicolas Chesneau, 1577), p. 470.

tion."[45] Ivollé did have reason to fear, although not until significantly later, and not from the king. In 1567, he fell into the hands of "heretics" on the outskirts of Auxerre, from whom he suffered great "outrages and excesses."[46] According to Goussard, a priest of Chartres and curé of Thivas, one of the "malign troop of heretics" who knew Ivollé took pity on the old man, "at least hoping to get some silver out of it,"[47] and he was ransomed. However, this only increased Ivollé's fervor, for his sermons were "…more animated and full of invective against the fury and the folly of the Calvinists…" He believed "God had not saved him so that he would keep quiet and rest but that rather he would defend the faith and confute the errors [of the heretics] more diligently than he had ever done before."[48] According to Goussard, who wrote the preface to Ivollé's sermons, "…those who survived (if one can even say that) were like a flock destitute of their pastors, abandoned to the rage of the wolves…"[49]

Indeed, the situation had worsened immeasurably. By October 1561, when 8000-9000 Protestants allegedly attended services outside the Porte St-Antoine of Paris, "…Catholic preachers raged against the Huguenots, urging their parishioners to take up weapons to defend their churches from the heretics. They even challenged the authority of the crown. A Carmelite preaching at St-Benoît reportedly compared the situation in the kingdom to that of two children playing with an apple who were about to let it be snatched by a third."[50]

Far from all Catholic preaching was (or was even considered to be) seditious or violent by this date or later. The greatest part of Ivollé's sermons on the mass are concerned with explaining true doctrine. Similarly, Etienne Paris (d. 1561), Dominican and auxiliary bishop of both Rouen and Orléans, authored numerous homilies, including a series against heresy, funeral orations, and Biblical expositions. His only extant sermons date from the early 1550s, and they do speak of heresy:

---

45 Ibid., p. 482.
46 Denys Goussard, "Preface and Epistre," to Dyvolé, *Dix sermons*, fol. Avi.
47 Ibid.
48 Ibid.
49 Ibid.
50 Diefendorf, "Prologue," p. 1074.

> In such company the Holy Spirit is found, not among those who are singular and partial in their beliefs and intentions, who separate themselves from the common doctrine of the Church Fathers, disagreeing with the commonly-held beliefs of the Church, distancing themselves from the common religion, and wanting through their headstrong behavior to appear special. This singularity is the daughter of pride…a shoot more pestilent than its root, engendering pertinacity, which is the mother of heresy.[51]

Elsewhere he attacks perpetrators of iconoclastic acts.[52] But on the whole, his sermons are dominated not by vitriol but by eloquence and orthodox Catholic teaching. Moderates would remain within the ranks of Catholic preachers, but as the wars began and continued, particularly during and after the reign of Henri III, they were as likely to suffer (although nonviolently) from the retributions of their co-religionists. The Minim friar Jean de Han, like Le Picart and others before him, paid dearly for his overt attacks on royal policy in 1561. During a Catholic riot at the Cemetery of the Innocents, Han counselled those listening to his sermons "…not [to] count on royal judges to punish Lutherans – [they] would have to take matters into their own hands."[53] But upon his death a half year later, "…crowds flocked to honour him…as a saint."[54] When in 1561-1562 the Jesuit Emond Auger (d. 1591) gave the Advent and Lenten series in Valence, he barely escaped hanging.[55]

Evangelical and Calvinist Preaching

It is virtually impossible to differentiate between the evangelical preaching that had been part of the French *préréforme* movement and early "reformed" preaching, at least in the 1520s and 1530s. All that can be said with any certainty is that there was no Lutheranism as such in France, except in the person of François Lambert

---

[51] Etienne Paris, *Homelies suyvant les matieres traictees es principales festes & solennitez de l'annee* (Paris: Robineau, 1553), p. 71.

[52] Ibid., p. 116.

[53] Davis, "Rites of Violence," p. 167.

[54] Marc Venard, "Catholicism and Resistance to the Reformation in France, 1555-1585," in Philip Benedict et al., eds., *Reformation, Revolt and Civil War in France and the Netherlands 1555-1585* (Amsterdam: The Netherlands Academy of Arts and Sciences, 1999), p. 135.

[55] Ibid., p. 138.

and a few others. Although innate French and Swiss ideas dominated the early French Reformation, this is not to suggest that Lutheran *theology* did not have an impact.

Perhaps the most well-known attempts at early "reform" with an
evangelical bent occurred in the diocese of Meaux under the episcopal leadership of Guillaume Briçonnet before 1520. Around
Briçonnet, whose intent seems to have been primarily to insure that
the Word of God was preached to his flock,[56] there gathered the
"Circle of Meaux." It included the famed humanist Jacques Lefè-
vre d'Etaples, Guillaume Farel, Gérard Roussel, Martial Mazurier,
Pierre Caroli, and many others, most of whom would at some point
or another find themselves in theological hot water as a result of
their views and, more importantly, their preaching. There can be
little doubt that unorthodox ideas flourished among the group, and
spread through preaching. Caroli denounced fasting, prayers to the
saints, and ecclesiastical compulsion, insisting provocatively considering the date that "…scripture is now understood better than ever
before…"[57] Jacques Pavannes preached that offerings to the saints
were heretical, and along with his friend Mathieu Saunier supported iconoclasm and attacked the mass.[58] In a statement that res-
onates with historical irony in view of what I have termed the
"river threat," Etienne Lecourt is said to have exclaimed: "If the
bones of Saint Peter were in my church, I would bury them
honorably in the ground; but if my parishioners were to venerate
them, I would myself take the bones and put them in a sack and
throw them into the river."[59] Despite Briçonnet's best intentions,
the *Bourgeois de Paris* probably expressed the sentiments most at the
time, including the authorities, felt in regard to the Circle: "…the
great majority of the group of Meaux were infected with the false
doctrine of Luther…"[60] Briçonnet himself admitted that *le menu
peuple* of the city were singing songs calling the theologians of Paris
hypocrites and bigots. By 1525, although he would continue his
efforts at reform from within, Briçonnet (under compulsion) or-

---

[56]   Herminjard, *Correspondance*, vol. 1, p. 157.
[57]   Charles Duplessis d'Argentré, *Collectio judiciorum de novis erroribus* (Paris: Cailleau,
1728), vol. 1, p. 26.
[58]   Ibid., pp. 33-34.
[59]   Ibid., p. 97.
[60]   V.-L. Bourrilly, ed., *Le journal d'un bourgeois de Paris sous le regne de François Ier (1515-
1536)* (Paris: Alphonse Picard, 1910), p. 233.

dered the priests and vicars of his diocese to insure orthodoxy.[61]

One sermon delivered in Grenoble in 1524 by Aimé Meigret was published in Lyon, probably the result of the city's proximity to Switzerland and the appearance in Lyon later that year of Marguerite de Navarre. Meigret's "orthodoxy" has been evaluated differently by those who have studied the sermon.[62] The sermon was announced well in advance, so one of his opponents, Claude Rollin, delivered a preemptive sermon. The result was predictable: when Meigret arrived to preach, the cathedral was overflowing with Catholics and evangelicals alike. Among the most prominent was the reformer Pierre de Sebiville, who remarked to the Dominican sitting next to him, "Wait until the end and you'll see he has great things to say and sustains the opinion of Luther."[63] In the sermon, Meigret argues that "…faith in Jesus Christ means to believe that we will never gain paradise except by the virtue of the faith…that we have in him."[64] Although there was nothing unorthodox in this view, Meigret's own words suggest that he meant them in the "new" way: "I know that this doctrine is new to you and that some of you will find it disagreeable …To what state of affairs have we come that when someone preaches and declares the gospel to you, you call him a heretic or a Lutheran, but someone who glorifies human tradition and inventions is in your opinion a preacher of the gospel?"[65] Meigret's fate is unknown: the *Bourgeois of Paris* claims he made an *amende honorable*, common in the 1520s,[66] but Faculty of Theology records suggest that he was imprisoned for a time.[67]

Three preachers of the 1530s and 1540s deserve special note – Gérard Roussel, Jean Michel, and Raphaël de Podio. It was largely Roussel, and his connections to the king and queen of Navarre,

---

[61]   For a fuller discussion of the Circle of Meaux, see Michel Veissière, "Croyances et pratique religieuse à Meaux aux temps de Guillaume Briçonnet (1525)," *Revue d'histoire de l'église de France* 67 (1981), 55-59.

[62]   The sermon was edited by Henri Guy, "Le sermon d'Aimé Meigret," *Annales de l'Université de Grenoble* 15 (1928), 181-212. See also Henri Hours, "Procès d'hérésie contre Aimé Meigret," *Bulletin de la Société de l'histoire du protestantisme français* 19 (1857), 14-43; Nathanaël Weiss, "La réformateur Aimé Meigret, *Bulletin de la Société de l'histoire du protestantisme français* 39 (1890), 245-269; Taylor, *Soldiers of Christ*, pp. 200-208.

[63]   Hours, "Procès," pp. 26-27.

[64]   Guy, "Sermon," p. 206.

[65]   Ibid., pp. 206-207.

[66]   Bourrilly, *Journal*, p. 154.

[67]   Farge, *Biographical Register*, p. 295.

who had roused the fury of Catholic preachers such as Le Picart, leading to their imprisonment and temporary exile. In 1525, Roussel had written to Briçonnet from Strasbourg about his excitement at the preaching he had heard there. As a member of the Circle of Meaux, he had challenged the preeminence of the Vulgate Bible, and in Lent of 1531, he had been accused by the theologians of Paris of preaching heresy in the presence of Marguerite. But in 1533, Siderander wrote to a correspondent in Strasbourg that "…so many people wanted to hear the sermons on the Word of God preached by Gérard that no sermons could be given, because 4000-5000 people were present. Three times the location had to be changed, and it was very difficult to find a space large enough to accommodate the crowd. However, he preached daily throughout Lent, with the king and queen present."[68] The overflowing crowds at the Louvre prompted Le Picart to preach in bitterness that "only old women come to my sermons–all the men go to the Louvre!"[69]Although Roussel was questioned, and Francis I ordered him held temporarily, the light measures taken against him infuriated the theologians of Paris. Thanks to the powerful influence of Marguerite, Bèze claims that soon thereafter he and others were "…announcing the truth a little more boldly than they had been accustomed to do."[70] However, even before the Affair of the Placards, but after the inaugural sermon preached at the University of Paris in 1533 by Nicolas Cop, circumstances had changed. Although Roussel had been forbidden to preach,[71] when he attempted to do so at Notre-Dame in April of 1534, the crowd clamored, "Down with him!" He was stoned before he was rescued by the authorities, and it was his last effort to preach in Paris.[72] With the Affair of the Placards and the eclipse of the influence of the king's sister, Roussel's star also went into decline, at least in the capital. Thanks to royal influence, however, he was promoted to the

---

[68]   Herminjard, *Correspondance*, vol. 3, p. 55.
[69]   Ibid, p. 161.
[70]   G. Baum and E. Cunitz, eds., *Histoire ecclésiastique des églises réformées au royaume de France. Édition nouvelle avec commentaire, notice bibliographique et tables des faits et des noms propres* (Paris: Fischbacher, 1883), vol. 1, p. 26.
[71]   Charles Schmidt, *Gérard Roussel: Prédicateur de la Reine Marguerite de Navarre* (Geneva: Slatkine Reprints, 1970), p. 107.
[72]   George Schurhmanner, *Francis Xavier: His Life, His Times. Vol. I: Europe, 1506-1541* (Rome: Jesuit Historical Institute, 1973), p. 202.

bishopric of Oloron in Béarn. But Roussel's death was as dramatic as his life, and emphasized how dangerous it had become for preachers, Catholic or evangelical, to spread the Word. In 1550, while preaching at nearby Mauléon-Licharre in southwestern France, Roussel was attacked when a Catholic in attendance wielding an ax used it on the pulpit. Roussel was trapped under the collapsed pulpit. Although pulled free by his supporters, he died as they were taking him home.[73]

Another case of great interest from this period is that of the preacher Jean Michel, whose sermons were usually delivered in the church of Notre-Dame-du-Fourchaud in Bourges, a university town in which Calvin had spent time. Connected with Marguerite since 1523 as her almoner, Michel's preaching at the cathedral of St.-Etienne was such that he was prohibited by the archbishop from further preaching.[74] But Michel continued his efforts well into the 1530s, angering the local priests. The result one Sunday in 1536 demonstrated the rising tide of violence:

> One day, one of the last, so that he would be hindered from preaching to the great crowd that had gathered to hear him, they began to chant the office of the dead at the hour when he habitually ascended the pulpit; but the hearers, already assembled, were highly irritated and made such a loud noise with their books that the frightened priests took flight. Hardly had the tumult been calmed when Jean Michel began, and following his normal custom, he recited the Lord's Prayer in French, without adding the *Ave Maria* to it. Immediately, Charles Bonin, lord of Corpoy and Procurer General of the Great Council…driven by his pious zeal, rose and began to pronounce in a loud voice the *Ave Maria*. He could not do so…the women themselves threatened to assault him with their taborets, and he barely escaped.[75]

But Michel's actions spoke louder than words. Condemned in January of 1537 to make an *amende honorable* before the cathedral of St.-Etienne, he escaped–to the Swiss cantons.[76] Apparently still seeking to spread his message, he returned to Bourges; in October of 1539 he was handed over to the secular arm, and was burned on Christmas eve outside of the Great Tower of Bourges.[77]

---

[73] Schmidt, *Roussel*, p. 164.
[74] Louis Raynal, *Histoire du Berry* (Bourges: Vermeil, 1844), vol. 3, pp. 301-302.
[75] Ibid., p. 339.
[76] Ibid., p. 340.
[77] Ibid., p. 341.

There are a number of similar cases from the 1530s, although most evangelical preaching took place in the provinces after the events of 1534. Around that time, Jacques Vallery, the vicar of the parish church of Privas, "openly preached Lutheran doctrines and presided over religious meetings in several houses…. [B]reaking with the Roman church, his group began to eat meat during Lent, and participated in seditious activities."[78] While Vallery was able to flee to Geneva, a fellow preacher of Privas, Jacques Chavanhas, was captured and taken to Toulouse, where he was executed.[79] Then

> [i]n the small village of Courthézon, a priest named Raphäel de Podio preached every day during Lent of 1544. According to an auditor, whose suspicions had been aroused, de Podio preached "that the host and sacrament of the altar was not the body of God, except in spirit; also, that when a person died, the same day his soul went to heaven or hell; to pray for that soul was a losing cause; to make gifts of silver, candles, or other goods to a church was useless and God wanted none of that; to go in homage to Notre-Dame or to other saints was idolatry; to go down on one's knees before images…and paintings served no purpose; holy oil is of no avail, it is nothing but water.[80]

Marc Venard points out that Podio clearly divided the parish, a situation that must have held in much of France during these and the years to come. Certain women of the town remembered him saying that there was no purgatory, that it was not necessary to pray for the dead, and that while he spoke constantly of Jesus Christ, he hardly mentioned the Virgin Mary.[81] According to a traveler, a female innkeeper of the town, supported by other women, said she wished he would go to the devil. She avowed that because of him there had been a huge commotion in her lodgings.[82] Others, however, feared speaking out against him, or supported him actively. When he was accused of preaching "false heretical and Lutheran doctrines," Podio simply changed his venue to private homes. Venard reports that every day many people went

[78] Eugène Arnaud, *Histoire des protestants du Vivarais et du Velay: Pays de Languedoc de la Réforme à la Révolution* (Geneva: Slatkine Reprints, 1979), vol. 1, p. 10.
[79] Ibid.
[80] Marc Venard, *Réforme protestante, Réforme catholique dans la province d'Avignon XVIe siècle* (Paris: Cerf, 1993), pp. 340-341.
[81] Ibid., p. 341.
[82] Ibid.

to his house, "within which they attended secret *prêches*. But some women were no less enthusiastic: 'There are those,' one said, 'who follow the doctrine of the said preacher and say that they are just as good as the Virgin Mary and that she had no more preeminence over them.'"[83] Although the chapter of Notre-Dame-des-Doms and others pursued the subject literally, Podio was able to leave town.[84] What this incident and others point to is the important role women played in the preaching event both before and after the Reformations. The greater attendance by women at sermons was regularly remarked upon by preachers in the late medieval period. Menot had claimed that for every one man at a sermon, "...you will find four women...;"[85] Maillard and Pepin had offered similar insights.[86] We have also seen that women were as likely as men to be involved in violent or seditious actions at sermons, as when Jean Michel's opponent was attacked by women wielding as weapons the stools on which they sat during sermons. In fact, although certainly not with the approval of Genevan authorities, two women named Marguerite and Jacquéline led *prêches* in Montélimar in 1556.[87]

Almost no printed Calvinist sermons have survived from sixteenth-century France, possibly because (except for Calvin himself), reformers did not share the zeal for publication of their sermons that had been and would be displayed by Catholics.[88] Censorship, the dangers involved, and a felt need for direct inspiration by the Spirit may have played a role. But the escalation of tensions after the implantation of the first Calvinist church in Paris in 1555, military disaster, and a more concerted effort by Genevan preachers after this date led to further outbreaks of violence against preachers, people, and holy objects. In the Dauphiné, the preaching of a "possible foreigner" on Easter Day 1558 who attacked Catholic beliefs, calling them superstition, idolatry and error, led to violence when the bishop attempted to silence the preacher. However, it was

---

83 Ibid., p. 342.

84 Ibid.

85 Nève, *Sermons choisis*, p. 416; cf. Ibid., 101;

86 Maillard, *Sermones de stipendio peccati*, fol. 337; Olivier Maillard, *Sermones dominicales* (Lyon: Stephan Gueygnardi, 1503), fol. 278; Guillaume Pepin, *Conciones quadragesimales ad sacros evangeliorum sensus pro feriis quadragesimae mystice et moraliter explicandos* (Antwerp: Guillelmus Lesteenius and Engelbertus Marnicus, repr. 1656), p. 60.

87 Arnaud, *Dauphiné*, vol. 1, p. 32.

88 Edmond Grin, "Deux sermons de Pierre Viret, leurs thèmes théologiques et leur actualité," *Theologische Zeitschrift* 18 (1962), 116-132.

the bishop and his attendants who barely escaped.[89] In 1560, *prêches* were regular occurrences in Montpellier. Calvinists there had taken over the church of Saint Mathieu forcefully, breaking statues and the crucifix. "The Augustinian who had preached at the church of Notre-Dame-des-Tables had been publicly contradicted with 'great tumult, clashes, shrieking, threats and beatings in the areas that were faithful to the party of the…Augustinian…'. The Protestants menaced the bishop, Guillaume Pellicier, and his clergy '…that they would kill them if they forbade them from preaching and meeting.' 'They had also,' stated the *parlement*, 'threatened with death the preacher of the church of Notre-Dames-des-Tables.' "[90] *Parlement* records from Pézénas record that the farms and houses where ministers had been lodged and preached were razed to the ground,[91] while at Anduze, the convent church was invaded by a mass of men and women shouting "[w]e want to having preaching done in this convent;" the next day they occupied the parish church where their minister preached.[92]

Catherine de Medici's attempt to reconcile the factions at the Colloquy of Poissy and the issuance of edicts of pacification after the wars had begun only exacerbated the situation. When Bèze preached publicly at the colloquy just outside Paris, he began and ended in a conciliatory manner:

> …[W]e do not say that in the Lord's Supper the bread is simply bread, but the sacrament of the precious body of Our Lord Jesus Christ, who was delivered for us; nor that the wine is simply wine, but the sacrament of the precious blood, which was spilled for us,… But if it has happened, or happens at some time, that some people using our doctrine as cover, are found guilty of rebellion against the least of your officials, Sire, we protest before God and Your Majesty that they are not our people, and that they will never have more bitter enemies…[93]

But amidst these otherwise mild words were ones that could not be accepted by any Catholic in 1561 regarding the meaning of the

---

[89] Arnaud, *Dauphiné*, vol. 1, pp. 31-32.

[90] Gabriel Loirette, "Catholiques et protestants en Languedoc à la veille des guerres civiles (1560)," *Revue de l'histoire de l'église de France* 23 (1937), 509-511.

[91] Ibid., p. 514.

[92] Ibid., p. 516.

[93] Théodore de Bèze, *Harangue des Protestants du Royaume de France…prononcee…en presence du Roy & de Monseigneurs de son Conseil, assemblés à Poissy, pour le faict de la Religion* (n.p., 1561), pp. 26, 37.

eucharist: "When one or the other of these two opinions will be demonstrated by holy scripture, we will be ready to embrace it and hold it unto death."[94] Mild words? Hardly, for they challenged the authority of both church tradition and by extension, that of The Most Christian King. In 1561, Calvinists who had been worshipping in the Faubourg Saint-Marcel felt their services were being disturbed by the ringing of bells at St.-Médard and went to ask that they be silenced. When the Catholics did not agree, a riot ensued, in which the parishioners felt they were under attack.[95] The Catholic version of the event was as follows:

> [The Protestants]…went in great numbers to the church of Saint-Médard, which they pillaged, mortally wounding several parishioners and smashing the images of the church. It happened that a poor baker of the parish, father of twelve children, seeing the massacre in the church, took the ciborium with the reserved host, saying to them, "My masters, do not touch this, for the honour of he who reposes within." But a wicked man ran him through with a halberd, killing him next to the high altar and said to him, "Is this your pastry God who now delivers you from the torments of death?" And they crushed under foot the precious body of Our Lord, and smashed the ciborium… The poor people, in fear of attack, retreated to the tower and rang the alarm bell but were not rescued… Two others were killed and several others wounded… The people of Paris were very aroused…[96]

Words delivered and actions taken by both sides had begun an escalating and inexorable cycle of rumor and violence that the Crown was unable to contain.

In that same year a religious riot occurred in Toulouse, where the "streets…were full of people singing the Psalms and the commandments of God resonated everywhere."[97] Three Catholic preachers were arrested for speaking out against Catherine and her softness on heresy, and the result was considerable bloodshed on both sides.[98] Temperate voices could still be heard: in 1561, the chancellor of France spoke to Charles IX in the following terms: "Gentleness will profit more than bitterness: let us rid ourselves of

---

[94]   Ibid, p. 30.
[95]   Diefendorf, *Beneath the Cross*, p. 61.
[96]   David Potter, ed., *The French Wars of Religion: Selected Documents* (New York: St. Martin's Press, 1997), p. 42.
[97]   Mark Greengrass, "The Anatomy of a Religious Riot: Toulouse in May 1562," *Journal of Ecclesiastical History* 34 (1983), p. 370.
[98]   Ibid., pp. 371, 385.

diabolical words, names of…factions and seditions, Lutherans, Huguenots and Papists; don't change the name of Christian, for look at how many evils have occurred in Italy under the name of Guelph and Ghibelline…"[99] Likewise, in a letter addressed to the reformed church at Nîmes in 1563, Pierre Viret (d. 1571) wrote "thank God there was no sedition…among you for the cause of religion, at least while I was among you."[100] But as Ann Guggenheim points out, Viret was likely dissembling, for before Christmas of 1561, "…some Calvinists forcefully occupied the Cathedral of Notre Dame and on Christmas Eve Viret agreed to preach there. By agreeing to preach in an illegally occupied building Viret gave his tacit consent to the seizure…"[101] The situation in 1561-1562 was not very different in Burgundy. Mack Holt recounts that "[a] Calvinist preacher harangued [the people] for more than an hour, insisting that the 'papists' only wanted 'to give us faggots in order to burn us.'"[102] The preaching and iconoclastic wars had begun in earnest. In 1562, "…many Catholics felt it was their duty 'to clean the whole province of Burgundy of this vermin of preachers and ministers…"[103] That they did not succeed is clear, for in Dijon in 1570, a Calvinist "baptized his dog in a public fountain in 1570 and forced the poor beast to 'drag a statue of St. Anthony through the city in contempt of the holy sacrament of baptism and the veneration of the saints."[104]

The Saint Bartholomew's Day Massacre of August 1572 did not end Calvinist preaching. But a combination of several factors—the decimation of Huguenot ranks in the wake of the massacres in Paris and the provinces, self-imposed exile, conversion, fear, and increasing use of the pamphlet as the weapon of choice in the propaganda wars—changed the amount, content, and tenor of Calvinist preaching in France. Catholics had gained the upper hand at

---

[99]   *Harangue, contenant la remonstrance faicte devant la majesté du Roy treschrestien Charles neufiesme, tenant ses grans Estatz en sa ville d'Orleans: par monseigneur le Chancelier de France* (Lyon: Benoist Rigaud, 1561), fol. Diiii.

[100]   Ann H. Guggenheim, "Beza, Viret, and the Church of Nîmes: National Leadership and Local Initiative in the Outbreak of the Religious Wars," *Bibliothèque d'humanisme et renaissance* 37 (1975), 40.

[101]   Ibid.

[102]   Mack P. Holt, "Wine, Community and Reformation in Sixteenth-Century Burgundy," *Past & Present* 138 (1993), 63.

[103]   Ibid., p. 69.

[104]   Ibid., p. 70.

least in the pulpit after 1572, and especially during the years of the Holy League, their preaching became increasingly radical and politicized.

Catholic Preaching, 1572-1610

It had taken Catholics longer to appreciate the value of print propaganda, but this changed during the 1560s. In the wake of the St. Bartholomew's Day Massacre, Catholic pamphlet literature at least matched that of their opponents, even if their pamphlets appear to have been less virulent than Catholic preaching,[105] at least in terms of attacks on royal policy. Unfortunately, relatively few Catholic sermons have survived from this period, with the notable exceptions of the sermons of Simon Vigor[106] as well as isolated sermons and homilies and a number of polemical funeral orations.[107] Charles Labitte's study of preachers during the League, originally published in 1841, remains the most complete study of Catholic preaching in this period.[108] Many sermons remain to be studied in manuscript form in regional archives, while countless others were destroyed during the Religious Wars, Revolution, and World Wars. Yet others were never printed, quite possibly for the same reason that Calvinists tended not to print their sermons – events were simply moving too quickly and an immediate and direct *political* response was needed. To the degree that pre-Reformation preachers were able to adapt sermons of the Church Fathers, medieval theologians, or great contemporary preachers to their needs, this was no longer possible in the highly-charged atmosphere in the decades after St. Bartholomew's Day. The enemy was now at least threefold – not only the Protestants, but the royal family, and even-

---

[105] James R. Smither, "The St. Bartholomew's Day Massacre and Images of Kingship in France: 1572-1574," *Sixteenth Century Journal* 22 (1991), 30n.

[106] See Diefendorf, *Beneath the Cross*, pp. 152-158; Barbara Diefendorf, "Simon Vigor: A Radical Preacher in Sixteenth-Century Paris," *Sixteenth Century Journal* 18 (1987), 399-410

[107] Larissa Juliet Taylor, "Funeral Sermons and Orations as Religious Propaganda in Sixteenth-Century France," in Bruce Gordon and Peter Marshall, eds., *The Place of the Dead: Death and Remembrance in Late Medieval and Early Modern Europe* (Cambridge: Cambridge University Press, 2000), pp. 224-239.

[108] Charles Labitte, *De la démocratie chez les prédicateurs de la Ligue* (Geneva: Slatkine Reprints, 1971).

tually those Catholics who were seen as collaborators – the *po-litiques.*

A study of the sermons of Simon Vigor (d. 1575), while radical in their time, makes them seem almost moderate when compared to the excerpts we have from sermons delivered in the late 1580s and 1590s. Horrified at the impending wedding of Marguerite de Valois with the "heretic" Henri de Navarre, Vigor predicted (wisely as it turned out), that "torrents of blood" would flow.[109] Speaking of Calvin's death, Vigor preached : "God sometimes sends to his creatures sicknesses that are indications and predictions of eternal damnation, just as he did to Antiochus and Herod, who died completely putrefied such that the worms left their bodies with such a great stink that no one knew how to endure it. Calvin died the same way…"[110] But he adds, "What is the cause of our [present] malady? ….[E]vils come from our sins. Most often such evils are inflicted on us by the devil for our sin."[111] Like his pre-war predecessors, Vigor actually spent considerable time in his sermons on reform of the church:

> …[T]o be the bishop of a diocese is to take care of those in it, to look at how they behave, to reform them and return them to their pristine state, and to inquire into what doctrine is being preached there. …Listen, you must be diligent and careful to watch over yourself and your flock… Because there will be a day when you render account for your deeds. [The good pastor] must, like a nurse who is busy looking over a small child, without having any other occupation, give him her breast, teaching him to walk and speak and eat. …Such is the vigilance of a someone who has people in his care that he always keeps an eye on them to teach, instruct, and correct.[112]

Even when speaking of discord, Vigor says, "God the creator is not only rendered wonderful in the fact that he created the world…but the beauty of the world consists of different things, often contrary, but they are so well united and conjoined that in this way the ex-

---

[109]   R. J. Knecht, "Defending the Faith in 16th-Century France," *Proceedings of the Huguenot Society of Great Britain and Ireland* 26 (1994-1997), 324.

[110]   Simon Vigor, *Sermons catholiques pour tous les iours de Caresme & Feries de Pasques, faits en l'Esglise S. Etienne du mont à Paris* (Paris: Michel Sonnius, 1588), fol. 87.

[111]   Ibid.

[112]   Simon Vigor, *Sermons catholiques sur les dimanches et festes depuis l'onziesme apres la Trinité iusques au Caresme* (Paris: Nicolas du Fossé, 1597), pp. 2-3.

quisite work of God is rendered the more amazing to us."[113] Such preaching was common even in the worst of times, although later Catholic preachers were often denied or received deferred preferments if their sermons appeared too mild. René Benoist, although he "…produced sweeping attacks on the 'blasphemies' of the heretics and their 'corruption' of the faith…his favorite subjects, the ones to which he returned time and again, were the sacrifice of the Mass and the real presence in the Eucharist."[114] Benoist proclaimed in one homily:

> We have not received the spirit of servitude so that we would fear, but the spirit of adoption of children by God. …We must therefore not fear, since the occasion of such great joy is announced and proposed to all nations, estates, sexes, and conditions.…It is therefore an occasion of great joy throughout the whole world.…Oh! What consolation, Christians, when by living faith we understand the compassion and grace of our God in the mission of Jesus Christ![115]

Benoist paid for his moderation later; although appointed Bishop of Troyes by Henri IV in 1593, he was never confirmed.[116] Speaking in a similar fashion, Leonard Janvier, canon of St-Lambert-en-Forêts, in a homily published in 1565, asked God to help the king by giving him good counsel, but also prayed for God "…not only to take care of our friends and benefactors, but also the enemies and persecutors of the honor of God. We will pray for the will to find true peace and harmony between us and our enemies, to remove from their hearts all hate and malevolence, to end all disputes, trials, wars, and battles…so that we will be able to leave in peace with God and with our neighbors."[117] So as we speak of the inflammatory rhetoric that dominated the pulpit, especially in the last years of Henri III and the period before Henri de Navarre converted to Catholicism, we must bear in mind that that is the preaching that made "news." Vigor, while telling his hearers that "…every true Christian must hate the enemies of God, traitors to

---

[113] Ibid., p. 459.

[114] Diefendorf, *Beneath the Cross*, p. 149.

[115] René Benoist, *Homélie de la Nativité de Iesus Christ, en laquelle est clairement monstré l'office du vray Chrestien* (Paris: Claude Frémy, 1558), fols. Avii–Aviii.

[116] Frederic J. Baumgartner, "Renaud de Beaune, Politique Prelate," *Sixteenth Century Journal* 9 (1978), 112.

[117] Leonard Janvier, *Prosne & exhortations accoustumees, avec prieres chrestiennes* (Paris: Thomas Richard, 1565), fol. 5.

him, the king and the country…I am not saying this so that we should sound the tocsin against them, nor to call on you to take up arms, but so that you will turn away from all association and communication with them."[118] Yet earlier in the sermon series, Vigor did say:

> It is necessary to remove the heretics, if they will not allow themselves to be converted. It is in the power of the king with the sword to exterminate them, and to excommunicate their ministers. But for those who do not have such power, what must they do? Pray….that God will exterminate them, and remove them. You will say I am cruel. …But what must we do? …O Lord God, how long will you wait before you avenge your blood which has been innocently spilled? Do you want to allow these murderers to reign forever? We pray to you, hurry up and get rid of them.[119]

In the aftermath of St. Bartholomew's, many Catholic preachers turned up the heat in their pulpit rhetoric. Arnaud Sorbin, who had preached at court since 1567, thanked God for having given Charles IX "the means to uncover and act against the secret conspiracies his enemies had planned"[120] – an overt reference to the massacres.

A further turning point in the political radicalization of Catholic preaching occurred with the execution of Mary Queen of Scots by Elizabeth I. The judicial murder of a former queen of France and a member of the Guise family outraged the French people. Renaud de Beaune delivered a funeral sermon for Mary, saying that her death was "… the regret of all France…"[121] According to de Beaune, Mary was a role model for English Catholics: "…seeing this poor captive princess…a million poor afflicted Catholics breathed in the hope that one day they would regain with her liberty the liberty of their religion…"[122] Recounting the tale of how Mary was "framed," de Beaune continues:

---

[118] Vigor, *Sermons…au Caresme*, p. 482.

[119] Ibid, pp. 40-41.

[120] Arnaud Sorbin, *Oraison funebre du treshault, puissant et treschrestien Roy de France, Charles IX, piteux & debonnaire, propugnateur de la Foy, & amateur des bons esprits; prononcee en l'Eglise Nostre dame de Paris le XII. de Iuillet, M.D.LXXIIII* (Paris: Guillaume Chaudière, 1574), fol. 3.

[121] Renaud de Beaune, *Oraison funebre de la tres-chrestienne, tres-illustre, tres-constante, Marie Royne d'Escosse, morte pour la Foy, le 18. Febrier, 1587, par la cruauté des Anglois heretiques, ennemys de Dieu* (Paris: G. Bichon, 1588), p. 13.

[122] Ibid., p. 19.

> But of what crime was she accused? Accused of being a Catholic! Oh happy crime! Oh desired accusation! …Cease your contrivances, don't fabricate any more testimonies, she avows this crime, she publishes it and preaches and protests that in spite of all with which you have tormented her in this her long prison, she has never wavered nor changed her faith. She is sworn to this religion, and will not change it for fear of death, torture, threats, or the infamy with which you have thought to defame her.[123]

De Beaune asks God, "…avenger of kings, who will give us today the tears to weep at this spectacle, and that one day you will give us the torches to set fire to and eradicate from the earth those who carried out such cruelty. Alas! They have made bonfires of joy…"[124]

But Mary's death in 1587 was nothing compared to the events that followed. The assassinations by Henri III at Blois of the Duc de Guise and the Cardinal of Lorraine led to unprecedented fury, expressed in Catholic pamphlets but most of all from the pulpit. We have very few extant sermons from this period, but numerous reports of them. As David Bell has shown, pamphleteers and preachers worked together to spread their message. "…Pierre de l'Estoile confided to his journal, 'The people never walked out of a sermon without having fire in their heads and a readiness to fall upon the *politiques.*' The preacher Panigarole later wrote: 'They preached twice a day in every church throughout the siege, and with such vehemence that they confirmed the people in this resolution to prefer death to surrender.'"[125] In 1589, the most radical of all the preachers, Jean Boucher, finished a sermon saying that Henri III "'…has the head of a Turk, the body of a German, the hands of a harpey, the garters of an Englishman, the feet of a Pole, and the soul of a true devil.'"[126] More scathing criticism could hardly be imagined. Although there are few mentions of possible regicide in the chronicles, at least two instances are well known. At Notre-Dame, Jean-François Pigenat asked "if someone could not be found among them zealous enough to avenge the great Lorraine

---

[123] Ibid., pp. 26-27.
[124] Ibid., p. 39.
[125] David A. Bell, "Unmasking a King: The Political Uses of Popular Literature Under the French Catholic League, 1588-89," *Sixteenth Century Journal* 20 (1989), 374.
[126] Ibid., p. 375

with the blood of a tyrant."[127] The preacher Jean Guincestre, who
had earlier compared the king to Herod,[128] questioned whether no
one had enough of a conscience…to kill him."[129] As Megan
Armstrong has shown, the Franciscan friary in Paris was often a
hotbed of political turmoil. It was "[t]he steps of the Cordelier
Church [that] provided the platform from which Madame de
Nemours, the mother of the assassinated Guise brothers, preached
in favour of the regicide of Henry III in 1589." [130] As witness to the
Franciscans' loathing of Henri and his deeds, they removed "…the
head from the King's portrait in July 1589 powerfully symboliz[ing]
the religious community's willingness to reject royal authority when
it seemed to jeopardize the spiritual health of their flock."[131] Indeed, someone did heed the message – the king was assassinated by
the monk Jacques Clément on August 1, 1589. A few preachers,
among them the Jesuit Auger, dared to give funeral sermons for
Henri. He was ostracized as a result. After Jean de la Barrière pro-
nounced a funeral sermon at Bordeaux, his monks rebelled against
him, and he was persecuted by *ligueurs* for at least a decade.[132] But
most Catholic preachers responded with celebration, however fearful they were at what lay ahead with the Protestant Henri de Navarre waiting in the wings.[133] The Bishop of Comminges preached
" '…oaths and blasphemies…exhorting people to arm themselves
for Jesus Christ…' "[134] Leaders of the *Seize* instructed preachers to
cover certain points in their sermons, justifying the actions of
Clément and comparing him with Judith, emphasizing that Henri
de Navarre could not succeed to the throne, and telling all who
supported Navarre that they would be excommunicated.[135] Boucher,

---

[127]   Labitte, *De la démocratie*, p. 45
[128]   Ibid., p. 43.
[129]   Mark Greengrass, "The Assassination of Henri III," *History Today* 39 (1989), 16.
[130]   Megan Armstrong, "The Franciscans in Paris, 1560-1600," Ph.D. thesis, University of Toronto, 1997, p. 12.
[131]   Ibid, p. 58.
[132]   Labitte, *De la démocratie*, p. 265.
[133]   As Armstrong has demonstrated, the Franciscan friars of Paris, including Jean
Garin, Maurice Hylaret, Robert Chessé, and Panigarole, had close ties to the Catholic
League. They were among "…the most intransigent opponents of Henry of Navarre's
accession to the throne, outlasting papal resistance to the point that their activities became an embarrassment to the pontiff." Armstrong, "Franciscans," pp. 58-59, 363.
[134]   Mark Greengrass, "The *Sainte Union* in the Provinces: The Case of Toulouse,"
Sixteenth Century Journal 14 (1983), 493.
[135]   Labitte, *De la démocratie*, p. 79.

according to l'Estoile, preached "nothing but killing."[136] But the enemy was now different. There were fewer Calvinists in France, if those who remained had become more militant, and Henri III was no more than a bad memory. Henri de Navarre remained, but to the most militant Catholic preachers, an equally potent threat was that posed by the *politiques*, who seemed willing to compromise what for *ligueurs* could never be compromised. In Paris in 1594, Renaud de Beaune (Archbishop of Bourges and later of Sens) and René Benoist were conjoined with Henri de Navarre in a popular verse:

> Of the three B's we must be on guard
> Of Bourges, Benoist and Bourbon
> Bourges believes in God compassionately
> Benoist preaches about him ingeniously
> But God will preserve us from this finesse
> And from Bourbon and his mass.[137]

Being a *politique* Catholic was equated with being the worst of heretics. As late as 1594, as Robert Harding has shown, "…preaching was the central religious and propaganda activity of the Confraternity in Orléans. … It was the violent sermons that the bishop and governor complained about in reports to the papal vice-legate. They claimed that the preachers accused the secular clergy of favoring heresy and inciting people to expel the bishop by force. On at least two occasions, in 1591 and 1594, sermons triggered pre-planned armed uprisings by the Confraternity aimed at taking control of the city."[138]

Of course the story of dangerous, inflammatory, and seditious preaching did not end with the coronation of Henri IV in February of 1594 or his entry into Paris a month later. Yet it was none other than Renaud de Beaune, appointed almoner to Henri IV, who probably composed and announced his conversion to Catholicism. Although called a Judas, a would-be antipope and worst of all, a *politique*,[139] de Beaune would survive, and the *politique* cause would

---

[136]   Quoted in Mark Greengrass, *France in the Age of Henri IV*, 2nd ed. (London and New York: Longman, 1995), p. 64.

[137]   Quoted in Baumgartner, "Beaune," p. 110.

[138]   Robert R. Harding, "The Mobilization of Confraternities Against the Reformation in France," *Sixteenth Century Journal* 11 (1980), 102.

[139]   Baumgartner, "Beaune," pp. 99, 104.

triumph. In responding to what was seen as a cancerous lesion destroying the sacred body, the most fanatical Catholic preachers had learned important political lessons, as Christopher Elwood has suggested, from their Calvinist counterparts: "The Catholic League's rejection of absolutism, although it served a fundamentally different religious vision, benefited significantly, albeit indirectly, from the critical approach to political power eucharistic doctrine facilitated."[140] But French society had changed by the seventeenth century, and although still afflicted by war and still overwhelmingly Catholic, was increasingly affected by the the political and cultural developments of *raison d'état*, science, and rationalism.

Preaching in the seventeenth century, when Tridentine reforms first were implemented in France, has been explored to the degree possible for both its literary merits,[141] and more importantly in the recent study by Thomas Worcester. While exploring the preaching of Jean-Pierre Camus, Worcester delves deeply into preaching and its cultural connections in seventeenth-century France.[142] He shows how one bishop used the printing press in early seventeenth-century France as a vehicle to promote his vision of the world. His findings are both ironic and natural in view of what has been covered in this chapter. Bishop Camus felt that there was "…no opposition between Catholic devotion and the best interests of the state; indeed these go hand in hand."[143] Indeed, in the funeral oration given by Jacques Suarez after the assassination of Henri IV in 1610, he averred that "…a state which did not protect religion would perish…just as religion would perish without the protection of the state."[144] Yet seventeenth-century preaching in France differed in many ways from what had come before, not only because church and state were far more in concert than they had been in the previous century, but because Tridentine preaching ideals were put into practice. This was the great age of Bossuet and other preachers

---

[140] Christopher Elwood, *The Body Broken: The Calvinist Doctrine of the Eucharist and the Symbolization of Power in Sixteenth-Century France* (New York: Oxford University Press, 1999), p. 171.

[141] Peter Bayley, *French Pulpit Oratory, 1598-1650* (Cambridge: Cambridge University Press, 1980).

[142] Thomas Worcester, *Seventeenth-Century Cultural Discourse: France and the Preaching of Bishop Camus* (Berlin and New York: Mouton de Gruyter, 1997).

[143] Ibid., p. 246.

[144] Armstrong, "Franciscans," pp. 50-51.

known for the elegance and eloquence of their sermons. As Worcester explains, Camus preached "…in a French flowing with word-plays and vivid imagery designed to both delight his audience and move them to repentance. Panegyric predominated as Camus placed before his hearers and/or readers images of conversion, love of God, sanctity."[145] Although there can be little doubt that some French preachers in the early modern period continued to follow some of the ideals (if not the style) of late medieval preaching and the political rhetoric that came to dominate France in the Religious Wars, we are by this point in a new space. It is one in which the notion of sacred rhetoric as eloquence (in order to move, persuade, and delight) became the goal of many if not most preachers. In the aftermath of war, assassinations, iconoclasm, and violence on an unprecedented scale, the changed nature of preaching toward support of one king, one law, and one faith is simple to understand. People were tired of war and hungry for peace, at least in their religious lives.

What can we learn, however, from the study of preaching in France during the time before age of absolutism? Perhaps the most obvious lesson is that for both Catholics and Huguenots, preaching mattered. It not only reflected the beliefs and interests of the society in which it took place, but had the power to influence that society in a very active way. Preaching was a dangerous vocation indeed. For preacher and hearer alike, sermons in the pre-modern period went far beyond the Augustinian ideals – they shaped the course of events, often affecting in a very personal way the lives (and in some cases deaths) of preachers and their audiences. As Natalie Zemon Davis observes, "…in sixteenth-century France, we have seen crowds taking on the role of priest, pastor, or magistrate to defend doctrine or purify the religious community – either to maintain its Catholic boundaries and structures, or to re-form relations within it."[146] The lines became very blurred in the second half of the sixteenth century in France, but the roles of preacher and audience would again become more sharply – however differently – defined in the centuries that followed.

---

[145] Worcester, *Seventeenth-Century Discourse*, p. 241.
[146] Davis, *Society and Culture*, p. 186.

Bibliography

Archives communales d'Amiens, BB14-17.

Armstrong, Megan, "The Franciscans in Paris, 1560-1600," Ph.D. thesis, University of Toronto, 1997.

Arnaud, Eugene, *Histoire des Protestants du Vivarais et du Velay: Pays de Languedoc de la Réforme à la Révolution* (Geneva: Slatkine Reprints, 1979).

— *Histoires des protestants du Dauphiné aux XVIe, XVIIe et XVIIIe siècles*, vol. 1: 1522-98 (Geneva: Slatkine Reprints, 1970).

Bakos, Adrianna, "The Historical Reputation of Louis XI in Political Theory and Polemic During the French Religious Wars," *Sixteenth Century Journal* 21 (1990), 3-32.

Baum, G., and E. Cunitz, eds., *Histoire ecclésiastique des églises réformées au royaume de France. Edition nouvelle avec commentaire, notice bibliographique et tables des faits et des noms propres* (Paris: Fischbacher, 1883).

Baumgartner, Frederic J., "Renaud de Beaune: Politique Prelate," *Sixteenth Century Journal* 9 (1978), 99-114.

Bayley, Peter, *French Pulpit Oratory, 1598-1650* (Cambridge: Cambridge University Press, 1980).

Beaune, Renaud de, *Oraison funebre de la tres-chrestienne, tres-illustre, tres-constante, Marie Royne d'Escosse, morte pour la Foy, le 18. Febrier, 1587, par la cruauté des Anglois heretiques, ennemys de Dieu* (Paris: G. Bichon, 1588).

Benoist, René, *Homélie de la Nativité de Iesus Christ, en laquelle est clairement monstré l'office du vray Chrestien* (Paris: Claude Frémy, 1558).

Bell, David A., "Unmasking a King: The Political Uses of Popular Literature Under the French Catholic League, 1588-89," *Sixteenth Century Journal* 20 (1989), 371-386.

Bèze, Theodore de, *Harangue des Protestants du Royaume de France...prononcee...en presence du Roy & de Monseigneurs de son Conseil, assemblés à Poissy, pour le faict de la Religion* (n.p., 1561).

— Bèze, *Le passavant de Théodore de Bèze, Epître de Maître Benoît passavant à Messire Pierre Lizet* (Paris: Isidore Liseux, 1875).

Bourquélot, Félix, ed., *Mémoires de Claude Haton* (Paris: Imprimérie Impériale, 1857).

Bourrilly, V.-L., ed., *Le journal d'un bourgeois de Paris sous le règne de François Ier (1515-1536)* (Paris: Alphonse Picard, 1910).

Calvin, John, *Tracts and Treatises in Defense of the Reformed Faith*, trans. Henry Beveridge (Grand Rapids: W. B. Eerdman, 1958).

— *Des scandales qui empeschent auiourdhuy beaucoup de gens de venir à la pure doctrine de l'Evangile, & en desbauchent d'autres* (Geneva: Jean Crespin, 1550).

Davis, Natalie Zemon, "The Rites of Violence," in *Society and Culture in Early Modern France* (Stanford: Stanford University Press, 1976), pp. 152-187.

Désiré, Artus, *Les regretz et complainctes de Passe partout et Bruitquicourt, sur la mémoire renouvellées de trespas et bout de l'an de feu tres noble et venerable personne Maistre Françoys Picart, docteur en théologie et grand doyen de Sainct Germain de l'Aucerroys* (Paris: Pierre Gaultier, 1557).

Diefendorf, Barbara, *Beneath the Cross: Catholics and Huguenots in Sixteenth-Century Paris* (New York: Oxford University Press, 1991).

— "Simon Vigor: A Radical Preacher in Sixteenth-Century Paris," *Sixteenth Century Journal* 18 (1987), 399-410.

— "Prologue to a Massacre: Popular Unrest in Paris, 1557-1572," *American Historical Review* 90 (1985), 1067-1091.

Doumergue, Emile, *Jean Calvin: Les hommes et les choses de son temps* (Lausanne: Georges Bridel, 1899).

Duplessis d'Argentré, Charles, *Collectio judiciorium de novis erroribus* (Paris: Cailleau, 1728).

Elwood, Christopher, *The Body Broken: The Calvinist Doctrine of the Eucharist and the Symbolization of Power in Sixteenth-Century France* (New York: Oxford University Press, 1999).

Dyvolé, Pierre, *Dix sermons de la Saincte Messe et de ceremonies d'icelle* (Paris: Nicolas Chesneau, 1577).

Farge, James K., *Biographical Register of Paris Doctors of Theology, 1500-1536* (Toronto: Pontifical Institute, 1980).

Greengrass, Mark, "The *Sainte Union* in the Provinces: The Case of Toulouse," *Sixteenth Century Journal* 14 (1983), 469-496.

—, "The Assassination of Henri III," *History Today* 39 (1989), 11-17.

— *France in the Age of Henri IV*, 2nd ed., Studies in Modern History (London and New York: Longman, 1995).

— "The Anatomy of a Religious Riot: Toulouse in May 1562," *Journal of Ecclesiastical History* 34 (1983), 367-390.

Grin, Edmond, "Deux sermons de Pierre Viret, leurs thèmes théologiques et leur actualité," *Theologische Zeitschrift* 18 (1962), 116-132.

Guggenheim, Ann H., "Beza, Viret, and the Church of Nîmes: National Leadership and Local Initiative in the Outbreak of the Religious Wars," *Bibliothèque d'humanisme et renaissance* 37 (1975), 33-47.

Guy, Henri, "Le sermon d'Aimé Meigret," *Annales de l'Université de Grenoble* 15 (1928), 181-212.

Harangue, contenant la remonstrance faicte devant la majesté du Roy treschrestien Charles neufiesme, tenant ses grans Estatz en sa ville d'Orleans: par monseigneur le Chancelier de France (Lyon: Benoist Rigaud, 1561).

Harding, Robert R., "The Mobilization of Confraternities against the Reformation in France," *Sixteenth Century Journal* 11 (1980), 85-107.

Herminjard, A.-J., *Correspondance des réformateurs dans les pays de langue français* (Geneva and Paris, 1886-1887).

Hilarion de Coste, F., *Le parfait ecclesiastique ou l'histoire de la vie et de la mort de François Le Picart, Seigneur d'Atilly & de Villeron, Docteur en Théologie de la Faculte de Paris & Doyen de Saint Germain de l'Auxerrois* (Paris: Sebastian Cramoisy, 1658).

Holt, Mack P., "Wine, Community and Reformation in Sixteenth-Century Burgundy," *Past & Present* 138 (1993), 58-93.

Hours, Henri, "Procès d'hérésie contre Aimé Meigret," *Bulletin de la Société de l'histoire du protestantisme français* 19 (1857), 14-43.

Janvier, Leonard, *Prosne & Exhortations accoustumees, avec prieres chrestiennes* (Paris: Thomas Richard, 1565).

Knecht, R. J., "Defending the Faith in 16th-Century France," *Proceedings of the Huguenot Society of Great Britain and Ireland* 26 (1994-1997), 317-329.

Labitte, Charles, *De la démocratie chez les prédicateurs de la Ligue* (Paris: Joubert, 1841).

Launoy, Jean de, *Regii Navarrae Gymnasii Parisiensis Historia* (Paris, 1677).

Le Picart, François, *Les sermons et instructions chrestiennes, pour tous les Dimenches, & toutes les festes des saincts, depuis la Trinité iusques à l'Advent*, 2 parts (Paris: Nicolas Chesneau, 1566).

Loirette, Gabriel, "Catholiques et protestants en Languedoc à la veille des guerres civiles (1560)," *Revue de l'histoire de l'église de France* 23 (1937), 503-525.

Maillard, Olivier, *Sermones de stipendio peccati* (Lyon: Stephan Gueygnardi, 1503).

—, *Sermones dominicales* (Lyon: Stephan Gueygnardi, 1503).

Mandrot, Bernard, ed., *Journal de Jean de Roye connu sous le nom de chronique scandaleuse, 1460-1483*, vol. 2 (Paris: Renouard, 1896).

Méray, Antony, *La vie au temps des libres prêcheurs ou les devanciers de Luther et de Rabelais: Croyances, usages et moeurs intimes des XIVe, XVe, et XVIe siècles*, 2 vols. (Paris: Claudin, 1878).

Nève, Joseph, ed., *Sermons choisis de Michel Menot* (Paris: Honoré Champion, 1924).

Oursel, Charles, *Notes pour servir à l'histoire de la Réforme en Normandie au temps de François Ier* (Caen: Henri Deslesques, 1913).

Paris, Etienne, *Homelies suyvant les matieres traictees es principales festes & solennitez de l'annee* (Paris: Robineau, 1553).

Pepin, Guillaume, *Sermones quadraginta de destructione Ninive* (Paris: Claude Chevallon, 1527).

— *Concionum dominicalium ex epistolis et evangeliis totius anni, pars hiemalis* (Antwerp: Guillelmus Lesteenius & Engelbertus Gymnicus, repr. 1656).

— *Conciones quadragesimales ad sacros evangeliorum sensus pro feriis quadragesimae mystice et moraliter explicandos* (Antwerp: Guillelmus Lesteenius and Engelbertus Marnicus, repr. 1656).

Potter, David, ed., *The French Wars of Religion: Selected Documents* (New York: St. Martin's Press, 1997).

Raynal, Louis, *Histoire du Berry*, vol. *3* (Bourges: Vermeil, 1844).

Roelker, Nancy Lyman, *One King, One Faith: The Parlement of Paris and the Religious Reformations of the Sixteenth Century* (Berkeley: University of California Press, 1996).

Samouillan, Alexandre, *Olivier Maillard: Sa prédication et son temps* (Toulouse: Privat, 1891).

Schmidt, Charles, *Gérard Roussel: Prédicateur de la Reine Marguerite de Navarre* (Geneva: Slatkine Reprints, 1970).

Schurhmanner, Georg, *Francis Xavier: His Life, His Times. Vol. I: Europe, 1506-1541* (Rome: Jesuit Historical Institute, 1973).

Smither, James R., "The St. Bartholomew's Day Massacre and Images of Kingship in France: 1572-1574," *Sixteenth Century Journal* 22 (1991), 27-46.

Sorbin, Arnaud, *Oraison funebre du treshault, puissant et treschrestien Roy de France, Charles IX, piteux & debonnaire, propugnateur de la Foy, & amateur des bons esprits; prononcee en l'Eglise Nostre dame de Paris le XII. de Iuillet, M.D.LXXIIII* (Paris: Guillaume Chaudière, 1574).

Sypher, G. Wylie, " 'Faisant ce qu'il leur vient à plaisir': The Image of Protestantism in French Catholic Polemic on the Eve of the Religious Wars," *Sixteenth Century Journal* 11 (1980), 59-84.

Taylor, Larissa Juliet, *Heresy and Orthodoxy in Sixteenth-Century Paris: François Le Picart and the Beginnings of the Catholic Reformation*, Studies in Medieval and Reformation Thought, 72 (Leiden: Brill, 1999).

— *Soldiers of Christ: Preaching in Late Medieval and Reformation France* (New York: Oxford University Press, 1992).

— "Comme un chien mort: Preaching about Kingship in France," *Proceedings of the Western Society for French History* 22 (1995), 157-170.

— "Out of Print: The Decline of Catholic Printed Sermons in France, 1530-1560," in Robin B. Barnes et al., eds., *Books Have their Own Destiny: Essays in Honor of Robert V. Schnucker* (Kirksville, Mo.: Sixteenth Century Essays and Studies, 1998), pp. 105-113.

— "Funeral Sermons and Orations as Religious Propaganda in Sixteenth-Century France," in Bruce Gordon and Peter Marshall, eds., *The Place of the Dead: Death and Remembrance in Late Medieval and Early Modern Europe* (Cambridge: Cambridge University Press, 2000), pp. 224-239.

Vacquerie, Jean de la, *Remonstrance adressé au roy, au princes catholiques, et à tous Magistrats & Gouverneurs de Republiques, touchant l'abolition des troubles & emotions qui se sont aujourd'huy en France, causez par les heresies qui y regnent & par la Chrestienté* (Paris: Jean Poupy, 1574).

Veissière, Michel, "Croyances et pratique religieuse à Meaux aux temps de Guillaume Briçonnet (1525)," *Revue d'histoire de l'église de France* 67 (1981), 55-59.

Venard, Marc, *Réforme protestante, Réforme catholique dans la province d'Avignon XVIe siècle* (Paris: Cerf, 1993).

— "Catholicism and Resistance to the Reformation in France, 1555-1585," in Philip Benedict et al., eds., *Reformation, Revolt and Civil War in France and the Netherlands 1555-1585* (Amsterdam: The Netherlands Academy of Arts and Sciences, 1999), pp. 133-148.

Vigor, Simon, *Sermons catholiques pour tous les iours de Caresme & Feries de Pasques, faits en l'Esglise S. Etienne du mont à Paris* (Paris: Michel Sonnius, 1588).

— *Sermons catholiques sur les dimanches et festes depuis l'onziesme apres la Trinité iusques au Caresme* (Paris: Nicolas du Fossé, 1597).

Weiss, Nathanaël, "La réformateur Aimé Meigret," *Bulletin de la Société de l'histoire du protestantisme français* 39 (1890), 245-269.

Worcester, Thomas, *Seventeenth-Century Cultural Discourse: France and the Preaching of Bishop Camus* (Berlin and New York: Mouton de Gruyter, 1997).

CHAPTER FIVE

THE SOCIAL HISTORY OF PREACHING: ITALY

Corrie E. Norman
(Converse College)

Perugia, 1448: Everyone was crying and shouting for about half an hour, "Jesus, have mercy!"
Venice, ca. 1525: Everyone who went ... experienced a miracle....
Rome, ca. 1576: And to heare the maner of the Italian preacher, with what a spirit he toucheth the hart, and moveth to compunction.... These things are handled with such a grace coming from the preachers mouth, that it calleth of al sortes great mulititudes, and worketh in their hartes marvelous effectes.[1]

Crying and shouting, the miraculous, marvelous effects – these are typical descriptions of preaching that come down to us from the three centuries between 1400 and 1700 in Italy. In these years, preaching was at the center of Italian culture and devotion. People, at least in the major urban areas, expected that they and their society would be dazzled, entertained, informed, even transformed, on a regular basis, by preaching. Thus they would come, sometimes in the tens of thousands if the sources do not exaggerate, to hear the Italian preachers. Denys Hay has observed the "pre-eminence" of preaching in the fifteenth century when the Franciscan Bernardino of Siena (d. 1444) and Dominican Savonarola of Florence (d. 1495) held forth. Many others less familiar to modern historians, such as the subject of the Perugian diarist cited above, Franciscan Roberto

---

[1] Diary of Graziani of Perugia on Roberto Caracciolo da Lecce in Roberto Rusconi, *Predicazione e vita religiosa nella società* (Torino: Einaudi, 1981), pp. 192-4. Giuseppe Musso, *Vita del Rev. Cornelio Musso* (Venice: Giunti, 1586), p. 4, in Corrie E. Norman, *Humanist Taste and Franciscan Values, Cornelio Musso and Catholic Preaching in Sixteenth-Century Italy* (New York: Peter Lang, 1998), p. 16. Gregory Martin, *Roma Sancta (1581)*, ed. George Bruner Parks (Rome: Edizioni di Storia e Letteratura, 1969), pp. 71-2, quoted in John W. O'Malley, *The First Jesuits* (Cambridge, Mass.: Harvard, 1993), p. 97.

Caracciolo da Lecce (d. 1495), were wowing Italian crowds as well.[2] As Frederick McGinness has documented, preaching in Rome even experienced a "brisk quickening in the era after Trent."[3] The great preachers of that time, whose names were known all over Europe by contemporaries, such as Francesco Panigarola, O.F.M (d. 1594) and later Paolo Segneri, S.J. (1694), are all but unknown today.

One could even say that Italian culture of the late medieval and early modern periods was a preaching culture in that preaching was one of the primary means of communication and acted as such on multiple levels. As the commentators put it, preaching involved "everyone"; it "calleth of al sortes great mulititudes." Preaching shaped the culture and individuals with its "marvelous effectes"; and the culture shaped it. As Robert Bonfil reminds, it is "an expression rooted in society's perception of its social identity."[4] It is equally important to remember, however, that for medieval and early modern preachers and hearers, preaching was first and foremost an expression of the divine; sacred mystery was the root of its power to transform and define.

If early modern Italy was a preaching culture, it was largely a home-grown one. Anne Thayer has observed that Italy exported much sermon literature but imported very little – especially not northern literature.[5] It had no need to do so, given the volume and quality of its own resources. This is significant for two reasons. First, it presents scholars of Italy with an opportunity to study the development of a form of cultural representation as "Italian" as the art of Caravaggio or the writing of Dante. Indeed, it was primarily as a form of Italian literature that early modern preaching was studied, when studied at all, in previous eras. Second, for historians of preaching in other regions, Italian preaching stands as a largely unexplored basis for comparison. For those specifically interested

---

    [2] Denys Hay, *The Church in Italy in the Fifteenth Century* (Cambridge: Cambridge University Press, 1977), p. 67, in Franco Mormando, *The Preacher's Demons: Bernardino da Siena and the Social Underworld of Early Renaissance Italy* (Chicago: University of Chicago Press, 1999), p. 3.

    [3] Frederick J. McGinness, *Right Thinking and Sacred Oratory in Counter-Reformation Rome* (Princeton, N.J.: Princeton University Press, 1995), p. 82.

    [4] Robert Bonfil, "Preaching as Mediation between Elite and Popular Cultures: The Case of Judah del Bene," in David B. Ruderman, ed., *Preachers of the Italian Ghetto* (Berkeley: University of California Press, 1992), p. 69.

    [5] Anne Thayer, "Sermon Collections: 1450-1520," *Medieval Sermon Studies Newsletter* (Spring 1998): 57-8.

in Italian religiosity, that it seemed to develop its own traditions independent of much of the rest of Europe, gives us a special lens into the peculiar nature of Italian devotion. (The exchange of sermon resources between Italy and Spain, and the Spaniards and Frenchmen who brought new orders of preachers to Italy were exceptions.)

Yet perhaps most importantly, even though Italians may have lacked an interest in preaching elsewhere, Italy was, as many an Italian preacher of the age put it, "the theater of the world." More specifically, all eyes were on Rome as the center of the Roman Catholic world, a world just in the process of being defined and much of that defining went out of the mouths of Italian preachers and found its way into the published sermon volumes that Catholics elsewhere craved. To have a history of early modern Catholicism, we have to have a history of Italian preaching, "to heare the maner of the Italian preacher," as did that most impressed Englishman Gregory Martin.

It is difficult to understand why Italian preaching has gone so long without becoming a focus of scholarship. For most of the twentieth century, scholars have neglected it. Preaching has been underutilized at best in the cultural histories of early modern Italy, its most common appearance being the occasional anecdote taken out of context. Ecclesiastical historians, particularly Jedin, have registered the significance of preaching for the sixteenth-century Church, and the preaching ministry of a few of its main protagonists has been underlined in biography, such has Paolo Prodi's chapters on preaching in the episcopacy of Gabriele Paleotti (d. 1597).[6] These, however, provide limited coverage of its scope. The area in which I argue that preaching primarily belongs, the history of devotion, was perhaps least attentive to it, while preaching was occasionally mined for theological history.

The various preaching orders have not, on the other hand, neglected their preaching traditions. Franciscans, particularly, and also Dominicans and Jesuits of the early twentieth century focused on reclaiming the history of the their great preachers, combing manuscript sources and relaying their discoveries in their journals.

---

[6]   Hubert Jedin, *A History of the Council of Trent,* trans. Ernest Graf, 2 vols. (London: Thomas Nelson and Sons, 1957-61). Paolo Prodi, *Il Cardinale Gabriele Paleotti,* 2 vols. (Rome: Edizione di storia e letteratura, 1959-67), especially volume 2, chapter 9.

While methodologically much of this work borders on hagiography and is of little use today, it provides helpful documentation. In the case of the Franciscans, for example, Anscar Zawart's *The History of Franciscan Preaching and of Franciscan Preachers* is invaluable if in great need of updating.[7] Little of the effort of the orders resulted, however, in monographic studies let alone comprehensive histories of preaching. Only in Arsenio D'Ascoli's *Predicazione dei Cappuccini nel Cinquecento in Italia* do we have an attempt to narrate the history of an order's preaching in early modern Italy.[8] Nor have those once well-known stars of the past received their due. Only three articles have been published on Panigarola in the twentieth century (1911, 1960, 1990).[9] Bernardino da Siena has fared a bit better with editions of his sermons and the publication of Marchesa Origo's biography in 1962. He was hardly forgotten after that, the subject of several conferences and seminal articles, but only in 1999 did Berdardino receive a long overdue book-length treatment by Franco Mormando.[10]

In sum, early modern Italian preaching has been a sorely understudied topic, neglected for other sources and subjects. Only in the past twenty-five years have we seen the stirrings of a revival of interest in Italian preaching, and we may yet see it produce excitement again. While we do not have a comprehensive picture of preaching in early modern Italy, the scholarship of the past twenty-five years has shed enough light on it that we can begin to see its outlines.

---

[7] Anscar Zawart, *The History of Franciscan Preaching and of Franciscan Preachers* : *A Bio-Bibliographical Study* (New York: J.F. Wagner, 1928).

[8] Arsenio D'Ascoli, *Predicazione dei Cappuccini nel Cinquecento in Italia* (Loreto: Libreria San Francesco d'Asissi, 1956).

[9] Roberto Rusconi, "Rhetorica Ecclesiastica: La predicazione nell'eta posttridentina fra pulpito e biblioteca," in *La Predicazione in Italia dopo il Concilio di Trento tra Cinquecento e settecetto. Atti del X convegno di Studio dell'Associazione Italiana dei Professor di Storia della Chiesa* (Napoli, 6-9 Settembre 1994), eds. Giacomo Martina, S.J. and Ugo Dovere (Rome: Edizioni Dehoniane, 1996), p. 21, cites Laura Zanette, "Tre predicatori per la peste: 1575-1577," *Lettere Italiane* 42 (1990), 430-59; and Giovanni Pozzi, "Intorno all' predicazione del Panigarola," in *Problemi di vita religiosa in Italia nella cinquecento. Atti del Convegno di storia della Chiesa in Italia* (Bologna, 2-6 Settembre 1958), ed. Convegno di storia della chiesa in Italia (Padua: Antinori, 1960), pp. 315-22, as the most recent. For other Rusconi works, see n. 18.

[10] Iris Origo, *The World of San Bernardino* (New York: Harcourt, Brace, 1962). Among the editions of Bernardino's works is the nine volume *Opera Omnia* (Quaracchi: Collegio San Bonaventura, 1950-65). See the bibliography in Mormando for the most complete list of works on Bernardino.

While we will never experience preaching as did Gregory Martin or the myriad Italian townspeople of his age, this essay will provide a glimmer of the liveliness of preaching for early modern people. My view is based primarily on developments of the preaching culture of Italy in the sixteenth and early seventeenth centuries. Even if our understanding remains limited until further primary research is completed, one thing is quite clear: there is something we can call an Italian preaching culture of the early modern period that grows out of and is contiguous with the preaching of fifteenth-century Italy despite important changes. This is confirmed by our Perugian, Venetian, and English witnesses. Any of their reports could have been made (and were) of preaching at any time in Italy in these centuries.

Continuity in the preaching culture of Italy in these three centuries rests on six shared assumptions in the general culture that remain constant, although the forms and theories associated with them and the structures and locations in which they appear vary over time. The first is that preaching should transform; it "toucheth" and "moveth." Second, the "wondrous effectes" of transformation are harmony in society and between society and the sacred; thus personal and communal "compunction," repentance, and the appeal for divine mercy are the most common themes. Third, moving stems from a combination of two things. The "spirit" or Word of God embodies itself in the preacher and is transmitted to the hearer through him; it "toucheth the harte," as Gregory said, more than mind. The preacher's rhetorical skill, "such a grace" as Gregory put it, works with divine grace in this process. Fourth, the messenger most likely to transmit the Word is the one whose image and action as well as words recall or even miraculously recreate those of the earliest apostles and prophets of God before the people. He is most likely to belong to one of the medieval mendicant preaching orders or one of the new orders that drew upon or shared their understandings of apostolic preaching. Fifth, preaching is an event where the sacred is made manifest. The "crying and shouting" of the crowds is the result of the activity of the Spirit through the preacher; but it occurs in ritualistic forms: the preacher sounds the message and the hearers respond with communal cries, "Jesus, have mercy!" Preaching occurs most often in liturgical settings and is tied to liturgical, sacramental, or devotional practice and is understood and experienced in similar ways.

Finally, audience as well as preacher and Spirit determined the nature of the preaching event. Their reactions, the degree to which they receive the words of the preacher, and their emotional and physical responses confirm the presence of the holy, showing the "marvelous effectes." And while preaching was a communal event for "everybody" and the Council of Trent encouraged the uniformity of content and style, the audience was not seen as monolithic. Preachers had to move "al sortes" – the audiences *within* the audience – people of different walks of life, abilities, and sensibilities even within the boundaries of shared culture and assumptions.

Although our witnesses to preaching in this period testified to continuity, most of the historians who have begun to revive interest in it in the last two and a half decades have focused on change. This is quite understandable given that these three centuries experienced tremendous changes, characterized by the historical nomenclature we ascribe to them: "late medieval," "Renaissance," "Pre-/Post Tridentine," "Counter," "Catholic Reformation;" "Catholic Reform," the "Baroque." Here it is helpful to focus on the emerging picture depicted by modern scholars.

Recent Historiography

Preaching in fifteenth-century Italy, according to the latest scholarship, was part of two worlds that overlapped in reality although seldom in scholarly treatments: the late Middle Ages and the Renaissance. Scholars focusing on the fifteenth century have tended to center their interest on the social history of the preacher's role and preaching in urban centers and the relationship of the friars to popular culture. Italians such as Carlo Delcorno, Roberto Rusconi, and the late Zelina Zafarana have been at the forefront of this work.[11] At least three important books from American authors also

---

[11]   Carlo Delcorno, *Giordano da Pisa e l'antica predicazione volgare* (Florence: Sansoni, 1975); "La città nella predicazione francescana nel quattrocento," *Quaderni del Monte* 3 (1984). See also the bibliographical article by Delcorno, "Rassegna di studi sulla predicazione medievale et umanistica," *Lettere italiane* 33 (1981), 235-76. Roberto Rusconi, *Predicazione*; "Dal pulpito alla confessione. Modelli di comportamento religioso in Italia tra 1470 e 1520 circa," in *Strutture ecclesiastiche in Italia e in Germania prima della Riforma*, eds. Paolo Prodi and P. Johanek (Bologna: 1984); "Il sacramento della penitenza nella predicazione di san Bernardino da Siena," *Aevum* 48 (1973), 253-86; "La

focus on this area. Donald Weinstein's *Savonarola and Florence* looks at the ill-fated Dominican's preaching and ministry in light of Florentine political and social crises. Bernadette Paton has studied the preaching and ministry of the friars in Siena with an eye toward their social teaching. And Franco Mormando's recent work on Bernardino da Siena focuses on the great preacher's "dark side" and its relationship to the definition of social deviance.[12]

Humanistic interest in classical rhetoric in Renaissance Italy greatly affected preaching. Scholars have depicted the preaching that resulted from the influence of humanism as both a rejection of the medieval *artes praedicandi* and a representation of new values and tastes based on ancient models. With the transition from late medieval to Renaissance, the interest in preaching shifted from Tuscany to Rome, from social history to rhetoric, and from popular to elite circles. The most important work on Renaissance preaching is the groundbreaking *Praise and Blame in Renaissance Rome* by John W. O'Malley, which documented the new preaching at the papal court from 1450 to 1521 and sparked interest in the history of Catholic preaching among a number of scholars.[13] O'Malley's interests were not just rhetorical; he looked at the role of the new preaching in articulating the religious and cultural milieu of the Renaissance papal court. This is a social history of another sort and a very important one, for this style transformed society at all levels after the Council of Trent. John McManamon, in his study of funeral oratory from 1374-1534, shows how the use of classical *epideictic*, "the art of praise and blame," also employed at the papal court, advanced humanistic ideals beyond the court.[14]

---

predicazione francescana sulla penitenza all fine del quattrocento nel 'Rosarium Sermonum' di Bernardino Busti," *Studia Patavina* 22 (1975), 68-95. Seminal essays of Zelina Zafarana are collected in *Da Gregorio VII a Bernardino da Siena. Saggi di storia medievale*, eds. O. Capitani et al. (Firenze: Scandicci, La Nuova Italia Editrice, 1987).

[12] Bernadette Paton, *Preaching Friars and the Civic Ethos: Siena, 1380-1480* (London: Centre for Medieval Studies, Queen Mary and Westfield College, University of London, 1992). Donald Weinstein, *Savonarola and Florence* (Princeton, N.J.: Princeton University Press, 1970). Cynthia Polecritti, *Preaching Peace in Renaissance Italy: Bernardino of Siena and his Audience* (Washington, D.C.: Catholic University of America Press, 2000), which I was unable to see before this chapter went to press.

[13] John W. O'Malley, *Praise and Blame in Renaissance Rome: Rhetoric, Doctrine, and Reform in the Sacred Orators of the Papal Court, ca. 1450-1521* (Durham, N.C.: Duke University Press, 1979).

[14] John M. McManamon, *Funeral Oratory and the Cultural Ideals of Italian Humanism* (Chapel Hill, N.C.: University of North Carolina Press, 1989).

Frederick McGinness has documented how preachers at the papal court and Rome after Trent used humanistic methods, proceeding from defensive "counter-reformation" rhetoric to the triumphant envisioning of a Roman Catholic worldview. As O'Malley before him, McGinness combed the archives of the Vatican and other sources to reconstruct the function of preaching in the social milieu of the Church, with the papal court as its central axis. He also builds on the analysis of rhetoric in the post-Tridentine period best represented to date in the magisterial work of Marc Fumaroli, *L'Age de l'eloquence*.[15]

Historiography, while making great strides in the last twenty years, remains incomplete and unbalanced. Research on preaching in early modern Italy has focused on the study of classical rhetoric and its application in sermons and preaching manuals. A clear picture is emerging of developments in form and style, their relationship to Tridentine agenda, and how sermons reflected the goals and tastes of elite practitioners and audiences, particularly at the papal court. If compared, however, to the scholarship on late medieval Italian preaching, where the focus has been on popular preaching and what sermons reveal about the broader society, there is much left to tell of the story of preaching in early modern Italy.

Further, while scholars have rightly remarked on monumental changes in sacred rhetoric, the continuity and stability of the Italian preaching tradition undergirding those changes has not been stressed enough. In my own study of Cornelio Musso (d. 1574), who was credited with putting the new humanistic rhetoric to work in Italian popular preaching, I found a leading figure who represents the complexities of preaching in the period. The one who produced "miracles" as an adolescent preacher in Venice, a star in the pulpits of Rome and other cities in his prime, and a favorite orator at the papal court throughout his career, Musso viewed his success as dependent on his adherence to the traditions of medieval Franciscan preaching as well as his new humanistic style.[16]

There is hope on a few fronts that the coming decades will see a more comprehensive view of early modern Italian preaching cul-

---

[15] McGinness, see n. 3. Marc Fumaroli, *L'âge de l'eloquence: Rhetorique et "res literaria" de la Renaissance au seuil de l'epoque classique* (Geneva: Droz, 1980).

[16] Corrie E. Norman, *Humanist Tastes and Franciscan Values: Cornelio Musso and Catholic Preaching in Sixteenth-Century Italy* (New York: Peter Lang, 1998).

ture. First, recent interest in the *mezzogiorno* and the popular missions of Orders has brought renewed attention to the importance of preaching. The rich archival sources for the Jesuits are especially promising.[17] Second, scholars of diocesan reform efforts are finding the role of preaching among other issues to be of central importance in the sources in episcopal archives. Work has concentrated on Borromean Milan. Cardinal Carlo Borromeo (d. 1584) and his nephew Federigo (d. 1631), however, were not the only bishops who left important writings on the ideals and realities of preaching. Setting the course for post-Tridentine developments were the early reform efforts of G. M. Giberti (d. 1543), Gasparo Contarini (d. 1542), and Marcello Cervini (d. 1555). The role of preaching in the episcopacies of Carlo Borromeo, Cornelio Musso, Girolamo Seripando (d. 1563), and Gabriele Paleotti have also received attention.[18] Perhaps the most important piece of the picture may yet come as scholars search diocesan records for evidence of parish preaching.

Finally, we can derive hope from the optimism of the man most knowledgeable about the culture of Italian preaching, Roberto Rusconi. In his numerous articles, Rusconi has laid the groundwork for almost every aspect of late medieval and early modern preaching, including the study of significant figures and movements, rhetorical developments, iconography, theology, the history of ministry and popular devotion, and social history.[19] His seminal article in

---

[17] Luigi Mezzadri, "Storiografia delle missioni," in Martina and Dovere, pp. 457-485, gives a comprehensive overview of recent scholarship; p. 476 n. 84 lists works on Jesuit missions.

[18] Francesco C. Cesareo, "Penitential Sermons in Renaissance Italy: Girolamo Seripando and the *Pater Noster*," *Catholic Historical Review* 83 (1997), 1-19. On Contarini and Cervini, see William J. Houdon, "Two Instructions to Preachers for Tridentine Reform," *Sixteenth Century Journal* 20 (1989), 457-470. John W. O'Malley, "St. Charles Borromeo and the *Praecipuum Episcoporum Munus*: His Place in the History of Preaching," in *San Carlo Borromeo: Catholic Reform and Ecclesiastical Politics in the Second Half of the Sixteenth Century*, eds. John M. Headley and John B. Tomaro, (Washington, D.C.: Folger Books, 1988), pp. 139-57. Adriano Prosperi, *Tra evangelismo e Controriforma: G.M. Giberti (1495-1543)* (Rome: Editione di storia e letteratura, 1969). Prodi, *Paleotti*. Gabriele De Rosa, "Il francescano Cornelio Musso dal Concilio di Trento alla Diocesi di Bitonto," *Rivista di storia della chiesa in Italia* 40 (1986), 55-91.

[19] Roberto Rusconi's seminal works on preaching are "Predicatori e predicazione," in *Storia d'Italia Annali* 4: *Intellettuali e potere*, ed. C. Vivanti (Torino: Einaudi, 1981), pp. 995-1012; and *Predicazione*, esp. pp. 283-327 for this period (see n. 1). See also "Predicazione," *Dizionario degli Istituti di Perfezione* VII (Roma: Edizioni Paoline, 1983), pp. 513-550; "Gli ordini religiosi maschili dalla controriforma alle soppressioni

Storia d'Italia and subsequent collection of primary sources provide the most comprehensive picture of preaching we have; but it has been twenty years since the publication of those works. In 1996, the most important Italian volume on early modern preaching since Rusconi's works of the early eighties appeared. In this collection of essays by interdisciplinary scholars, Rusconi expresses his optimism that we can compose a comprehensive picture of preaching in this period through work that includes "religious, social and literary" considerations and integrates "jurisdictional, doctrinal, and devotional" aspects.[20] Then, all that will hold us back are the limitations of the sources.

Sources

The lack of sources on preaching precludes a full picture of Italy's preaching culture. But along with diocesan, monastic, and papal records, preaching treatises and accounts of various sorts provide rich information. With the countless manuscript and *incunabular* sermons, published editions of many of these from the sixteenth century, the often multiple editions of the great preachers of the sixteenth and seventeenth centuries, we have a wealth of sermon material from the period.

The dearth of scholarship on preaching stems first of all from a failure to examine sermons as evidence of a culture of preaching. In the existing scholarship, there is often limited citation or discussion of actual sermon material. The few editions of fifteenth-century preachers that exist are old and in need of updating. The only recent critical edition known to me is the 1989 work of Delcorno on Bernardino's 1427 Siena sermons.[21] I know of no published translation of a full-length sermon from sixteenth-century Italy.[22] There is no catalogue of early modern Italian sermons, so scholars

---

settecentesche. Cultura, predicazione, missioni," *Clero e societa nell'Italia moderna,* ed. Mario Rosa (Roma-Bari: Laterza, 1992), pp. 207-74.

[20]   Rusconi, "Rhetorica," in Martina and Dovere, pp. 42-44.

[21]   Bernardino da Siena, *Prediche volgari sul Campo di Siena 1427,* ed. Carlo Delcorno, 2 vols. (Milan: Rusconi, 1989).

[22]   An edited English translation of a Savonarola sermon appears in John C. Olin, ed., *The Catholic Reformation: Savonarola to Ignatius Loyola* (New York: Fordham, 1992), along with other documents related to preaching.

are left to their own devices in searching out primary sources with few aids.[23]

Besides locating sources, the greatest difficulty comes in determining exactly how these sources relate to actual preaching. Most late medieval sermons survive in Latin reductions, although unless intended for a clerical or university audience, they usually would have been preached in a mix of Latin (mostly for scriptural references) and vernacular. They are most often little more than outlines of the original sermons, leaving little evidence of the life once in them. They are not intended to reflect an event but rather to serve as topical models for other preachers. Most often they were done by the preacher himself and provide plans for cycles of sermons for Lent, Advent, or for the entire year. Occasionally in these rather dry scholastic accounts, one can glimpse the liveliness of a Bernardino or Caracciolo, but generally they leave much to the imagination.

Even the vernacular sermons could hardly be considered exact reports. Scribes, appointed by the preachers or on their own, took down the sermons as *reportationi* as they were preached. For example, using notarial methods, Savonarola's devotees took down his sermons and put them immediately into print.[24] What the scribes captured depended on their intentions and interests as well as their capacities and methods. Making a profit (copies of sermons were sometimes sold on the spot to pious laity who could afford them) and personal devotion (preachers encouraged literate hearers to take down their words for later reflection) often took priority over historical recording; yet to the extent that they reveal the range of uses of and interests in preaching, they tell us something about the

---

[23]   Sources most helpful for locating sermons and related primary sources include: Paul Oskar Kristeller, *Iter Italicum* (Leiden: E.J. Brill, 1965-7), Fernanda Ascarelli, *Le cinquecentine romane: Censimento delle edizioni romane del XVI secolo possedute dalle biblioteche di Roma* (Milan: Etimar, 1972); Anne Schutte, *Printed Italian Vernacular Religious Books 1465-1550: A Finding List* (Gevena: Droz, 1983); and Zawart (n. 7). See also the bibliography of Fumaroli (n. 15), and the appendix in McGinness (n. 3) The articles on specific preachers in *Dizionario biografico degli italiani* (Rome: Istituto della Enciclopedia italiana, 1960-), are generally quite useful.

[24]   Roberto Rusconi, "Da costanza al Laterano: La 'Calcolata devozione' del ceto mercantile-borghese nell'italia del Quattrocento," in *Storia dell'Italia religiosa*, ed. André Vauchez (Rome: Laterza, 1993), vol. 1, p. 532.

preaching culture.[25] While they may not present a complete picture of preaching or even an "accurate" account of all that was said by the preacher, the reportations often include details about the event or reflect the preacher's spontaneity in ways that the Latin sermons do not.

Reportationi are much rarer in the sixteenth and seventeenth centuries.[26] As Tuscan Italian became a more acceptable language for preaching among elites, the publication of sermons in Italian increased, although many still were translated into Latin for wider usage abroad. Yet it is still not likely that sermons were reproduced in print exactly as they were preached for a number of reasons. Some preachers worked from an outline, especially when preaching before "the people." The manuscript records of Bishop Paleotti's sermons, for example, contain outlines of sermons preached in parishes. His Latin sermons for elite audiences were more complete.[27] His popular sermons were more extemporaneous; such sermons would have been difficult to reproduce *verbatim* after the fact.

Even if the preacher did scrupulously compose his text before preaching, it does not guarantee that what appears in print is exactly what was preached. In 1583, Borromeo had Panigarola accompany him on a diocesan visitation. After Panigarola's first sermon, Carlo took him aside and ordered the greatest preacher of the day to revise his sermons, devoting the majority of his time to "something easy and devout."[28] Panigarola's published version, *Cento Ragionamenti*, contains "the mass of topics" and those that "his most illustrious lordship" had wanted said."[29]

Editors and publishers as well as the preachers often had a heavy hand in printed versions of sermons. The earliest volumes of Cornelio Musso's sermons were surely published as Musso intended. We know that he edited them himself, worked closely with the publisher, and even stopped the presses on one edition when he

---

[25] Stanislao da Campagnola, "La Predicazione Quaresimale: Gestione, evoluzione, tipologie," in Martina and Dovere, p. 262 and Rusconi, *Predicazione*, p. 176; for examples, pp. 177-8. See Mormando's discussion of the *reportationi* of Bernardino, pp. 44-45.

[26] Carlo Delcorno, "Forme della predicazione cattolica fra Cinque e Seicento," in *Cultura d'élite e cultura popolare nell'arco alpino fra Cinque e Seicento*, ed. Ottavio Besomi and Carlo Caruso (Boston: Birkhaeuser Verlag, 1995), p. 280.

[27] Prodi, *Paleotti*, vol. 2, pp. 88-9.

[28] Ibid.

[29] Ibid.

discovered that the publisher had made a change in the index without consulting him. Musso died before finishing his work on his Roman Lenten sermons, however, and the task fell to two editors. The preface to one of the volumes congratulates the last editor for his excellent job of reconstruction, given the poor condition of some of Musso's remaining manuscripts.[30]

As with medieval sermons, the sermon books of the early modern period were printed for a variety of reasons that affected their resemblance to actual preaching. The bishop of Milan, Carlo Borromeo, had his own sermons of 1583-4 edited and translated into Latin for use abroad as preaching models. After his death, other sermons, even further removed from live preaching, according to Prodi, were published by family members who were apparently most interested in enhancing their family prestige.[31]

As preachers such as Musso and Panigarola who employed classical rhetoric became admired for their eloquence, a main aim of publishing sermons became marketing them as literature. They were to be enjoyed for their style and language as reading. Published sermons were to be the private devotional matter of educated elites as well as literary models. Well aware that their sermons would be scrutinized as literature and convinced that eloquence was essential in order for them to affect their intended audience, preachers revised and embellished them. In a rare case in which we have a reportation as well as the preacher's manuscript edition and the published sermon, the path of a sermon from preaching to print is clear. Girolamo Mautini da Narni (d. 1632) was preacher to the papal court for much of the early part of the seventeenth century. Vicenzo Criscuolo has compared the three versions of a sermon preached by Narni at the court in 1609, aligning the versions in parallel columns. Large lacunae exist in the reportation compared to the other versions. While Narni's and his editor's versions are very close, the editor trimmed Narni's version in several places.[32]

The sermon volumes of early modern Italy persist with two of the main goals of medieval printed sermons—serving as models for

---

[30] Norman, pp. 5-6.
[31] Delcorno, "Forme," pp. 282-4.
[32] Vincenzo Criscuolo, *Girolamo Mautini da Narni (1563-1632): Predicatore Apostolico e Vicario Generale dei Cappuccini* (Roma: Istituto Storico dei Cappuccini, 1998), pp. 223-300.

preachers and devotional material for readers; however, they combine these interests. Unlike the medieval Latin sermon models intended for clergy, sixteenth-century published sermons were more
likely to be expanded and refined with the pious reader in mind
rather than abridged forms of preaching. What printed sermon
volumes reveal for certain is the "polyfunctional" nature of sermons in early modern culture, as Delcorno has put it.[33] While they
remain perhaps our best sources for the culture of preaching and
ought to be the starting place for research, they need to be studied
in conjunction with other types of sources.

Treatises and Other Arts of Preaching

Between the 1570s and the eighteenth century, over 1200 works on
sacred rhetoric appeared.[34] They served to flesh out the directives
on preaching from the Council of Trent, which gave few specific
guidelines on the practice of preaching. They brought into clear
relief the humanistic methods that had already begun replace the
medieval scholastic sermon among cutting edge preachers. They
also reveal the pastoral psychology of the Post-Tridentine era and
the attitudes toward various types of practitioners and audiences
held by the reformers of preaching. Italians, especially members of
the traditional preaching orders, were in the vanguard of Catholic
writing on preaching, even before Trent. Thus new ideas mixed
with traditional thinking and practice of the orders.[35]

While members of the orders were the most significant theorists
as well as practitioners of preaching, Trent had clearly emphasized
the responsibility of bishops in the regulation of preaching. Bishops
such as Carlo Borromeo inspired and mandated works on preaching and even took the task upon themselves. The bishop's *Instructiones praedicationis verbi Dei* (1573) and subsequent works became

---

[33]   Delcorno, "Forme," pp. 284-5.
[34]   Giacomo Martina, "Presentazione," in Martina and Dovere, p. 10.
[35]   John W. O'Malley, "Form, Content, and Influence of Works about Preaching
before Trent: The Franciscan Contribution," in *I frati minori tra '400 e '500. Atti del XII
Convegno Internzionale* (Assisi, 18-20 ottobre 1984), ed. Centro di Studi (Assisi: Centro di
Studi, 1985), pp. 27-50.

models. In 1576, a number of works that point to the influence of his episcopate appeared in Italy and elsewhere.[36]

The treatises often had different audiences in mind and thus varied in focus and instruction. From Panigarola we have two treatises: a "practical" guide in *Modo di comporre una predica* and a more theoretical work, *Il Predicatore*. They varied greatly in length, from Musso's three-page directive to his clergy in the diocese Bitonto, to Narni's twenty-page treatise on sermon composition, to the multi-chaptered *Il Predicatore*.[37]

Other types of preaching aids also began to appear after Trent. The Dominican Vincenzio Ferrini produced *Della lima universale de'vitii* in the late 1590s. The volume is basically a compendium of quotable quotes on various topics associated with vices or various types of sinners. In the preface, he explains that he has collected the wisdom of some forty of the "most celebrated authors" and "most excellent preachers of our age" for use by those who have little time or access to the "almost infinite" number of works on preaching. It was intended for use by preachers and pastors and also for "all those that strive to rid themselves of vice."[38] Among the things that the *Lima* reveals is a continuity of focus on mercantile and court culture carried over from late medieval preaching.

Such sources are especially important for constructing a view of parish preaching. We know of very few sermons from parish preachers in Italy before 1750. Beside diocesan mandates or records, preaching aids designed for parish use are the best sources. The sources assume that parish priests who did preach (not all did), would be less capable than the preachers of the orders. They might read a published sermon or they might follow a guide such as Gabriele Inchino's *Vie del Paradiso* (1607), which provided sermon models directed at both regulars and parish priests. Rusconi reported that Inchino marked the margins of his text with "P" for *predicatore*

---

[36] Rusconi in Martina and Dovere, pp. 15-6. Delcorno, "Forme," pp. 292-3. See also O'Malley, "St. Charles Borromeo."

[37] Cornelio Musso, *Synodus Bituntina*, ed. Giuseppe Musso (Venice: Giolito, 1579), pp. 391-2; Girolamo Narni, *Modo breve et facilissimo di compore le prediche conforme allo stile moderno che riguarda l'utile e non il puro diletto*, in Criscuolo, pp. 137-53; Francesco Panigarola, *Modo di comporre una predica* (Padova, 1599) and *Il Predicatore* (Venice: Ciotti, 1609).

[38] Vincenzio Ferrini, "Ai cortesi lettori," *Della lima universale de'vitii* (Venice: Gionti, 1617). First published in 1596.

and "C" for *curate*, "taking account of their respective competencies."[39] It also seems that parish priests continued to rely on traditional resources for the most part. In examining the book lists of parish priests (which many bishops required in the late sixteenth century), Rusconi found the majority of texts on preaching to be of late medieval origin. Roberto Caracciolo, for one, had not yet been forgotten. His Latin sermons were reprinted in the sixteenth century and used as models by parish priests. The holdings of monastic libraries (required by the Index) also reveal that where the works of the proponents of the new rhetoric and Tridentine ideals existed, they were shelved alongside those of their medieval predecessors and outnumbered by them. As Rusconi concludes, many if not most preachers whether regular or secular seem to have been exposed mostly to late medieval preaching resources and were using them to accomplish post-Tridentine goals.[40] This should serve as a caveat against basing conclusions on the ideals of the sacred rhetorics without checking them against accounts of practice.

The three quotations beginning this essay come from other types of sources that we might group together as "accounts" of preaching that are found in works primarily about other topics or in diaries, letters, or itineraries. As Campagnola observed, none of the published sermons we have "reflect in the least part" the fascination of hearers that are reported by these sources.[41] While clergy such as the Jesuit Gregory Martin often comment on preaching, these accounts are where we find the most direct evidence of lay opinion, such as the report of the lay witness to Caracciolo's preaching. Even when recorded by clergy, they can be invaluable to relaying the reactions of the masses, although through an ecclesiastical filter.

Diary accounts can be particularly revealing of the preaching event even when they say little about the content. They serve not only to supplement sermons but also reveal that preachers and audiences may have viewed different things as most significant about preaching. The diarist who left his testimony about Caracciolo's Lenten cycles in 1448, for example, focused on the activities surrounding preaching: the daily processions, the numbers and sponta-

---

[39] Rusconi in Martina and Dovere, p. 37.
[40] Ibid., pp. 23-28.
[41] Campagnola, p. 253.

neous outbursts of the people, and the friar's dramatic departure.[42] Almost a century later, a member of the entourage of Vittoria Colonna described the Lenten preaching of Bernardino Ochino (d. 1564) in Rome from the perspective of the court's itinerary: they dined, went to the Office, the preacher began at the "second hour of evening" and preached for four hours during which the Marchesa listened from Cardinal de Medici's balcony; then they went home to bed. What of the sermon besides its length? It ended after four hours only because Ochino could no longer be heard for the crying of the crowd.[43]

Comparison with a preacher's itinerary reveals the different concerns lay people and preachers may have had. An Observant Franciscan at the end of the fifteenth century records the length of his sermons, a common factor in accounts of preaching (four and one-half hours on average in this case). Yet his concerns about length do not reflect the interests of the two previous reports. They were interested in length as an indicator of the audience affect and activity. This preacher is concerned that he never manages to get through his outline before running out of time. Further indicating his primary interest in content, he records his sources.[44]

Another type of account of preaching by or for the laity is the devotional book based on preaching. Lay people, as well as spiritual advisors, undertook such projects for themselves, encouraged by preachers.[45] While other accounts focus on the activity of preaching, these reveal the content that most impressed lay people and the close relationship between preaching and devotion. Zafarana found in the "spiritual diary" of the Florentine Margherita di Tommaso Soderini a daily account for five years of the "consolation" she found in preaching at Santa Maria del Fiore in the late fifteenth century.[46] A Florentine manuscript of unknown origin also found by Zafarana records sermons heard from 1467 to 1502, "practically an entire life." While it lists the names of the preachers and often refers to them, the manuscript is organized by topic rather than sermon. Zafarana speculates that this work may have been for another

---

42   Rusconi, *Predicazione*, pp. 192-4.
43   G.B. Belluzzi in D'Ascoli, pp. 431-2. Lent of 1535.
44   Rusconi, *Predicazione*, pp. 198-9.
45   For an example, see ibid., p. 177.
46   Zafarana, "Per la storia religiosa di Firenze nel Quattrocento: Una raccolta privata di prediche," in Capitani, pp. 280-1.

woman's devotional use, for not unlike later catechisms, it was organized to serve as a guidebook to practical Christian living. [47]

Letters from the period sometimes contain accounts of preaching. In fact, some "letters" are really short discourses on a famous
preacher's rhetorical skill. For example, several manuscript versions
of such a letter by the courtier Lelio Guidiccioni about Girolamo
Narni's preaching are housed in the Vatican Library. Sources like
these are forerunners of Federigo Borromeo's account of the great
preachers of the age, published in 1632.[48] They were intended for
a cultured audience and highly stylized; yet they often reveal aspects of popular preaching that the published sermons cannot, such
as the mannerisms and voice of the preacher. In their accounts of
popular audience reactions and the testimonies of elite connoisseurs
of rhetoric, cultured fans like Guidiccioni also reveal the commonly
held assumption about what was most essential to good preaching:
the ability to move all types of people.

Purpose

The main purpose of preaching throughout this period was to
move listeners to change their lives. The impetus for this came from
two directions, with somewhat different vocabularies and agendas.
First, going back to the apostolic preaching of the medieval mendicants, was the goal of leading hearers to repentance. For that reason, Francis had instructed his followers to preach "vices and virtues, punishment and glory." Franciscans as diverse as Bernardino
da Siena and Cornelio Musso were faithful to Francis's instructions
as were many of other allegiances throughout the period.[49]

Humanism and rhetorical theology also promoted the goal of
moving. As O'Malley put it, the preachers at the Renaissance papal
court saw their use of rhetoric in service of "the single goal of aid-
ing... listeners in their efforts to master the most important art of all

---

[47]   Ibid., pp. 282-5.
[48]   Letter of Lelio Guidiccioni to the Bishop of Novara, 1611 (later versions also
exist). See Criscuolo, pp. 379-84, Federigo Borromeo, *De sacris nostorum temporum
oratoribus* (Milan: 1632).
[49]   *Regula Bullata*, Chapter 9: "announce to them vices and virtues, punishment and
glory with brevity of words...," *Seraphicae Legislationis Textus originales* (Quaracchi, 1847),
p. 44, my translation.

—the art of good and blessed living...."[50] While the foci may be different—moving to do penance and moving in a more general sense to upright living—generally a moral message, aided by emotive rhetoric designed to elicit transformation, was common to both. Of course, there were other goals as well, and sometimes these might overtake moving as the primary purpose. The scholastic forms that the friars used lent themselves more readily to teaching or proving and thus often appear more like doctrinal lectures than moral exhortation. The preachers at the papal court were to discourse on the "Christian mysteries"; thus their sermons were also "doctrinal." The teaching of doctrine, however, was in service of the goal of "moving and pleasing."[51]

Furthermore, papal court preaching in the Renaissance primarily fit into the oratorical genre known as "demonstrative." That is, it was to please, to delight with its grand discourses on the majesty of God. The sermons of the mendicant preachers, as Francis's words indicate, were to inspire hope *and* fear with their discussions of the consequences of vice and virtue. McGinness observes that by the mid-sixteenth century, however, the goal of preaching at the court and elsewhere was generally understood to be "persuasion" that might be accomplished in a variety of rhetorical forms drawn from the classical orators and the Church Fathers, but that maintained the focus that Francis articulated.[52]

These goals continued to converge in the wake of Trent. The first Tridentine decree on preaching cited the Franciscan Rule on the topics of preaching and the goal of moving to repentance.[53] Subsequent episcopal teachings echoed this theme as did the sacred rhetorics. The fact that some of the greatest mendicant preachers of the day also became bishops propelled the idea further into the dioceses. The new orders of the sixteenth century would take up where the older orders left off. Along with the Capuchins, the Jesu-

---

[50] O'Malley, *Praise and Blame*, p. 124.

[51] Ibid.

[52] On the connection between purpose and rhetorical forms in preaching, see McGinness, pp. 55-60.

[53] "Preachers of the Word," Fifth Session, Chapter 2, Council of Trent,1546: "feed the people... by teaching them those things that are necessary for all to know in order to be saved, and by impressing upon them with briefness and plainness of speech the vices that they must avoid and the virtues that they must cultivate, in order that they may escape eternal punishment and obtain the glory of heaven," *The Canons and Decrees of the Council of Trent*, ed. H.J. Schroeder (Rockford, Ill: Tan Books, 1978), p. 26.

its in particular took their cues from the purpose of the older preaching orders.[54] It would find new expression in their preaching missions. Although the missions served a variety of purposes at times, Rusconi notes that Italian missions were "primarily...public penitential ceremonies."[55] The missions' goal was conversion, brought about by penitential preaching and reinforced by catechism, devotional practices, and the examples of the missionaries. Thus preaching was "at the center" of a number of ministries intended to produce changed lives.[56] While the forms developed, the intention did not change from the fifteenth century. That cyclic Lenten preaching done by the members of the orders became "even more central an element of public life" in the sixteenth and seventeenth centuries is strong evidence that the penitential nature of the preaching culture persisted.[57]

Content

While the goal of moving hearers to repentance put the focus on virtue and vice as the subjects of preaching, many others topics were also tied to it. Hardly a single topic is not discussed somewhere in the preaching sources. But most sermon topics can be categorized under one of two headings. They either point toward social transformation, harmony in community, or they point to spiritual transformation, harmony between God and society or the individual. Most sermons tend to cover both, relating them to specific vices and virtues, for they were seen as inherently bound together.

Scholars have long noted the rich social, economic, and political content of the late medieval Italian sermons of Bernardino and others. Arguing against violence and for charity toward the poor, connecting various crises and natural disasters to dissension be-

---

[54]   John W. O'Malley, *The First Jesuits* (Cambridge, Mass.: Harvard University Press, 1993), p. 94, makes the connection between the Jesuits and the friars. On p. 96, he notes that moving was the primary purpose of Jesuit preaching.

[55]   Rusconi in *Storia d'Italia* 4, p. 1007.

[56]   Giuseppe Orlandi, "La Missione Popolare: strutture e contentuti," in Martina e Dovere, p. 530.

[57]   Michele Miele, "Attese e direttive sulla predicazione in italia tra cinquecento e settecento," in Martina and Dovere, p. 84.

tween members of society and society and God, and admonishing family members of their responsibilities to each other and God were the stock of their preaching. Post-Tridentine preachers continued the message. Although early modern published sermons often edited out much of the specific social content, preaching was still associated with societal and spiritual restoration. Bishops like Paleotti and Musso preached their inaugural sermons in their dioceses on peace, much as the itinerant medieval friars would announce their presence in a place by preaching peace. In seventeenth-century Piedmont, violence tended to abate during the missions.[58] Sixteenth- and seventeenth-century preachers still railed against the uncharitable rich in specific detail. Even the Apostolic preachers, appointed to be the personal preachers to the papal court, preached vehemently against luxuriating in splendor while the poor starved. Narni told the court of Paul V that the testimony of the poor at the final judgment against its luxury would be "as gold and silver."[59] It was the crisis of plague in Milan that prompted Carlo Borromeo to begin preaching to his people. His nephew Federigo's ministry and preaching in time of plague would eventually be immortalized in a masterpiece of Italian literature, Manzoni's *Promessi sposi*. While vastly different in style, Panigarola's plague preaching carried the same penitential message as that of Carraciolo's 100 years earlier.[60]

While scholarship on Christianity and the family in early modern Italy has not kept pace with studies on Germany and England, sources indicate that there is ample material on the family in Italian preaching. Chavarria chronicles the developments in ecclesiastical attitudes toward women and children that are reflected in seventeenth- and eighteenth-century sermons. While most interested in observing change, she confirms the continuity of preaching on the family from the late Middle Ages to the modern period in at least one significant way. Preachers often encouraged youths to rebel

---

[58] Luigi Mezzadri, "Storiografia delle missioni," in Martina and Dovere, p. 467.

[59] Girolamo Narni, *Prediche fatte nel Palazzo Apostolico* (Rome: Stampa Vaticana, 1632), p. 244.

[60] I examined Panigarola's sermon on the plague ("La Peste") from *Prediche di Monsig. Revermo. Panigarola, vescovo d'Asti fatte dai lui straordinariamamente e fuor de'tempi quadragesimale* (Venice: Ciotti Senese, 1599); and Caracciolo's *Sermones de timore divinorum judiciorum* (Naples, 1473). See Zanette (n. 9) on Panigarola's and F. Borromeo's plague preaching.

against the values and desires of their elders. They reinforced their preaching with graphic stories of familial tragedy. The seventeenth-century preacher Stefano Pepe told of the suicide of a young girl forced into a convent without a vocation by her parents upon the marriage of her older sister. Her suicide note read, "See this child murder, mother, as your tribute to the devil."[61] More often, children were encouraged to defy their families by delaying marriage or taking up the spiritual life. Jesuit sermons, particularly, Chavarria reports, "painted a desolate picture of marriage and rich image of religious life."[62]

Looking back to late medieval preaching on the family, the focus on youth and admonition of parents is common. Bernardino often railed against parents, especially mothers, for their bad examples and encouragement of vices in their children.[63] In the sixteenth century, Seripando required that the children of Salerno attend his sermons, ordering the schoolmaster to see to it. Cesareo marks his "constant attention and reference... to youth" seeing it as major focus of Seripando's episcopal reform program. Once again, his preaching often puts children at odds with their parents, warning them against the "pernicious customs" of their elders: "The devil speaks in your ears and says, 'Do you want to be better than your elders? Do as they do.'"[64] In these cases, it appears that the preachers abandon the message of social harmony in favor of harmony between individuals and God. But according to Chavarria, what they attempt to do is to create a harmonious "uniform" society based on clerical values rather than the family values of the culture. Their goal was to transform the family into the "guarantor of subordination of its members to norms of comportment dictated by the clergy...."[65] She attributes this to Trent; however, Mormando finds the same goal in Bernardino. Paton finds that preachers less zealous than Bernardino were more willing to negotiate community morés.[66]

---

[61] Elisa Novi Chavarria, "Ideologia e comportamenti familiari nei predicatori italiani tra cinque e settecento. Tematiche e modelli," *Rivista storica italiana* 100.3 (1988), 691.

[62] Chavarria, p. 691.

[63] Mormando, pp. 135-7.

[64] Cesareo, pp. 17-18.

[65] Chavarria, p. 706.

[66] Paton, p. 332.

What we know is that Trent placed a new emphasis on uniformity of belief and practice that carried over into preaching ideals. This is reflected in the two Tridentine decrees on preaching, some seventeen years apart. The first decree's emphasis on preaching "vices and virtues" comes in the context of limiting evangelical preaching on scripture and doctrine. A new generation of leaders in 1563 focused on preaching as a tool for shoring up what remained of the Catholic fold.[67] Thus while in 1546, the council urged avoiding theological discussions in favor of moral preaching, at the end of the Council preaching was connected to teaching right belief as well as virtuous living.[68] Symptomatic of this new emphasis on doctrine in preaching was the publication in 1590 in Venice of the Roman catechism with a guide to its use for parish preaching. [69]

Sermons throughout the period covered the most pressing doctrinal issues of the age. Already before 1550, we find catechetical preaching with sermon cycles based on the Lord's Prayer, the Creeds, and other significant statements of the Faith. The Eucharist is a constant topic of early modern preaching. There is an abundance of doctrinal content, spelling out the difference between orthodoxy and heresy; but sermons still focus more on lifestyle and inspiration. Seripando's sermon cycles on the Creed and Lord's Prayer included explanation of sacramental doctrine. Cesareo describes the scene in which the bishop sits with the faithful standing around him while he teaches the faith to them in these "conversations." He argues, however, that Seripando was not just teaching; rather these sermons were designed to "foster a penitential spirit that would move the listener to lead a better Christian life."[70] It is typical to see in early modern sermons what begins as doctrinal discussion for the head move into a devotional message for the heart calling for repentance. Narni says repeatedly that it is more important to manifest the work of God's love in the world than to understand its "substance." The "most noble and necessary

---

[67] Rusconi, *Predicazione*, p. 286.
[68] Rusconi in Martina and Dovere, pp. 18-9. For example, the Decree on Reform, Twenty-fourth Session, Chapter 4, mandates preaching on Sundays and holidays, and is followed in Chapter 6 by the mandate to explain the Mass and festivals "in the vernacular tongue" during the services, Schroeder, pp. 195-8.
[69] Rusconi, *Predicazione*, p. 288.
[70] Cesareo, p. 4.

theme... for the Christian orator," according to Narni, is "penitence" because that is the theme "Christ first preached." [71]

Campagnola's study of early modern Lenten cycles confirms the
continued penitential emphasis. Confession and Eucharist receive
much attention, but vice preaching comes first.[72] In *Nota delle prediche
che sogliono farsi nelle nostre missioni*, the eighteenth-century Jesuit
Alfonso de Liguori summed up the topics that preachers were
obliged to discuss: "Mortal sin, death, judgment and hell, confession, Mary and prayer" are necessary, with "the mercy of God,
divine call, the importance of salvation, the vanity of temporal
goods..." also recommended. Sermons, Alfonso continued, should
move "hearers to a good confession and secure the fruit with a conversion of life" and should always end with a call to contrition.[73]
Paolo Segneri similarly advised other preachers to emphasize vice,
especially in the last half of the sermon. Jesuits used the *Spiritual
Exercises* of the first week as a structure for penitential preaching. In
1549, Landini wrote to Ignatius, "...in that meditation on the three
sins of death, judgment and hell, all the people tremble and he who
doesn't is well mad."[74] It was a new package for an old message.

Roberto Caracciolo had relied heavily on medieval scholastic
proof texts; and Musso began each of his forty sermons in his cycle
on the Creed with a classical illustration. Yet for Italian preachers
throughout this period, preaching was biblical. As Frederick
McGinness has observed about post-Tridentine preachers' attitude
toward scripture, "...every word and symbol there provided an illu-
minating and precise commentary on their own times and on human motivations."[75]

Early modern preachers drew their inspiration not only from the
humanist emphasis on scripture and the return *ad fontes* but also
from the apostolic ideal of the medieval orders. Further, they
tended to think of the relationship between the Bible and preaching
similarly. Fabris's examination of the use of scripture in preaching
after Trent found the abundance of scriptural proof texts, biblical
vocabulary and imagery, and the pervasive tendency to allegorize

---

[71] Narni, *Prediche*, pp. 252, 322.
[72] Campagnolo, p. 260.
[73] Cited in Orlandi, pp. 523-4
[74] Orlandi, p. 518.
[75] McGinness, p. 98.

scripture that also characterized medieval preaching.[76] There were some developments that reinforced the significance of the Bible in preaching. Preachers who abandoned the scholastic form often adapted the patristic homiletic form that structured sermons more closely on scripture. Trent reinforced the connection by relating its pronouncements on preaching and scripture.[77]

Even before Trent's conclusion, reform-minded bishops emphasized scripture as the content of preaching. Rusconi notes an understanding of reform from Giberti to Paleotti and Borromeo that included "...a style of preaching founded on explanation of Gospel."[78] Seripando held that bishops, above all, were to "pastor the sheep in the field of Holy Scripture."[79] But the basic interpretation of the content of the Bible and its relationship to preaching remained constant. Trent and the bishops emphasized the practical morality they found in the Gospel, over against the abstract doctrine of Pauline theology stressed by evangelicals. Bernardino, echoing Francis, had said that there was "no other gospel than that a man would...leave vice and follow virtue, fear punishment and love glory."[80] Preachers of the next two centuries would follow suit.

Spirit-Word-Rhetoric

To understand the relationship of preaching to scripture, however, we have to look to an underlying assumption held by Catholics in this period. Preaching, first and foremost, was only effective when inspired by the Spirit of love who speaks the Word of God through the preacher. While there is no systematic "theology of the Word" in early modern Catholic thought, this implicit understanding of the Word can be traced back at least to the preaching Orders. Franciscan preachers, from Anthony to Bernardino to Musso, described the relationship of Christ the Word to preaching in the

---

[76] Rinaldo Fabris, "Uso Della Bibbia nella predicazione dal concilio di Trento alla fine del settecento," Martina and Dovere, p. 79.

[77] Fabris, p. 50.

[78] Rusconi, *Storia d'Italia* 4, p. 95.

[79] Fabris, p. 51.

[80] Zelina Zafarana, "Bernardino nella Storia della predicazione popolare," *Bernardino predicatore nella società del suo tempo* (Todi: Accademia Tuderina, 1976), p. 57. From Sermon 28, Florence, 1524.

same way. The Spirit comes into the preacher, exciting him, he gives voice to the Word both in his speech and action, and through him, the Word reaches the hearer's heart more than ear, moving the hearer.[81]

The Word could be manifest in a variety of ways, including scripture and preaching. While Catholics spoke of preaching explaining scripture, they did not always seem to make a sequential connection between the Word in scripture and the Word in preaching. There were venues for teaching scripture, such as the sacred lectures that Jesuits and others conducted, but that was not the primary role of preaching. As Narni explained, "the immense fire of the ...love of God... goes out through various doors... with miracles, preaching, illumination of the blind, justification of sinners, multiplication of bread, resurrection of the dead and with so many other signs that were written."[82] Preaching, like miracles and scripture, was a means by which Christ's Word profoundly effected those it touched. Musso described the connection between various forms of the Word poetically:

> You want knowledge, behold the tongue;
> You want charity, behold the fire;
> Fire on tongues, tongues on fire;
> Wise love, amorous wisdom of the holy apostles;
> Spirit, fire, love are one thing only;
> Thus are tongue, sermon, doctrine the same thing.[83]

Italian preachers, however, were more likely to compare preaching to the Eucharist than to scripture, holding that they were the most effective vehicles of the Word. They understood preaching to do what the mass also did: make Christ present to bring the holy into the midst of humanity. As Narni put it, the preacher's job was "to manifest to the people the inventions of God."[84] The preachers, moved by the Spirit, put the holy before their hearers through their vivid words, actions, and images as surely as the priests' words did

---

[81] Norman, pp. 40-44.
[82] Narni, *Prediche*, p. 326.
[83] Musso cited in Norman, 44. From a Pentecost sermon preached in Bari, 1556, in *Prediche*, vol. 3 (Venice: Giolito, 1568), p. 296.
[84] Narni, *Prediche*, p. 256.

in the Mass. Like the words of the liturgy, the preacher's vocabulary was primarily biblical. Fabris's conclusion mentioned above confirms this understanding of the connection between scripture, preaching and the Word: the use of scripture was primarily by direct evocation through quotation or example. To explain scripture in preaching was to use it to make the divine accessible to people. That was the "miracle" they experienced. One admirer of Narni reported hearing these remarks among the crowd after Narni preached: "Did you hear God speak?" and "Every word is a sermon!"[85] Making the divine appear, however, also necessitated a use of language and style that helped elicit the Holy.

Language and Style

There is a continuous interest in questions involving language and rhetoric through the early modern period in Italy. As Giombi states, the period sees the "progressive affirming of the vernacular" for preaching.[86] The great preachers of the fifteenth century had mixed Latin and various forms of the vernacular in their preaching, an attempt to preserve the appropriate language of theology and scripture and to relate it to the people at the same time. Gradually Tuscan came to dominate as the pastoral need for "clearly comprehensible" preaching and desire for uniformity coupled with the growing aesthetic sense of Tuscan's superiority.[87] Although some questions about language persist into the seventeenth century, by the mid-sixteenth century, the focus shifted to style, that is, how to use the ancient Latin rhetorical models for contemporary Italian preaching. This would become the work of Italian sacred rhetoricians after Trent.

Cornelio Musso was the first according to contemporary observers to preach eloquently in Italian. Almost ten years before the close of Trent, a Paduan scholar, Bernardino Tomitano, composed a brief description of Musso's preaching. Tomitano declared Musso, "a master and model of ornament, who with both beautiful ar-

---

[85] Criscuolo, p. 393.
[86] Samuele Giombi, "Livelli di cultura nell'trattatistica sulla predicazione e l'eloquenza sacra del XVI secolo" in Besomi and Caruso, p. 251.
[87] Ibid., pp. 251-2.

rangement and infinite abundance of examples, knows how to explain the mysteries of God, the secrets of nature, and the precepts
of religion."[88] From the rest of Tomitano's description it becomes
clear that Musso's ability "to explain the mysteries" depended on
the vividness of his "abundance," which touched hearers by ap-
pealing to their senses and bringing subjects to life—manifesting the
sacred to them. Tomitano compared Musso's "word pictures"
(*ecphrasis*) to the paintings of the most skilled artists of the day:

> I do not know speaking truthfully, what Titian or what Michelangelo
> could do with the brush and colors on the canvasses to better depict
> bodies than he, who by the sublime spirits of his ingenuity makes appear
> to us with the senses the glory of that invisible life of heaven, which here
> through shadows and similitudes alone we judge.[89]

Reminiscent of the reports of Musso's effect in Venice, Tomitano
reported that he had seen crowds so caught up in Musso's preaching that they did not "just forget about eating, drinking, sitting,
walking, sleeping...but of even being alive in this life."[90] Musso's
rhetoric enabled his audience to look at the baby Jesus through
Simeon's eyes or to witness the frightful scene of the Second Coming. By manifesting the sacred models to them, he not only put the
Word before them, he called them to partake of it, by identifying
with the sacred models. In keeping with the affective devotional
model of late medieval Italy, Musso drew his hearers into the biblical scene as in the following example where Christ speaks directly
to them:

> *Tristis est anima mea usque ad mortem.* Behold his voice tired and sorrowful.
> *Tristis est anima mea usque ad mortem.* "My children, from this hour, I will
> know nothing but trouble and sorrow; all my joy is finished, no longer
> will I have any consolation, now begins my martyrdom, you won't see
> me happy ever again, my sorrows will continue to increase until I come
> thus to death. My body you see here will be lashed, these my eyes, these
> my ears, this my face, all this my flesh will be full of torture. Have pity
> on me, my children, because *Tristis est anima mea usque ad mortem....*" Oh,
> such words would move a tiger to pity and they don't move you, Chris-
> tians? And they don't move you, Christians? Feel, feel that sadness in

---

    [88] Bernardino Tomitano, *Discorso sopra l'eloquentia e l'artificio delle prediche, e del predicare
di Monsignor Cornelio Musso* (Venice, 1554), 2, cited in Norman, p. 57.
    [89] Tomitano, 3, cited in Norman, p. 63.
    [90] Ibid.

you, transfer that sorrow to your heart. Don't just understand, don't just meditate, feel it, experience it, taste it![91]

Musso was a skilled practitioner of what Deborah Shuger sees as a main focus for the sacred rhetorics that would come after him: how vivid style could convey the "impassionating divine word" from preachers to hearers.[92]

Musso would be the first of many; his protegé Panigarola would not only outshine Musso in fame but also exceed Musso's style with an even more luxuriant use of metaphor, allegory, and imagery. Yet the Council of Trent had already decreed that "briefness and plainness of speech" was the most suitable approach for preaching in 1546. Musso himself, in his discussions of preaching, would follow the teaching of his Franciscan heritage and Trent by advocating a simple style enlivened not by rhetoric but the Spirit alone. This ambivalence lingered into the late sixteenth century; although as the proliferation of sacred rhetorics shows the trend was "harvesting the fruits of Renaissance humanism for the mission of the Church."[93]

We know that sophisticated allegory, sumptuous language, and dramatic style were in high demand through the complaints of bishops about their popularity. The primary criticism stemmed from suspicion about preachers' and audiences' motives. Everyone from an orator of high style such as Musso to an advocate of plainness such as Filippo Neri (d. 1595) warned preachers about "searching in some pompous way [for] the vain applause of the people."[94] Entertainment-seeking audiences and egotistical preachers threatened to empty preaching of its transformative power. Some bishops, following Trent, sharply contrasted the simple moralistic preaching the Council called for with rhetoric. Borromeo thought "metaphorical style" to be as dangerous as "prophecy" and "subtle questions" and condemned the use of all three in preaching.[95]

---

[91] Cornelio Musso, *Prediche sopra il simbolo de gli apostoli, le due dilettioni, di Dio, e del prossimo, il sacro decalogo, e la passione di nostro Signor Gesu Christo....* 2 vols. (Venice: Giunti, 1590), vol. 2, p. 610. From a Passion Sermon preached in Rome, 1542.

[92] Deborah K. Shuger, *The Christian Grand Style* (Princeton, NJ: Princeton University Press, 1988), p. 108.

[93] McGinness, p. 60.

[94] Giombi, p. 260.

[95] Ibid., p. 266.

On the other hand Borromeo and others realized the need to capture the attention of hearers through imagery, example, and narrative to which they could relate. Borromeo held up Christ as a model, who used "metaphors, examples and similitudes from his context to make his disciples understand."[96] Bernardino and other popular preachers of the preceding century had done this by using the language of streets. This did not seem appropriate to late sixteenth-century leaders either. While the impetus to use an attractive style was similar, to enhance the manifestation of the Holy and transformation of the hearers, post-Tridentine leaders were too imbued with the taste for better language and uniformity to turn back. Borromeo warned preachers not to allow the "dignity" of preaching to lapse. In his *Instructiones praedicationis verbi Dei* of 1573, the bishop recommends "a *via media*" – neither the "refined" and "precious" language of elites or the coarseness of street dialect. He calls this "popular" preaching although, as Giombi points out, it is not the language of the people. Borromeo found agreement in fellow bishops and reformers like Neri.[97] Sacred rhetoricians also followed suit. In his *Divinus Orator* of 1595, the Jesuit Ludovico Carbone juxtaposed the genus he called the *barbarum dicendi* with the *obscurum dicendi*.[98] Preaching was to be "in the middle," an oft-used phrase in this period. That is, it should neither be the language of the elite nor the lowly, but a language defined by the Church.

Practice often showed how difficult this was to accomplish. The missionaries to the *mezzogiorno* and elsewhere succeeded to the extent that they were able to adapt their rhetorical training to local dialects and contexts. The rhetorically-trained, stylistically sophisticated preachers were in great demand. By the 1570s, even those bishops who idealized a simple type of catechetical sermon realized that there was a growing awareness and desire for the high style, pushed in part by published sermons, and thus sought out the help of the stars. Of course, this did not always go smoothly, as Borromeo and Panigarola discovered during the Visitation of 1583.

Borromeo and others worried that message, style, or language inappropriate to the audience's station might scandalize, confuse, or bore. Perhaps worse, they feared it might titillate, feeding an

---

[96] Ibid., p. 256.
[97] Ibid., pp. 256-257.
[98] Ibid., p. 258.

equation of preaching with entertainment and preachers as show-men who manifest affectation rather than the effects of God. Yet, given the popularity of preachers like Panigarola, could it have been that the passionate, abstract, melodious and vivid preaching gave the people what they wanted and what the churchmen thought they needed? Not entertainment or teaching but the mira-cle of divine transforming presence?

While Trent and the bishops warned about overly theatrical, stylized preaching, the shared assumption that preaching should move people through evocation of the divine pushed preaching in another direction more in keeping with the sensual, emotive trends in Eucharistic devotion. The simple gospel that the bishops stressed ironically provided "an inexhaustible arsenal of themes and ico-nographic subjects" that preachers could "visualize" in highly embellished speech. The apex of this sensibility is exemplified in "conceit" preaching, where the preacher builds his sermon around images rather than a narrative or teaching of scripture.[99] As the following example from Panigarola's Pentecost sermon illustrates, sight, sound, and movement announce the presence of the divine to the heart through the senses. Panigarola's skill for crafting rich imagery is based in the richness of the words and images of scrip-ture (in italics), which here, punctuate to and fro movement of holy "wind" (*vento*) and "fire" (*fuoco*) that swirl and flash before us. The ability to understand the language completely is not necessary for the hearer (or reader) to comprehend Panigarola's message:

> Impetuosissimo **vento**, e ardentissimo **fuoco**: **Vento** che e una delle piu ricche goioie del thesoro di Dio, *qui producit ventos de thesauris suis.* **Fuoco**, che e una delle piu acute spade della guardia di Dio; *ignis ante ipsum pracedet, et inflammabit in circuitu inimicos ejus.* **Vento**, che muove, muove le procelle in mare: *spiritus procellarum.* **Fuoco**, che abbrugia queste selve in terra; *ignis, qui comburit silvam.* **Vento** che dissipa la polve; *sicut pulvis quem proijcit ventus.* **Fuoco**, che consuma le spine; *sicut ignis in spinis .* **Vento**, che con l'humor infresca; *flabit spiritus ejus, et fluent aquae.* **Fuoco**, che con l'ardor riscaldar; *nec est, qui se abscondat a calore ejus.*[100]

---

[99] Rusconi, *Storia d'Italia* 4, pp. 1003-4.

[100] Francesco Panigarola, "Della venuta dello Spirito Sancto in vento e in fuoco … fatta in S. Pietro di Roman, l'anno 1589," in *Prediche*, f. 1.

The Ritual Character of the Event

Preaching was an event for people in early modern Italy. Diary accounts and other sources by lay people emphasize the event character of preaching; they focused more on what happened than on what was said. Recalling the account of Ochino's preaching that the Colonna entourage experienced after a dinner, we might be tempted to equate preaching culture with entertainment, as many churchmen feared the populace did. People were attracted to the spectacle of preaching. The reality of preaching's attraction, however, is more complex than its entertainment value, although its theatrical qualities were a big part of not only what drew the crowds but what moved them. To understand this, we must keep in mind what it meant to be religious in early modern Italy. Italian devotion was vivid and dramatic; it focused on imaginative identification with the holy models of scripture or the saints. It imaginatively recalled holy places. It involved either active participation in recreating the holy stories literally or active telling of and listening to the sacred stories. Both brought the sacred to life; and devotional practices often combined activity and active attention through reading or listening, viewing or meditating. The point was for people to encounter the holy and be transformed. It was not just theater. Discussing sacred drama, Narni explains that Christ "assists by his presence" those who recreate the events of his earthly life with devotion. Such presentations are "true, living, animated, spiritual" not "dead, fictive or material" as a scene in a play that only pretends.[101] Narni means that Italian devotion was not just theatrical, it was ritualistic. It attempted to bring devotees into the presence of the holy through reliving sacred narratives. The preaching event always had the potential to be miraculous.

Chief player in the sacred drama was the preacher. His gestures and actions, dress, demeanor and iconography, the language and rhetorical style that evoked sacred models all recalled a Jeremiah, Paul, or Francis. Even less overtly, however, preaching was ritualistic. For example, preachers and reports of preaching give very consistent accounts of the ritual actions of preachers. Paolo Segneri describes how a preacher should begin his sermon. Before rising to

---

[101]   Narni, *Prediche*, p. 328.

the pulpit, he was to bow and reverence the Sacrament or the crucifix; he then acknowledged the audience and raised his hands in
prayer to God. He bowed again to the cross and said the *Ave Maria*
loud enough for the audience to hear. Before rising, an assistant
removed his mantle. He rose into the pulpit, where he uncovered
his head before citing the theme and beginning the sermon.[102]
Other scholars have pointed out the significance of gesture and
protocol in the early modern world. Here, however, I read the activity primarily as a sequence designed to connect the Divine and
the people. The preacher approached the Divine himself, he
showed the people to the Divine and offered supplication on their
behalf to Christ and his Mother, inviting the hearers through his
voice to participate in summoning the Virgin. Having received the
Word for the people, he "revealed" it in a series of actions as he
neared the articulation of the Word from on high in the pulpit.
Narni, whose description is very similar to Segneri's, further advised preachers to heighten the intensity of the moment that the
Word was revealed by gradually raising the voice and hand together: "begin with a moderate voice…say four to six words, and
begin a little movement with the right hand, placing the index and
thumb together; then, with the other fingers separated and arched,
accompany the word with gesture."[103] Thus the preacher's voice
and gesture would rise gradually to reveal the Word just as the
preacher's body had.

Preachers also behaved ritualistically in carving out sacred space
from the mundane. In his missions, Paolo Segneri would sometimes
create a sacred spot for his preaching out of ordinary terrain. After
mass, he would lead the people in procession to a high spot in the
countryside "where he could be seen and heard well." He might
further define the space with an awning or a mat and, no doubt,
stake it out with the cross he would carry.[104] Having transformed an
ordinary hill into a holy mount, Segneri would begin his sermon.

While the preacher was central to the ritual, it depended on
communal effort as well. An account of Caracciolo's Lenten ser-

---

[102] Fabiano Giorgini, "Le Forme penitenziali durante le missioni popolari," in
Martina and Dovere, p. 124.

[103] Narni, *Modo*, in Criscuolo, p. 144.

[104] Bernadette Majorana, "Elementi Drammatici della predicazione missionaria:
Osservazioni su un caso gesuitico tra XVII e XVIII secolo," in Martina and Dovere,
p. 130.

mons in Perugia in 1448 illustrates how Caracciolo's message was
embodied in the community. Around 1500 people began showing
up two hours before the sermon in anticipation. Caracciolo led a
procession "of the whole town," which culminated in the sermon.
Caracciolo preached on "holy peace" and at the climax, held up a
crucifix. The diarist notes the crowd's reaction: "Everyone was crying and shouting for about half an hour: 'Jesus, have mercy.'"
Then, four citizens were chosen by the community to make a gesture of peace.[105] There are several elements in this preaching event
that are of significance and that persist in Italian preaching at least
into the eighteenth century. With cross, action, and Word, the
preacher in the image of the apostles shows Christ and calls the
community to repentance. It was essential, however, that the community participate. First the procession gathered the community
together, with each person in appropriate station. Its movement
around the town evoked the sacred by marking off the space for the
holy.

At the sign of the Cross, the sacred was manifest, and the entire
community gave the ritual response, crying for peace with God.
The four peacemakers further sanctified the community in their
reconciliation as ritual representatives of the entire town. Their activity marked the ritual resacralization of the community.

The use of the cross, as noted earlier, was especially important.
In ritual terms, it is a "hierophany," a manifestation of the divine
acknowledged as such in high ritual moments. This is clear in the
directions of later preachers. Narni, for one, advises other preachers when reaching the peak of reprehending vice, "to raise your
voices and to grab the Crucifix, embrace it and to touch the
wounds." Especially on important occasions or in trying to "convert prostitutes" or "reconcile enemies," Narni says that "it is good
to raise Christ from his place... to take him in hand and show
him."[106]

Ritual participation of the community in a variety of ways reinforced the message of the sermon by bringing it to life, especially at
the holiest times of year, where the most significant divine activities
are recalled. Caracciolo, again, "made a representation" after
preaching on Good Friday. A stage was erected in the center of the

105   Rusconi, *Predicazione*, pp. 192-4.
106   Narni, *Modo*, in Criscuolo, p. 144.

piazza. As the preacher held up the crucifix at the door of one church, the divine appeared at the door of another across the piazza: a barber acting as the naked Christ, with crown of thorns and carrying the cross, "his flesh flagellate and bleeding." As the Christ processed, "Mary" dressed in black and weeping appeared, then "Magdalen," "John," "Nicodemus," and "Joseph" in turn. As the holy figures come to the life, the crowd responds by wailing.[107]

Sacred representations continued to be a part of the preaching event, especially during Holy Week. Preachers like Musso who could put the scenes before his hearers' eyes with words alone also had recourse to enactment on special occasions. One of his Holy Week sermons in Rome contained an extended dialogue that recalled not only the sacred narrative but also linked it to classical tragedy. Christ, our "Julius Caesar" was eulogized by Musso's "Anthony," while the audience was thrust into the role of "Brutus" the betrayer. The highlight came when "Anthony" displayed the bloody tunic of "Caesar."[108]

The ritual embodiment of penance required by the sermons was acted out at its most extreme in physical discipline. While acknowledging that public penance combined with preaching had been a reality since at least the twelfth century in Italy, Giorgini states that it reached its apex in the Jesuit missions of the seventeenth century. In Segneri's *Pratica delle missioni*, he gives detailed directions to other Jesuits on how to organize processions, use images, and practice discipline in combination with preaching.[109] Bodily discipline was especially common in the missions of southern Italy. In some cases, everyone could participate according to his or her state in life. The Missionaries and some men would flagellate themselves, ashes on their heads, chains on their feet. Women might carry crosses on their shoulders. The children would wear small crowns of thorns and carry small crosses in hand.[110] In other instances, representatives acted on behalf of the whole community. After the sermon, the preacher would dismiss the women. Some men were separated out from the others in a part of the church. The preachers told this group to do penance for "their conversion and for that of hardened

---

[107]   Rusconi, *Predicazione*, p. 192.
[108]   Norman, p. 77.
[109]   Giorgini, p. 496 n. 8.
[110]   Giorgini, p. 496.

sinners of the country." The men would beat themselves and cry, "Pardon me, Lord, have mercy! Peace! Restitution!" During the flagellation the missionaries would pray and recite Psalms.[111]

Most often however, the preacher and his assistants were likely not only to bear the Word and embody it, but also to bear its consequences in their own bodies on behalf of the community. For Segneri it "wasn't enough" to ask for divine mercy, the preacher should also "satisfy justice" through bodily discipline; "the tongue alone is not enough, the hand is also needed...."[112] Preachers sometimes entered churches or *piazze* wearing chains or carrying a cross.[113] They sometimes beat themselves before preaching or at the high point of their sermons.[114] S. Alfonso, after preaching on dirty speech and blasphemy, dragged his tongue across the floor of the church to "clean up" these sins.[115]

Majorana argues that the use of such discipline, while obviously designed to work up the audience, is best explained as "ritual-drama." It "incarnates and makes manifest a most profound sense of the vocation and obedience of the missionary." This is, she continues, "a religious and social project that involves the laity as much as the clergy." The missionary takes on the cross quite literally and the people's response of horror, fascination, guilt, and repentance confirm the experience of the holy.[116] In this respect, the preacher acts ritualistically as "priest" mediating the divine through his own sacrifice.

Spiritual transformation was confirmed ritualistically in preaching and associated devotions and in the liturgies and sacraments of the Church. For early modern Italians, preaching and the sacraments of confession and the Eucharist were intricately connected, even when preaching took place outside of the liturgical setting. The connection between preaching and confession is obvious – it is at the root of the purpose and content of preaching and evidenced in the penitential ritual activities that so often accompany preaching.

Preaching and the Eucharist became increasingly connected in the early modern period as Catholic Eucharistic piety flourished.

---

[111] Giorgini, p. 495.
[112] Ibid., p. 499.
[113] Ibid., p. 494.
[114] Majorana, pp. 130-1.
[115] Giorgini, p. 495.
[116] Majorana, p. 150.

Eucharistic doctrine and devotion were often discussed in sermons, but the connection goes further. Preaching and adoration of the Eucharist are parallel rituals that manifest the holy, often in the same liturgy. This connection is nowhere more vivid than in the *quarant'ore* or "Forty Hours" preaching performed especially by Jesuits and Capuchins. The sanctified Host was displayed for continual public adoration for forty days, while preachers exhorted almost non-stop, spelling each other in turn.[117]

An example cited by Frederick McGinness illustrates the relationship between devotion to the Eucharist and preaching. Advertising for the *quarant'ore* held in 1608 at San Lorenzo in Damaso in Rome read, "When all are kneeling and the doors are closed, the music will begin in order to elevate the souls to God. Then Father Fedele will deliver the sermon, and it will serve as a mediator between the soul and God, in order to reconcile everyone with His Divine Majesty; and each will be disposed as God our Lord will inspire."[118] The sermon, like the Eucharist, mediates the Word to the soul.

Intense drama, powered by sounds, sights, and motions that "elevate the soul" were essential to an experience of the Holy in preaching or the Eucharist in Baroque Italy. Emotive ritual practice was not new with the Baroque, but found new forms, more intense and systematized (ritualized) than earlier. This was true for the development of the preaching missions. The papal court exhibited similar changes. O'Malley noted that the developments in sacred rhetoric in the Renaissance courts paralleled a "progressive liturgical solemnization" there.[119] Different sensibilities are found at the Baroque court, but developments in preaching and liturgy continued to parallel each other. Both made manifest the ideology of a new Roman Catholicism that glorified order and reveled in dramatic expression.[120] The papal court was a "reflection and image of the heavenly court."[121] The liturgical practices and preaching there were designed to reflect it. That is, they serve as "paradigmatic models" of the sacred for Catholics everywhere.

---

[117] O'Malley, *First Jesuits*, p. 92.
[118] McGinness, pp. 84-5.
[119] O'Malley, *Praise and Blame*, p. 10.
[120] See McGinness, esp. Chapter 4, pp. 87-91, on the relationship of preaching and liturgy to the Baroque and Catholic ideology.
[121] O'Malley, *Praise and Blame*, p. 10.

While Baroque sensibilities were not unique to Italian preaching, the flamboyant style was often credited to Italians. In the north, a theatrical and highly emotive mission preaching style, known as the "Italian method," was attributed to Italian Jesuits and considered highly effective. It was not for everyone, however. A papal diarist in the early seventeenth century recorded the reaction of some French courtiers at the apostolic court as they listened for the first time to a famous Italian preacher. They "laughed" at his preaching, particularly at his "exaggerated" actions and facial expressions.[122] Audiences in Italy expected such exaggeration. Whether they were elites on the cutting edge of Baroque culture or not, they expected the extraordinary in-breaking of the holy and assumed it came in glorious intensity.

Audience

Preaching was a ritual event that involved the active participation of audience as well as preacher in the evocation of the holy through dramatic expression. Yet scholars have often complained that our sources for preaching, especially sermons, tell us little about real people and real social situations. At best, they tell us what a clerical elite thought about lay society. Between the "homogenization" of preaching as a tool for Catholic uniformity and the "literaturizing" of it, some scholars believe that published sermons after Trent are devoid of evidence of real life.[123] While often disappointing as sources of social history, sermons are excellent sources of lived religion when approached cautiously. They are the scripts of sacred drama. They were intended not to reveal "facts" about daily life but rather to make present the "truth" through sacred narrative. They illustrate sacred roles both directly and indirectly for the actors – audiences and preachers – who came to preaching events expecting to play their parts. Preachers portrayed themselves as "Isaiahs" wailing against the Israelites; audiences were to respond in kind to the "prophets" by playing the part of the errant chosen. The playwright in this case was also the star; the drama only worked, however, when all the actors were able to grasp their parts

---

[122] Campagnolo, p. 266.
[123] Delcorno, "Forme," p. 291.

and were willing to play them. The people had to be convinced to see themselves in their roles; they had to be moved to collaborate with the preacher and with the Word. Thus sermons had to provide appropriate meaning-making models; sacred roles had to overlap with social roles. In a highly stratified society, this meant that preachers had to play to the audiences within the audience. For early modern Italian preachers, reaching their audience*s* and communicating with them appropriately was a primary and problematic concern for which variant strategies were developed. This is revealed in discussions about preaching and in the structure of sermons.

Medieval sermons explicitly addressed various states of society; the *artes* advised preachers how to tell different types of people about the same subjects. While the Latin *sermo modernus* was geared to a learned and/or clerical audience, popular preaching used a mix of both Latin and vernacular and a modified form and style coupled with practical examples. Giombi notes that this is "a strong signal of compromise with local parlance."[124] It also means, however, that elites and people were sent not the same message with different words, but rather, different messages.

We have already discussed the linguistic and stylistic developments that kept this issue alive in the early modern period. The divisions of Christendom only made the matter more pressing and complex. In 1541, Contarini composed his brief *Instructio pro praedicatoribus* which advocated simple moral preaching for the people while the "difficulties of faith" might be discussed before the educated and religious elite. The idea of different messages for different levels of society came to be known as the "double truth" strategy.[125] Contarini's ideas on preaching reflect pressing concerns about the spread of Protestant ideas. He advised against discussing theologically hot issues at all before those who might be confused by them, as Trent would two decades later.[126]

By the middle of the century, however, most of those concerned with preaching spoke in terms of one message preached with different styles appropriate for particular audiences. After Trent, the basic tenets of Catholic orthodoxy as well as piety and moral reform

---

[124] Giombi, p. 250.
[125] Rusconi, *Storia d'Italia* 4, pp. 988-90.
[126] Houdon, p. 466.

were to be preached to all; yet all concerned knew that also meant preaching for a variety of audience levels. Narni advised other preachers to balance attracting the educated among the audience with speaking in such a way that the simple might "carry away most of the sermon" for further "contemplation" at home.[127]

While Narni stressed balance, Cardinal Borromeo's preaching ideal centered on the development of parish preaching by those who knew the local population rather than the "canned" preaching of itinerants who too often spoke over their heads. In his *Instructione* of 1573, he stressed "knowing the environment, local traditions, and character of the inhabitants" as well as "age, social condition and intellectual preparation" of hearers. Only through attention to such particulars and adjusting speech accordingly would the preacher be successful. Among his specific instructions is the avoidance of Latin citations when preaching to peasants.[128] As the Jesuit Luigi Giuglari wrote in the second half of the seventeenth century, "the quality of who hears prescribes the of style of the one who speaks." The same truth he spoke of "gravely" to his prince, he embellished in another manner for the people.[129]

Preachers and preaching theorists often discussed the connections between style of preaching, location, and occasion. Delcorno cites two examples. Panigarola in *Il Predicatore* distinguished among a sermon in a great pulpit, the familiar homily that could be made anywhere and other types of preaching. High style was appropriate only in high places and for particularly solemn occasions such as the Passion.[130] Different types of preaching designated by different names also indicate different audiences. Giorlamo Comboni di Salo' is called "*Predicatore*" in the title of his 1622 sermon collection; but he qualified the address by saying that "he has as much regard for the simple as the learned... and thus each of his "*prediche*" was crafted so that it could be divided into three "*sermoni*," making length a factor that separated types of audiences as well.[131]

Giombi also cites two relevant examples. Botero (d. 1617) described two ways of preaching, which he called "Advent and Lent"

---

[127] Narni, *Modo*, in Criscuolo, p. 139.
[128] Ibid., pp. 264-5.
[129] Ibid., p. 259.
[130] Delcorno, "Forme," p. 277.
[131] Ibid.," p. 278.

modes. The "Advent" preaching style was for urban populations with a relatively educated elite and consisted of "high oratory" spoken in "Tuscan." "Lent" preaching was for rural peasants, was plain, and used local dialect.[132] The Franciscan Luca Baglione, in the earliest of the Italian preaching treatises, divided the classical goals of preaching by audience types. "Nobles" and "the middle" are to be "delighted" first. Only then should preachers "turn to the others." As long as the nobles stay and approve, he reasons, the lowly will remain.[133] Preaching was to include mixed messages for mixed audiences with primary attention to those of higher social status. Some significant assumptions are reflected here. First, change must take place at the top first. Second, the lower classes might come to preaching to be in the presence not only of the divine but also of the local gods; they might stay as much out of deference to nobles as the divine.

Preaching in different ways, using different styles in different locations, equating length of sermon with level of audience, and adjusting the purpose according to audience type inevitably meant that different messages were transmitted to different audiences. Whether bishops, preachers, and theorists admitted it or not, the truth was "double." Theory and practice were often at odds.

Miele argues that Borromeo and Paleotti exhorted their priests to a "biblical-catechetical-pastoral" style of preaching consistent with the evangelical preaching advocated earlier by Giberti and Seripando and opposed Contarini's notion of two types of preaching for different audiences.[134] Yet Paleotti's own efforts reflect mixed feelings about mixed messages. In his synod in 1569, he emphasized the Tridentine injunction to preach practical matters of lifestyle and simple doctrine and to "accommodate hearers, who mostly cannot understand high and difficult things."[135] Prodi tells us that Paleotti himself spent a great portion of his year in visitation accompanied by preaching and also preached in his cathedral. In the cathedral, he preached in Latin from written texts with specific source citations. Paleotti defended the use of Latin in sermons, ac-

---

[132] Giombi, p. 269.

[133] Ibid, p. 270. Luca Baglione, *L'arte di predicare* (Venice, 1562).

[134] Michele Miele, "Attese e direttive sulla predicazione in italia tra cinquecento e settecento," in Martina and Dovere, p. 94.

[135] Prodi, *Paleotti*, vol. 2, p. 79.

cording to the capacities of hearers and circumstances. He connected this to content. Classical Latin, he said, was the language of
the learned for "difficult and high things" which ought to be excluded from vernacular.[136] In his visitation sermons, however, he
"treats scripture in the language of daily life," using examples from
agriculture and speaking from notes without citations.[137] According
to Prodi, Paleotti preached as he conducted his pastoral ministry:
he made contacts with people not as "uniform sheep" but in "determined categories of society."[138] Paleotti's directions for the implementation of Tridentine rules on marriage illustrate this further.
The regulations are accompanied by a collection of twenty model
sermons in Italian, by various authors of varying styles and difficulty. As the introduction explains

> And because people to whom one must preach vary, poor, rich, learned,
> unlearned, noble, ignoble, those in cities and those in the country, there-
> fore, here are various sorts [of sermons] together, some doctrinal, some
> moral, some more familiar than others, some longer and some shorter:
> for the purpose that from one banquet full of various foods anyone can
> choose the one that best suits the subjects to whom he must speak....[139]

The complexity of the preacher's job becomes much more apparent as we observe two of the greatest preachers of the period struggle to reach a multiplicity of audiences in their sermons. Cornelio
Musso's sermons are alive with direct address to his hearers. In a
random sample of twenty sermons from throughout his career,
there were approximately three direct addresses per page. Other
devices such as constant use of the imperative and imaginary dialogues or monologues also help make Musso's sermons, even in
print, "conversations," as he most commonly referred to them.

While he uses certain addresses for his entire audience, most
commonly "*ascoltanti*" (hearers) and "*christiani*," Musso speaks first
to a high audience; in the twenty sermons that I have charted, he
directly addresses nobles 128 times. Indirect evidence also affirms
his special interest in reaching the wealthiest, most powerful, and

---

136 Giombi, p. 254; Prodi, *Paleotti*, vol. 2, pp. 89-90.
137 Prodi, *Paleotti*, vol. 2, p. 110.
138 Ibid., p. 85.
139 Introduction, *Del Sacramento del matrimonio avvertimenti alli Reverendi Curati con la gionta di varii sermoni da potersi usare nella celebratione de delli matrimonii. Di ordine di Monsignor illusmo. e Rever. Cardinal Paleotti Arcivescovo di Bologna* (Venice: Angelieri, 1607).

best educated. His examples and analogies reflect the special interests of the upper classes. Yet there is other evidence that shows his
awareness and concern about having a little something for everyone. Musso never preaches only to the learned. Typically, he speaks
first to them and then changes his focus by saying, "I don't want to
prove or clarify this anymore, *dotti*."[140] He then moves on to simpler
matters, exhortation, and addresses to "Christians" or "Hearers"
in general.

Audience is the overarching structural factor in Musso's preaching, influencing both form and content. In the second sermon of a
Lenten cycle that he preached in Rome in 1539, Musso divides the
sermon equally between clergy and laity.[141] The first half of the sermon is a mini-guide to preaching intended for the clergy. The second is a virtues-and-vices mini-sermon preached on the text of the
day. But it was not always the people who got the fire and brimstone. In a Saturday sermon on the Canticle of the Virgin, he nar-
rated the text and then urged the Roman people to praise God in
imitation of the Virgin. Then, the intention changed, based on the
audience and the text of the day, Mark 6, the story of Jesus calming
the storm: "Clerics, prelates, priests, I say to you that the ship of
Christ is in peril because of your bad lives." [142]

As this illustrates, the use of scripture and biblical interpretation
was related to the preacher's audience dilemma. Seripando, noting
that his people had trouble understanding Paul, shifted to the
"words that came out of Christ's own mouth."[143] Federigo Borromeo warned about the use of biblical allegory for the simple.[144]
But theory and practice did not always agree. Paolo Segneri is a
case in point. In the preface to his Lent sermons of 1642 preached
in Venice, Segneri acknowledged that the "great people" prefer
"brilliant and subtle" interpretations, yet he says that he will preach
"imitating Jesus" with the literal sense for the people. Fabris notes,
however, that while Segneri's sermons are in a "simple style," he
employs allegory.[145]

---

[140] For example, in *Simbolo*, pp. 73 and 79.
[141] Cornelio Musso, *Delle prediche quaresimali…sopra l'epistole e sopra l'vangeli corrente per i giorni di quaresima* (Venice: Giunti, 1586), vol. 1, pp. 68-82.
[142] Musso, *Quaresimale*, vol. 1, pp. 98-112.
[143] Fabris, p. 51.
[144] Giombi, pp. 264-5.
[145] Fabris, p. 67.

Fabris's study of the use of scripture in early modern Italian preaching reveals that the use of complex allegory was common. He walks carefully through Musso's 1550 sermon to the Murati nuns of Florence, examining his use of scripture and observing that the entire sermon is permeated with biblical "expressions and figures."[146] While he notes that Musso primarily employs the Pauline text in the first part of the sermon and the Gospel and Old Testament readings in the second, Fabris overlooks Musso's use of these texts to structure the parts of his sermon for different audiences. Musso acknowledges the nuns in the first two parts, which contain complex allegories and multiple references to classical texts; but his message to them only comes with his simpler narrative treatment of the gospel story in the third part of the sermon. The nuns more often function as object lessons, even when he "addresses" them. As Musso told them, they teach "more by example than he can by words."[147] Addressing them, he uses their example to reach to another audience, the noble and educated Florentine laity present.

Musso's earliest published sermon, preached late in Advent in 1530 in Padua, illustrates more explicitly his attention to different audiences. In the first part of the sermon, Musso discusses theological points abstracted from the Gospel of the day, John 1:1, but sets out his main purpose as "singing," setting the appropriate mood for the occasion. In the second part, however, he explains to the scholars of Padua why he used the John text rather than the lesson from Isaiah 9 as his theme: "Because I find myself today in this Athens, I want to begin by the platonic method, from things intelligible and then descend to the sensible." John, he continued, wrote in style appropriate to convince "those heretics schooled in the philosophy of the day."[148] He goes on to argue about the nature of the Trinity and divine incarnation, employing complex argument and allegory. He ends the section by asking the learned to "cede to my dear people, who expect to hear about the birth of our Christ."[149] The third

---

[146] Fabris, p. 52.

[147] Cornelio Musso, "Prediche fatta in Firenze nella chiesa delle Murate... sopra l'evangelo delli due discepoli che andavano in Emaus. Nelle quale se tratta delle allegrezze del christiano," *Prediche*, vol. 1 (Venice: Giolito, 1556), pp. 226-78. Quotation, p. 239.

[148] Cornelio Musso, "Predica... della Natività," *Prediche*, vol.4 (Venice: Giolito, 1568), pp. 50-103. Quotations, pp. 62 and 64.

[149] Musso, *Prediche*, vol. 4, p. 73.

part of the sermon then takes off from the Lucan account of the nativity into a literal narrative that weaves the history of Padua with the Roman Empire under Augustus and the kingdom of Christ. He rounds it off with a call to praise as in the beginning. Thus his overall purpose is to set a mood of praise, but he does so in different ways, illustrated with different sources for the learned and unlearned.

Musso's protegé Panigarola also attempted to address different audiences by varying biblical usage. Fabris noted that Panigarola's sermon on the marriage at Cana, preached at St. Peter's in 1586, is structured on the division of the Gospel text into two parts. The first part of the sermon discusses Jesus' words to his mother while the second treats the allegorical sense of the marriage.[150] Panigarola, like Musso, may be accommodating different audiences. In the proem, Panigarola addresses two types of hearers: "Illustrious Lords" and "you who hear me." In the first part of the sermon, he addresses both audiences twice. When he addresses "hearers," he asks simple questions about the water-turned-wine: "You recall, hearers, how things were just after the Israelites came out of Egypt? You recall that they needed or made signs?" His question to the learned is more sophisticated: "But what is it, oh learned ones, that makes nature change essential form in the same material...?" [151] Panigarola continued to build a complex allegory with multiple references to the church fathers and Latin quotations, sometimes following the direct exegesis of Augustine.

Panigarola changed subjects and main audience in the second part, noting that scripture provided something for everyone (in contrast to the difficult interpretation he pursued previously):

> There is no doubt hearers that in whatever state you are, even joined to sin, one can hope for salvation: if you want soldiers saved and dear to God, the Centurion was a soldier; if artisans and fishers, there were many apostles and Paul himself who worked with his hands. If rich, rich was Abraham; if poor, poor was Lazarus...if young, Daniel; if old, Melchizedek, if a converted sinner, the thief; if a penitent woman, Magdalen. But in the end, all are reduced to three states: virgins, married and widows... and to give hope to all those states that in anyone of them one can find health: for the virgins, in the virgin birth, for the

---

[150] Fabris, p. 53.
[151] Francesco Panigarola, "Prediche della utilitá delle nozze di Cana Galilee...," *Prediche*, pp. 153-4.

widow, from Anna who gave praise and for the married, today, at the marriage one wants to find it.[152]

Panigarola continues with his message to the "married," addressing the "*Romani,*" but this part is only one-third as long as the first. He rounds out the message as his teacher Musso did: "What do you say men? What do you say, women? Do you want to be saved? Do you want heaven?… Then obey the commandments of God; serve his precepts, cooperate with your free will, so that... finally you will be changed... from water to wine."[153]

Musso and Panigarola, praised and blamed for highly sophisticated styles and language thought only appropriate for connoisseurs by some, provided mixed messages for mixed audiences through structure and biblical interpretation while capturing and holding attention with vivid style. People generally stood through preaching. Sermons could be quite long and were divided into parts (often with breaks in between). There were other things to catch hearers' attentions (often complained about by preachers). The constant repetition, lyrical phrases, and direct addresses in early modern preaching indicate not just stylistic preference but pastoral necessity. Preachers had to hold an audience's attention; they also had to jar it at significant times. Shouting when excoriating vice, high drama at pivotal points, the vivid narrative, as well as the visible message embodied by the preacher himself were bound to command the attention of everyone. There were things that attracted everyone, but there were also messages tailored more particularly.

Discerning target audiences in early modern sermons can be complicated. Audience address is not always a clear indicator, as in the example of Musso's sermon "to" the Murate nuns. Another "audience" that is more often object than subject is the poor. Zafarana found that medieval preachers such as Giacomo della Marca treated the poor cursorily while focusing on merchants and nobles in detail.[154] Early modern preaching, at least in the urban centers, seldom contained direct address to the poor. In all of Musso's preaching, for example, the poor are addressed directly only twice. When they appear in sermons, they are usually used as

---

[152] Panigarola, *Prediche*, pp. 158-9.
[153] Ibid., p. 160.
[154] Zelina Zafarana, "Predicazione francescana ai laici," in Capitani et al., p. 183.

living indictments of the rich and spurs to their spiritual advancement.

Preaching: Medium of Exchange or Social Control?

Preachers, Tridentine regulation, and the bishops were involved in the production of preaching. Was the script simply written for lay people who heard the sermons? Or, did they have a hand in production of the preaching event as well? Preachers were concerned with reaching various audiences; did sermons reflect only clerical perceptions of the needs of the laity or did they reflect the perceptions of audiences as well? I have already noted the importance of laity in the ritual event of preaching as well as the demands of the lay market for published sermons. Many scholars, however, have seen preaching primarily as a tool of social control that colored society in light of ecclesiastical ideals. "The ultimate and unspoken goal of Bernardino's public mission, according to Mormando, "was the furtherance of the great medieval dream of a total Christian theocracy, that morally and socially homogeneous society in which Christian doctrine had the first and final word."[155]

The dream of social hegemony was never realized through preaching because, as a medium of communication, it involved exchange. Even in the attempt to get across a message aimed at eliminating popular culture, Bernardino had to use its language, stories, and shared assumptions. In the process, the values reflected in these media were transmitted as well as disputed. Further, Bernardino and other preachers were also part of that culture. Paton's study of preaching in late medieval Siena concluded that preaching involved two-way "traffic" in culture and ethics. Preachers "served to popularize and vernacularize the learned Latin tradition... while at the same time imbibing aspects of lay and civic culture and incorporating them into their message." Preaching was a "catalyst" by which values were "transmitted" as well as "transferred."[156] Preachers stood in both worlds. Bernardino helped to push market values while railing against them because he used the *lingua franca* of a market society; he shared it with his audience.

---

[155] Mormando, pp. 47-8.
[156] Paton, p. 84.

Paton has also shown how looking only at the most famous
preachers might skew our understanding of preaching. The likes of
Bernardino and Savonarola stood out in part because they were
extreme. They may have appeared that way to many of their colleagues as well. "Many preachers," she argues, "were willing to
accommodate social practices if they were not seen to be overtly
harmful to the common good." On familiar topics such as prodigal-
ity and vanity, the sermons she examined show that "mendicant
teaching on any given topic was less fixed and homogenous than is
commonly supposed." Thus people may have been left to choose
among the various opinions of the friars and others.[157]

Mormando and Paton agree about the extremity of Bernardino's
preaching. Mormando draws a poignant picture of a man driven
by fear and personal discipline to exaggerated notions of piety.
Paton suggests that while friars generally were concerned with social issues such as "maintaining peace, justice and goodwill in the
community," extremists such as Bernardino attempted to effect "a
penitential consciousness akin to their own" in everyone.[158] For
Bernardino, this morality extended to social issues that the Church
hierarchy of the time showed little concern for, such as witchcraft.[159]

Medievalists have made more progress on the idea of exchange
than those who study early modern preaching. Scholars have argued that sixteenth-century "counter-reform" preaching, and especially post-Tridentine preaching, shared a vision of cultural hegemony similar to Bernardino's; only now, vernacular preaching was
part of the institutional machinery being developed by the church
hierarchy to accomplish it. In Bernardino's day, it had involved a
mixed language that reflected cultural exchange. Coletti argues that
the vernacular used in early modern preaching was not a language
of two-way communication that encouraged give and take; it was
a "literary" one, spoken by preachers but not by the people. Thus,
it replaced the "mediating" function of preaching with "the art of
verbal manipulation" that intended not so much "to communicate
but to move." At the same time, Trent and subsequent episcopal
injunctions against preaching on subtle doctrines before the people

157 Ibid., pp. 332-3.
158 Ibid., p. 333.
159 Mormando, p. 225.

also discouraged thinking. Baroque preaching became "a spectacle of language" where words might evoke emotion but did not supply meaning.[160] What Coletti's argument misses is the shared assumptions of a highly ritualized Baroque culture that expressed meaning on a variety of levels. Reacting to social control theories of Delumeau and Ginzburg, Mezzadri reminds us that even attempts at social control involved positive exchange and did not always clash with popular culture. While the theatricality of the mission preaching could be interpreted simply as a manipulative tool, he argues that the missions also "were an injection of hope on a closed and uncertain horizon."[161] People in the poorest regions of Italy may have taken the transformative rituals and messages of preaching missions to heart in ways that the missionaries intended, but more likely, they took what they could translate most directly to their experiences and needs while rejecting, compromising, or ignoring the rest once the preaching event concluded. As Mario Iadanza comments, the missions were "great collective rite(s) expressing a community and a culture."[162]

The most obvious relationship of preaching to social control was its connection to the Inquisition. Romeo has found, however, that preachers were "little disposed or little prepared" to collaborate with the Holy Office against lay people. In early modern Italy, preachers themselves were more likely to be accused of heresy than accusers. Lay people rarely accused clergy. Accusations tended to come from the clergy, especially the professional preachers, against other professional preachers (itinerants), usually on charges of unorthodox or dangerous theological preaching.[163]

Scholars of popular culture have repeatedly bemoaned the lack of "folk elements" in early modern preaching, attributing this to the "suspicion of every lay expression of culture not under ecclesiastical control and thus susceptible to becom[ing] a vehicle for heresy" and fear of the Holy Office.[164] Precisely because of that fear, however, new preaching aids appear that deal with popular culture. The Capuchin Valerio da Venezia, for example, produced *Prato*

---

[160] Colletti cited in Giombi, p. 258.
[161] Luigi Mezzadri, "Storiografia delle missioni," in Martina and Dovere, p. 465.
[162] Iadanza cited in Mezzadri, p. 483.
[163] Giovanni Romeo, "Predicazione e inquisizione in Italia dal Conciol di Trento alla prima meta del seicento," in Martina and Dovere, p. 235.
[164] Delcorno, "Forme," p. 291.

Fiorito in 1606, which would become one of the great market suc-
cesses of religious literature in seventeenth-century Italy. The *Prato*
focuses in part on magic, witchcraft, and possession and is based on
contemporary sources as well as traditional material. Works like this
reflect sharing and cultural exchange, mixing clerical adaptation
and invention with popular belief and practice.[165]An example of
this complex sharing can be seen in Panigarola's preaching on heresy from a sermon of 1582: "When you see a layman, a merchant,
an artisan, a woman who want to interpret scripture, flee as if it
were a fire." Panigarola plays on common notions of "monstrous
inversions" of the social order to build his argument about unau-
thorized teaching. The climax he employs uses the most shocking
inversion of all—the woman interpreting scripture usurps the leadership of the church![166]

Lay culture and clerical accommodation to it could be repressed
by Post-Tridentine attempts at social control. In 1595 Giovan
Battista Greco was arrested for "dirty speech" in his preaching at
the church of Santa Maria dei Meschini. According to witnesses,
Greco preached that women were permitted to communicate after
having sex with their husbands; in fact, "because holy matrimony
is a sacrament" itself, he reasoned that a woman might take the
sacrament as many times as she had experienced intercourse.
Greco had been a popular preacher in the Naples area for seventeen years; no doubt such preaching pleased many of his people.
Many parish preachers like Greco may have held opinions more in
keeping with their people and influenced by their experiences with
people than with the positions of the higher-ups in the Church.
Unlike the professional itinerants who were most often accused of
doctrinal errors, when parish preachers were accused, the accusations tended to center on unorthodox moral preaching related to
everyday issues like sexual practice. Greco's preaching career ended
when the archbishop intervened, silencing this expression of accommodation with his people.[167]

It is also important to remember however, that lay people often
wanted to accommodate the Church because they understood its
teachings to be of central importance to their well-being. While

---

[165] Ibid., p. 300.
[166] Ibid., pp. 297-8.
[167] Romeo, pp. 240-1.

preaching was chiefly an experience of action and emotion, people did also listen to the theological content, and tried to make sense of it for themselves. There are reports of common people debating theological positions, of shoemakers, tanners, and washerwomen discussing theological points made in sermons even long after the preacher had moved on to another locale. Romeo gives the example of a group of Neapolitan women returning from church who stopped a priest they recognized in the street to ask about the upsetting words they had just heard in the sermon of a Capuchin preacher. They reported: "We poor people can't be saved because the Padre preacher said that whoever does not know the Holy Trinity cannot be saved."[168] Romeo cites this story as an example of how little lay people might have understood of essential church doctrine being preached. But is it not also an example of lay initiative in theological matters? The women were skeptical about what they heard from the preacher. They wanted to believe in the possibility of their own salvation. Thus, they turned to another official of the church to clarify their theological dilemma.

It is difficult to know the effect of preaching, especially over the long term. But one example brings home the legacy of early modern preaching in Italy and the power of lay initiative. Boaga reports that when he visited Sardinia in 1964, he was surprised to find a Carmelite Marian confraternity there that was not recognized by the order. He discovered that it had been founded by Carmelite missionaries who had been there in 1636, after which they discontinued their ministry. The confraternity had kept going, the Marian devotions being passed orally among the laity, all those years.[169] Giuseppe De Rosa's definition of popular culture is helpful here: "In traditional Catholic countries, popular religion is not religion different from the religion of the church, but the religion of the church seen and practiced by the Christian people."[170]

---

[168] Ibid., p. 238.
[169] Emmanuele Boaga, "Il Frate predicatore in Italia tra cinquecento e settecento: il caso dei carmelitani," in Martina and Dovere, pp. 230-1.
[170] Cited in Mezzadri, p. 482.

Was the Preaching Culture a Culture of Fear?

One of the issues related to social control that has occupied historians of early modern preaching in the last few years has been
whether preaching propagated a "culture of fear." Italian preachers, with their dramatic style, give plenty of evidence for what has
come to be called the "Delumeau thesis." Indeed, how well a
preacher could scare his audience appears to be one of the measures of his effectiveness. The greats of the fifteenth century were
known for their abilities to blend fear of judgment and hell with the
social conditions of their hearers to provoke change through fear.
At the other end of our period, the missionaries remained consistent with the medieval friars' agenda. The Lazzarists held that,
"more fear than love" should be preached. Redemptorists held that
their first task in transformation was "to make them feel the terror
of judgment."[171]

If the "Delumeau thesis" is correct, why? First, fearful preaching reflects the preachers' perceptions of society and of themselves.
Mormando underlines how real the power of the devil was for
Bernardino. Carlo Borromeo, who recommended that his preachers "exaggerate the torments of hell," understood himself to be in
a battle with Satan.[172] In the 1583 visitation, he declared that his
purpose was to "reconquer" the place that has been taken by the
devil. The signs were clear to him: heresy, card playing, dancing,
drunkenness, and witchcraft abounded. Vice and heresy became
equated and the bishop engaged in a fierce battle exacerbated
by the ravages of the plague in the region, an omen of God's
wrath.[173]

The preacher's fear was part of a collective fear. He may not
have created it as much as he played on and increased it. People
expected such negative preaching, especially in certain contexts.
Certain liturgical times were most appropriate for preaching on
judgment, particularly Advent and Lent and especially Holy Week.
Since Lent and Advent cycles predominate among printed sermons,
this may skew our understanding of preaching. Also "revivalist"
mission preachers were expected to deliver a fire and brimstone

---

[171]   Orlandi, p. 530.
[172]   Campagnola, p. 265; Mormando, p. 91.
[173]   Delcorno, "Forme," pp. 292-3.

sermon; they announced it in their demeanor and the people knew how to react.

The connection between confession and the communal nature of preaching should be considered here as well. Virulent preaching was intended to lead to and was accompanied by confessional ministry. Paton explains that preaching "depended on the pressure of the collective conscience, and the shame it induced in the individual malefactor, to bring about moral reform...." Confession could deal on a more personal level with individuals, providing catharsis.[174] As I have shown in the ritualistic responses to preaching, catharsis often took place communally as part of the preaching. Pastoral psychology was involved as well. Missionaries such as the Redemptorists, as Orlandi has observed, thought that people's faith was "superficial" and assumed that they needed to stress the fearful aspects of their message.[175] Many preachers thought that it took intense preaching to change their audiences.

No doubt some preachers were more fear inspiring than others. Cesareo holds that Seripando's sermons differ in "character and in tone from many of the penitential sermons preached throughout Italy during the Renaissance." While other preachers emphasized "penitential mortification," the bishop focused on "inner renewal" and geared his penitential preaching to the "building up" of his flock. [176] Yet balanced preaching is stressed in the most important preaching documents of the period. This understanding of preaching goes back to the inherent balance in the Franciscan Rule, "vices and virtues, punishment and glory," a phrase adopted by the Council of Trent. While Delumeau sees the Council promoting fearful preaching, others find balance in Tridentine and subsequent legislation.[177] Many early modern preachers and theorists support this notion. Capuchin Mattia Bellintani in the early seventeenth century recommends "moral exaggerations in which... one shows the ugliness of vice in order to reprehend and the beauty of virtue in order to exhort."[178] Earlier, Musso's sermons show conscientious attempts at balance. Even in an Ash Wednesday sermon where

---

[174] Paton, p. 59.
[175] Orlandi, p. 521.
[176] Cesareo, p. 3.
[177] Miele, p. 97.
[178] Campagnola, p. 266.

fearful preaching might be most appropriate, Musso, commenting that "God made man in balance," used two different biblical texts to construct two parts of a sermon, each eighteen pages in length, one hopeful and one fearful. For Musso the Word, Christ, preached a balanced message and scripture provided balance as well.[179] Preachers worried about those who might take the fearful message too hard as well as those (the majority) who needed it drummed into them. Narni warned, "Never induce sinners to desperation… because you close the heart and it won't admit the reign of grace; but give them hope."[180]

While some preachers attempted to balance every sermon or sermon to context and audience, others sought to balance fierce preaching with other types of ministries. The Jesuit missions incorporated balance into the very structure of their work. Typically, missionaries traveled in pairs, one acting in the role of "*il dolce*" and the other "*il terribile.*" The sweet one taught while the terrible one was the preacher.[181] As a late seventeenth-century Jesuit document explained, the sermon was "to move the will to compunction by detesting vices, loving virtue and changing ways… thus …the sermons should be usually of… the price of the soul, the gravity of sin, the necessity of penitence, the rigor of divine justice, death, judgment, hell, eternity and the like." It would make sense then that Delumeau would find that fearful subjects dominate mission sermons. As Orlandi argues, however, one needs to balance the assessment of preaching with that of other pastoral activities.[182]

Conclusions and Trajectories

Preaching remained a consistent and significant vehicle of communication for the Church, the people, the sacred, and the culture through late medieval and early modern Italy. Continuity in purpose, content, and ritual-event character, dilemmas about style and rhetoric, and the expectations of preachers and audiences defined preaching in the period just as surely as the profound changes that

---

[179]   Norman, pp. 100-1; Musso, *Prediche*, vol. 1, pp. 100-71.
[180]   Narni, *Modo*, in Criscuolo, p. 148.
[181]   Orlandi, p. 520.
[182]   Ibid., p. 533.

took place in those centuries. Much work remains to be done in these areas. The creation of research aids on preaching and sacred rhetoric could expedite matters.

Along with the trajectories already established, new methodological perspectives offer promise. In general, religious studies methodologies have been largely absent from the research on early modern preaching. Phenomenological and ritual studies in particularly lend themselves to the study of preaching in this period.

More attention should be given to the visual and spatial aspects of preaching, not as background information but as primary. Given the overlapping assumptions that rhetoricians, musicians, and artists held about Baroque style, the architectural and artistic dimensions of preaching events ought to be examined more closely. The liturgical setting is also an important source for preaching. Most sermons begin with some reference to the liturgy or the significance of the day. We tend to pass these by quickly but for preachers and audiences they provided the framework for most preaching events. Thus those who study preaching should acquaint themselves with current work in the study of art, architectural, liturgical and music histories. Art depicting preaching events in this period has yet to be studied comprehensively, although Rusconi's articles on the medieval iconography of preaching have provided an excellent foundation for future work.[183]

Especially important for filling in our picture of Italian preaching culture are two areas of research that offer important perspectives often lost in the shadow of patriarchal Christianity. First, preaching was not just a vehicle of communication for Christianity. David Ruderman, Marc Saperstein, and others are beginning to piece together the history of Jewish preaching in Italy. Early modern It-

---

[183] Roberto Rusconi, "Women's Sermons at the End of the Middle Ages: Texts from the Blessed and Images of the Saints," in *Women Preachers and Prophets through Two Millennia of Christianity*, eds. Beverly Mayne Kienzle and Pamela J. Walker (Berkeley: University of California Press, 1998), pp. 173-91; "I 'falsi credenti' nell'iconografia della predicazione (secoli XIII-XV)," in *Cristianitá ed Europa: Miscellanea di studi in onore di Luigi Prosdocimi*, ed. Cesare Alzati (Rome: herder, 1994,) pp. 313-37; "Giovanni da Capestrano: iconografia di un predicatore nell'Europa del '400," in *Predicazione francescana e societá veneta nel Quattrocento*," 2nd ed., Atti del II convegno internazionale di studi francescani, Padua, March 26-28, 1987 (Padua: Centro studi antoniani, 1995), pp. 25-53.

aly was also the "age of sermons" for Italian Jews. [184]Jewish preaching needs to be studied further in its own right and for its own significance; however, comparative work on Jewish and Christian preaching in the period could prove especially fruitful for understanding the significance of this medium in early modern Italian society. Preaching provided a vehicle of exchange between the two communities. Often, this was coerced exchange as Jews were forced to attend Christian preaching. Christian preaching about Jews was tragically a means of Christian domination and the persecution of difference. Yet Jews and Christians, particularly elite practitioners and connoisseurs of preaching, also chose to attend the sermons of each other's famous preachers, and to learn from each other.[185] The popular Jewish preacher, Leon of Modena, borrowed from Panigarola's work in his own preaching treatise; Christians came to hear his oratory.[186] Jewish and Christians preachers had many of the same dilemmas and held many of the same values. The Jewish *darshan* paralleled the Christian orator as a mediator between levels of culture.[187] Leon of Modena worried, as did many Christian orators, about the tension between using eloquent Hebrew and communicating with the people. He warned Jewish preachers not too "soar to high" above their heads.[188] The Jewish preacher was a "*shofar*" to the Christian preacher's "trumpet;" he was a prophet announcing vices and virtues. And as Christian preachers used the Jew, Jewish preachers, according to Saperstein, used the Christian "as a rhetorical goad to bring the listeners back to their own tradition."[189]

Gender analysis of the culture of preaching both expands and alters the picture of preaching in current scholarship. While attention to female audiences has become a commonplace of medieval preaching, the reasons are multiple and complex. First, women

---

[184]   Ruderman, p. 3 (see n. 4). Marc Saperstein, *Jewish Preaching, 1200-1800: An Anthology* (New Haven, Conn.: Yale University Press, 1989). Saperstein includes sermons of two preachers from this period, Leon of Modena and Judah Moscato, and an excellent introduction.

[185]   Saperstein, p. 27; Ruderman, p. 1. On Jesuit preaching to Jews see O'Malley, *First Jesuits*, p. 191.

[186]   Johanna Weinberg, "Preaching in the Venetian Ghetto: The Sermons of Leon Modena," in Ruderman, pp. 108-110.

[187]   Ruderman, p. 3.

[188]   Saperstein, "Introduction," in Ruderman, p. 51.

[189]   Saperstein, *Jewish Preaching*, p. 30.

were addressed because they came to sermons. Preaching was one of the few permissible reasons for women to enter public space. Their presence in public sacred space, however, was highly charged. This is illustrated amply in the artistic portrayals of open-air preaching, where women are usually depicted separated from men by a curtain. Randolf has also observed that women were usually segregated in the northernmost and darkest part of the church during services, limiting their access and limiting access to them. Paradoxically, mendicant preachers highlighted women's presence by railing against the vanity of women and against the "idolatry" of mothers who brought their daughters to church for display.[190] Women in many cases were, then, the objects rather than, or as well as, the subjects of preaching. Preachers competed with women for the attention of men in their audiences. The male gaze was redirected to view women in a darker light by the preachers.[191]

While all women could be fodder for the preachers as object lessons, nuns and prostitutes provided particularly useful object lessons for preaching virtue. Prostitutes, like Jews, were compelled to attend sermons in some cities.[192] No doubt their presence prompted others to attend and preachers took full advantage. In a sermon in Rome in 1541, Musso gives a lengthy altar call to prostitutes.[193] Yet in the end, they become symbols of penitence for the crowd. "Come on, come on youths, men, and women!" he cries after he tells the repentant prostitute what to say in asking forgiveness. Note that her words should include, "You won't ever spurn a man or a women, Lord, who comes to you with living faith."[194]

In 1540, Musso preached a sermon to the *convertite* in Rome.[195] These newly reformed prostitutes-turned-nuns provided a special opportunity for Musso to reach his target audience. He begins his sermon by setting out the "silly" way in which he, acting as a nursemaid, must preach to these newborn converts, speaking in a high

---

[190]   Adrian Randolph, "Regarding Women in Sacred Space," in *Picturing Women in Renaissance and Baroque Italy*, ed. Geraldine A. Johnson and Sara F. Matthews Grieco (Cambridge: Cambridge University Press, 1997), pp. 21-28 on segregating women; p. 35 on mothers and daughters.

[191]   Randolph, p. 38.

[192]   O'Malley, *First Jesuits*, p. 179.

[193]   Musso, *Simbolo*, vol. 2, Sermon 34, p. 526.

[194]   Ibid., p. 527.

[195]   Musso, "Delle santa oratione," *Prediche del rev. Cornelio Musso...di nuovo poste in luce...* (Venice, Giolito, 1586).

voice. Yet the structure of the sermon reveals that the *convertite* were
not the only audience he planned to reach that day. In setting out
how he must talk to these "infants," he begs the indulgence of the
patrons of the convent, the more mature "mothers and fathers." By
page four of the sermon, he regularly shifts audiences from sisters
to patrons; but the content does not change from its penitential
focus. The presence of these new nuns gives him an opportunity to
preach about humility and prayer to a group that probably needs
to hear about it more than they do. Further, it gives him the opportunity to do so without offending the patrons at the same time. A
pastoral strategy for elites may be reflected here. Panigarola advised
against preaching directly to nobles about their vices, suggesting
they would be more likely to hear a message put indirectly as his
teacher Musso did in this sermon.[196] For Musso, the sisters' good
example, but more especially their failures and ignorance made
them part of the content intended for another audience.

Women could function as a sort of "everyman" at times for
preachers; their inclusion in addresses indicates that the lowest
common denominator in terms of education and status, and that
includes spiritual status, is being targeted. When Musso speaks in-
clusively, for example, he is talking about the bare bones of Christianity—the basics that everyone should and could understand. He
tells the Romans, "All men have always wanted...to know something of this... For me, I know, that there isn't a woman among
you, who with a thousand other things on your mind doesn't have
this desire too, wanting to understand something of the other life."
Women are the best example of "men" unable to be saved by intellect: "Women then, are all occupied with the active life, they can't
attend, even if they wanted to, to learning.... God couldn't have
done better, for our health, than to find this way of making us all
believe... Believe, believe everybody...!"[197]

In the most extreme cases, preachers turned women into personi-
fications of the fear and insecurity embedded in the culture.
Preachers could have a heavy hand in promoting witchcraft accusations. Mormando concludes that Bernardino fanned fears of collu-
sion between the devil and "witches" where there had been little

[196]   Panigarola, *Il Predicatore*, vol. 2 , p. 416.
[197]   Musso, *Simbolo* vol. 1, p. 177; pp. 36-7.

worry over witchcraft previously.[198] Panigarola's equation of heresy with the image of a woman preaching is another case of such objectification.

Women, however, were not just the lowest common denominators or the objects of sermons intended primarily for men. They were addressed in their own right as well. That nuns and laywomen alike faithfully recorded sermons for their private devotion and preservation, and were a substantial part of the market for published sermons, indicates that they understood preaching to be addressed to them. Preachers talked to and about women at the same time. As O'Malley relates, while Jesuit preaching missions to urban prostitutes (something of a Jesuit specialty) probably were also addressed to others, particularly wealthy laywomen who might serve as sponsors for *convertite*, the ministry was directed at the prostitutes and their conversion first.[199]

Preachers addressed women so much in part because they saw them "as [more] prone to moral weakness" than men.[200] Chavarria sees the gradual development of a "new image" of woman as a tool for the church in the home that is more positive.[201] Looking back to the fifteenth century, however, Paton observes that preachers addressed women as "the mainstays of the domestic unit and the primary operators of the subtle network of underground civic communication" as well as excoriating their weaknesses.[202]

Preachers addressed women because they could reach another audience: the men in their lives. As Paton points out, however, women were not just tools for the Church to transmit its values to their men. The friars knew that women had to be convinced in their own right because they themselves were "powerful cultural catalysts."[203] While the friars' theory of power like that of society was based on patriarchal hierarchy, they adjusted their message to the reality of women's influence. Chavarria argues that preachers after Trent may have actually empowered women in their preaching on women as the religious center of the home at a time when noble

---

[198] On Bernardino and witchcraft, see Mormando, Chapter 2.
[199] O'Malley, *First Jesuits*, pp. 179-82 on their ministry to prostitutes.
[200] Paton, p. 57.
[201] Chiavarria, p. 686.
[202] Paton, p. 57.
[203] Ibid., p. 58.

families were attempting to limit women's power within the family.[204]

Women were not only influential in relaying the message of preaching to their families, but served as patrons and instigators of preaching events. In 1546 a Dominican preacher "was summoned to Salerno" by Isabella Villamarino, wife of the prince, who was concerned with the spread of heretical ideas "being discussed by all ranks of society."[205] It is important to note here that not only was she transmitting the sermon to the people; but she also was transmitting important information to the preachers. Women who kept their ears to the ground may have been important sources for preachers; even as the preachers punished them for this by preaching against their gossip.

Despite the horror of Panigarola and others, the idea of women's preaching was not unknown in medieval and early modern Italy. Images of women discharging the office of preacher abound in popular devotional literature, sacred poetry and drama, religious art, the liturgy, and sermons. Roberto Rusconi has documented the ubiquity of the image of Mary Magdalene as the *apostola apostolorum* exhorting the faithful, as well as images of other preaching female saints such as Catherine of Alexandria and Martha. Holy women of the late Middle Ages such as Catherine of Siena were quite often depicted preaching. Rusconi concludes that "[i]t would have been difficult for such artworks to reflect a practice, such as preaching by women, that was not officially recognized, or at least tolerated, by ecclesiastical institutions."[206] That lay people considered great saintly women as preachers is evident in the following note written to a fifteenth-century Italian merchant, Datini, from a friend, Mazzei. Writing about the preacher Dominici whom he had recently heard, Mazzei compared him to two models, one male and one female: "You think you are hearing one of Francis's disciples and himself reborn. We all cry and stand stupefied at the clear virtue that he shows, like saint Bridget."[207] Given the equation of preaching in example and words, Mazzei seems to think of Bridget as much as Francis as a preacher here.

---

[204]   Chavarria, pp. 688-90.
[205]   Cesareo, p. 5.
[206]   Rusconi in Kienzle and Walker, p. 174.
[207]   Rusconi, *Predicazione*, p. 174.

Very little work has been done on women's preaching in Italy.
Valerio has identified some women who preached with the support
or approval of clergy. The nun Caterina Vannini (d. 1606), in reply-
ing to a request from Federigo Borromeo for her opinion on his
sermons, spoke from "her own experience." She suggested that he
might be briefer. She tells him when she preaches to her nuns that
she "goes no more than an hour;" after that it does no one any
good.[208] In Rome, Caterina Paluzzi (d. 1645) preached for at least
twenty-five years, from 1620-45, mostly to the nuns of Santa Cecil-
ia in Trastevere, often with cardinals and other clergy in attendance. Unfortunately, we have no sermons, only this testimony:
"Suor Caterina often preached in the choir, taking the theme of the
gospel or some lesson from the Holy Office, especially on saints'
days or feasts of the Madonna. She expounded it so in her preaching that she moved us all to tears, giving us so much edification
from its marvels."[209] The story of Paola Antonia Negi (d. 1554)
shows what was more likely to happen when a woman attempted
to preach outside of the convent. In 1552, she was examined by the
Inquisition and condemned for "usurping for herself a divine role."
She testified to her confidence that God calls all regardless of gender to be apostles, referring to Mary Magdalene and Catherine of
Alexandria.[210]

Let us return to Rusconi's call for a picture of preaching based
on interdisciplinary interests and research, a broad use of sources,
and attention to parish preaching as well as preaching of the orders. Parish preaching has remained largely in the shadows of the
colorful preaching events of Lenten cycles and missions. Yet parish
preaching, because of its local context, should be central to any
understanding of the preaching culture.

I close with an example of how interdisciplinary research, attention to often overlooked sources and careful reconstruction can put
parish preaching at the focal point. Among the episcopal records in
Milan, Wietse De Boer discovered what might on cursory examination have appeared to have been hardly worth attention: a short
sermon by Girolamo di Basti, curate of Malgrate, preached in Oc-

---

[208] Adriana Valerio, "La Predicazione femminile dagli anni pre-tridentini alla
prima metá del seicento" in Martina and Dovere, p. 193.
[209] Valerio, pp. 190-1.
[210] Ibid., pp. 186-90.

tober of 1574. The beginning of the sermon offers little promise. Girolamo praises his bishop Carlo Borromeo for attempting to "do away with ignorance in the brains" of curates; but he says he is too old and unlearned to change.[211]

De Boer found two copies of the three-page sermon. Checking the records of Di Basti's library holdings, he concluded that the priest had merely copied into Italian a Latin sermon of Vincent Ferrer's found in the only sermon book among his fourteen-book collection. This is exactly what we might expect from an aged and ill-trained priest, exactly what reforming bishops like Borromeo strived to change: canned, irrelevant preaching. As De Boer observes, he chose an "arid" late medieval sermon "far from the… simplicity and attention to practical ends" that Borromeo wanted in parish preaching.[212]

De Boer searched further, however, and discovered that Di Basti's sermon was not exactly what it seemed at first glance. The biblical theme is Mark 6:47 which initiates the story of Jesus' walk on water. Ferrer's sermon based an allegory, the "boat of penitence," on the text. This theme was important in the confraternal piety in the diocese. Further, the tone of the sermon fit the disciplined piety that was the Borromean ideal and addressed the practice of confession. As De Boer observes, "His public probably was much more sensitive to his content than a modern reader could imagine."[213] De Boer further connected diocesan documentation of the competing interests within the church hierarchy and diocese with the sermon content; the preacher did not work in "neutral circumstances."[214] Girolamo was not as ignorant as he claimed and not as irrelevant as we might think. His simple effort fit his and his audience's changing circumstances during Borromeo's episcopate and offers us a more complex picture of preaching in his culture.

In one of her seminal articles on Bernardino, Zafarana remarked that preaching is not the "expression of a single personality" but "the fruit of a milieu and the result of a work in some measure col-

---

[211]   Wietse De Boer, "Il curato di Malgrate, or il problema della cultura del clero nella Milano della controriforma," *Studia Borromaica* 12 (1998), 138.
[212]   Ibid., pp. 140-1.
[213]   Ibid., pp. 142-3.
[214]   Ibid., pp. 148.

lective."[215] While preachers such as Bernardino, Musso, and Panigarola shared the culture of their hearers, what made them stand out then and now was their charisma, the "miracles" they could perform like no one else in their ages. They are representative and yet they are not. No doubt many others such as the curate of Malgrate wait in the shadows for us to look closer, not for the most luminous expressions of the preaching culture, but rather, for the earthy tones of collective culture at its most basic communal level.

Bibliography

Ascarelli, Fernanda, *Le cinquecentine romane: Censimento delle edizioni romane del XVI secolo possedute dalle biblioteche di Roma* (Milan: Etimar, 1972).

Boaga, Emanuele, "Predicazione: Dal concilio di Trento al CIC," in *Dizionario degli Istituti di Perfezione*, vol. 7 (Rome: Edizioni Paoline, 1983), pp. 545-550.

Cesareo, Francesco C., "Penitential Sermons in Renaissance Italy: Girolamo Seripando and the *Pater Noster*," *The Catholic Historical Review* 83 (1997), 1-19.

Chavarria, Elisa Novi, "Ideologia e comportamenti familiari nei predicatori italiani tra cinque e settecento. Tematiche e modelli," *Rivista storica italiana* 100 (1988), 691.

— "Pastorale e devozioni nel XVI e XVII secolo," in *Storia del Mezzogiorno*, ed. G. Galasso and R. Romeo (Rome: Editalia, 1991), pp. 369-413.

Criscuolo, Vincenzo, *Girolamo Mautini da Narni (1563-1632): Predicatore Apostolico e Vicario Generale dei Cappuccini* (Rome: Istituto Storico dei Cappuccini, 1998).

D'Ascoli, Arsenio, *Predicazione dei Cappuccini nel Cinquecento in Italia* (Loreto: Libreria San Francesco d'Asissi, 1956).

De Boer, Wietse, "Il curato di Malgrate, or il problema della cultura del clero nella Milano della controriforma," *Studia Borromaica* 12 (1998), 137-53.

De Rosa, Gabriele, "Il francescano Cornelio Musso dal Concilio di Trento alla Diocesi di Bitonto," *Rivista di storia della chiesa in Italia* 40 (1986), 55-91.

---

[215] Zafarana, "Bernardino nella storia della predicazione popolare," in Capitani, pp. 277-8.

Delcorno, Carlo, "Forme della predicazione cattolica fra Cinque e Seicento," in *Cultura d'e'lite e cultura popolare nell'arco alpino fra Cinque e Seicento*, ed. Ottavio Besomi and Carlo Caruso (Boston: Birkhaeuser Verlag, 1995), pp. 275-302.

— "Rassegna di studi sulla predicazione medievale et umanistica," *Lettere italiane* 33 (1981), 235-76.

Dizionario biografico degli italiani (Rome: Istituto della Enciclopedia italiana, 1960-).

Fumaroli, Marc, *L'âge de l'éloquence: Rhétorique et "res literaria" de la Renaissance au seuil de l'époque classique* (Geneva: Droz, 1980).

Frugoni, Chiara, "L'iconografia e la vita religiosa nei secoli XIII-XV," in *Storia dell'Italia religiosa*, vol. 1, ed. André Vauchez (Rome: Laterza, 1993), pp. 485-504.

Giombi, Samuele, "Dinamiche della predicazione cinquecentesca tra forma retorica e normativa religiosa: le istruzioni episcopali ai predicatori," in *Cristianesimo nella Storia* 13 (1992), 73-102.

— "Livelli di cultura nella trattatistica sulla predicazione e l'eloquenza sacra del XVI secolo," in *Cultura d'elite e cultura popolare nell'arco alpino fra Cinque e Seicento*, eds. Ottavio Besomi and Carlo Caruso (Boston: Birkhaeuser Verlag, 1995), pp. 247-73.

Houdon, William J., "Two Instructions to Preachers for Tridentine Reform," *Sixteenth Century Journal* 20 (1989), 457-470.

Howard, Peter Francis, *Beyond the Written Word: Preaching and Theology in the Florence of Archbishop Antoninus, 1427-1459* (Florence: L.S. Olschki, 1995).

Jedin, Hubert, *A History of the Council of Trent*, trans. Ernest Graf, 2 vols. (London: Thomas Nelson and Sons, 1957-61).

Kristeller, Paul Oskar, *Iter Italicum* (Leiden: E.J. Brill, 1965-7).

McGinness, Frederick J., "Preaching Ideals and Practice in Counter-Reformation Rome," *Sixteenth-Century Journal* 11 (1980), 109-127.

— *Right Thinking and Sacred Oratory in Counter-Reformation Rome* (Princeton, N.J.: Princeton University Press, 1995).

McManamon, John M., *Funeral Oratory and the Cultural Ideals of Italian Humanism* (Chapel Hill, NC: University of North Carolina Press, 1989).

Martina, Giacomo and Ugo Dovere, *La Predicazione in Italia dopo il Concilio di Trento tra Cinquecento e settecetto. Atti del X convegno di Studio dell'Associazione Italiana dei Professor di Storia della Chiesa*, Napoli, 6-9 Settembre 1994 (Rome: Edizioni Dehoniane, 1996).

Mormando, Franco, *The Preacher's Demons: Bernardino da Siena and the Social Underworld of Early Renaissance Italy* (Chicago: University of Chicago Press, 1999).

Norman, Corrie E., *Humanist Taste and Franciscan Values, Cornelio Musso and Catholic Preaching in Sixteenth-Century Italy* (New York: Peter Lang, 1998).

— "The Franciscan Preaching Tradition and Its Sixteenth-Century Legacy: The Case of Cornelio Musso," *The Catholic Historical Review* 85 (1999), 208-32.

— "Showing the Inventions of God: Preaching and Ritual on Holy Thursday at the Court of Paul V," in Kathleen M. Comerford and Hilmar M. Pabel, eds., *Early Modern Catholicism: Essays in Honor of John W. O'Malley, S.J.* (Toronto: University of Toronto Press, 1991).

O'Malley, John W., "Content and Rhetorical Form in Sixteenth-Century Treatises on Preaching," in *Renaissance Eloquence: Studies in the Theory and Practice of Renaissance Rhetoric*, ed. James Murphy (Berkeley, CA: University of California, 1983), pp. 238-52.

— *The First Jesuits* (Cambridge, Mass.: Harvard University Press, 1993).

— "Form, Content, and Influence of Works about Preaching before Trent: The Franciscan Contribution," in *I frati minori tra '400 e '500. Atti del XII Convegno Internzionale*, Assisi, 18-20 ottobre 1984, ed. Roberto Rusconi (Assisi: Centro di Studi, 1985), pp. 27-50.

— *Praise and Blame in Renaissance Rome: Rhetoric, Doctrine, and Reform in the Sacred Orators of the Papal Court, ca.1450-1521* (Durham, NC: Duke University Press, 1979).

— "St. Charles Borromeo and the Praecipuum Episcoporum Munus: His Place in the History of Preaching," in *San Carlo Borromeo: Catholic Reform and Ecclesiastical Politics in the Second Half of the Sixteenth Century*, eds. John M. Headley and John B. Tomaro (Washington, D.C.: Folger Books, 1988), pp. 139-57.

Paton, Bernadette, *Preaching Friars and the Civic Ethos: Siena, 1380-1480* (London: Centre for Medieval Studies, Queen Mary and Westfield College, University of London, 1992).

Polecritti, Cynthia, *Preaching Peace in Renaissance Italy: Bernardino of Siena and his Audience* (Washington, D.C.: Catholic University of America Press, 2000).

Pozzi, Giovanni, "Intorno all'predicazione del Panigarola," in *Problemi di vita religiosa in Italia nella cinquecento. Atti del Convegno di storia della Chiesa in Italia*, Bologna, 2-6 Settembre 1958, ed. Convegno di storia della chiesa in Italia (Padua: Antinori, 1960), pp. 315-22.

Prodi, Paolo, *Il Cardinale Gabriele Paleotti*, 2 vols. (Rome: Edizione di storia e letteratura, 1959-67).

Prosperi, Adriano, *Tra evangelismo e Controriforma: G.M. Giberti (1495-1543)* (Rome: Editione di storia e letteratura, 1969).

Publiese, O. Zorzi, "Two Sermons by Giovanni Nesi and the Language of Spirituality in Late Fifteenth-Century Florence," *Bibliotheque d'Humanisme et de Renaissance* 42 (1980), 641-56.

Randolph, Adrian, "Regarding Women in Sacred Space," in *Picturing Women in Renaissance and Baroque Italy*, eds. Geraldine A. Johnson and Sara F. Matthews Grieco (Cambridge: Cambridge University Press, 1997), pp. 17-41.

Ruderman, David B., ed., *Preachers of the Italian Ghetto* (Berkeley: University of California Press, 1992).

Rusconi, Roberto, "Da costanza al Laterano: La "Calcolata devozione" del ceto mercantile-borghese nell'italia del Quattrocento," in *Storia dell'Italia religiosa*, ed., Andre Vauchez, vol. 1 (Rome: Laterza, 1993), pp. 506-32.

— "Dal pulpito alla confessione. Modelli di comportamento religioso in Italia tra 1470 e 1520 circa," in *Strutture ecclesiastiche in Italia e in Germania prima della Riforma*, eds. Paolo Prodi and P. Johanek (Bologna: 1984).

— "I 'falsi credentes' nell'iconografia della predicazione (secoli XIII-XV)," in *Cristianitá ed Europa: Miscellanea di studi in onore di Luigi Prosdocimi*, ed. Cesare Alzati (Rome: Herder, 1994), pp. 313-37.

— "Gli ordini religiosi maschili dalla controriforma alle soppressioni settecentesche. Cultura, predicazione, missioni," in *Clero e societa nell'Italia moderna*, ed. Mario Rosa (Roma-Bari: Laterza, 1992), pp. 207-74.

— "Giovanni da Capastrano: iconografia di un predicatore nell'Europa del '400," in *Predicazione francescana e societá veneta nel Quattrocento" Atti del Il convegno internazionale di studi francescani, 1987* (Padua: Centro studi antoniani, 1995, 2nd edition), pp. 25-53.

— "Predicatori e predicazione," in *Storia d'Italia Annali 4: Intellettuali e potere*, ed. C. Vivanti (Torino: Einaudi, 1981), pp. 995-1012.

— "Predicazione," *Dizionario degli Istituti di Perfezione*, vol. 7 (Roma: Edizioni Paoline, 1983), pp. 513-550.

— "La predicazione francescana sulla penitenza all fine del quattrocento nel 'Rosarium Sermonum' di Bernardino Busti," *Studia Patavina* 22 (1975), 68-95.

— *Predicazione e vita religiosa nella societa* (Torino: Einaudi, 1981).

— "Il sacramento della penitenza nella predicazione di San Bernardino da Siena," *Aevum* 48 (1973), 253-86.

— "Women's Sermons at the End of the Middle Ages: Texts from the Blessed and Images of the Saint," in *Women Preachers and Prophets through Two Millennia of Christianity*, eds. Beverly Mayne Kienzle and Pamela J. Walker (Berkeley: University of California Press, 1998), pp. 173-91.

Saperstein, Marc, ed., *Jewish Preaching, 1200-1800: An Anthology* (New Haven, Conn.: Yale University Press, 1989).

Schutte, Anne, *Printed Italian Vernacular Religious Books 1465-1550: A Finding List* (Gevena: Droz, 1983).

Weinstein, Donald, *Savonarola and Florence* (Princeton, N.J: Princeton University Press, 1970).

Westervelt, Benjamin Wood, "The Borromean Ideal of Preaching: Episcopal Strategies for Reforming Pastoral Preaching in Post-Tridentine Milan, 1564-1631," Ph. D. diss., Harvard University, 1993.

Zelina Zafarana, *Da Gregorio VII a Bernardino da Siena. Saggi di storia medievale*, ed. O. Capitani et al. (Florence: Scandicci, La Nuova Italia Editrice, 1987).

Zanette, Laura, "Tre predicatori per la peste: 1575-1577," *Lettere Italiane* 42 (1990), 430-59.

Zawart, Anscar, *The History of Franciscan Preaching and of Franciscan Preachers: A Bio-Bibliographical Study* (New York: J.F. Wagner, 1928).

CHAPTER SIX

PREACHING THE WORD IN EARLY MODERN GERMANY

Susan C. Karant-Nunn
(University of Arizona)

Throughout the high and late Middle Ages, penitential preachers crisscrossed the German countryside, pausing to declaim where they could find an audience. To the basic message of repentance, the mendicant revolution of the thirteenth century added that of correct doctrine as a necessary antidote to apparently rampant heresy.[1] The regular availability of sermons increased markedly, for a defining assignment of the friars was to preach. The more compelling among them, such as Meister Eckhart (1260-1328) and Berthold von Regensburg (1210-72), attracted throngs. Simultaneously, cities and donors began to establish preacherships, usually in the cathedral or other main church, and chose the best available sacred rhetoricians to fill them.[2] Johann Geiler von Kaisersberg (1445-1510) and Huldrych Zwingli (1484-1531) were among these. Many people heard these men with enthusiasm, but we cannot be certain how much they did this out of a genuine desire to improve their lives and how much in order to break the tedium of their routine. Very likely, motives combined. All the really popular preachers, those whose names have come down to us, possessed a charisma that itself drew listeners.

---

[1] D. L. D'Avray, *The Preaching of the Friars: Sermons Diffused from Paris before 1300* (Oxford: Clarendon Press, 1985); Nicole Bériou and David D'Avray, eds., *Modern Questions about Medieval Sermons: Essays on Marriage, Death, History and Sanctity* (Spoleto: Centro italiano di studi sull' Alto medioevo, 1994).

[2] For a summary of the numbers and functions of early sixteenth-century German *Prädikaturen*, see Steven E. Ozment, *The Reformation in the Cities: The Appeal of Protestantism to Sixteenth-Century Germany and Switzerland* (New Haven: Yale University Press, 1975), pp. 38-42; also works on particular regions, such as Rudolf Herrmann, "Die Prediger im ausgehenden Mittelalter und ihre Bedeutung für die Einführung der Reformation im ernestinischen Thüringen," *Beiträge zur thüringischen Kirchengeschichte* 1, 1 (1929), 20-68.

On the eve of the Reformation, the impulse to integrate the Catholic Church into society – to "domesticate" the clergy – coincided not only with princes' and patricians' political aspirations but also with an evident yearning to know more about religion. The chasm that separated the laity from the clerical estate needed to be narrowed, in part so that religious information was no longer the purview of a separate order that doled it out to its spiritual inferiors, the laity, as its members saw fit. One aspect of the upsurge in late medieval piety was a passion for direct access to the biblical Word. This assertion of the untrained intellect was a manifestation of self-confidence, of an expansive post-plague mentality. People adjusted their earthly horizons to encompass more of the extra-European world, and they wanted to penetrate the heavenly sphere as well. They asked a dual-sided question: how can I live satisfactorily on earth, and how can I live eternally in heaven? In those days, the here and the hereafter formed an integrated whole.[3] Works of art present to us the crowds of people, including old men and young mothers nursing babies, who surrounded the pulpits, where these existed, to hear the Word. Those who could not stand for the considerable length of time that preachers held forth, brought along low, collapsible stools and hunkered down upon them. Initially only canons and other high-ranking clergy, magistrates, and the nobility had permanent seating in churches.

The sermon was essential in establishing and spreading the Reformation movement. By means of numerous maps and charts, Manfred Hannemann has shown us in concrete terms how preaching shaped events.[4] While Bernd Moeller has told us, "No book, no Reformation," it might be just as apt to say, "No sermon, no

---

[3] I am once again taking exception to the interpretation of Steven Ozment, who follows Étienne Delaruelle and others concerning "the burden of late medieval religion" per se (*The Reformation in the Cities*, esp. pp. 15-32), although some scrupulous souls such as Martin Luther and Katharina Schütz Zell may have felt that the doctrine of justification by faith lifted a great burden from their shoulders (Elsie Anne McKee, *Katharina Schütz Zell: The Life and Thought of a Sixteenth-Century Reformer* [Leiden: Brill, 1999], 1, p. 307). See also Ozment's *The Age of Reform 1250-1550: An Intellectual and Religious History of Late Medieval and Reformation Europe* (New Haven: Yale University Press, 1980), pp. 208-209, 222.

[4] Hannemann, *The Diffusion of the Reformation in Southwestern Germany, 1518-1534* (Chicago: Department of Geography, University of Chicago, 1975), passim.

Reformation."[5] The majority of sermons preached were never printed.

The many elements that came together under the rubric of anticlerical sentiment at the end of the Middle Ages were the products of ecclesiastical contumely toward civic well-being and of abuse of official Catholic teaching.[6] Where these were kept within tolerable bounds, revolution was less likely to break forth. Further, even where it did, virtually every "anticleric," whether a clergyman himself or a layperson, envisioned a calm, reordered Christendom in which godly pastors tended their human flocks.[7] Part of the shepherd's duty was to preach: more people than before desired to *know* about their faith.

This wish, possibly more widespread among urban than rural dwellers, coincided very nicely with the emerging theological precept of *sola scriptura*. Foreshadowed by John Wyclif (1325-84) and Jan Hus (1372-1415), and underscored by the humanists' call *ad fontes*, Martin Luther (1483-1546) cut off papal authority in declaring that the Scriptures alone contained everything that God chose to reveal about Himself to His human creatures. In a largely illiterate society, how were the unschooled to overcome the chasm that separated them from the printed text? Robert Scribner has shown us how even the cheapest woodcuts transmitted a world of thought, in addition to the practice of reading aloud in taverns and at spinning bees.[8] These mechanisms, albeit useful and ongoing within Lutheranism, were hardly adequate to the goal of implanting the

---

[5] See the essays by Moeller, R. W. Scribner, Thomas A. Brady, Jr., and Steven Ozment on this subject in Wolfgang J. Mommsen, ed., *Stadtbürgertum und Adel in der Reformation: Studien zur Sozialgeschichte der Reformation in England und Deutschland* (Stuttgart: Klett-Cotta, 1979), pp. 25-48.

[6] For an introduction to multiple aspects of the anticlerical phenomenon, see the essays in Peter A. Dykema and Heiko A. Oberman, eds., *Anticlericalism in Late Medieval and Early Modern Europe* (Leiden: Brill, 1993); and for the views of one author, Hans-Jürgen Goertz, *Pfaffenhaß und groß Geschrei. Die reformatorischen Bewegungen in Deutschland 1517-1529* (Munich: C. H. Beck, 1987). In his own contribution to Dykema and Oberman, Goertz points out the complexity of anticlericalism ("'What a Tangled and Tenuous Mess the Clergy Is!': Clerical Anticlericalism in the Reformation Period," pp. 499-519), here at p. 503.

[7] Susan C. Karant-Nunn, "Clerical Anticlericalism in the Early German Reformation: An Oxymoron?" in Dykema and Oberman, *Anticlericalism*, pp. 521-34, here at pp. 532-33.

[8] R. W. Scribner, *For the Sake of Simple Folk: Popular Propaganda for the German Reformation*, Cambridge Studies in Oral and Literate Culture 2 (Cambridge, Eng., and New York: Cambridge University Press, 1981).

Word of God in the understanding and in the heart of every Christian. Unstructured settings left too much room for misinterpretation, even personal invention. The people must be carefully taught. Further, God delivered to individuals His great gift of justifying faith by means of the Word. The elect were fertile ground for this fructifying activity of the Holy Spirit even as they listened to the Gospel being preached. The Reformers took it for granted that no false exposition of God's Word could produce this result. The Scripture must be preached "loud and clear," as they confidently put it, without any human embroidery.

Within this conceptual framework, the torch plainly passed from the transubstantiating priest, whether or not he occasionally preached, to the explicator of Scripture. How securely it can be maintained that the people themselves were disillusioned concerning the priest's magical powers continues to be debated.[9] My own judgment is that a sizeable majority would have been content to retain transubstantiation so long as they gained, in addition, regular instruction from the pulpit, as well as the integration of the clergy into the citizenry. The governors of the state and of the new churches did not consult the masses before reaching their decisions.

The surging popular interest in learning about their religion and the Reformers' conviction that pastors must preach intersected. A number of practical obstacles loomed between the faithful and the realization of their ambitions. Even in Saxony, where the Lutheran Reformation first took mature shape, much reform of the parishes lay unfinished at the time of Luther's death and the ensuing War of the League of Schmalkald (1546).[10]

If the middle of the sixteenth century witnessed much official

---

[9]   At least implicitly, the literature on iconoclasm takes it for granted that the destruction of sacred artifacts revealed, in the minds of the perpetrators, a rejection of the *sacral* powers of priests. In certain individuals, this may have been true. The attachment to magical practices that visitation protocols reveal, however, would suggest that transubstantiation itself was not the salient issue, but rather the economic, judicial, ethical, and moral abuses of the Catholic ecclesiastical system. These violations of civic values had surely come to be symbolized by sacred artifacts.

[10]   Gerald Strauss has described church leaders' discouragement at mid-century as they realized that the "conversion" they had expected the preaching of the Word and other forms of religious instruction to effect had not widely occurred (*Luther's House of Learning: Indoctrination of the Young in the German Reformation* [Baltimore: Johns Hopkins University Press, 1978], pp. 300-308). They abandoned any lingering qualms about allying themselves with the enforcing state – although the state itself had hardly been waiting in the wings for an invitation.

discouragement over the prevailing dearth of lay knowledge and religious dedication, those who felt downcast hardly slackened their efforts. From this time on, authorities pressed on clergy harder than before their duty to preach often, correctly, persuasively, watchfully, and on several specific occasions that were connected to the life course. The sermon became a central ritual artifact.

Frequency of Preaching

As the Reformation got underway, and before it had made extensive headway across the German landscape, the first teams of parish inspectors or visitors sought to compel those Catholic parish priests who were willing to accommodate themselves to the new demands – and who thus could be permitted to remain in their posts – to preach every Sunday. Whether this had been their custom or not varied greatly, but a look at the early visitation protocols suggests that all had customarily resorted to homiletics chiefly on the highest feast days, such as between Palm Sunday and Easter. Few curers of souls had been able to evade the obligation to convey Christ's Passion to the faithful, even though, unprepared as many were, they had to resort to books of postils or brief reiterations of familiar messages.

Beginning in 1528 in territories subject to the Elector of Saxony, and armed with printed copies of the 1527 "The Visitors' Instructions to the Pastors in Electoral Saxony" ("Unterricht der Visitatoren an die Pfarrherrn im Kurfürstentum zu Sachsen"), visitation committees compelled those clergy who desired to avoid expulsion to commit the contents to memory. "The Visitors' Instructions" was the first document intended to convey Lutheran teachings to the incumbent priesthood. Earlier unsystematic reconnaissance visitations had shown that merely verbal instruction by the visitors could not in itself quickly produce doctrinal skill. Having studied this text, each cleric had to demonstrate his initial mastery by preaching a sermon on an assigned topic, often some aspect of justification by faith.[11] This tenet of the new faith set it most clearly

---

[11]   See my longer description of these initial encounters in *Luther's Pastors: The Reformation in the Ernestine Countryside* (Philadelphia: American Philosophical Society, 1979), pp. 24-27.

apart from most late medieval Catholic belief, which stressed the necessity of good works. Only when the priests had digested this precept could they be entrusted with the Sunday inculcation of the laity. Throughout reforming Germany, only when this dominical preaching was securely in place could the governors of the fledgling churches move on to demand of the new pastors more frequent and varied instruction of parishioners. In the early decades of Protestantism, however, the variability of sermons was restricted by the need to repeat the most fundamental of themes until, at last, the members of the congregations had absorbed them – one hoped.

After 1529, with the issuance of Luther's *Longer Catechism* and his *Shorter Catechism*, Elector Johann and the heads of the Ernestine church and visitation began to expect pastors and other preachers to expound on the catechism separately. Luther had been disillusioned and embittered by conditions in the parishes, which he had observed during participation in the first Saxon general visitation. These moved him to prepare his catechisms in the first place. He revealed his mood in his introduction to the longer version:

> We have no small cause for promoting the catechism so energetically and for desiring and requesting others to do so. For we see that unfortunately many preachers and pastors hereabouts are very negligent and despise both their office and our teachings, some out of great craftiness, but others out of unvarnished laziness and attention to filling their bellies, the attitude of these suggesting that they were pastors or preachers for their bellies' sake and didn't have to do anything except make use of parish property as long as they lived, just as they were accustomed to do under the pope.[12]

The Reformers had initially wished to engage adults in weekly catechism classes but soon found that the catechetical sermon, along with the firm expectation of attendance, was the only means of systematically teaching mature parishioners. The latter associated formal instruction with the low status of childhood. With ongoing threats of punishment, they could be impelled to send their young offspring and servants to classes, but they would not go themselves. They could only be reached by means of a second, obligatory Sunday sermon devoted to the rudiments of the faith. This new category and endeavor were interposed in the Sunday program with difficulty, but within Saxony and Hesse and other early established

---

[12] WA 30/1:125, my translation.

Lutheran societies, the catechetical sermon was in place before mid-century.[13] It essentially doubled the burdens of preaching and of attending church. These sermons were often placed on Wednesday or Sunday afternoons. Parish visitation committees rigorously inquired whether such sermons were held and reliably heard, and where needed, they took measures to remedy laxity.

In rural parishes, these two sermons constituted the routine preaching and attendance obligations of clergy and laity respectively. In the urban setting, where there were often more than one parish and a number of deacons or preachers to assist the pastors, sermons were available at least several days a week and at various times of day. In 1529, the Saxon visitors established the following schedule for the city of Torgau:

Sunday
   Pastor to preach Gospel in city church (*Pfarrkirche*) at usual morning hour.
   First deacon to preach Gospel in monastery early in the morning.
   Second deacon to preach catechism in city church in the afternoon.
Monday
   First deacon to preach on Matthew early in the morning.
Tuesday
   Same as Monday.
Wednesday
   Pastor to preach in the morning from one of the books of Moses or other Old Testament book.
Thursday
   Second deacon to preach in the morning from one of Paul's letters.
Friday
   Same as Thursday.
Saturday
   No service.[14]

---

[13]   Robert J. Bast has reminded us that catechetical literature focused on the Ten Commandments was plentiful in the late Middle Ages, but there were evidently too few and infrequent arenas for conveying official conviction to the common laity (*Honor Your Fathers: The Emergence of a Patriarchal Ideology in Early Modern* Germany [Leiden: Brill, 1995], passim). Prior to teaching the laity, the ordinary priesthood had to be instructed. Bast has delineated the role of Jean Gerson in stimulating greater clerical attention to the rudiments of the faith. I hope that Mary Jane Haemig's Ph.D. dissertation will soon appear: "The Living Voice of the Catechism: German Lutheran Catechetical Preaching, 1530-1580," Harvard Divinity School, 1996.

[14]   Karl Pallas, *Die Registraturen der Kirchenvisitationen im ehemals sächsischen Kurkreise*, 6 vols. (Halle, 1906-1914), 4, p. 4, my translation.

In Altenburg, Georg Spalatin (1484-1545) imposed the following regimen on himself and his colleagues:

> *Sunday*
>> Morning
>>> Pastor and preacher alternate from week to week between city church (*Pfarrkirche*) and castle church.
>> Afternoon
>>> Preacher and first deacon alternate from week to week between city church and castle church.
> *Monday*
>> Preacher to preach every week in castle church plus every other week in city church.
>> First deacon to preach the other Mondays in city church.
> *Tuesday*
>> Preacher in city church.
>> Second deacon in castle church.
> *Wednesday*
>> Afternoon
>>> First deacon preaches catechism in castle church.
>>> Second deacon preaches catechism in city church.
> *Thursday*
>> Pastor in castle church.
>> Preacher in city church.
> *Friday*
>> Preacher in castle church.
>> First deacon in city church.
> *Saturday*
>> First deacon in castle church.
>> Second deacon to preach the shorter catechism and otherwise, for the sick in the hospital.
>> Every Monday and Friday morning, at 5:00 in summer, at 6:00 in winter, somebody must preach in the city church "for poor servants who cannot otherwise attend."[15]

Sermons were probably not much over one hour in length. As the sixteenth century wore on, authorities of church and state had added so many edifying and exhortatory texts to the divine service that they found it necessary to explicitly limit preaching to a maxi-

---

[15] Thüringisches Hauptstaatsarchiv Weimar, Reg. Ii 1, fol. 408. My translation. Here I cannot resist referring the reader to T. H. L. Parker, *Calvin's Preaching* (Louisville, Ky.: Westminster/John Knox, 1992), even though Geneva was not part of the German-speaking world. The eventual effects of Calvin's faith upon Germany, radiating outward from Geneva, are beyond dispute.

mum of an hour, and in some places to forty-five minutes or even half an hour.

Correctness of Preached Doctrine

The theologians who directed the established Reformation churches were mightily concerned lest the clerics in their supervision preach false doctrine. They, after all, had lived through the period of "wild growth" (*Wildwuchs*) from about 1518 until after the suppression of the Peasants' War, when many felt inspired to pronounce their own versions of the Word of God.[16] The variety of their teachings was far greater than Bernd Moeller imagines and than extant printed works reveal.[17]

Another cause of the authorities' worries was that the early Protestant clergy, whether inherited from a displaced Catholicism or appointed in the immediate aftermath of the Reformation upheavals, had little pertinent higher education. The majority of first-generation pastors had served as priests in the same locales. Even where they had attended a university, the education they received was mainly unrelated to the task of running a parish church; it might, indeed, have better equipped them subtly to *oppose* the new teachings. Most priests, however, had learned their profession by serving as a kind of apprentice (*famulus*) to an expe-

---

[16] Franz Lau first uses the term *Wildwuchs* in idem and Ernst Bizer, "Reformationsgeschichte bis 1532," in *Reformationsgeschichte Deutschlands. Ein Handbuch* (Göttingen: Vandenhoeck & Ruprecht, 1964), pp. 3-66.

[17] Moeller, "Was wurde in der Frühzeit der Reformation in den deutschen Städten gepredigt?" *Archiv für Reformationsgeschichte* 75 (1984),176-93; and my earlier response: Susan C. Karant-Nunn, "What Was Preached in German Cities in the Early Years of the Reformation? *Wildwuchs* versus Lutheran Unity," in *The Process of Change in Early Modern Europe: Essays in Honor of Miriam Usher Chrisman*, eds. Phillip N. Bebb and Sherrin Marshall (Athens, Ohio: Ohio University Press, 1988), 81-96. Moeller has recently affirmed his position on the basic theological (Lutheran) uniformity of the German Reformation in Bernd Moeller and Karl Stackmann, *Städtische Predigt in der Frühzeit der Reformation: Eine Untersuchung deutscher Flugschriften der Jahre 1522 bis 1529* (Göttingen, Germany: Vandenhoeck & Ruprecht, 1996). Cf. the essays in Berndt Hamm, Bernd Moeller, and Dorothea Wendebourg, *Reformationstheorien: Ein kirchenhistorischer Disput über Einheit und Vielfalt der Reformation* (Göttingen: Vandenhoeck & Ruprecht, 1995).

rienced clergyman.[18] In addition, there were numerous handbooks for priests, which told them how to carry out their office.[19] These emphasized the correctness of the liturgy. After the Reformation was put in place, there was in the short term no formal curriculum for the training of pastors. The sons of well-off and prominent families might go beyond the basic arts curriculum and study theology as soon as they perceived their inclination toward the clerical vocation. But those who gained some formal acquaintance with Protestant theology quickly moved into urban posts, leaving most of the countryside unimproved until the seventeenth century.

How, then, to guarantee the orthodoxy of sermons? This was a challenge that could be met by no simple mechanism. The emerging churches confronted this problem with a set of intertwined techniques. The cities of Germany ordinarily had a number of villages, including the village parishes, under their supervision. The urban clergy both officially and informally kept an ear attuned to the pulpit performances of their more junior as well as their rural colleagues. As ecclesiastical structures evolved, senior urban pastors could be named superintendents and be given the oversight of their lesser colleagues. In this and similar capacities, these leading clerics dropped in on sermons, with or without notice. Visitation committees periodically made their rounds, imposing preaching as one of the requisite demonstrations of pastors' and deacons' suitability for reappointment. Especially in view of the lack of replacements, supervisors met infractions with forbearance and patient correction, admonishing all their charges to further, regular study. To this end, parsonages *had* to have separate chambers to which clergy could withdraw to their books from the household hullabaloo. Toward the close of the century, as their economic status stabilized, pastors were increasingly likely to have a tiny collection of books to which they could turn. This often included a volume of Luther's postils,

---

[18]   Karant-Nunn, *Luther's Pastors*, pp. 13-21; Friedrich Wilhelm Oediger, *Über die Bildung der Geistlichen im späten Mittelalter* (Leiden: Brill, 1953), esp. "Das notwendige Wissen," pp. 46-57. Bernard Vogler, *Le clergé protestant rhénan au siècle de la Réforme, 1552-1619* (Paris: Ophrys, 1976), begins a full generation after the start of the Reformation and thus presents somewhat more advanced conditions than would have prevailed at the beginning of the sixteenth century.

[19]   Peter A. Dykema, "Handbooks for Pastors: Late Medieval Manuals for Parish Priests and Conrad Porta's *Pastorale Lutheri* (1582)," forthcoming in Andrew C. Gow and Robert J. Bast, eds., *Continuity and Change: Studies in Honor of Heiko Augustinus Oberman on His Seventieth Birthday* (Leiden: Brill, forthcoming October 2000).

though seldom for the entire year. Where there was a Bible, this was usually provided by the parish itself.

None of these measures fully satisfied theologians in the age of orthodoxy, however, which was characterized by vicious doctrinal strife. The spirit of the time demanded additional guarantees that every preached word conformed to the overseers' expectations. In such an atmosphere, only the verbatim reading of printed prayers and sermons could assuage theologians' anxieties. As a result, liturgical rubrics provided sermons and other parts of the service of worship for pastors to pronounce aloud. The irony is plain: a better-trained pastorate was made to revert to the late medieval pattern of reading out loud the sermons of reliable divines! Such sermons were plentifully available, for it became fashionable in Lutheran– but not in Calvinist–lands for the occupants of prestigious pulpits, whose orthodoxy went mainly unchallenged, to collect their homilies and submit them for publication. Hundreds of thousands of sixteenth-century printed sermons have consequently survived, and they evidently graced the domestic devotions of literate urban families. Some of these may have been employed in rural pulpits; certainly Luther's own postils still served there.[20]

The late sixteenth century was, then, an age of concern about the content of sermons. Those ministers who were attuned to their superiors did not mount the pulpit and expound on the Bible at will. Luther had done this, but his more ordinary successors could only seize such liberty at their peril.

Powers of Persuasion

Not only the content of sermons was at issue. Preaching was needed to rouse parishioners from the torpor that routinely overcame them after they took their places in church. One of the side-benefits of the Lutheran retention of standing, kneeling, and singing was that it postponed the temptation to fall asleep–postponed it until the hour of the sermon. The dead in the graveyard might be

---

[20]   An example of this genre, which was clearly intended to guide less well prepared clergymen, is Caspar Huberinus [superintendent in Oehringen, d. 1553], *Postila Teutsch, Vber alle Sontägliche Euangelion, vom Aduent biß auff Ostern, Kurtze vnd nützliche Außlegung* (Nuremberg: Johann Daubman, 1548).

thought of as holy sleepers, but those snoring in their pews definitely could not. English Puritan congregations sometimes had beadles, part of whose duties was to keep people awake during the sermon, but to my knowledge, German churches did not. How, then, was the Holy Spirit to do its work of rooting faith in the worshipper? How were the ignorant to gain instruction? Early modern people had no concept of subliminal hearing.

The task of holding the attention of the laity rested on the sermonizers. Without formal training in homiletics, the grammar school- and university-educated pastor could at least recall his lessons in rhetoric. Perhaps Philipp Melanchthon (1497-1560) had preaching, too, in mind as (in 1519, 1521, and 1531) he prepared editions of his textbook on rhetoric for publication.[21] For this humanist-Reformer, the well-being of society rested in the hands of the good man (*vir bonus*), who could hardly fulfill his essential functions without the ability to mold public opinion by means of speech.[22] Melanchthon's schoolbooks quickly made their way to the heart of the basic arts curriculum, but the subject of rhetoric itself had been there since the revival of the *trivium* (grammar, dialectic, and rhetoric) centuries earlier. In the Reformation context, the role of the preacher was easily conflated with that of the secular speaker: each was, within his sphere, to manifest the virtues of the Renaissance *good man* and so to shape and elevate society.

Bruce Tolley has described the studies of future clergymen in the seminary (*Stift*) in Tübingen at the end of the sixteenth century. Material learned from lectures in both theology and rhetoric was rehearsed, and mastery ultimately demonstrated, by means of the very traditional disputation and the more Renaissance-influenced declamation. The young men apparently read Calvinist works in order to make them the targets of their polemics.[23] A rudimentary homiletics grew naturally within this context, and during this late Reformation period, according to Tolley, the seminarians each gave about three practice sermons per year. This paucity, he opines, "perhaps accounts for the poor evaluations that some of the candi-

---

[21] Within the newer literature are Joachim Knape, *Philipp Melanchthons "Rhetorik,"* (Tübingen, Germany: Max Niemeyer Verlag, 1993); Olaf Berwald, *Philipp Melanchthons Sicht der Rhetorik* (Wiesbaden, Germany: Harrassowitz, 1994).

[22] Berwald, pp. 32-36.

[23] Tolley, *Pastors and Parishioners in Württemberg during the Late Reformation 1581-1621* (Stanford, Calif.: Stanford University Press, 1995), pp. 32-35.

dates for the pastorate received from the consistory."[24] Luise
Schorn-Schütte provides evidence of the late arrival of a formal
homiletics requirement for all who would enter the pastorate. Until
at least the late seventeenth century, theological mastery and a
moral life remained the salient qualifications for the Lutheran
clerisy.[25] The abilities especially of rural pastors to penetrate the
somnolence of their audiences varied greatly. The most naturally
gifted preachers, like Zwingli, moved with greater ease from country to city posts. Peasants sometimes pointed out to visitors that
they avoided sermons because these were so dull.

Pastors as Moral Guardians

The preaching function cannot be detached from the larger configuration of obligations that the sixteenth-century Protestant clergy
bore. In their sermons, on whatever topics, preachers presented to
their hearers both explicitly and implicitly a model of the Christian
life that they, the clerics themselves, were intended to embody. Part
of the responsibility of clergymen, whether from the pulpit or in
their daily interactions with the laity, was to render the laity more
than nominally Christian.

In Zwinglian, Lutheran, and later also in Calvinist lands, the
preachers' rising status in relation to the laity is symbolized by the
pulpit. The clergy were no longer technically elevated by their special miraculous powers and their ability to mediate between human
beings and the Divine. Instead, the pulpit physically raised them
above the heads of their neighbors. During the sixteenth century,
this piece of ecclesiastical furniture became not only ubiquitous but
higher in altitude, artistically elaborated in Lutheran and Catholic
parishes, and costly. Further, these structures were not peripheral
but penetrated to the heart of the pews. This was done ostensibly
so that everyone could see and hear, and surely this intention was
genuine. But if we consider that in this period, pews were built
nearly everywhere and people expected to sit and to *stay* in them

---

[24]   Ibid., pp. 34-35.
[25]   This was true in Basel as well, as Amy Nelson Burnett's unpublished paper,
"Funding Future Pastors: The Financing of Theological Education in Sixteenth-Century Basel," makes clear.

until dismissed by the benediction, we may perceive another disciplinary dimension in the program of those who determined the arrangement of the local sanctuary. The poverty of a community was a hindrance, but it did not stop the general evolution of church interiors. Congregations were more or less willing but nonetheless captive audiences. Refusal to attend the sermon and to receive the Lord's Supper became, in this authoritarian era, a punishable offense – indeed, it occasionally met with exile. More often, those who were chronically lax, provided their behavior did not represent outright doctrinal recusancy, were buried without the traditional ceremonies (in late medieval Catholicism summarized with the words *crux, lux, dux* – cross, light, procession). Calvinism eliminated these rituals as idolatrous, in any case, but developed in excommunication and rigorous penitential observances its own means of removing the nonconformist from the Christian commonality. The arrangement of Calvinist sanctuaries in the sixteenth and seventeenth centuries reflects a nearly exclusive orientation toward the very prominent pulpit.[26]

The man who preached, then, spoke as an authority and scrutinized the demeanor of his charges as he held forth. The bodies of the audience were held in place, their faces directed toward the pulpit. All the same, the more popular preachers knew how to appeal to the laity by larding their rhetoric with meaningful exempla, now cleansed of the more fanciful late medieval stories that Luther and the other Reformers had decried. Johannes Mathesius (d. 1565), pastor in the silver-mining town of Joachimsthal, drew on the experiences of miners and their families, and on one occasion even donned the garb of a miner.[27] Such preachers possessed an ability to hold their listeners spellbound. Gifted, sensitive clerics clearly won their congregations' enthusiasm and steadfast loyalty.

In the stern atmosphere of the late sixteenth and early seventeenth centuries, the sermonizing encounter was only one of several in which the laity and their ministers engaged one another; and

---

[26] Paul Corby Finney, ed., *Seeing Beyond the Word: Visual Arts and the Calvinist Tradition* (Grand Rapids, Mich.: William B. Eerdmans, 1999), those parts on the early period of Calvinism, passim.

[27] For example, the whole series of sermons built around mining themes: *SA-REPTA* [sic] *Oder Bergpostil, Sampt der Jochimßthalischen kurtzen Chroniken . . .* (Nuremberg: Johann vom Berg and Vlrich Newber, 1562), subsequently published in at least four further editions.

these other encounters must be considered in reconstructing the place of the preacher in society. Clergymen who exercised the cure of souls had always occupied a middle ground between secular authority and people. Even where their social provenance and their humble preparation for the priesthood hardly set them apart from the ordinary laity around them, owing to their sacred status they had access to their more lofty neighbors and could provide a channel of communication between ranks as disparate as nobles and peasants. Above all, literacy being relatively scarce outside the cities, a common cosmic view, including acceptance of a hierarchical and animated universe, bound the echelons together.

Although attaining its objectives took up much time and unflagging effort, the Reformation was everywhere determined to enlist the clergy in the grand enterprise of reconciling religious ideals and the convictions, manifested by the behavior, of Christians.[28] Even though abandoning the enumeration of sins in confession, Lutheran ecclesiastics wished to know the inner state of members of the visible church, and this best revealed itself in deportment. Before as after the Reformation, preachers touted piety, love, and service of neighbors, a certain self-abnegation, and the moderation of sexual, violent, and self-serving impulses. All of these principles had biblical support, and the Reformers took the enforcement of these rules as their God-given duty. In close cooperation with the state, superintendents and consistories henceforward watched the clergy watching the people. Under the circumstances, princes and magistrates strove to render the parish clergy scions and agents of the moral as well as the secular order.[29] They prepared them for this new role by requiring a higher degree of training in the liberal arts and theology for entering the ministry. This improvement in education is visible in the visitation protocols not later than the early seventeenth century. At the same time, a greater percentage of the pastorate derived from Germany's cities and towns than in earlier times. The advancing Reformation may be seen in part as a

---

[28]   Bruce Gordon, "Preaching and the Reform of the Clergy in the Swiss Reformation," in Andrew Pettegree, ed., *The Reformation of the Parishes: The Ministry and the Reformation in Town and Country* (Manchester.: Manchester University Press, 1993), pp. 63-84, on this point at p. 80.

[29]   See Luise Schorn-Schütte's summation, "Priest, Preacher, Pastor: Research on Clerical Office in Early Modern Europe," *Central European History* 33 (2000), 1-40, here at p. 36.

campaign of acculturation in the countryside, an urban *Drang nach aussen*.[30] If such aggrandizing, incorporative motives were unconscious, they are nonetheless visible everywhere. Ecclesiastical and worldly authorities required pastors to assist them in identifying transgressors, and they made no clean distinction between spiritual and civil sins. In the pulpit, the preachers searched their neighbors' faces not just for alertness and comprehension but also for the will to live out the values expounded.

Within Lutheran parishes, those who preached knew each soul intimately from a daily acquaintance and especially from periodic exchanges in the confessional. This was ordinarily true in Catholic regions as well, except that Capuchin and Jesuit preachers might hold forth in communities where they were not also residents and confessors.[31] Under Calvinism, which abolished auricular confession, elders assisted the clergy in apprising themselves of the moral condition of every inhabitant. Yet, I do not suggest that relations were hostile between preachers and their fellows. There is some evidence of a revived anticlericalism during this coercive age, but many communities probably managed to resolve tensions between clergy and laity.[32] Pastors who made themselves despicable were bound to suffer unpleasant consequences in their daily lives, and as practical men they found ways of accommodating the world view of those in their care. They were perpetually suspended between popular and official values.

---

[30] I take this to be the fundamental message of Robert Muchembled, *Popular Culture and Elite Culture in France 1400-1750*, trans. Lydia Cochrane (Baton Route, La.: Louisiana State University Press, 1985), and I agree with it. I do think that Muchembled differentiates too baldly between the popular culture and the elite culture of the title.

[31] Cf. W. David Myers, *"Poor, Sinning Folk": Confession and Conscience in Counter-Reformation Germany* (Ithaca, N. Y.: Cornell University Press, 1996).

[32] R. W. Scribner, "Anticlericalism and the Reformation in Germany," in idem, *Popular Culture and Popular Movements in Reformation Germany* (London and Ronceverte: Hambledon Press, 1987), pp. 242-56, esp. pp. 252-56. This inspired my own "Neoclericalism and Anticlericalism in Saxony, 1555-1675, *Journal of Interdisciplinary History* 24 (1994), 615-37; and possibly also Scribner's student, C. Scott Dixon, "Rural Resistance, the Lutheran Pastor, and the Territorial Church in Brandenburg Ansbach-Kulmbach, 1528-1603," in Andrew Pettegree, ed., *The Reformation of the Parishes: The Ministry and the Reformation in Town and Country* (Manchester, Eng.: Manchester University Press, 1993), pp. 85-112; Sabine Holtz, *Theologie und Alltag: Lehre und Leben in den Predigten der Tübinger Theologen 1550-1750* (Tübingen: J. C. B. Mohr [Paul Siebeck], 1993), pp. 351-52. See also Amy Nelson Burnett, "Basel's Rural Pastors as Mediators of Confessional and Social Discipline," *Central European History* 33 (2000), 67-86.

Preaching and Rites of Passage

The century from 1550 to 1650 and beyond witnessed a massive flowering of the Lutheran sermon as an edifying and, in its printed form, literary genre. In Catholic and Calvinist regions, as frequent as preaching now also was, the sheer volume of published sermons attained nothing like that found in Lutheran domains. Not even all of the sermons of John Calvin (1509-64) have been published.[33] Why this should be remains something of a mystery.

Within Lutheranism, as shown above, the initial stress was upon the correct, persuasive explication of the faith to unsophisticated audiences, and, in line with theological conviction, the awakening of faith through the hearing of the Word. Both of these goals were achievable by means of the paired regular Sunday sermon, which dealt with the full range of themes that could be built upon biblical texts, and the catechetical sermon. By mid-century these were seen as inadequate to the task of converting people's hearts. A confessionalizing, indeed veritably missionizing church bureaucracy now demanded that pastors and deacons also preach on other key occasions that, owing to their nature, would sooner or later involve nearly every parishioner: at weddings and at funerals. Calvin, meanwhile, prohibited both forms and relied instead on the recitation of those scriptural passages that served his evangelical counterparts as texts. While no one has yet plumbed the volume of extant printed wedding homilies, Rudolf Lenz has ventured a highly informed guess that about a quarter of a million funeral sermons have survived.[34] Both wedding and funeral sermons that were published were presented by Lutheran Germany's leading divines and usually marked the nuptials or the passing of individuals of higher

---

[33] See Parker, *Calvin's Preaching*, pp. 65-75. Bernard Roussel and Larissa Taylor have informed me that in France, neither Catholic nor Huguenot sermons were often published after the 1530s. This is understandable in the Huguenot case, particularly as these nonconformists' position deteriorated. On France, see Taylor's two books: *Soldiers of Christ: Preaching in Late Medieval and Reformation France* (New York: Oxford University Press, 1992); and *Heresy and Orthodoxy in Sixteenth-Century Paris: François Le Picart and the Beginnings of the Catholic Reformation*, Studies in Medieval and Reformation Thought 77 (Leiden: Brill, 1999).

[34] Lenz, *De mortuis nil nisi bene? Leichenpredigten als multidisziplinäre Quelle unter besonderer Berücksichtigung der historischen Familienforschung, der Bildungsgeschichte und der Literaturgeschichte*, Marburger Personalschriften-Forschungen 10 (Sigmaringen, Germany: Jan Thorbecke, 1990), pp. 20-21.

social standing. In some parishes, elite citizens had to pay an extra fee to the pastor for a full-blown and original sermon. Nevertheless, a modest, routinized preaching was expected to take place at the marriages and interments of unexceptional people. Such sermons explained already well-known Bible passages.

Implicit in the wide dissemination of published sermons is the conviction that reading, too, could engender faith in the literate Christian. A prosperous urban class must have been buying these volumes for their household devotions, and possibly, too, as a means of displaying to visitors their piety and intellectual capability. Finally, as already suggested, the contents of these books were to serve as models to less qualified clergymen.

I have written elsewhere about wedding sermons for what they (and other sermons) reveal about the preachers' social convictions, and for their part in a campaign to define gender roles.[35] In brief, it increasingly fell within the purview of pastors to further instruct couples on their proper relationship than had been accomplished in the late Middle Ages by the recitation of the Genesis verses about Adam and Eve or expositions of the Wedding at Cana.[36] Just why a longer, more emphatic exposition of late medieval values seemed now to be needed lay within the clerical mentality of the day, which was not satisfied with the degree of conformity to its model that traditional accounts had won. Women and men were too flexible in their relations, and societal disorder was enraging God, whose vengeance loomed over all. Preachers were enjoined to rectify this problem by describing truly Christian deportment to couples and their guests. To the modern reader, the messages are paradoxical: they enthusiastically advocate marriage as an estate to be entered by practically every adult, but at the same time they

---

[35] "*Kinder, Küche, Kirche*: Social Ideology in the Sermons of Johannes Mathesius," in Andrew C. Fix and Susan C. Karant-Nunn, eds., *Germania Illustrata: Essays on Early Modern Germany Presented to Gerald Strauss*, Sixteenth Century Essays & Studies 18 (Kirksville, Mo.: Sixteenth Century Journal Publishers, 1992), pp. 121-40; "'Fragrant Wedding Roses': Lutheran Wedding Sermons and Gender Definition in Early Modern Germany," *German History* 17 (1999), 25-40.

[36] On changes in the nuptial rites in general after the Reformation, see my *The Reformation of Ritual: An Interpretation of Early Modern Germany* (London and New York: Routledge, 1997), pp. 6-42; and Lyndal Roper, "'Going to Church and Street': Weddings in Reformation Augsburg," *Past and Present* 106 (1985), 62-101.

often express a severe mistrust of women.[37] They have abandoned the Catholic preference for the celibate life, yet they continue the pattern of misogyny laid down centuries earlier by a clergy that undergirded its own abstinence with harsh rhetoric. Of course, each preacher revealed his own personal qualities in his sermons. Certain preachers, such as Caspar Huberinus, Paul Rebhun, and Johannes Mathesius were more stringent in their views of women, however little they might have recognized this label; and Johannes Freder (Ireneus) and Cyriakus Spangenberg were more generous.[38]

It did not behoove Lutheran preachers to make women the objects of such thoroughgoing reprehension that men hesitated to marry. Nevertheless, Reformation clerics often concertedly disseminated the rhetorical patterns long established by late medieval divines. According to these, women, as the weaker vessels and daughters of Eve, had to know their place, which was invariably the home. Here and in public they wore headbands that denoted their subordination to their husbands, and they bowed their heads (*tücken*; in modern German *ducken*) before them. They used whatever resources their spouses gave to them and managed their housekeeping, however meagerly. They did not go out to work, for women's gainful employment would make their husbands beholden to them. Men were the lions, the majesty, the sun, the abbots of the domestic monastic establishment; women's authority was delegated to them and not theirs by right.

The preachers did seek – not unlike some of their predecessors – to foster mutual love and trust among their charges. This was to be achieved by means of wives' complete submission and husbands'

---

[37] Another summary of the images of women presented in sermons is to be found in Helga Schüppert, "Frauenbild und Frauenalltag in der Predigtliteratur," in *Frau und spätmittelalterlicher Alltag* (Vienna: Österreichische Akademie der Wissenschaften, 1986), pp. 103-56. See also the essays in Rüdiger Schnell, ed., *Text und Geschlecht: Mann und Frau in Eheschriften der frühen Neuzeit* (Frankfurt/Main: Suhrkamp, 1997); and most recently, idem, *Geschlechterbeziehungen und Textfunktionen: Studien zu Eheschriften der Frühen Neuzeit* (Tübingen: Max Niemeyer, 1998).

[38] I have made this remark in greater detail in "'Fragrant Wedding Roses'," pp. 27-28, and provided references to the literature on these men. Particularly valuable to anyone thinking of researching this topic is the bibliography prepared by Erika Kartschoke, ed., *Repertorium deutschsprachiger Ehelehren der frühen Neuzeit*, vol. 1, pt. 1, *Handschriften und Drucke der Staatsbibliothek zu Berlin/Preußischer Kulturbesitz (Haus 2)* (Berlin: Akademie Verlag, 1996).

conscientious forbearance. Men should "look through their fingers" at their mates—that is, they should refuse to perceive all their wives' shortcomings, for otherwise they would be perpetually discontented. They should love their wives as they loved themselves; husband and wife were one flesh, and no man should hate his own body.

Despite the endurance of this role-defining ideology into the nineteenth and even the twentieth century, some qualitative changes can be observed. Preachers gradually admitted a more emotional, even erotic love to the proper bond between spouses. This shift is perceptible in the wedding sermons of the early seventeenth century. Rudolf Lenz goes too far in denying that personal inclination and affection were to be found in the early modern family.[39] Luther's own insistence upon the inevitability of sexual desire helped to prepare for this trend, although in his own time, Luther found it necessary to insist that he had not married out of love; in 1525, the year he married Katharina von Bora, he defined *love* as sexual desire. The pastorate also came to admit that a good deal of the malfunctioning of marriage lay in the responsibility of husbands, who were too often drunken and who beat and abandoned their wives more frequently than wives their husbands. Still, the astute cleric knew from long experience, including his own marriage(s), that harmony was ultimately the achievement of both partners, and that heartfelt love greatly facilitated it.

The second great life-course venue of preaching in the age of orthodoxy was the funeral.[40] Even before death, the pastor or the deacon was to appear at the dying person's bedside and preach to her, the family, servants, and neighbors on some aspect of repentance and reliance upon the atoning act of Christ on the cross. This was the preliminary segment of a homiletic program of preparing the laity for a proper death. The rituals of the dying chamber implicitly express uncertainty about the salvation of those who died an *improper* death. Calvin, in eliminating deathbed and most funerary rituals, conformed practice more completely to his conviction that God determined people's destinations "before the foundation of the world." In addition, some people thought that the preaching at the

---

[39] "'Ehestand, Wehestand, Süßbitter Stand'? Betrachtungen zur Familie der Frühen Neuzeit," *Archiv für Kulturgeschichte* 68 (1986), 371-405, here at pp. 384-85.

[40] I have written about death and dying in *The Reformation of Ritual*, pp. 138-89.

graveside inevitably produced encomia, or inflated descriptions of the virtues of the deceased, which militated against proper humility in the listeners.

Eulogies or not, funeral sermons became an institution in Lutheran lands. Ideally, they were intended to impress human mortality upon those who were present: the best preparation for death lay in living with the outcome in mind. In this respect, Protestant culture displayed continuity with medieval conviction. In their rhetoric, preachers repeatedly characterized life on earth as "this vale of tears" (*dieses Jammerthal*), departing remarkably little (except for the pontiff's condemnation of marriage and reproduction) from Innocent's III's treatise, "On the Misery of the Human Condition," of about 1195.[41]

The Preaching of Easter Week

An unavoidable paschal task of even the humblest of late medieval parish priests was to impress upon his congregation the dire agony that Christ had endured for the sake of its eternal well-being. This duty coincided with the time when nearly all Latin Christians, in compliance with the decrees of the Fourth Lateran Council (1215), fulfilled their annual obligation to confess and receive the eucharist. During Easter Week, the churches were packed. People came not only because they were told to do so; part of the attraction of this week was precisely the dramatic depiction of the Lord's suffering and the communal grief and repentance that this unleashed. An ardent personal identification with Christ in His ordeal lay at the heart of the widespread high and late medieval religious expressiveness that we know as *affective piety*.[42]

---

[41]   Lothario dei Segni, *On the Misery of the Human Condition*, ed. Donald R. Howard (New York: Bobbs-Merrill, 1969).

[42]   Carolyn Walker Bynum has popularized this concept in, for example, *Jesus as Mother: Studies in the Spirituality of the High Middle Ages* (Berkeley, Calif.: University of California Press, 1982), esp. pp. 3-21, 77-81, 105-109, 129-135, and in a chapter entitled "Jesus as Mother and Abbot as Mother," pp. 110-69 and 264-65. Bynum (personal communication) attributes the "discovery" of this mode of piety to André Wilmart, *Auteurs spirituels et textes dévots du moyen âge latin: Études d'histoire littéraire* (Paris: Bloud et Gay, 1932); Louis Gougaud, *Devotional and Ascetic Practices in the Middle Ages* (London: Burns, Oates & Washbourne, 1927); Marie Dominque Chenu, *La théologie au douzième siècle*, Études de philosophie médiévale 45 (Paris: J. Vrin, 1957); and André Vauchez, *La*

Jesuit, Capuchin, and other Counter-Reformation preachers actively sustained this kind of arousal and made it a prominent feature of Catholic identity and commitment during this period. In keeping with Luther's pointed disapproval, Protestant authorities scorned it and at least initially discouraged overlong, overly moving homiletics. The Lutheran Johann Kymeus declared mockingly,

> It was the ultimate goal of those who preached the Passion [to consider] how one could move the people to crying, to howling, and to lamenting over the unkind Jews and hard-hearted people who took the life of Christ, God's Son. But the recognition of sin and faith, which one ought chiefly by means of the Passion to bring about–this remained behind.[43]

Nevertheless, among Lutheran Passion sermons of the late sixteenth century there is great variability in the amount of attention paid to the minutiae of Christ's suffering as opposed to the abstract doctrine of the atonement and its benefits for humankind. Where the older pattern remained intact, this was probably owing to the convergence of two psychological traits: that of the preachers, whose faith disposed them to sympathize profoundly with the Son of God and to try to impart that zeal to those in their care; and that of many hearers, who welcomed the traditional melodrama and catharsis of Holy Week.

In his own Passion sermons, Calvin abandoned the recital of Jesus' agony and turned instead to a studied concentration upon the unworthiness of each and every one of His listeners. The emotion that Calvin, and possibly also his followers (whose surviving sermons are all too few), strove to elicit was extreme self-deprecation.[44]

An aspect of Lutheran and Catholic Passion sermons that abso-

---

spiritualité au moyen âge occidental: VIIIe-XIIe siècles (Paris: Presses universitaires de France, 1975).

[43] From a collection of Passion sermons by Urbanus Rhegius, Johann Kymeus, Johannes Bugenhagen, and Martin Luther, Passional Buch. Vom Leiden vnd Aufferstehung vnsers Herrn Jhesu Christi . . . (Wittenberg: Georg Rhaw, 1540), fol. x. On emotion, see Susan C. Karant-Nunn, "'Gedanken, Herz und Sinn': Die Unterdrückung der religiösen Emotionen," in Bernhard Jussen and Craig M. Koslofsky, eds., Kulturelle Reformation (Göttingen: Vandenhoeck & Ruprecht, 1999), pp. 65-90; and my forthcoming essay, "Patterns of Religious Practice: Nontheological Features," in Thomas A. Brady, Jr., ed., volume of essays to appear in 2001.

[44] I have used Jean Calvin, Plusieurs Sermons de Iejan Calvin touchant la diuinite, humanite, et natiuite de nostre Seigneur Iesus Christi . . . (n. p.: Conrad Badius, 1558), pp. 28-267, which are the Passion sermons.

lutely demands further study is their explicit anti-Semitism. It may well prove that Passion preaching, with its ongoing immoderate allegations of Jewish guilt for Christ's execution, was a vehicle for sustaining medieval prejudices not only in the early modern era but in the modern one as well. Only in their preparations for the performance of the year 2000 did the script writers of the famed Oberammergau Passion play choose to eliminate the worst anti-Semitic expressions from their text.

Preaching and Society

In the age of Reformation and Counter-Reformation, preaching emerged as a mode of communication more prominent than before or since. In practice, its functions were far more numerous than simply to inculcate correct belief and confessional identity upon the laity. In a time lacking electronic media and in which governors had no qualms about imposing requisite church attendance upon all subjects, the spoken sermon reached a large segment of the Protestant populace. We may well assume that in systematically and repeatedly publicizing theologians' beliefs and social values, it gradually influenced – though it never fully formed – people's convictions.[45] This cannot have been achieved within one or two generations, and the mid-sixteenth century is too early a terminus from which to judge the Reformation's success or failure.

Sermons did much else. They steeled their hearers in times of war. They moved them to hate the Turks. They helped communities to deal with the ravages of disease. They urged prayers for the well-being of princes and magistrates and their families. In the midst of all of these functions, they informed people of current events. Churches were, in any case, often those village and urban structures in which the terms of engagements were reached, worldly contracts agreed upon, meetings held, and announcements made.[46]

---

[45]   On the power of the sermon, see Elfriede Moser-Rath, "Familienleben im Spiegel der Barockpredigt," in Werner Welzig, ed., *Predigt und soziale Wirklichkeit: Beiträge zur Erforschung der Predigtliteratur*, Daphnis, Zeitschrift für mittlere deutsche Literatur 10 (1981), 47-65, esp. p. 65.

[46]   Elfriede Moser-Rath asserts that Bavarian Protestant sermons of the baroque period yield little to the folkloric researcher, because the preachers did not relate Scripture to the daily lives of the people (quoted by Leonhard Intorp, *Westfälische Barock-*

The premises lent their sanctity to numerous occasions, although after the Reformation, these edifices were locked up more and more frequently between services of worship.

Sermons attuned the lay ear to a higher form of its native language than it would otherwise have regularly heard; and through their citation of the Lutheran Bible and other vernacular translations, they fixed New High German within the popular ken. This linguistic fact, however, could lead us to believe that clergymen, in their homiletic role, simply acted upon their audiences: they informed, they indoctrinated, they judged. In practice, communication is an exchange between two or more parties. Sabine Holtz has rightly described the sermon as existing "at the boundary [*Nahtstelle*] between theology and everyday life."[47] In order to succeed, preachers had to respond to the physical circumstances, the social structure, and the cultural assumptions of their hearers. No printed sermons can relay to modern researchers the dynamics, the conditions of interchange between the homilist and the community on a particular occasion. Lacking this information, we can hardly penetrate to the core of meanings within the communicative moment. All the same, we must acknowledge these multiple valences. Preachers could not simply harangue their audiences. They had to build upon a foundation of common understanding, incorporating the language and exempla of everyday life. They could not only look down from the pulpit to judge people's moral condition. They tailored their remarks to their particular congregation in its current vicissitudes. They took cues from the glances and expressions of their neighbors. They invented sermons that met local needs. They responded . . . or they failed.

Acknowledgements

Thanks to Peter A. Dykema and John M. Frymire for reading an earlier version of this essay critically and giving me the benefit of their expertise.

---

predigten in volkskundlicher Sicht [Münster/W.: Aschendorff, 1964] , p. 8). I find this hard to believe, for many Protestant sermons are replete with popular references and turns of phrase.

[47] Holtz, *Theologie und Alltag*, p. 6.

Bibliography

Bériou, Nicole and David D'Avray, eds., *Modern Questions about Medieval Sermons: Essays on Marriage, Death, History and Sanctity* (Spoleto: Centro italiano di studi sull' Alto medievo, 1994).

Burnett, Amy Nelson, "Funding Future Pastors: The Financing of Theological Education in Sixteenth-Century Basel," unpublished paper.

— "Basel's Rural Pastors as Mediators of Confessional and Social Discipline," *Central European History* 33, 1 (2000), 67-86.

Cruel, Rudolf, *Geschichte der deutschen Predigt im Mittelalter* (Hildesheim: Georg Olms Verlagsbuchhandlung, 1966. Reprint of original 1879 edition).

Dixon, C. Scott, "Rural Resistance, the Lutheran Pastor, and the Territorial Church in Brandenburg Ansbach-Kulmbach, 1528-1603," in *The Reformation of the Parishes: The Ministry and the Reformation in Town and Country*, ed. Andrew Pettegree (Manchester: Manchester University Press, 1993), pp. 85-112.

Dykema, Peter A., "Handbooks for Pastors: Late Medieval Manuals for Parish Priests and Conrad Porta's *Pastorale Lutheri* (1582)," in *Continuity and Change: Studies in Honor of Heiko Augustinus Oberman on His Seventieth Birthday*, eds. Andrew C. Gow and Robert J. Bast (Leiden: Brill, 2000).

Gordon, Bruce, "Preaching and the Reform of the Clergy in the Swiss Reformation," in *The Reformation of the Parishes: The Ministry and the Reformation in Town and Country*, ed. Andrew Pettegree (Manchester: Manchester University Press, 1993), pp. 63-84.

Haemig, Mary Jane, "The Living Voice of the Catechism: German Lutheran Catechetical Preaching, 1530-1580," Ph.D. diss., Harvard Divinity School, 1996.

Hamesse, Jacqueline, Beverly Mayne Kienzle, Debra L. Stoudt, and Anne T. Thayer, eds., *Medieval Sermons and Society: Cloister, City, University* (Louvain-la-Neuve: Fédération Internationale des Institutes d'Études Médiévales, 1998).

Hamm, Berndt, Bernd Moeller, and Dorothea Wendebourg, *Reformationstheorien: Ein kirchenhistorischer Disput über Einheit und Vielfalt der Reformation* (Göttingen: Vandenhoeck & Ruprecht, 1995).

Hannemann, Manfred, *The Diffusion of the Reformation in Southwestern Germany, 1518-1534* (Chicago: Department of Geography, University of Chicago, 1975).

Herrmann, Rudolf, "Die Prediger im ausgehenden Mittelalter und ihre Bedeutung für die Einführung der Reformation im ernestinischen Thüringen," *Beiträge zur thüringischen Kirchengeschichte* 1, 1 (1929), 20-68.

Holtz, Sabine, *Theologie und Alltag: Lehre und Leben in den Predigten der Tübinger Theologen 1550-1750* (Tübingen: J. C. B. Mohn [Paul Siebeck], 1993).

Izbicki, Thomas M., "Pyres of Vanities: Mendicant Preaching on the Vanity of Women and Its Lay Audience," in *De ore Domini: Preacher and Word in the Middle Ages*, eds. Thomas L. Amos, Eugene A. Green, and Beverly Mayne Kienzle (Kalamazoo, Michigan: Medieval Institute Publications, 1989), pp. 211-34.

Karant-Nunn, Susan C., " 'Fragrant Wedding Roses': Lutheran Wedding Sermons and Gender Definition in Early Modern Germany," *German History* 17, 1 (1999), 25-40.

— "*Kinder, Küche, Kirche*: Social Ideology in the Sermons of Johannes Mathesius," in *Germania Illustrata: Essays on Early Modern Germany Presented to Gerald Strauss*, ed. Andrew C. Fix and Susan C. Karant-Nunn, Sixteenth Century Essays & Studies 18 (Kirksville, Missouri: Sixteenth Century Journal Publishers, 1992), pp. 121-40.

— *Luther's Pastors: The Reformation in the Ernestine Countryside* (Philadelphia: American Philosophical Society, 1979).

— "Neoclericalism and Anticlericalism in Saxony, 1555-1675," *Journal of Interdisciplinary History* 24, 4 (1994), 615-37.

— "What Was Preached in German Cities in the Early Years of the Reformation? *Wildwuchs* versus Lutheran Unity," in *The Process of Change in Early Modern Europe: Essays in Honor of Miriam Usher Chrisman*, eds. Phillip N. Bebb and Sherrin Marshall (Athens, Ohio: Ohio University Press, 1988), pp. 81-96.

Lenz, Rudolf, *De mortuis nil nisi bene? Leichenpredigten als multidisziplinäre Quelle unter besonderer Berücksichtigung der historischen Familienforschung, der Bildungsgeschichte und der Literaturgeschichte*, Marburger Personalschriften-Forschungen 10 (Sigmaringen, Germany: Jan Thorbecke, 1990).

Moeller, Bernd, "Was wurde in der Frühzeit der Reformation in den deutschen Städten gepredigt?" *Archiv für Reformationsgeschichte* 75 (1984), 176-93.

— and Karl Stackmann, *Städtische Predigt in der Frühzeit der Reformation: Eine Untersuchung deutscher Flugschriften der Jahre 1522 bis 1529* (Göttingen: Vandenhoeck & Ruprecht, 1996).

Moser-Rath, Elfriede, "Familienleben im Spiegel der Barockpredigt," in *Predigt und soziale Wirklichkeit: Beiträge zur Erforschung der Predigtliteratur*, ed. Werner Welzig, special issue of *Daphnis: Zeitschrift für mittlere deutsche Literatur* 10, 1 (1981), 47-65.

Myers, W. David, *"Poor, Sinning Folk": Confession and Conscience in Counter-Reformation Germany* (Ithaca, New York: Cornell University Press, 1996).

Oediger, Friedrich Wilhelm, *Über die Bildung der Geistlichen im späten Mittel-alter* (Leiden: Brill, 1953).

Ozment, Steven E., *The Age of Reform 1250-1550: An Intellectual and Religious History of Late Medieval and Reformation Europe* (New Haven, Connecticut: Yale University Press, 1980).

— *The Reformation in the Cities: The Appeal of Protestantism to Sixteenth-Century Germany and Switzerland* (New Haven, Connecticut: Yale University Press, 1975).

Parker, T. H. L., *Calvin's Preaching* (Louisville, Kentucky: Westminster/John Knox, 1992).

Schorn-Schütte, Luise, *Evangelische Geistlichkeit in der Frühneuzeit: Deren Anteil an der Entfaltung frühmoderner Staatlichkeit und Gesellschaft*, Quellen und Forschungen zur Reformationsgeschichte 62 (Gütersloh, Germany: Gütersloher Verlagshaus, 1996).

— "Priest, Preacher, Pastor: Research on Clerical Office in Early Modern Europe," *Central European History* 33, 1 (2000), 1-40.

Schüppert, Helga, "Frauenbild und Frauenalltag in der Predigtliteratur." In *Frau und* spätmittelalterlicher *Alltag* (Vienna: Österreichische Akademie der Wissenschaften, 1986), pp. 103-56.

Scribner, R. W., "Anticlericalism and the Reformation in Germany," in idem, *Popular Culture and Popular Movements in Reformation Germany* (London and Ronceverte: Hambledon Press, 1987), pp. 242-56.

— *For the Sake of Simple Folk: Popular Propaganda for the German Reformation*, Cambridge Studies in Oral and Literate Culture 2 (Cambridge, England, and New York: Cambridge University Press, 1981).

— "Preachers and People in the German Towns," in idem, *Popular Culture and Popular Movements in Reformation Germany* (London and Ronceverte, West Virginia: Hambledon Press, 1987), pp. 123-43.

Taylor, Larissa Juliet, *Soldiers of Christ: Preaching in Late Medieval and Reformation France* (New York: Oxford University Press, 1992).

— *Heresy and Orthodoxy in Sixteenth-Century Paris: François Le Picart and the Beginnings of the Catholic Reformation*, Studies in Medieval and Reformation Thought 77 (Leiden: Brill, 1999).

Tolley, Bruce, *Pastors and Parishioners in Wurttemberg during the Late Reformation 1581-1621* (Stanford, California: Stanford University Press, 1995).

Vogler, Bernard, *Le clergé protestant rhénan au siècle de la Réforme, 1552-1619* (Paris: Ophrys, 1976).

CHAPTER SEVEN

SWITZERLAND

Lee Palmer Wandel
(University of Wisconsin, Madison)

Preaching, as distinct from a printed sermon, occurs in a particular moment in time, within a particular living community, in a place with particular physical and historical definition. Each preacher spoke to, thundered at, excoriated, exhorted, implored, gestured before a specific human community. No one audience was the same as the next: each had social, political, and historical specificity. Effective preachers were not charismatic in the abstract – their charisma was inseparable from an ability to reach their audiences. Those audiences were not passive recipients of texts of fixed content, but listeners and nodders, nay-sayers and dozers, whose reactions were embedded in their own lives, their own experiences and inner landscapes.

To turn to the human contingencies of preaching is to confront the limits of historical sources and methods.[1] We know from criminal records and chronicles that preaching transformed: hundreds of ordinary Christians found "true belief" in the sermons of dozens of preachers; some were moved to acts of violence; others to reorder their lives – to leave spouses, children, homes in pursuit of "true Christianity." Those records suggest that preaching was the single most important cultural form in the Reformation. And yet, those records, which intimate the scope of preaching's importance, are also practically all we can know about its influence. For the sixteenth century in particular, rare is the witness who speaks elo-

---

[1] For two very different efforts to explore the interplay of preaching and audience, see Monika Hagenmaier, *Predigt und Policey: Der gesellschaftspolitische Diskjurs zwischen Kirche und Obrigkeit in Ulm 1614-1639* (Baden-Baden: Nomos, 1989); and Norbert Schindler, "Die Prinzipien des Hörensagens: Predigt und Publikum in der Frühen Neuzeit," *Historische Anthropologie* 1 (1993), 359-93.

quently to the effect of a sermon, who speaks in detail about the moment of preaching. We have hundreds of printed and manu-script sermons – notes taken by followers, students, colleagues – of perhaps a half dozen of the most famous preachers. But those writ-ten texts bear at best an oblique and indefinite relation to the event of preaching. Words were and are not fixed entities; an audience brought to a sermon a plethora of experiences, associations, reso-nances from their individual and collective lives.[2]

We do not know, in other words, what any one Christian heard. It is important to state that from the outset. A printed sermon can tell us what the preacher said – if indeed the transcript is accurate, if indeed the recorder's intent was to capture the delivered sermon, as distinct from an idealized sermon for a broader readership. But each sermon was heard by an aggregate of distinctive human be-ings of unique and distinguishing experiences – of differing social place and profession, of differing literacy and informal education, of differing political stature, of different ages, and sex, with all the attendant distinctions of gender in the early modern period.

With that caveat, we can nonetheless seek to recapture some as-sociations, articulated by contemporaries at the time, that would have been a part of public discourse, familiar to the residents of Swiss cities and villages, that would have echoed for them as they listened to the preaching. Let us begin, therefore, with the broadest common denominator for all audiences: the actual individuals within any one audience could come from anywhere, but they were gathered in a church, a garden, a home, or a field in what is mod-ern-day Switzerland. The audiences of this chapter, in other words, listened from a place of unique political consonance in early mod-ern Europe – especially for such key terms as divine law, brotherly love, neighbor.[3]

"Switzerland" is and was a unique political construction. By 1500, in the histories they wrote of their origins, the "cantons" that

---

    [2] Hans-Georg Gadamer, "Klassische und philosophische Hermeneutik (1968)," repr. In *Gadamer Lesebuch* (Tübingen: J. C. B. Mohr, 1997), pp. 32-57.
    [3] On the political consonances of Reformation preaching, see Peter Blickle, *The Revolution of 1525*, trans. Thomas A. Brady, Jr. and H.C. Erik Midelfort (Baltimore: Johns Hopkins University Press, 1981), and *Gemeindereformation; Die Menschen des 16. Jahrhunderts auf dem Weg zum Heil* (Munich: Oldenbourg Verlag, 1985); and Thomas A. Brady, Jr., *Turning Swiss: Cities and Empire, 1450-1550* (Cambridge University Press, 1985).

had formed the "Confederation" had already articulated much of which they understood themselves to be "Swiss." In 1291, the "forest cantons" of Uri, Schwyz, and Unterwalden formed a "Perpetual Alliance," swearing mutual assistance in the struggle to preserve their traditional rights against the Habsburg dynasty. In that beginning were a cluster of perceptions fundamental to the Swiss political identity that would be ratified with the Peace of Westphalia in 1648: small, essentially autonomous jurisdictional and legal units – cantons – allied to preserve ancient, largely communal rights, against a legal lord viewed as foreign, expansionist, and hostile to those rights. The "Swiss Confederation" did not exist as a "state" until the Treaties of Westphalia, but those treaties simply recognized what had been a political reality for a century or more and a political dream for far longer. For magistrates, peasants, craftsmen, herdsmen, fishermen, and nobles throughout the alpen and lake countries of the lands between Bavaria and Swabia to the north, Austria to the east, Venice and Milan to the south, and Savoy to the west, "the Confederation" was no diplomatic alliance among subject cities and regions of the Emperor, but a binding of cantons – uniquely "Swiss" – in the express protection of "traditional rights."

The preaching of concern in this chapter took place within a political context that was, at the time, represented as unique to early modern Europe. Neither monarchy along the English or French model nor city-state along the Italian model, the "Confederation" comprised a range of political entities. Some cantons had their origin as Imperial Free Cities: Zurich, Bern, Zug, and Shaffhausen. Until the Treaties of Westphalia in 1648, these cities remained nominally subject to the Emperor. Other cantons had their origin as ecclesiastical foundations around which cities grew: Lucerne and Basel. Their relations to bishops, abbots, and other ecclesiastical lords shaped how they pursued reform as well as the culture of preaching in the town. The core of the original Confederation had been the so-called forest cantons: Uri, Schwyz, and Unterwalden. These cantons had been subject to the Habsburg house of Austria. Over the years, they were joined by other cantons that, like them, were predominantly rural: Solothurn, Fribourg, Glarus, and Appenzell. These cantons set themselves apart from the city cantons. They were governed not by merchants or guildmasters, but by peasants, and they were proud of their communal political ideals.

These dramatically different political entities were united in an alliance that emphasized traditional freedoms and privileges over against their lords. Each had chosen, explicitly, to defy Habsburg claims for specific kinds of sovereignty in the lives of their subjects. The Confederation was constituted of units of governance each of which was prepared to go to war to preserve its jurisdictional autonomy in questions of economy, politics, morality, and religion. Each canton was both discrete and distinct, legally and jurisdictionally – each would address preachers and preaching within the parameters of that complex political identity.

Preaching took place within a broad and general public discourse within and among the cantons, in which certain kinds of autonomy were being articulated, and in which "brotherly love" resonated with political ideals of equity or parity. Equally, however, in the early modern period, the cantons distinguished explicitly and publicly among themselves – differences of wealth, economy, and political institutions mattered.[4] Urban cantons had more sorts of people who practiced a wider range of crafts: fishing and weaving, like rural villagers, but also typesetting and paper processing, goldsmithing and engraving, cabinetry and glass painting. The larger city cantons of Zurich, Bern, and Basel were centers of publishing and commerce, as well as marketplaces for local agricultural produce. Basel had a university, the oldest in Switzerland, and was a center of humanist scholarship. All three were home to significant artists and artisans, whose work adorned printed pamphlets and books, and churches and private homes. The economy of the forest cantons was largely animal husbandry: shepherds and goatherds, dairy production and fishing.

Wealth and commerce belonged to the cities. That had consequences for preaching. In cities, either private individuals, often merchant families, or organizations, such as guilds, endowed preaching positions. These positions, which seem to have originated in the fifteenth century, were funded specifically for the purpose of preaching to the laity. Some were attached to the cathedral in episcopal sees, some to the major church of a town. These positions were created in addition to the normal preaching duties of parish priests. They were often inspired by the preaching orders, the Do-

---

[4] Jean-François Bergier, *Die Wirtschaftsgeschichte der Schweiz von den Anfängen bis zur Gegenwart* (Zürich, 1983).

minicans and Franciscans, who had houses in all the major cities of
the Confederation and a good number of the towns by the end of
the fifteenth century. Important for preaching in the sixteenth century and beyond, these posts were intended to be exclusively
preaching posts: the preaching, in other words, was not to be part
of the larger canvas of the Mass, not to be subsumed within the
liturgy. These preaching posts established preaching itself as an
autonomous event, which occurred not in a piazza, as with
Savonarola or Bernardino of Siena, but within that structure for
the rhythmic practice of worship, the church.

Basel was the earliest Swiss city to have such preaching posts.
Preaching positions were endowed at the Minster in 1455/56 and
1467, and at the Magdalen chapel of the parish church St. Peter's
in 1507. Lucerne (1471), Winterthur (1475), Bremgarten (1487),
Chur (1491/2), Fribourg (1497), and Bern (1509) each had one.[5]
These posts were frequently attached to a specific altar within the
parish or main church of a town. In German-speaking Switzerland,
before 1530, some fourteen full-time, and one each Advent- and
Lenten preaching posts were endowed – not nearly as many as in
Württemberg at the same time.[6]

These posts were filled by many different sorts of preachers.
Some belonged to religious orders – Dominicans, Franciscans,
Augustinians – while others were secular priests. Some were trained
in classical languages, others held doctorates in theology. Preaching
was not restricted to these posts. Preaching could also take place in
the marketplaces of towns or the commons of villages, within the
frame of the liturgy, and on feast days. But these posts ensured that
preaching, quite apart from the liturgical year and the cadences of
the liturgy, took place, within the shelter of the churches in which
the positions were endowed, and consistently, whether weekly or
daily, according to the specific wishes of the donor. Many of the
most famous preachers in early modern Switzerland held these
posts: they were hired for their manifest gifts as preachers, not for

---

[5] Eduard Lengwiler, *Die vorreformatorischen Prädikaturen der deutschen Schweiz von ihrer
Entstehung bis 1530* (Freiburg in der Schweiz: Kanisiusdruckerei, 1955), p. 20.

[6] "[Württemberg] zählte damals 137 Städte; davon besassen 42, also 30.66%, ein
Predigtamt. In der Schweiz hingegen, mit 87 Städten, machten die 14 vollwertigen Pre-
digerstellen nur 16.1% aus, somit fast einmal weniger als in Württemberg." Lengwiler,
p. 21.

pastoral or liturgical service, but to preach. About the preachers we know a good deal more than of their audiences.

In 1519, Huldrych Zwingli was called to the position of People's Priest at the Great Minster in Zurich.[7] It was a preaching position, specifically for the laity, and he began his job with a sermon on Matthew. That moment has long been seen as the beginning of Reformation in Switzerland: Zwingli began not with a traditional form of sermon – a homily or an exhortation – but with the words of Scripture itself, the first Gospel, taking his congregation into the act and the electricity of biblical exegesis.

In Zwingli's first performance as a preacher in Zurich are captured many elements: a medium-sized town, a place of ancient and complex religious landscape, a human community of competing visions of Christianity, and the Reformation's particular attentiveness to the words of the different books of the Bible. Zurich was not one of the largest cities in the Confederation: at 10,000 residents, Basel was at least twice as large in population; Geneva would swell to perhaps three times the population of Zurich, with the influx of French refugees at mid-century. In 1519, Zurich was a relatively prosperous town of some 5000 residents, governed, like most Imperial Free Cities, by guilds and patricians – urban nobility – in a Town Council of two chambers, Small and Large Councils.

On the eve of the Reformation, the churches of Zurich, as in every early modern city, were the epicenter of urban life: places for worship, commerce, charity, and the formal affirmation in baptism and marriage of ties of kinship, protection, and affiliation. St. Peter's was probably the oldest parish church in Switzerland. The Great Minster had been founded by Charlemagne; opposite it across the Limmat, the Benedictine convent, the Minster of our Lady, had been endowed by his nephew, Ludwig the German. Charlemagne granted the Great Minster the rights of baptism, burial, tithing, and the care of souls, which made the Minster second parish church in Zurich. The Minster of Our Lady had been granted the right of minting coins. The three great medieval preaching orders established houses in Zurich soon after each one's institution: they were the oldest foundations for their orders in Switzerland. The Dominicans arrived in 1229; the Franciscans in 1238.

---

[7] On Zwingli's preaching in Zurich, see Hans-Christoph Rublack, "Zwingli und Zurich," *Zwingliana* 16/5 (1985), 393-426.

Until the early years of the sixteenth century, the Franciscans were much loved in Zurich: many residents were buried in the cloister, and the people of Zurich held services and commemorated feast days in the Franciscan church. The Augustinians arrived about 1270. [8] In 1480, the Pope designated Zurich's seven churches – the two Minsters, St. Peter's, the Water Church, the Dominican, Franciscan, and Augustinian cloisters – as seven holy places pilgrims could visit and receive the same indulgences as a pilgrim could receive in Rome.

There were two parishes in Zurich, one on each side of the Limmat. These were the anchor of lay religious life: the daily Mass; communion; the celebration of feast days, each with its own particular cadences of processions, Mass, sermon, and communion; as well as the place for private prayer, meditation, and devotion. The laity of Zurich also used the Franciscan church and the Minster of Our Lady for a range of religious activities, including hearing sermons and attending Mass; these, too, were a part of the landscape of religious life for the people of Zurich.

In all of these churches, preaching took place. That preaching took place, in other words, within structures of differing scale, imagery, – Charlemagne, for instance, stood on the exterior of the Great Minster – stained glass, and of different functions. Some were cloister churches, with their particular connotations of a life lived under a rule, either an enclosed life, such as that led by the Benedictine nuns of the Minster of Our Lady, or a mendicant life, modeled on Christ's apostolic poverty and homelessness, such as that of the Dominicans, Franciscans, and Augustinian canons. Some were parish churches, with their deep integration into both a parish, a particular geography of religious life, and the neighborhoods that constituted that parish: the gardeners' quarter, or the carpenters' quarter, for St. Peter's Church, or the merchants' neighborhood, for the Great Minster.

Preaching, in other words, took place in overlapping but distinctive human landscapes. Most often, it took place within a church. As the case of Zurich suggests, however, no two churches were the same. In Zurich, people might attend sermons in their own parish. If they were parishioners of St. Peter's, they might also choose to

---

[8]   Rudolf Pfister, *Kirchengeschichte der Schweiz*, vol. I (Zurich, 1964), pp. 237-8, on the Franciscans; pp. 263-6, on the Dominicans.

go to the Great Minster to hear Zwingli. So, too, the people of Zurich chose to hear sermons in the churches of the religious, those who lived under a rule. These were not churches primarily intended for the laity, but the lay men and women of Zurich could attend sermons in the churches of the Dominican, Franciscan, Augustinian cloisters or of the Benedictine convent. There they would listen to a preacher within a space that was designated as belonging to an order, yet open in this way to the laity. In each instance, that church had been built, was physically a presence, within a specific neighborhood and "watch." In each instance, the building was a part of the geography of the familiar – the windows one passed on the way to the grain market, the walls one passed on the way to the fish market, the portals one passed on the way to the workshop or the guildhall or to one's relatives or companions.

So, too, preaching existed in many different relations to the structures of devotional life. Sometimes the sermon was delivered within the structure of the Mass. Increasingly at the end of the fifteenth century, preaching took place, as it did with Zwingli's first preaching in Zurich, autonomous of the liturgy. Each town had its own relics, its own particular sacred history, of acts of martyrdom, of miracles, of acts of benefice and charity. Zurich had been founded on the site of the martyrdom of the two Roman saints, Felix and Regula; their relics formed the material center of the devotional life of the town. Other saints, such as those of Basel, were known not for martyrdom, but for acts of charity. The models of holy life, in other words, differed from place to place. A sermon's invocation of sacrifice echoed differently in Zurich than in Basel. In Zurich, murals of the two saints' martyrdom informed collective religious life of exemplary acts.[9] In Basel, carved statues evoked acts of beneficence and caritas.

The Canons of the Minster who hired Zwingli were largely patrician and religiously conservative. They believed in hiring him they were bringing in a promising young biblical scholar whose knowledge of Greek was growing, whose reputation as an inspiring preacher had begun to spread, and whose birthplace, the mountain village of Toggenburg, made of him more of a Swiss loyalist than many other preachers. They were not prepared for what they got.

---

[9]   On the many exemplary functions of martyrs, see Brad Gregory, *Salvation at Stake: Christian Martyrdom in Early Modern Europe* (Cambridge, MA, 1999).

Heinrich Bullinger, Zwingli's friend and successor in Zurich, offers us a glimpse of Zwingli's own style of preaching, a fleeting insight into one of the most charismatic and effective preachers of an age of preachers:

> In his sermons he was most eloquent (*flyssig*), simple, and understandable, so that many heard him willingly, and there was a great rush of people to his sermons... His speech was graceful and sweet. For he spoke idiomatically and was unwilling to use the usual pious chatter, the confusion thrown down from the pulpit, or unnecessary words.[10]

And its effect:

> There was soon a rush of all sorts of people, in particular the common man, to these evangelical sermons of Zwingli's, in which he praised God the Father, and taught all people to place their trust in God's Son, Jesus Christ, as the single Savior.[11]

Increasingly in the sixteenth century, men and women in cities throughout Europe chose to attend sermons at churches—and fields—outside their parish, as they sought to hear specific preachers famous for their preaching. When Zwingli took up his post as Lay Priest in Zurich in January 1519, he captured the people of Zurich's attention, drawing the devout and the curious first from throughout the city, then from the surrounding countryside.

Zwingli captured their attention by breaking the traditional order of sermons, which had followed specific texts of Scripture set to specific days in the liturgical year. Prior to the Reformation, those endowed preaching posts had made possible sermons autonomous of the liturgical calendar. Zwingli's sermons moved past even that autonomy: they were not pendant on any liturgy or liturgical cycle, but centered explicitly and dramatically on the text of Scripture—autonomous of the ritual year and treating the text of Scripture as possessing its own autonomy and integrity. He began with the first words of the first Gospel, Matthew, which he then explicated, continuing through the Gospel to its end. In the weeks that followed, he moved in this same way through Acts, then the Epistles

---

[10] Heinrich Bullinger *Reformationsgeschichte*, ed. J.J. Hottinger and H. H. Vögeli (Frauenfeld: , 1838), vol. I [hereafter B], p. 306. When Carlstadt visited Zurich, by contrast, many found his speech unintelligible, see *Aktensammlung zur Geschichte der Zürcher Reformation in den Jahren 1519-1533*, ed. Emil Egli (Zurich, 1879; Aalen, 1973)[hereafter EAk], 2002 (all references are to document numbers).

[11] B, p. 12.

to Timothy.[12] He taught his congregation to hear the words of Scripture, to hear the "Word of God," as he would call them again and again, not excerpted to fit a particular time of year or in snippets, but as texts, narratives, whose meaning one worked to discern, and whose meaning pertained to the conduct of daily life.

Zwingli, himself a gifted preacher, understood well the efficacy of preaching. He sought first to achieve the freedom to preach the text of Scripture, then to control how that preaching was done and toward what ends. In his sermon, "The Shepherd," delivered at the Second Disputation and published in March 1524, Zwingli outlined what he believed to be the responsibilities of the preacher to his congregation. Acting as a "true shepherd" meant preaching the true Word of God; seeking in deed and in word to teach his "flock" how to live by the two commandments of Christ; and then leading them to maintain that life.[13]

In Zurich, the Word of God was preached in all the churches, to the full congregation on Fridays as well as Sundays and all holy days, and to any who were interested on other days of the week as well. Zwingli, his close associates and friends, Leo Jud and Heinrich Engelhard, and later in the century, Bullinger, as well as dozens of preachers throughout the countryside, preached week after week, each in his church.[14] In Zurich, the pastors looked to the Old Testa-

---

[12] Bullinger describes what Zwingli preached his first four years in Zurich (B, p. 51).

[13] "Der Hirt," in *Huldreich Zwinglis Sämtliche Werke* [hereafter Z], vol. III (*Corpus Reformatorum*, vol. 90), eds. Emil Egli, Georg Finsler, and Walther Köhler (Leipzig, 1914), pp. 1-68. On 30 June 1530, Zwingli published a second treatise, "Concerning the Preaching Office," in response to the preaching of Anabaptists. In it, he was more concerned with the abuse of the preacher's authority within his congregations than with detailing further the nature of the office and its responsibilities. Like Luther, he was confronted with two "abuses" he had helped to engender: the great autonomy and authority of preachers in the early years of the Reformation and the singular authority of Scripture, which Zwingli had called for, led to individual preachers inviting their communities to rebel against all authority, including the magistracy of Zurich, which supported Zwingli's vision of Reformation, and to find their authority in their differing readings of Scripture. See "Von dem Predigtamt," Z IV, eds. Emil Egli, Georg Finsler, Walther Köhler, and Oskar Farner (Leipzig, 1927), pp. 369-433.

[14] For a list of the clergy in Zurich in 1525, EAk 889. For lists of clergy, both Catholic and Reformed, in the canton as well as the town, who attended the First Synod on April 21, 1528, see EAk 1391. For a list of preachers in the canton of Zurich, 1532-1580, see Bruce Gordon, *Clerical Discipline and the Rural Reformation: The Synod in Zurich, 1532-1580* [Zürcher Beiträge zur Reformationsgeschichte 16] (New York: Peter Lang, 1992), Chapter 6.

ment prophets as their model of style of speaking and of dress. They thundered from the pulpit, their manner of delivery "biblical" rather than "classical." They dressed in austere black scholar's robes, self-consciously contrasting their persons with the colorful priests' albs, stoles, and robes.

The preachers in Zurich were doctors, learned not so much in theology as in the languages and literature of the Bible. All participated in the *Prophezei*, the sole purpose of which was the close study of the Bible in its three languages: Hebrew, Greek, and Latin.[15] Zwingli had organized it in 1525, primarily to train boys and young men in the philological and textual skills of biblical scholarship. It became a vital center of biblical study in Zurich. It met every day but Friday and Sunday at 8 a.m., in the chancel of the Great Minster.[16] The preachers of Zurich brought their deep knowledge of the languages of the Bible to a close consideration of texts read sequentially, thereby deepening their own understanding of the text and teaching young men of Zurich how to listen more closely to sermons.

"Scripture," the written Word, became the "Gospel," the spoken Word.[17] It acquired a new kind of effect, a theatrical presence, as its very words were spoken, *performed*. Each week, parents as well as children would stand or, if they brought their own stools, sit in the church and listen to sermons of varying length. No longer merely the point of departure for sermons, the "Word of God" became the centerpiece and substance of sermons.[18] Here was no text interspersed in the fabric of the liturgy, but "the Word": God speaking in His Son's embodied voice and actions and through His Son's disciples to humanity. And as various testimonies indicate, people believed they could hear Christ speaking, and felt themselves confronted directly with the content of his ethical imperatives and his prescriptions for Christian behavior.

---

[15]   On the Prophezei, see especially Gottfried Locher, *Die Zwinglische Reformation in Rahmen der europäischen Kirchengeschichte* (Göttingen, 1979), pp. 161-3; and "In Spirit and in Truth: How Worship in Changed at the Reformation," in *Zwingli's Thought: New Perspectives* (Leiden: Brill, 1981), pp. 27-30.

[16]   *Johannes Kesslers Sabbata*, ed. Emil Egli and Rudolf Schoch, Historische Verein des Kantons St. Gallen (St. Gall, 1902), pp. 203-4.

[17]   Cf. Marjorie O'Rourke Boyle, *Erasmus on Language and Method in Theology* (Toronto: 1977).

[18]   Cf. John O'Malley, *Religious Culture in the Sixteenth Century: Preaching, Rhetoric, Spirituality, and Reform* (Brookfield, Vt.: 1993), chs. 3-5.

As that "Word" was preached, it acquired sound: it was heard through human voices by living communities. Indeed, for Zwingli, only the faithful *could* hear the true content of this "external Word," the read or preached Word of God – that "Word" was subject to "that word the heavenly Father preaches within our hearts."[19] In keeping with the radical freedom he accorded the working of the Holy Spirit, Zwingli held that preaching could not bring about faith nor could the "external Word," the aural experience of the text of Scripture, effect faith. It could and did help to form faith, however, to educate people in God's will.

"Reformation" meant that only the "Word of God" might be preached. In the wake of the Second Disputation in October 1523, the town council began what would be continuing efforts to assure the true representation of Scripture. All pastors were to preach "the holy Gospel clearly and truly according to the spirit of God":[20]

> Take care that God's Word is faithfully preached among you…and when you see how this alone brings glory to God and the salvation of souls, then further it, regardless of what this one or that one may say. For the Word of God makes you pious, God-fearing people.[21]

We have the texts of seven of Zwingli's sermons,[22] but those texts seem to be not verbatim records of what was preached. They seem to be later versions of a text that had been preached, revised, lengthened, expanded, altered in any number of ways.[23] Those texts, as any who have seen more than one performance of any play

---

[19] "Quod eo verbo, quod celestis pater in cordibus nostris predicat," Z III, p. 263.
[20] EAk 436. For later efforts to call preachers back to the true Word of God, see, for example, EAk 1536. In October, 1532, the Zurich town council issued yet another mandate for the "restitution and improvement of certain deformations and abuses now committed by the servants of the Word of God." (EAk 1899)
[21] Zwingli, "A Faithful and Solemn Exhortation to the Swiss Confederates," quoted in Locher, "In Spirit and in Truth," p. 4.
[22] "We do not possess a single manuscript of Zwingli's sermons. He always spoke extemporaneously, and did so daily throughout the years. The writings that have come down to us are mostly in Latin (used as a form of shorthand) and only partially fashioned. A series of special sermons, which he developed and published by request, grew into doctrinal writings."(Locher, "In Spirit and in Truth," p. 9)
[23] The relation among performance of a sermon, manuscript text of a sermon, and printed text of a sermon is highly problematic. Some printed sermons are transcriptions of notes a member of the audience, who may have been untrained in the craft of recording oral sermons; others are texts that were never performed. We cannot even be sure that those sermons that are in the hands of preachers were themselves ever performed as they were written.

or oration know, only give clues to the performance itself. Where were the inflections, the pauses, the thundering emphases? Where the exultant facial expressions? Where did the preacher bow his head? Where did he extend his hands in supplication or raise them in invocation? Printed sermons offer us the content as a flat textual, printed representation, but they cannot signal the inflections, the facial gestures, the sweep of a hand. And those untraceables brought that text a life and a significance for the audience who not only heard the words, but *saw* the preacher embodying those words.

In 1528, the town council instituted the synod, which would oversee not only the content of the sermons of all preachers in the canton, but the orthodoxy of their liturgical practices and the propriety of their conduct of their public and private lives.[24] This move would be echoed across European Christianity. At Trent, Catholics instituted measures to ensure consistent training of parish priests and to monitor both the conduct of all the clergy and the orthodoxy of the preaching to the laity. These bodies, whose functions were both educational and disciplinary, became normative in the later part of the sixteenth century. While they did not immediately achieve the uniformity of conduct and the consistent orthodoxy of preaching that was their goal and their purpose, they began a two-century process that did, in the end, achieve a certain homogeneity, long after the period of this volume.

Heinrich Bullinger arrived in Zurich before Zwingli's death and assumed leadership of the Zurich community at Zwingli's death. Bullinger is better known for the corpus of his writings – a large number of which were translated into English and helped to shape the English Reformed tradition – than for his preaching. But among Bullinger's written legacy are exempla of Reformed sermons, published at the *Decades* between 1549 and 1551.[25] These sermons are all the more valuable, since so few sermons of Reformed preachers other than Calvin were published. Seven transcriptions of Zwingli's sermons were published, which may not be transcriptions of actual performances. One of Oecolampad's sermons was published under his own hand. Of Oswald Myconius and Johannes Zwick, we have

---

[24] EAk 1391, 1714, 1757, 1899, 1941. For accounts of sermons the town council found heterodox, see, for example, EAk 938. On the synods in Zurich, see Gordon.
[25] Walter Hollweg, *Heinrich Bullingers Hausbuch* (Neukirchen: Moers, 1956).

none. Jacob Funkli, preacher in Biel, published the only extant sermon of Ambrosius Blarer in 1561. Of the Strasbourg circle, none of Capito's, none of Hedio's were published. William Farel, Peter Viret, and Theodore Beza did not publish any of their sermons in their lifetimes.[26] Bullinger's *Decades*, therefore, served singularly the purpose of providing preachers with both the form and the material for their sermons.

Most major German-speaking Swiss cities were home to one or more preachers who worked, most often through preaching, to bring religious practices, conduct, welfare policy, and governance into accord with a particular understanding of the Bible and its commands.[27] Heinrich Lüti, whom Zwingli had called to Zurich as an assistant to his position as people's preacher in 1520, preached in Winterthur from 1523 to 1537, actively working from the pulpit to bring that town's lived Christianity into accord with one found in Zurich. Of so many of those preachers, we have only the briefest traces: a record of the appointment, a passing mention in a later chronicle. In Diessenhofen, Lazarus Sigg held the endowed preaching post from 1507 to 1529. It would seem he preached an evangelical message: a subsequent history of Protestantism claims him.

In Bern,[28] Berchtold Haller was appointed to an endowed preaching post in 1519 and worked until his death seventeen years later to institute a vision of Christianity deeply influenced by Zwingli. Like Zwingli, he worked both from the pulpit and through the town council, using his considerable powers as a preacher in the church and in the town council chambers to shape not simply policy, but opinion – the people of Bern's understanding of what it meant to be a Christian and of "true Christianity." He is credited, for example, with the central role in calling a disputation in Bern in 1528, which then resulted in reforms to Christian practices closely following those in Zurich.[29] Haller's particular fusion of preaching and policy-making culminated in the *Berner Synodus*, the Church Order for Reformed Christianity in Bern, which he wrote

---

[26] Ibid, pp. 1-6.

[27] For the list of preachers who held endowed posts, see Lengwiler, pp. 79-92.

[28] On the efforts to regulate morals in the countryside of Bern, see Heinrich Richard Schmidt, *Dorf und Religion: Reformierte Sittenzucht in Berner Landgemeinden der Frühen Neuzeit* (Stuttgart: Gustav Fischer Verlag, 1995).

[29] J. Wayne Baker, "Berchtold Haller," in the *Oxford Encyclopedia of the Reformation*, ed. Hans J. Hillerbrand (New York, 1996) [Hereafter OER].

with Wolfgang Capito in 1532, in the wake of Zwingli's death at Cappel.

To Basel, twice Zurich's size in population, a major publishing center, and a university town, Johannes Oecolampad brought his skills in the biblical languages.[30] Like so many preachers of the sixteenth-century, Oecolampad was not born in the town where he acquired prominence as a preacher.[31] He was born Johannes Huszgen in Weinsberg, in the Palatinate, and there he first preached in a post endowed by his parents. Oecolampad was called to Basel in 1515 by the great publisher, Johannes Froben, in order to help Erasmus with his edition of the Greek New Testament. Oecolampad was among the most learned of the Protestant preachers, having studied Hebrew with the great Hebraicist, Johannes Reuchlin, written a Greek grammar, and published editions of the works of the Greek fathers. When Oecolampad returned to Basel in 1522, the city had already been much influenced by the reform movement in Zurich that Zwingli led. In his first years in Basel, he lectured on Isaiah at the university, published a series of lectures on Paul's Epistle to the Romans, and preached. In 1523, the town council of Basel issued a Preaching Mandate, insisting that all preaching had to be grounded in the words of Scripture.

In a recent article, Amy Nelson Burnett has delineated the education of pastors in Reformation Basel. [32] That education she divides, in agreement with older scholarship, into two levels: the schooling of boys and adolescents; and a formal instruction in theology. That education does not divide simply between the medieval Latin schools for the children of prosperous bourgeois and those intended for the clergy, on the one hand, and the university on the other. Instead, Burnett argues, the education divides between those subjects necessary to the pastoral responsibilities of Reformed min-

---

[30] On the Reformation in Basel, see Hans R. Guggisberg, *Basel in the Sixteenth Century: Aspects of the City Republic before, during, and after the Reformation* (St. Louis, 1982); Paul Roth, *Die Reformation in Basel* (Basel, 1936); Rudolf Wackernagel, *Geschichte der Stadt Basel*, vol. III (Basel, 1968).

[31] On Oecolampad, see Karl Hammer, "Der Reformator Oekolampad, 1482-1531," in *Reformiertes Erbe*, ed. Heiko Oberman, vol. I (Zurich, 1992), pp. 157-70; E. Gordon Rupp, *Patterns of Reformation* (London, 1969); Ernst Staehelin, *Das theologische Lebenswerk Johannes Oekolampads* (New York, 1971).

[32] Amy Nelson Burnett, "Preparing the Pastors: Theological Education and Pastoral Training in Basel," in *History Has Many Voices: Essays in Honor of Robert M. Kingdon*, ed. Lee Palmer Wandel [Sixteenth Century Studies Monographs, forthcoming].

isters and those for theological understanding, which, she suggests, did not necessarily improve pastoral skills. Those subjects which served pastoral purposes largely followed a Liberal Arts education: a knowledge of Latin and Greek for the study of the Bible; of rhetoric for effective preaching, as well as the arts of consolation, for the bereaved, the ill, the distraught, and of exhortation, for the frail, the truculent, or the intransigent. Once the young men had acquired these fundaments, they turned exclusively and intensively to the study of theology. In Basel, in other words, training in languages, in grammar, and in rhetoric, preceded what was perceived as specialized education in theology; and in sixteenth-century Basel, pastors did not need to understand the deeper mysteries of theology in order to preach and to minister to their congregations.

Those preachers who called themselves "evangelical" did not differ from medieval or Catholic preachers because they quoted scriptural texts in their sermons. Late medieval preachers such as Geiler von Keisersberg had done so. Preachers in Rome did so.[33] Evangelical preaching was distinguished by the way in which scriptural texts were treated in the sermons. Evangelical preaching was to be founded in close study of the Bible in its historical languages, a knowledge informed by the very historicity of language itself, the ways in which words connote differently at different times. Evangelical preachers were distinguished by a particular conceptualization of *how* the Bible was to be preached. Zwingli, Oecolampad, Swiss Anabaptists, Jud, Bullinger, treated the text of Scripture not only as sacred, but as sacrosanct. It was brought forward in the text of the sermon, transformed from exempla – of conduct, of ethics, of God's love – to the living Word of God. As such, Scripture itself was to be listened to. The relation of preacher to Scripture was that of philologist and textual scholar to a text of gravitas, of singular integrity and significance. The Word of God was not to be used to illustrate a human point, but was itself to be the focus of intense concentration, careful and methodical study, of a very special kind of listening and considering. The evangelical sermon was an exercise in exegesis, in explicating what God had meant when, through diverse human voices, he spoke to the faithful. The Word of God

---

[33] John O'Malley, *Praise and Blame in Renaissance Rome: Rhetoric, Doctrine, and Reform in the Sacred Orators of the Papal Court, c. 1450-1521* (Durham, N.C:. Duke University Press, 1979).

was not a flat text, but a living communication, which required discipline and learning and an intense attentiveness to be heard. Preaching was contingent in many different ways: preachers spoke to a human community living within a particular social, political, even devotional context, at a moment in time, about a text to whose own history those preachers were particularly attentive.

The Word of God was living, not only in being spoken, but also in its relation to everyday life. "Evangelicals" held all aspects of life to the test of Scripture. For all, Scripture was to exist in close and dynamic relation to the daily lives of each individual Christian, not a template for conduct, but an ethic each Christian had learned and, to a greater or lesser extent, mastered, through weekly, even daily attendance of sermons. They differed among themselves, what was to be the relation of Scripture to the life of the faithful Christian. Zwingli, Haller, Oecolampad, and Bullinger posed a complex hermeneutical relation between the life of the Christian and the text of Scripture: Scripture required an informed listening, to hear the historical consonances of the text. Anabaptists sought a closer mimesis to Scripture: adult baptism, a true supper around a table, communal economy.

No community of believers speaks more dramatically to the efficacy of preaching than the Anabaptists. Anabaptists were to be found in most towns and in hundreds of villages, yet they had no church building that was their own to use, no legal sanctions, no public space in which they were granted the right to worship, to pray, or to hear sermons.[34] And yet, Anabaptism grew with a stunning speed, as dozens of artisans, peasants, even merchants and some nobles embraced the apostolic simplicity of the life it proffered. They met clandestinely, in private homes or in fields, and there "some good brothers and sisters," in the typical formulation, listened to someone preach. We have eloquent evidence of the conversions, dozens upon dozens, that followed upon that preaching— primarily in testimonies from the trials of Anabaptists for heresy.[35]

---

[34] Claus Peter Clasen, *Anabaptism: A Social History, 1525-1618* (Ithaca & London: Cornell University Press, 1972); James M. Stayer, *Anabaptists and the Sword* (Lawrence: Coronado, 1976).

[35] See Michele Zelinsky, "The Anabaptists. A Special Case?" *Religion as a Civic Virtue: Religious Identity and Communal Relations in Augsburg 1517-1555* [Ph.D. diss., University of Pennsylvania, 2000], pp. 88-116; *Quellen zur Geschichte der Täufer in der Schweiz*, 4 vols. (Zurich: Theologischer Verlag, 1952-74).

Of the content of the preaching, we know only that it was scriptural
–"the Word of God." And we know that it turned souls and minds,
to take up a way of being a Christian at odds with both secular and
ecclesiastical authorities across Europe.

Perhaps most important for our purposes, those trial records provide the most substantive evidence of itinerant preachers, who
traveled from town to village, preaching to the faithful gathered in
homes and fields. Word went out in advance that the preaching
would take place – often, preaching was sporadic, according to the
itinerary of the preachers and the degree of danger involved in con-
gregating. These preachers were most often laymen, and even some
women, who were "moved by the Spirit": theologically untrained,
literate only in the Bible's text, which they knew in translation, not
in those scholarly languages. Many were not formally trained in the
ars praedicandi; they did not choose from among a range of formal
structures and styles of presentation, but spoke extemporaneously,
with immediacy, from the text of Scripture itself, allowing "the
Spirit" to guide their reading and their interpretation of the text.

The sixteenth century witnessed great preaching of a range of
styles, manners, and models. One community made it a central
mission to train, discipline, and send forth preachers to evangelize
Christians throughout Europe: Geneva. Geneva trained the first
generation of Reformed preachers, and sent them to France, the
Low Countries, Scotland to preach, to convert, to institute
Churches. That so many succeeded for so many years in such hostile political environments speaks to what they learned in Geneva.

The interdependencies of preaching and political identity in Geneva differed from those in Zurich or Bern. Legally, Geneva was
not a member of the Confederation of Swiss Cantons until the set-
tlements of the Napoleonic Empire in 1815. In 1500, Geneva was
the capital city of an episcopal principality, whose closest political
ties were to the larger and prosperous Duchy of Savoy, its neighbor
to the west.[36] The two states had become closely interdependent;
the *vidomne* in Geneva was appointed by the Duke and assisted in
the prosecution and punishment of crime in the principality whose
capital was Geneva. The Duke's representatives, in other words,

---

[36] For the following, see Robert M. Kingdon, "Geneva," in the OER; E. William
Monter, *Calvin's Geneva* (New York, 1975); William G. Naphy, *Calvin and the Consolidation
of the Genevan Reformation* (New York, 1994);

resided in Geneva and oversaw the administration of justice. In the sixteenth century, however, were laid the diplomatic, military, and religious alliances that would draw Geneva eastward, make of it more "Swiss" in its political and religious identity than "French."

In the sixteenth century, the magistrates of Geneva moved to gain autonomy, first from the bishop, and therefore from his political ally, the Duke of Savoy. How they pursued that autonomy shaped religious life in the city. [37] The magistrates formed alliances with Lausanne and Bern. The latter of the two proved decisive in Geneva's pursuit of autonomy: Bern offered military support, with which the magistrates voted formally to eject the prince-bishop and his retinue – in all, roughly 10% of the entire population of the city at that time. With that support, they assumed control of taxation, defense, minting coin, foreign relations, and the prosecution and execution of all justice within the city walls.

Bern's own religious commitments, perhaps beginning but certainly not ending with the importation of the evangelical preacher, Gaspard Megander, influenced how Geneva chose to address the vacuum left by the departure of the episcopal clergy. Bern's troops were evangelical by the time they entered Geneva to protect the city. Bernese troops forced the cathedral St. Pierre to open its doors to their evangelical preacher, Megander, who preached each morning in German. Megander was the first publicly recognized evangelical preacher in Geneva. Though the Genevois could not understand his German, the devotion of the troops to him was marked – not the content of Megander's sermons, but their visible effect captured attention.

Geneva came to "Reformation" through what Robert Kingdon has called a "revolution." When the General Council of Geneva expelled the prince-bishop and his retinue, it drove out those who had administered not simply religious, but also social, economic, and political jurisdictions of the prince-bishop. The magistrates of Geneva confronted a vacuum at the center of collective life. They needed people to fill all those essential functions of the clergy: mar-

---

[37]   The relation between Reformation and the pursuit of political autonomy is much debated in the literature. The chronology of events suggests that the magistrates' pursuit of autonomy from the bishop preceded the public endorsement of evangelical preaching, but the lessons of the scholarship in other cities suggests that the pursuit of political autonomy is not easily severed from a desire for reform of worship and ethics.

riage, charity, and justice. In other words, the General Council of Geneva deposed its clergy, then brought in new clergy to perform the functions left vacant by that expulsion.

Why did the magistrates choose evangelical preachers? In part, the answer lies in the military presence of Bern, in part, in the visible effect of Megander's preaching. But within Geneva, there was also growing a small group of lay men and women who thought of themselves as "evangelical" and formed a party for "reform". One incident gives us a feel for that party.[38] On April 15, 1533, a group of some forty Genevois gathered in the garden of the noble, Etienne Dad, to "hear the Word of God." Master Garin rose on a bench near a table, on a crude cabinet that had been raised in the garden, and "began to preach and discourse."[39] Not all were enthusiasts. One man cried out, "Those preachers who say they are the servants of God, that is nothing, for God has no need of servants…and the church that they say is the temple of God is not the house [maison] of God." And yet, those forty gathered privately to hear the Word of God preached and to partake of the first Reformed Supper. Master Garin preached again later that day in the garden, and again on Monday. Among those gathered in the garden were artisans of modest profession and women, two of whom were members of one of the most influential families in Geneva: the mother and daughter of Ami Perrin.

In its first formal invitation to a member of the clergy, Geneva's Council manifested the influence of Bern, certainly, but primarily of Zwingli. The invitation was to preach the true Word of God, and it was extended to William Farel, a French evangelical known for his zeal and his evangelism. Farel "preached not only in public, but went from house to house, admonishing, thereby converting a number."[40] The resonance of preacher and audience was almost immediately evident: in 1536, a general assembly of citizens declared that Geneva was to live according to the Gospel, renounced the Mass, and called for the Reformation of Christian life. Two months after the general assembly's vote, Farel persuaded a 27-year-old French lawyer to abandon his trip to Basel, to remain in

---

[38]   For the following, see Victor van Berchem, "Une prédication dans un jardin (15 avril 1533), in *Festschrift Hans Nebholz* (Zurich, 1934), pp. 14-20.
[39]   Van Berchem, p. 19.
[40]   Ibid., p. 2.

Geneva, and there to join the enterprise of Reformation. Farel did so on the recommendation of the Strasbourg evangelical community, who had discerned in John Calvin extraordinary spiritual and administrative gifts. Calvin had not planned to remain in Geneva: like so many who came to Geneva, he was a refugee from the growing persecution of evangelicals in his native France. But Farel proved persuasive and John Calvin stayed.

In hindsight, Calvin dominates our view of sixteenth-century Geneva. Certainly, Calvin's preeminence is deserved: even contemporaries such as Martin Bucer, who knew Luther and Zwingli as well, acknowledged Calvin's particular clarity of thought, his precision and elegance of expression in Latin, and his extraordinary gift for conceptualizing how one might organize human communities to sustain and nourish faith and to bring human conduct into accord with Christ's teachings as Calvin understood them. Yet he arrived, the younger and far less experienced French evangelical. He was soon joined by a "Company of Pastors," who collectively, in church after church, day after day, preached the Word of God. In so doing, they collectively worked to move the Genevois to bring their conduct and their belief into accord with the words of Scripture as that Company understood them.

Over the course of the sixteenth century, Geneva was home to some of the greatest preachers of early modern Europe: William Farel, John Calvin, Pierre Viret, Theodore Beza, John Knox. These men preached to a very different audience from those in Basel, Bern, or Zurich. Calvin was one of the earliest French-speaking refuges to arrive in Geneva, but over the course of the sixteenth century, Geneva became a major center for French refugees on the Continent. With the influx of refugees, Geneva grew to a population in 1550 of about 13,000 inhabitants.[41] The Company of Pastors preached, in other words, to a great many people who were not citizens of the town, had not been born there, nor grown up in its neighborhoods and parishes, but came there, having left behind their homes, a good deal of their property, often family and neighbors, and moved to a new state and a community of Christians who were strangers to one another. Their preaching sought to build communities of the faithful whose unity resided not in lan-

---

[41] Bergier, p. 44.

guage or in political identity or in home or in neighborhood, but in creed and liturgy.

In Geneva was forged a community of believers who did not share place of birth, dialect, kinship or social status. That community was forged primarily through institutions articulated by Calvin. His influence was singular in shaping not simply the city's religious life, but its morals and its legal institutions. Expelled with Farel in 1538 by a hostile town council, Calvin alone was invited back in 1541, and granted the authority to institute reform in the city. One of his first acts was the Ecclesiastical Ordinances, which instituted four offices: pastors, who were to preach the Word of God and administer the sacraments; doctors, who were to teach the Word of God, ultimately, in 1559, in an Academy founded for that purpose; elders, who were to discipline the community through the Consistory; and deacons, whose responsibilities were largely charity.

The Ordinances made manifest how Calvin understood preaching to be at the very center of Christian life. For Calvin, the pastors were a distinct office, whose primary activity was preaching – not the range of pastoral activities parish priests had held. That preaching, moreover, was to be informed by an education Calvin also instituted, first in the form of the office of doctors. The Consistory has been the subject of considerable scholarship and lies, for the most part, beyond the parameters of this study. It is of interest because it provides hard evidence that magistrates as well as pastors held preaching to be absolutely at center in the formation of Christian life.[42] The Consistory monitored attendance at sermons, asking the heterodox if they were attending sermons, returned to that question in later interviews, and in admonishing each transgressor articulated as the corrective a more frequent and concentrated attendance at preaching.[43] Preaching in Geneva was the centerpiece of the effort to make the Word of God living in the heart of each Christian. While the Consistory monitored, admonished, and, in extreme cases, disciplined, preaching, for Calvin, was the main vehicle for the reformation of character and conduct.

---

[42]   Thomas Lambert, *Preaching, Praying, and Policing in Sixteenth-Century Geneva* Ph.D. diss., University of Wisconsin, Madison, 1998.

[43]   Eric Goddard, seminar paper, Spring 2000. See also, *Registres du Consistoire de Genève au Temps de Calvin*, eds. Thomas Lambert and Isabella Watt, under the direction of Robert M. Kingdon, Volume 1 (1542-1544) (Geneva: Droz, 1996).

Within Geneva, people could hear Reformed preaching every day of the week and on most days, more than one sermon, should one so choose.[44] On an average Sunday, there were a total of eight full services at the three parish churches of Geneva: St. Peter, St. Gervais, and St. Germain. There was an early service at 4 or 5 in the morning; the main service at 9, when Calvin preached at St. Peter's; at noon; and between 2 and 4 in the afternoon. There were also several services on Wednesdays. At every service, the sermon was the centerpiece. Communion was offered only four times a year. Baptisms took place when necessary, usually at the noon service on Sundays. But at every service, one of the Company of Pastors preached. Every preacher was held to an hour limit; the Consistory minutes reveal individuals standing up and leaving as soon as the hourglass ran out. Everyone, moreover, was required to attend church at least once a week. The Consistory preferred that the Genevois attend their own parish churches, but some did not, and those especially devout, who sought to hear a sermon every day, had to travel to different churches—in no one church were sermons given seven days a week. The success of preaching can perhaps best be measured by the fact that crowding became a problem in the churches. St. Gervais, for example, had a capacity of some 800 persons, which was exceeded in the sixteenth century when Viret or one of the other popular preachers preached there.

For Geneva, as for hundreds of other cities, no record of the actual content of most of the preaching survives. For Geneva, as for a small handful of cities, one preacher alone was marked for posterity by his contemporaries; only John Calvin's sermons were deemed worthy of preservation and record for posterity. Soon after Calvin began preaching, people began taking notes of his sermons.[45] Some 3000 of those sermons were recorded, though we no longer have records for all those sermons. We know that Calvin followed the discipline of the *lectio continuo*: for each day of the week he preached, he picked one book from the Bible and spent much of the year going through it, passage by passage, week after week. He read a book from the New Testament or one of the psalms on Sundays, a book from the Old Testament on weekdays. He would read from Scrip-

---

[44] For the following, see Lambert.
[45] T.H.L. Parker, *Calvin's Preaching* (Louisville, KY: Westminster/John Knox Press, 1992).

ture a passage of between one and twelve verses, on average, two
to four. He read directly from the Bible, which lay on the pulpit
before him. He then used the allotted time to explicate that passage. He explained the terms. Then he went through the entire passage, explaining its sense; occasionally, he would add a pointed application to current events. He interrupted this routine to preach
sermons appropriate to the season on Good Friday, Easter, and
Pentecost, usually drawing upon appropriate texts from Matthew
or Acts of the Apostles.

Calvin seems not to have been the most popular preacher in
Geneva; Viret was. But Calvin was one of the reasons French refuges came to Geneva; and the Consistory records are filled with
testimonies of those natives of Geneva who came to hear his sermons. He was a passionate preacher, of uncommon clarity. He was
a master of the French language. Francis Higman credits Calvin
with the invention of the short French sentence. His sermons were
always extemporaneous: he read from Scripture and explicated as
he stood before his congregation. And yet, so deep were his rhetorical gifts that his sermons were always simple and clear. He understood how to structure his speech for aural comprehension. From
the pulpit, he abused the truculent, cajoled the timid, excoriated
the arrogant, and gave to the Word of God a searing as well as a
consoling voice.

In Geneva, Calvin articulated and instituted a particular vision
of the preacher and of the unique efficacy of the spoken Word of
God that would shape Christian communities across the globe. In
1559, Calvin founded the Genevan Academy.[46] In its first five
years, the Academy matriculated 339 students, of whom the overwhelming majority, between 61.4% (in 1564) and 86.3% (in 1562)
were French.[47] Next in numbers were students from the Piedmont,
the Swiss Cantons, and the Netherlands.[48] French Reformed communities sent their young men to Geneva, to study theology and to
learn the true liturgy. In the first years of the Wars of Religion,
eighty-eight ministers left Geneva to lead congregations in France.[49]

---

[46] Karin Maag, *Seminary or University? The Genevan Academy and Reformed Higher Education, 1560-1620* (Scolar Press, 1995).
[47] Ibid., pp. 28-9.
[48] Ibid., pp. 30-32.
[49] Robert M. Kingdon, *Geneva and the Coming of the Wars of Religion in France 1555-
1563* (Geneva: Droz, 1956), p. 6.

Not all seem to have been trained in the Academy, but Calvin viewed Geneva as a center for the training of preachers, informally through their experience of the Christian community in Geneva, with its daily preaching, its Consistory, and its practice of worship, and formally, through the educational program of the Academy, which Theodore Beza saw to completion. Calvin's correspondence speaks to a vision of preaching conducted throughout the world, in every language, a preaching distinguished by its adherence to the true Word of God and, perhaps most of all, by its demand for the inculcation of that Word into the conduct of daily life.

Preaching in the sixteenth century was most audible in those communities, such as Zurich, Basel, and Bern, which by legislative fiat altered the forms and practice of ancient Christianity to accord with those visions evangelical preachers were promulgating. We know so little of preachers in the Swiss cantons who remained loyal to Rome. In St. Gall, Wendelin Oswald sought the reform of his own order, the Dominicans. Also in St. Gall, Adam Moser used his endowed post to ridicule Protestants. Fribourg, Lausanne, St. Gall, and Uri all remained loyal to Rome; the configuration of political and ecclesiastical authority certainly had something to do with that loyalty, but were there also preachers who encouraged their congregations to continue to find in Rome spiritual leadership, in the Mass, true communion?

In historical hindsight, modern day Switzerland is known for its Reformed preaching. From Zurich, Huldrych Zwingli influenced preachers throughout German-speaking Europe, more immediately and palpably in Swabia and Bavaria, the southern reaches of modern-day Germany. His successor in Zurich, Heinrich Bullinger, helped to shape the Protestant churches in England, both through personal correspondence and through the English translation and publication of some of his works. Best known remains Calvin, however, who was never "Swiss," either by birth – he was born in Picardy – or by adopted home: in his lifetime, Geneva did not view itself as a Canton. And yet, the Reformed tradition, as it is practiced in modern day England, the Netherlands, Scotland, and America traces its origins to "Switzerland," and all that connotes.

Bibliography

Blickle, Peter, *Gemeindereformation. Die Menschen des 16. Jahrhunderts auf dem Weg zum Heil* (Munich: Oldenbourg Verlag, 1985).

Brady, Thomas A., Jr., *Turning Swiss: Cities and Empire, 1450-1550* (Cambridge: Cambridge University Press, 1985).

Bullinger, Heinrich, *Reformationsgeschichte*, eds. J.J. Hottinger and H.H. Vögeli, 3 vols. (Frauenfeld, 1838).

Burnett, Amy Nelson, "Preparing the Pastors: Theological Education and Pastoral Training in Basel," in *At the Frontiers of the Reformation: Essays in Honor of Robert McCune Kingdon*, ed. Lee Palmer Wandel, Sixteenth Century Essays and Studies (St. Louis, forthcoming).

Chenevière, Charles, *Farel, Froment, Viret: Réformateurs Religieux au XVIe siècle* (Geneva, 1835).

Gordon, Bruce, *Clerical Discipline and the Rural Reformation: The Synod of Zurich, 1532-1580* (New York: Peter Lang, 1992).

Guggisberg, Hans, *Basel in the Sixteenth Century: Aspects of the City Republic before, during, and after the Reformation* (St. Louis, 1982).

Hammer, Karl, "Der Reformator Oekolampad, 1482-1531," in *Reformiertes Erbe*, ed. Heiko Oberman, Vol. I (Zurich, 1992), pp. 157-70.

Hollweg, Walter, *Heinrich Bullingers Hausbuch* (Neukirchen: Moers, 1956).

Johannes Kesslers Sabbata, eds. Emil Egli and Rudolf Schoch (St. Gall, 1902).

Kingdon, Robert M., *Geneva and the Coming of the Wars of Religion in France 1555-1563* (Geneva, 1956).

Lambert, Thomas, *Preaching, Praying, and Policing Sixteenth-Century Geneva*, Ph.D. diss., University of Wisconsin, Madison, 1998.

Lengwiler, Eduard, *Die vorreformatorischen Prädikaturen der deutschen Schweiz von ihrer Enstehung bis 1530* (Freiburg in der Schweiz, 1955).

Locher, Gottfried, *Die Zwinglische Reformation in Rahmen der europäischen Kirchengeschichte* (Göttingen, 1979).

— "In Spirit and in Truth: How Worship in Zurich Changed at the Reformation," in *Zwingli's Thought: New Perspectives* (Leiden: Brill, 1981), pp. 1-50.

Longère, Jean, *La prédication médiévale* (Paris, 1983).

Maag, Karin, *Seminary or University? The Genevan Academy and Reformed Higher Education, 1560-1620* (Aldershot: Scolar Press, 1995).

Naphy, William G., *Calvin and the Consolidation of the Genevan Reformation* (New York, 1994).

Nauta, D., *Pierre Viret (1511-1571): Medestander van Calvijn* (Kampen, 1988).

Oxford Encyclopedia of the Reformation, 4 vols., ed. Hans J. Hillerbrand (New York, 1966: articles "Geneva," by Robert Kingdon; "Berchtold Haller," by J. Wayne Baker.

Parker, T.H.L., *Calvin's Preaching* (Louisville, KY: Westminster John Knox Press, 1992).

Pfister, Rudolf, *Kirchengeschichte der Schweiz*, vol. I (Zurich, 1964).

Registres du Consistoire de Genève au temps de Calvin, eds. Thomas Lambert and Isabella Watt, under the direction of Robert M. Kingdon (Geneva, 1996).

Rublack, Hans-Christoph, "Zwingli und Zurich," *Zwingliana* 16/5 (1985), 393-426.

Rupp, E. Gordon, *Patterns of Reformation* (London, 1969).

Staehelin, Ernst, *Das theologische Lebenswerk Johannes Oekolampads* (New York, 1971).

Wackernagel, Rudolf, *Geschichte der Stadt Basel*, vol. III (Basel, 1968).

CHAPTER EIGHT

THE BORING OF THE EAR: SHAPING THE PASTORAL VISION OF PREACHING IN ENGLAND, 1540-1640

Eric Josef Carlson
(Gustavus Adolphus College)

In 1552, Bernard Gilpin – a man so highly regarded that he was called the "Apostle of the North" – preached to the court of Edward VI. In his sermon, Gilpin asserted that "a thousand pulpits in England are covered with dust. Some have not had four sermons these fifteen or sixteen years ... and few of those were worthy of the name of sermons."[1] Skepticism is certainly reasonable in the face of what is a fairly typical example of the polemical depiction of late medieval preaching by supporters of reform. But well-crafted polemic can be a very powerful thing. Centuries after they were penned or spoken, their intended audience long dead, the words of sixteenth-century English reformers such as Gilpin retain the power to seduce. According to these polemicists, the Reformation brought the preaching of God's word to pulpits up and down the land – pulpits erected by the devout men and women who built the medieval parish churches of England, but thereafter allowed them to gather dust and cobwebs. Only the Lollards, who anticipated the themes of the reformers but were persecuted even unto death for their precocity, offered true preaching to the people. The medieval church offered "mumbling massmongers"[2] instead of powerful preachers, and empty rituals with no power to save instead of faithful preaching that was not only "the chiefe worke of the Ministerie" but also the ordinary means by which "men are

---

[1] Quoted in Susan Wabuda, "The Provision of Preaching during the Early English Reformation: With Special Reference to Itineration, c. 1530 to 1547," Ph.D. diss., University of Cambridge, 1992, pp. 6-7. See also D. Marcombe, "Bernard Gilpin: Anatomy of an Elizabethan Legend," *Northern History* 16 (1980), 20-39.

[2] Thomas Becon, *Prayers and Other Pieces*, ed. John Ayre (Cambridge: The University Press, 1844), p. 160.

brought to salvation [and] without [which] ordinarily men cannot attaine to salvation."[3]

Not surprisingly, such a simplistic dichotomy has not survived the critical scrutiny of historians. Familiarity with the life of Margery Kempe, for example, has made clear that medieval lay people could hear a good deal of orthodox preaching, particularly in urban centers such as York and King's Lynn. Although Kempe complained that she could not hear as much preaching as she desired and lamented in her prayers that "all the clerics that preach may not satisfy" her appetite for sermons,[4] she was able to attend a remarkable number of sermons, especially due to the presence of itinerant friars active throughout England.

Acknowledging the existence of a good deal of orthodox preaching in the medieval church should not, however, draw us to the opposite extreme of minimizing the change effected by the Reformation, especially the magnitude of the change in the relationship between preacher and audience. The reformed English church adopted a new pastoral ideal in which preaching assumed the highest priority and a palpable sense of urgency. With the abrogation of auricular confession, preaching became the principal way by which lay Christians might be brought to repentance for their sins, without which there was neither faith nor salvation – a belief that was bolstered by a number of scriptural passages that preachers frequently trotted out for support. Adding to the urgency for the preachers was their belief that God would hold each of them accountable for the soul of every member of their congregations.

Upon the firm foundation of this sincere understanding of their duty and of the means at their disposal, late sixteenth- and early seventeenth-century English preachers built a new relationship with their hearers – one in which they were effectively the indispensable agents of salvation. Arthur Dent, in that most popular of devotional works *The Plaine Mans Pathway to Heaven*, wrote:

> Faith commeth by hearing the word preached, then I reason thus: No preaching, no faith; no faith, no Christ; no Christ, no eternall life.... If

---

[3]   George Downame, *Two Sermons, the one commending the Ministerie in generall: The other defending the office of Bishops in particular* (1608), pp. 26-7. Unless otherwise noted, the place of publication for all pre-1640 books is London.

[4]   *The Book of Margery Kempe*, trans. B. A. Windeatt (New York: Penguin Books, 1985), p. 181.

we will have heaven, we must have Christ. If we will have Christ, we must have faith. If we will have faith, we must have the word preached. Then I conclude that preaching ... is of absolute necessity into eternall life.[5]

To accomplish the heady goal of saving the people, preachers had to preach more often and more effectively, and audiences had truly to listen. If faith came by hearing, the true Christian must be like the servant described in Exodus 21, whose commitment to the perpetual service of his master was sealed when the master brought him to the door of the house and pierced his ear with an awl. "Whoever he is that enters into Gods service," wrote Richard Crooke, "hee must have this marke, even an open eare, and it must be boared at the Doore of Gods house, that he may be readier to heare, then to offer the Sacrifice of fooles."[6]

Preaching in England before the Reformation

The contrast between hearing the Word of God and offering "the Sacrifice of fooles" was, of course, an attack on the medieval church and its "mumbling massmongers"–another piece of Reformation polemic, the other bookend in the matched set that frame my introduction. But if Gilpin's sermon, quoted at the beginning of this chapter, is polemical–and it certainly is–that does not mean that it has nothing important to tell us about late medieval preaching in England.

First, Gilpin's reference to four sermons is deliberate. In 1281, Archbishop Pecham established the requirement that all priests with *cura animarum* were to preach (or find someone to preach in their place) to their congregations on the Creed, the Ten Commandments, the Seven Works of Mercy, the Seven Deadly Sins, the Seven Virtues, and the Seven Sacraments. This was to happen four times a year. This requirement, binding only on the southern province of the church, was later extended to the northern prov-

---

5 Arthur Dent, *The Plaine Mans Pathway to Heaven* (1625), pp. 336-7.
6 Richard Crooke, "To the Christian and Benevolent Reader," in Stephen Egerton, *The Boring of the Eare* (1623), pp. A6r-A6v.

ince as well.[7] Bishops regularly attempted to enforce it (though with what success will be seen below) so it was an accepted standard by which Gilpin could evaluate the provision of preaching.

Even when there were sermons, Gilpin suggested that they often did not really count because they were of the wrong sort. Certainly by Edwardian reformers' standards that was true. Miracle stories and saints' lives were the stuff of medieval sermons, particularly those based on the most common sermon collections, such as Mirk's *Festial*. While penitence and conversion were undeniably important in sermons by some friars,[8] and humanists such as John Fisher were producing sermon collections with a stronger scriptural focus,[9] contemporary observers give us reason to believe that more priests relied on the *Legenda Aurea* and collections of ready-to-use sermons like *Dormi Secure*.[10] It is worth observing that the Lollards, whose place in the history of English preaching is undeniable, did not criticize the church for neglecting to offer sermons, but rather for failing to offer the *right sort* of sermons. The Wycliffite sermons that we now have in superb scholarly editions were intended to provide an alternative to *bad* preaching, which existed in enough abundance to demand attention.[11] But if all of this is true, how can Gilpin be right to speak of layers of dust covering English pulpits?

Gilpin's assertion might actually have been literally true, even in places well supplied with preaching. As Julia Merritt has pointed out, by way of explaining various Jacobean parochial experiments in moving the pulpit and modifying the placement of pillars in the church, medieval church interiors "were not especially well suited to the needs of parishioners attempting to hear a minister preaching a lengthy sermon."[12] In fact, much late medieval preaching

---

[7]   Peter Marshall, *The Catholic Priesthood and the English Reformation* (Oxford: Clarendon Press, 1994), p. 88.

[8]   Clarissa Atkinson, *Mystic and Pilgrim: The* Book *and the World of Margery Kempe* (Ithaca, NY: Cornell University Press, 1983), p. 115.

[9]   Maria Dowling, "John Fisher and the Preaching Ministry," *Archiv für Reformationsgeschichte* 82 (1991), 287-309; Wabuda, "Provision of Preaching," pp. 59-66.

[10]   Marshall, *Catholic Priesthood*, p. 87.

[11]   Pamela Gradon and Anne Hudson, eds., *English Wycliffite Sermons*, 5 vols. (Oxford: Clarendon Press, 1983-96); Anne Hudson, *The Premature Reformation: Wycliffite Texts and Lollard History* (Oxford: Clarendon Press, 1988).

[12]   J. F. Merritt, "Puritans, Laudians, and the Phenomenon of Church-Building in Jacobean London," *Historical Journal* 41 (1998), 946.

seems to have taken place not inside the church but in an outdoor venue. The most famous example is Paul's Cross in London, but smaller country churchyards were also used. It is unsurprising, therefore, that G. R. Owst used a manuscript illustration of a friar preaching in a churchyard for the frontispiece of his classic study, *Preaching in Medieval England*.[13]

Outdoor preaching meant that the sermon was detached from the Mass, which may have had consequences for public interest and attendance, at least in England, where there seems not to have been any parallel to the popularity of continental preachers such as Bernardino da Siena or Girolamo Savonarola.[14] Preachers *were* being sent out to preach in country parishes – and increasingly so in the late fifteenth and early sixteenth centuries. One noteworthy innovation, to which Susan Wabuda has called attention, is the use of cathedral, collegiate, and chantry clergy as itinerant preachers. For example, Lady Margaret Beaufort's chantry clergy were always to include a preacher who was mandated to deliver sermons in parishes in Hertfordshire, Cambridgeshire and Lincolnshire in which Lady Margaret had land or influence.[15] However, the problems faced by these preachers may be inferred from the example of John Veysey, licensed in 1487 to preach throughout the province of Canterbury. An indulgence of forty days was offered to those who heard his sermons in a state of grace, making clear that church authorities knew that sermon-hearing was seen as a voluntary exercise that might require some extra incentive.[16]

John Bromyard, a fourteenth-century Dominican friar, accused the English of being the worst sermon-goers in the world, generally preferring alehouses to sermons. Peter Marshall has demonstrated that this claim cannot be dismissed as self-serving hyperbole, because it can be confirmed by a range of sources. In 1481, for example, the "most part" of the parishioners of Bishophill (Yorkshire) was reported for not coming to sermons. Marshall finds the more

---

[13] Illustration from Fitzwilliam Museum MS 22, in G. R. Owst, *Preaching in Medieval England. An Introduction to Sermon Manuscripts of the Period c.1350-1450* (Cambridge: Cambridge University Press, 1926; repr. New York: Russell & Russell, Inc., 1965), frontispiece.

[14] John A. F. Thomson, *The Early Tudor Church and Society, 1485-1529* (London: Longman, 1993), p. 316.

[15] Wabuda, "Provision of Preaching," pp. 129, 135.

[16] Thomson, *Early Tudor Church*, pp. 315-16.

typical silence of visitation records revealing as well. He argues that most people simply did not care about the inadequacies of preachers or the absence of preaching. They were much more concerned with the provision of sacraments: "Thomas Becon might argue that 'one faithful preacher ... is better than ten thousand mumbling massmongers,' but it is doubtful whether a majority of [his] contemporaries would have concurred."[17]

The Brigittine monk Richard Whitford, whose orthodoxy was unquestioned, wrote that lay people should "ever keep the preachings rather than the masse, if by case they may not hear both."[18] Whitford was by no means alone; in fact, his words are strikingly similar to those of Bernardino of Siena.[19] But it is doubtful that most parish clergy would have agreed – and it seems incredible to expect them to echo these sentiments in their congregations. Instead, most clergy understood their most important role to be as it was described in medieval teaching aids such as the *Lay Folk's Catechism* and the *Quattuor Sermones*. These texts, designed to help instruct the laity about the sacraments, explained the sacrament of holy orders as that which empowered the priest to minister the sacraments. Preaching was not mentioned. Therefore, as Marshall argues with some understatement, "whether the preaching ideal could have become fully incorporated into the popular perception of the priestly vocation in this period remains highly doubtful."[20]

The Preacher's Tale

The English Reformation cannot, therefore, be credited with introducing occasions for public preaching, official commitment to regular preaching (however unevenly enforced) or even orthodox statements of the centrality of preaching. What, then, did change as a result of the English Reformation? It is beyond the scope of this essay to study changes in the doctrinal content and the rhetorical

---

[17] Marshall, *Catholic Priesthood*, pp. 90-1, 107.
[18] Richard Whitford, *A Werke for Housholders* (1530), fol. D4r.
[19] Atkinson, *Mystic and Pilgrim*, p. 115. For other examples, see Marshall, *Catholic Priesthood*, pp. 88-9.
[20] Marshall, *Catholic Priesthood*, pp. 95, 113-14.

structure of sermons.[21] The focus here will be on a fundamental change in the image of the minister's duties. With the Mass abrogated and mandatory auricular confession abolished, priests became ministers and ministers were preachers above all else. As a result, preaching came to occupy a central place in English culture, occurring on more occasions than ever before. Moreover, although medieval friars *may* have preached repentance in their sermons, there were other avenues to that destination in the medieval church. After the Reformation, that was effectively no longer the case and sermons, identified as the means to call people to the reconciliation with God necessary for salvation, were delivered with a new sense of urgency. To bring these issues into focus, we begin with the example of one of the most widely-respected preachers of the Elizabethan period.

By 1584, Richard Greenham had been the rector of Dry Drayton, a small parish roughly five miles northwest of Cambridge, for over a decade. During those years, he had earned a reputation as a model godly minister. Given his reputation and his proximity to the university, Greenham drew many young men to Dry Drayton who were eager to learn from him in order to prepare for their own future pastoral activity. One of those men kept a notebook in which he recorded Greenham's advice on many subjects, from the sublime to the banal, as well as details of Greenham at work.[22]

Preaching is a central concern of his disciple's notes. He described Greenham preaching in his parish several times each week, with weekday sermons beginning shortly after dawn so the villagers could attend before beginning their work in the heavy wet clay of Dry Drayton's fields. His sermons had virtually nothing in common with the learned lectures delivered at Cambridge and much in common with the dramas performed on the stages of Southwark's thea-

---

[21] J. W. Blench, *Preaching in England in the Late Fifteenth and Sixteenth Centuries. A Study of English Sermons 1450-c.1600* (New York: Barnes & Noble Inc., 1964) is still useful in this regard.

[22] On Richard Greenham, his ministry and his disciples, see Kenneth L. Parker and Eric J. Carlson, *'Practical Divinity': The Works and Life of Revd Richard Greenham* (Aldershot, Hants. and Brookfield, VT: Ashgate, 1998). The volume includes a critical edition of a manuscript record of Greenham's sayings preserved in the John Rylands Library (English MS 524); citations below are to our edition, since it is more easily accessible than the manuscript.

tres – a common characteristic of the most highly regarded preachers of the era.[23] Like an actor on stage, Greenham did not preach
from notes – though this did not mean, as some complained, that he
and other ministers "speak even whatsoever commeth into ther
mouths...." Rather, he asserted, "they speak that, which many
years they have studied for, which earnestly they have prayed for,
which by woful experience they have bought, and by a painful life
dearily paied for."[24] Like an actor confronting stage fright,
Greenham experienced "very sharp and trembling fears in the
flesh" before preaching, which he identified as "the very mallice of
sathan," trying to prevent him from delivering "necessary doctrine."[25] His delivery was also more that of the actor than the lecturer. Greenham preached with such energy "that his shirt would
usually be as wet with sweating, as if it had been drenched in water,"[26] and he brushed aside suggestions that he should dampen
"his great zeal and fervency of speaking."[27]

Greenham understood preaching to be part of a great cosmic
drama, because it was "the instrument which God hath appointed
to pull his people into the sheepfold of Jesus Christ, where they are
without daunger of destruction." A congregation without preaching
was like a flock of sheep scattered and threatened by wolves, "wan-
dering abroad to [its] owne destruction."[28] Since preaching was
"the most principal means to increase and beget faith and repentance in Gods people," Greenham believed that "where this ordinary means of salvation faileth, the people for the most part perish."[29] Since God's Word would not preach itself any more than
sheep would herd themselves to a safe haven, preachers bore a terrible responsibility. God held every minister accountable for every
soul entrusted to him, and it was the minister's most pressing burden "to watch over the souls of his people, to be so careful over

---

[23] Bryan Crockett, *The Play of Paradox: Stage and Sermon in Renaissance England*
(Philadelphia: University of Pennsylvania Press, 1995), esp. pp. 7-13; Francis Bremer
and Ellen Rydell, "Puritans in the Pulpit," *History Today* 45 (1995), 50-4.

[24] Parker and Carlson, *Practical Divinity*, p. 199.

[25] Ibid., p. 208.

[26] Samuel Clarke, "The Life of Master Richard Greenham," from *The Lives of
Thirty-Two English Divines*, 3rd ed. (London, 1677), p. 12.

[27] Parker and Carlson, *Practical Divinity*, p. 143.

[28] Richard Greenham, *The Workes of the Reverend and Faithfull Servant of Iesus Christ M.
Richard Greenham*, 4th ed. (1605), p. 778.

[29] Parker and Carlson, *Practical Divinity*, p. 339.

them, as that he will not suffer one through his negligence to perish."[30]

To save his flock, it was principally "necessarie that the Minister
of God, doe very sharply rebuke the people for their sinnes, and
that he lay before them Gods grievous judgements against sinners."[31] But Greenham recognized that rebuking sinners was a duty
fraught with danger and one that required great skill if it were not
to wreck the preacher's relations with his parish. Greenham's irenic
temperament was legendary in the Elizabethan church and he
urged ministers to find a balance between being "zealous against
the sinne" and "comiseration of the person," but "comiseration"
was ultimately less important than censure because "to censure
parishioners was to save them."[32] While some argued that such admonition was meddling, Greenham replied that that was the reasoning of Cain:

> We having learned not the practise of the world, but the practise of the
> word, looke for another judgement, and breaking through all such
> shadowes, wee dare and must be busie with our brother. And if neede
> be, we will sharply deale with him, as plucking him out of the fire. We
> may not under the colour of peaceableness, muzzle our mouthes; if I
> have an eye on the church, I must poynte at sinne; if I be an hand in the
> church, I must plucke it out: for every sinne not admonished is inrolled
> among our sinnes.[33]

The minister "must not be ashamed to rebuke and reprove such as
will not bee obedient to the Gospell, but remaine still wallowing in
their sinne: and if that holesome admonitions will not serve, he
must not spare to thunder out the just judgements of God against
them, untill he hath beaten them down to hell with the terror
thereof...."[34]

The effect of such preaching might be electrifying. Once, for
example, a woman hearing Greenham preach "burst out into des-
perate crying, that shee was a damned soule." The preacher left his
pulpit to console her, saying "woman didst thou not come into this

---

[30] Richard Greenham, *The Workes of the Reverend and Faithfull Servant of Jesus Christ M.
Richard Greenham, Minister and Preacher of the Word of God*, 5th ed. (1612), pp. 342, 358.
[31] Ibid., p. 392.
[32] Peter Iver Kaufman, *Prayer, Despair, and Drama: Elizabethan Introspection* (Urbana
and Chicago: University of Illinois Press, 1996), p. 52.
[33] Greenham, *Workes* (1605), p. 277; Parker and Carlson, *Practical Divinity*, p. 67.
[34] Greenham, *Workes* (1605), p. 782.

place to hear of thy sins and of the forgivenes of them in christ: bee of good comfort, and as thou seest thy sins so shalt thou hear pardon of thy sins."[35] This was hardly a regular event, nor did he expect that it would be. Greenham encouraged his students to be patient and persistent, comparing the preacher to a farmer who "would long after hee had sowen looke for the increas, not measuring the fruit of his labor by the time present but by the tyme to come...."[36] And much of sown seed, falling on barren or rocky ground, would never bear fruit. Not all would be saved by his preaching, but his duty was to deliver the message and he did not need to fear God's judgment if he carried that out to the best of his ability. Greenham said, "I drive men out of themselves and send them to christ if they wil, but if they refuse they go worthily to hel...." Thus, as his disciple observed when recording those words, "to whom hee could not bee the messenger of salvation for ther unbeleef, unto them hee was an instrument of condemnation prepared for them."[37]

Greenham had a genuine talent for this sort of preaching. His contemporary and posthumous reputations demonstrate that he was by any reasonable measure considered a success in his ministry, and modern scholarship supports those judgments.[38] Not every preacher had his good sense or good fortune. A few miles from Dry Drayton, in southeastern Cambridgeshire, Greenham's contemporary Simon Hacksuppe saw his ministry ruined in part by local reaction to his assault on local sinfulness. From 1583 to 1605, Hacksuppe was the rector of Weston Colville and during his tenure this was among the most troubled parishes in the diocese of Ely. Almost immediately after he arrived, his churchwardens reported Hacksuppe for railing against his neighbors during sermons. In 1591, he was presented for brawling with a local gentleman, Edward Stonehouse, in the parish church. In 1597, Elizabeth Martin and Helen Humphrey were presented for railing against Hacksuppe, as was the wife of Richard Webbe in 1600. These last three

---

[35]   Parker and Carlson, *Practical Divinity*, p. 252.
[36]   Ibid., p. 147.
[37]   Ibid., pp. 146-7, 195.
[38]   John Primus is more negative, but his analysis is based on an incomplete and somewhat uncritical reading of the sources: Primus, *Richard Greenham: Portrait of an Elizabethan Pastor* (Macon, GA: Mercer University Press, 1998). See my review in *Sixteenth Century Journal* 30 (1999), 239-41.

cases were not presented by the churchwardens, but most likely by Hacksuppe himself. It was not the first time; in 1591, for example, he had circumvented the wardens, presenting parishioners for such offenses as sleeping during the service, nonattendance, and working on the Sabbath.[39] Hacksuppe took his duty to correct sin a step beyond reprehending sin (and perhaps individual sinners) from the pulpit, and undertook the business of disciplining people through the church courts as well. In doing so, he violated long-standing norms of practice – for social discipline was the responsibility of the laity through the parish churchwardens[40] – and fatally undermined his ministry.

For another of Greenham's contemporaries, William Storr of Market Rasen (Lincolnshire), preaching was quite literally fatal to his ministry. Storr was murdered by one of his parishioners, who had become unhinged as a result of an August 1602 sermon given by Storr on the text from the prophet Isaiah: "Except the Lord of Hosts had left unto us a very small remnant, we should have been as Sodom, and we should have been like unto Gomorrah." During the sermon, a young man named Francis Cartwright "seemed to note it diligently with his pen, but as the stomake filled with rawe humors corrupteth all good nourishment that commeth therin, so this mans mind fraught with rancour, & malice, wrested al things he heard into the worse sense as purposely spoken against him...." Eight days later, Cartwright saw Storr walking in the town. He dashed into a cutler's shop, bought a sword, overtook Storr, and stabbed and slashed the defenseless minister several times. Storr lingered for several days before dying of his wounds; Cartwright escaped with the help of friends, "enemies to the Ministerie of the Gospel," who argued that he had been provoked by Storr's "evill words."[41]

If Greenham's success with preaching was not typical, neither was Storr's gruesome misfortune. The majority of England's preachers labored somewhere in the vast middle ground between

---

[39] Cambridge University Library, Ely Diocesan Records, D/2/17a, fol. 5v; B/2/11, fols. 165r-165v, 205r; B/2/16, fol. 135r; B/2/17, fol. 215r.

[40] Eric Josef Carlson, *Marriage and the English Reformation* (Oxford: Blackwell, 1994), pp. 142-80.

[41] Anon., *The Manner of the Crvell Ovtragiovs Mvrther of William Storre Mast. of Art, Minister, and Preacher at Market Raisin in the County of Lincolne Committed By Francis Cartwright. one of his parishioners, the 30. day of August Anno. 1602* (Oxford, 1603), fols. A2v-A4r.

the two. But whatever their fates, the preachers of the Elizabethan and Jacobean church worked from a very different starting point than did their late medieval precursors. The vision of preaching articulated by Greenham was representative of this new ideology, particularly as it described a new-found urgency in the preacher's relationship with his hearers. A late medieval preacher would have wandered lost in the mental world of his successors.

Preaching and the English Reformation

These new priorities were evident quite early in the course of the Reformation. In *The Institution of a Christian Man* (also known as *The Bishops' Book*) of 1537, the exposition on the sacrament of orders began with a list of the purposes for which Christ and the apostles thought that there should be ministers in the church. The first was "to preach and teach the word of God unto his people." Ministers were "to feed Christ's people ... with their wholesome doctrine; and by their continual exhortations and admonitions, to reduce them from sin and iniquity, so much as in them lieth, and to bring them unto the perfect knowledge, the perfect love and dread of God, and unto the perfect charity of their neighbours."[42] In the Ordinal of 1550, after the laying on of hands, the bishop presented ordinands with a Bible and a chalice saying, "Take thou authority to preach the word of God, and to minister the holy Sacraments in this Congregation."[43] The Thirty-Nine Articles, which became the standard statement of the core beliefs of the English church, described the visible church as "a congregation of faithful men, in the which the pure word of God is preached, and the sacraments be duly ministered."[44]

---

[42] *Formularies of Faith*, ed. Charles Lloyd (Oxford: The University Press, 1856), p. 101. The priorities in the list were not changed in any substantive way in *A Necessary Doctrine and Erudition for any Christian Man* (or *The King's Book*) of 1543, although the passages about feeding with wholesome doctrine and exhorting were deleted and replaced by a mandate to pray for the church and especially for their flock. Ibid., p. 278.

[43] *The Two Liturgies, A.D. 1549, and A.D. 1552: With Other Documents Set Forth by Authority in the Reign of King Edward VI*, ed. Joseph Ketley (Cambridge: The University Press, 1844), p. 179.

[44] David Cressy and Lori Anne Ferrell, eds., *Religion and Society in Early Modern England: A Sourcebook* (London: Routledge, 1996), p. 64. The wording is identical to that first used in the Edwardian articles of 1553.

Preaching—which had never received attention in earlier explications of the priestly office—was first among ministerial duties in every official statement from the commencement of the English Reformation. Moreover, although the authors of *The Bishops' Book* referred to both word and sacraments as the "ordinary mean or instrument" by which people were made "partakers of the reconciliation which is by Christ," they followed this with a passage, in part a paraphrase of Romans 10: 14, which made clear that the word was foremost in their thinking:

> And how can men believe in him, of whom they never heard tell? And how should men hear tell of God, unless there be some men to shew and preach unto them of him? ... And therefore it is said by the prophet Esai [i.e., Isaiah], Blessed be the feet of those preachers, which, being authorized and sent by God, do preach and shew unto us the peace and benefits which we receive by Christ.

While administering the sacraments remained prominent among ministerial duties, *The Bishops' Book* and *The King's Book* "appeared to make [the priest] into a mere cypher" in that role by stressing that he was only an instrument "of God, who himself was the sole worker of the sacraments."[45] In their sacramental functions, ministers seemed to have been demoted from manufacturers to deliverymen.

Between the time of *The Bishops' Book* and the Thirty-Nine Articles, the ranks of the sacraments had been reduced in a way that brought the English into line with other reformed churches. Most outstanding of the changes, from the perspective of preaching ministers, was in the status of auricular confession. Confession was still available but no longer mandatory, nor was it a sacrament. There was not even consensus in orthodox circles about whether confession had to be to a minister.[46]

The Roman church had understood the sacrament of confession as the place in which the priest exercised the power of the keys, granted to the church by Jesus, through the words of absolution. When the English church rejected auricular confession, it did not renounce the power of the keys. Instead, it was redefined. According to John Jewel, in his *Apologie ...of the Churche of Englande,*

---

[45] *Formularies of Faith*, pp. 101-4, 279-80; Marshall, *Catholic Priesthood*, pp. 116-17.
[46] See Eric Josef Carlson, "Confession and Absolution in the English Church, 1530-1640" (forthcoming).

> And touching the keys ... Christ's disciples did receive this authority, not that they should hear private confessions of the people, and listen to their whisperings, as the common massing priests do everywhere now-a-days ... but to the end they should go, they should teach, they should publish abroad the gospel ... and that the minds of godly persons, being brought low by the remorse of their former life and errors, after they had once begun to look up into the light of the gospel and believe in Christ, might be opened with the word of God, even as a door is opened with a key.[47]

Conformists and nonconformists agreed on this point. Richard Hooker described sermons as the "keyes to the kingdom of heaven" and Greenham called the Word the "gate of heaven" while "the keies thereof are given to the true Ministers of Gods word."[48] John Donne set out this new teaching on the keys most fully:

> There is no salvation but by faith, nor faith but by hearing, nor hearing but by preaching; and they that thinke meanliest of the Keyes of the Church, and speake faintliest of the Absolution of the Church, will yet allow, That those Keyes lock, and unlock in Preaching; That Absolution is conferred, or withheld in Preaching, that the proposing of the prom-ises of the Gospel in preaching, is that binding and loosing on earth, which bindes and looses in heaven.[49]

Locating the power of the keys in preaching naturally led to pri-macy for the sermon over and against the sacraments. According to the standard formulation of Bishop Jewel, the ministry of the reformed church consisted in both preaching the word of God and administering the sacraments, but the "principalist part of this of-fice is to preach repentance; that so we may amend our lives, and be converted unto God." It was for this that Christ had sent forth his disciples.[50] Richard Rogers identified three means appointed by

---

[47] John Jewel, *The Works of John Jewel*, ed. John Ayre (Cambridge: The University Press, 1848), 3, p. 61.

[48] Richard Hooker, *Of the Laws of Ecclesiastical Polity, Book V*, ed W. Speed Hill. The Folger Library Edition of the Works of Richard Hooker, vol. 2 (Cambridge, MA: Harvard University Press, 1977), p. 87; Greenham, *The Workes* (1605), p. 779. Even those who later challenged the role of preaching acknowledged this view; John Downe cited the passage from Hooker quoted above: *Certaine Treatises* (Oxford, 1633), p. 39.

[49] John Donne, *The Sermons of John Donne*, eds. George R. Potter and Evelyn Simp-son, 10 vols. (Berkeley and Los Angeles: University of California Press, 1953-62), 7, p. 320.

[50] Jewel, *Works*, 3, pp. 1130-1.

God for our growth in godliness: "the Ministery of the Word, read, preached, and heard," the sacraments, and public prayer. Of these three, Rogers asserted that the Word – particularly the Word preached – was rightly listed first because it contained everything necessary for salvation and that "God hath appointed this preaching of his Word, to perfect the faith of his Elect."[51] This view united conformists and nonconformists.[52]

For some preachers, the link between sin and preaching was so strong that they identified the first sermon with the first sin. John Frewen wrote that "the firste preacher that ever was uppon the earth was God himselfe, he preached to Adam in Paradise that comfortable Gospell, the seede of the woman, shall break the serpents heade." Over fifty years later, John Stoughton preached that "Paradise was the first Parish, that had a Sermon in it, and Adam was the first auditor, that heard a Sermon in Paradise, and the fall of man, was the first Text of the Sermon, that Adam heard, and God was the first Preacher of a Sermon upon that Text…."[53]

More commonly, however, preachers started with the first preacher of the Gospels, John the Baptist, and his message. Both Edward Philips and John Stockwood, for example, called attention to John's relentless preaching of repentance. Bishop Hugh Latimer pointed out that Christ's "first sermon" was the same as John's: ' "Do penance; your living is naught; repent.' Again, at Nazareth, when he read in the temple, [he] preached remission of sins, and healing of wounded consciences…." Stockwood, noting that Jesus followed John's example, told contemporary preachers to do likewise, preaching "the Gospel of the kingdome, that is to say reconciliation with God, repentaunce and forgivenesse of sinnes, & faith in Christ."[54] This was, as Jewel argued, nothing less than Christ's intention in calling men to ministry: like John the Baptist and Jesus

---

[51]   Richard Rogers, *Seven Treatises* (5th ed., 1630), pp. 281-4.

[52]   Parker and Carlson, *Practical Divinity*, p. 339.

[53]   John Frewen, *Certaine Faithfull Instructions* (1587), p. 302; John Stoughton, *Five Sermons on II Cor. V. XX.* (also known as *The Preachers Dignity, and Duty*) in *XV. Choice Sermons, Preached Upon Selected Occasions* (1640), p. 47. On the other hand, Richard Bernard argued that preaching originated before the Fall, when God taught Adam and Eve both the Law and the Gospel: *The Faithfull Shepheard* (1607), p. 1.

[54]   Edward Philips, *Certaine Godly and Learned Sermons* (1605), p. 93; John Stockwood, *A very fruiteful Sermon preched at Paules Crosse* (1579), fols. 34r, 38r-39v; Hugh Latimer, *Sermons and Remains*, ed. George Elwes Corrie, 2 vols. (Cambridge: The University Press: 1844-5) 1, p. 209.

himself when he began to preach, "he willed [ministers] to call the people to repentance, and to preach the kingdom of God. ... The principalest part of this office is to preach repentance; that so we may amend our lives, and be converted unto God."[55] Stoughton believed that not only the preacher's vocation but the entire sense of God's word could be found in the call to preach reconciliation in 2 Corinthians 5: 20. For Stoughton, this was "a little Bible [in which] all the letters are compendiously abbreviated in these few characters [and] all the silver sayings reduced to this golden sentence...." It was through preaching, not Rome's "eare-confession," that people were reconciled to God, wrote Andrew Willet, and through preaching that "the great worke of mans salvation" (as Henry Airay called it) was accomplished.[56]

In order to bring about this repentance and reconciliation, preachers had to speak often and forcefully about the sins of the people in their congregations. This was not an easy task, and many writers identified it as the principal cause of the contempt with which ministers were often treated. According to Stephen Gosson, for example,

> It is the very case oftentimes, if the preacher come to you with a painted fire, and stroake your spleene, and tell you that all is well, because you are predestinate you shall goe to Heaven sleeping, as men carried in a Coach without any action or motion of your owne, we shall never be gainsaide. But come to you with a true fire, and tell you muste worke out your salvation with feare and trembling, you beginne to murmur, because you are contrarie unto us.[57]

Griffith Williams lamented that although many people had "itching eares" and sought "heapes of teachers," they sought only those "after their owne lustes, men-pleasers, time-servers, delicate Physitians" who offered no cures for the diseases of their souls but only

---

[55] Jewel, *Works*, 2, pp. 1130-1. See also Frewen, *Certaine Fruitfull Instructions*, p. 304; William Perkins, *A Golden Chaine* in *The Works of William Perkins*, ed. Ian Breward (Abingdon, Berks.: The Sutton Courtenay Press, 1970), p. 237.

[56] Stoughton, *Five Sermons*, p. 7; Andrew Willet, *Synopsis Papismi*, 5th ed. (1634), p. 734; Henry Airay, *Lectures Upon the Epistle to the Philippians* (1618), p. 73.

[57] Stephen Gosson, *The Trumpet of Warre* (1598), fol. 63v. See also, for example, Bernard, *Faithfull Shepheard*, p. 71. I will address this issue in greater detail in "The Myth of Anticlericalism in the Elizabethan and Early Stuart Church" (forthcoming).

"those sweet bits, that will please their palates; for fear of ... making them Sermon-sick."[58]

Such preaching was worse than useless. It was one of the surest signs of "carnall securitie" that one favored a ministry that "will soothe [the people] up in their sinfull courses, and let them sleepe securely in their wickednesse," according to John Downame, when what was needed was preaching "which is that Plow and Harrow that breaketh up the fallow grounds of our hearts, and that bruiseth them and maketh them contrite ... that Hammer which breaketh these rockes in pieces, and that Fire which melteth and dissolveth those mettals that cannot be broken."[59] This did not exhaust the catalog of metaphors deployed to explain the nature of this preaching. Airay, for example, said that the preacher's goal was to "launce our sores unto the bottome, that so we may be thoroughly healed."[60] What all of these images share is a sort of violence, which is precisely what John Brinsley called for: a "holy violence," made necessary by the urgency of the case. "Cruell is that mercy," wrote Brinsley, "that suffers a man rather to bee drowned than to pull him out of the water by the hayre of his head."[61] If the preacher was to speak with "holy violence," attendance could best be described as "holy masochism." For Elnathan Parr, the person who came to a sermon, came "to bee sacrificed"—that is, to "suffer the sacrificing knife to cut the throat of [his] lusts." Although such a prospect was unpleasant, Parr advised his readers to "be not angry when thy sinnes are toucht, [but] lye as still as Isaak did when he should be made a sacrifice, if though desirest to be saved."[62] Only if "our filth is laid open before our eyes," wrote Bishop Jewel, can we be made "to see ourselves, to know our weakness, to repent our sins, to believe the forgiveness of our sins, and to turn to God."[63]

Nor could the preacher denounce sin once (or even occasionally) from the pulpit and move on to more pleasant topics. Rather, such

---

[58] Griffith Williams, *The Best Religion* (1636), p. 154.

[59] John Downame, *A Treatise of Securitie* in *A Guide to Godlynesse* (1622), pp. 39, 69-70.

[60] Airay, *Lectures Upon the Epistle to the Philippians*, p. 457.

[61] John Brinsley the Younger, *The Preachers Charge. And Peoples Duty* (1631), p. 16.

[62] Elnathan Parr, *The Workes Of that faithfull and painefull preacher, Mr. Elnathan Parr*, 3rd ed. (1632), p. 133.

[63] Jewel, *Works*, 2, p. 1033. For further discussion of this theme, see Kaufman, *Prayer, Despair, and Drama*, pp. 41-102.

preaching had to be constant because so many of the hearers were
"thick" (according to George Herbert) and "dull … and drowsie"
(according to William Ward).[64] In order to make an opening
through which the Spirit might enter, Donne argued that it was not
enough merely to knock and request entry into the soul. Rather, the
preacher had to batter the soul.[65] Even penitent Christians needed
constant reminders of the need for repentance, since there would
inevitably be "slippes and falles." As Richard Stock noted, even "he
that is in the best estate in this life is but as a ship, which if it be
neglected it will rot in the haven, and if it bee kept never so carefully, it will still need some repairing."[66]

This was tricky business. The first danger was that the preacher
would be accused simply of railing against his neighbors. When
Richard Bernard urged preachers to take care to know his audience
well, like "a Physician skilfull of his patients disease," so that he
might not deserve accusations of railing, he wrote from personal
experience.[67] To avoid such accusations, Downame advised each
preacher to show that he acted only out of love for his flock, being
"mooved in all things to seeke their good, and to preferre their salvation before his owne private profit. The which love in the teacher,
his instructions and comforts, but also his admonitions and
reproofes, seeing they come not out of any spleene, but out of
meere love, and fervent desire of saving their soules."[68]

The minister who could demonstrate "a Fatherly and motherly
affection" to his people had, according to Frewen, the best chance
of avoiding the second danger: that rather than being reconciled to
God, the people would as a result of the minister's "oversharpe
reprooving and rebuking" be either angered or driven to despair.[69]
On the other hand, too much caution in rebuking sinners could be

---

[64]   George Herbert, *A Priest To the Temple, Or, The Countrey Parson His Character, And
Rule of Holy Life* in *The Complete English Works*, ed. Ann Pasternak Slater (New York: Alfred
A. Knopf, 1995), p. 204; William Ward, *A Sinners Inditement* (1613), fol. B5r.
[65]   Donne, *Sermons*, 7, p. 396.
[66]   Richard Stock, *The Doctrine and Use of Repentance*(1616), p. 194. See also William
Hopkinson, *A Preparation into the waye of lyfe* (1581), fols. B1r-B1v; John Mayer, *Praxis
Theologica* (1629), pp. 184-6.
[67]   Bernard, *Faithfull Shepheard*, p. 73. On Bernard's problems in his own parish, see
Parker and Carlson, *Practical Divinity*, pp. 65-6.
[68]   Downame, *Guide to Godlynesse*, p. 484.
[69]   Frewen, *Certaine Fruitfull Instructions*, p. 294.

just as counterproductive. Parr set out the preacher's dilemma with admirable precision:

> In this, two sorts of Ministers much faile: First, those which are so tender and studious to please, that they are loath to speake any but sweet words, though men rot in their sinnes. Secondly, those which are as farre on the other extreme, accounting all prefacing and loving speaking to be dawbing, and no sentence to be zealously delivered, unlesse Damnation and damned be at the end of it: whereby many times they drive them farther from Christ, whom they would have converted unto him.[70]

It was no mean feat to condemn sin "but scare none from the Church [and] give no occasion by your preaching to runne out of the gates of Sion."[71] But this is precisely what ministers had to find a way to do.

Ward tried to explain how to strike the proper balance. He noted that Christ himself was known both to curse and to speak comfortably. Therefore, in their own preaching "promises and threatnings in a christian proportion, according to the occasion, should be mingled together." Frewen described the two voices that the minister needed to have: "a sweet and amiable voyce to drawe those to the flocke which yealde themselves teachable, and ... a loude voyce to cry out against all them that scatter the flocke."[72] Although it was fairly common to describe preachers with the biblical image of "sons of thunder,"[73] gentleness could in practice be the more productive approach. Leonard Wright, for example, pointed out

> that as little children may not alwaies be fed with vineger and sharp sauce, but rather with milke and sweet pap: so though somtime it be necessary to bruise and mollifie the hard stony affections of mens hearts, with the rigor of Gods fearefull judgements: yet rather to water them often with the sweet comfortable dew of his mercies in Christ, according to the wise physician, who tempereth his bitter medicines with sweet sirops.[74]

Richard Truman used similar imagery. He lamented that there were many preachers "who deale harshly and barbarously," doing more harm than good because their "salve proves worse then the

---

70 Parr, *Workes*, p. 74.
71 William Jones, *Commentary upon the Epistle ... to the Hebrewes* (1635), p. 641.
72 Ward, *Sinners Inditement*, p. B2v; Frewen, *Certaine Fruitfull Instructions*, p. 300.
73 For example Donne, *Sermons*, 7: 396; Downame, *Treatise of Securitie*, p. 70.
74 Leonard Wright, *A Summons for Sleepers* (1615), p. 49.

sore." Rebuking sinners required gentle preparation, a "loving pre-
amble … to hide the hooke of reprehension, to catch the soules of
them we fish for." Like the fisherman who conceals the hook in his
bait, physicians who "give bitter pills to queasie stomacked patients" wrap them in something sweet "to the intent they may take
them without offence." Kind and gentle words, Truman concluded,
could soften up the heart, in the same way as rain softens the earth,
making it easier to pluck the weeds of sin "and to receive the good
seede of wholsome reproofe."[75]

Greenham, as we have seen, recognized the dangers of harsh
preaching but favored erring on the side of severity rather than
gentleness. In giving this advice, he reminded fellow ministers that
"every sinne not admonished is inrolled among our sinnes."[76] The
urgency with which preachers undertook their mission was informed by this belief that they could be held accountable for every
person under their charge. William Jones wrote that it was the minister's duty to watch over the souls of his parishioners "as the henne
watches for the chickens against the kite." Because of this, he en-
treated lay people to

> suffer us to meddle with you, to reprehend that which is amisse in you:
> for we must give an accompt for you. Therefore we cannot let you alone,
> wee cannot, nay, wee must not permit you to sleepe in your sinnes: wee
> must lift up our voices as trumpets to waken you, because we are to give
> accompt for you.[77]

Preachers accepted that some would refuse to hear their message.
There were those, as Stock put it, who "by their owne peevish-
nesse" did not attend sermons or "having eares not boared, but
given to drowsines and sleepinesse" attended but did not hear. The
condition of such people was, as Samuel Gardiner described it,
"exceeding daungerous" because contempt for the ministry of the
Word "is the next dore to damnation it selfe."[78]

God would not punish ministers for this willful refusal to repent.
Rather, God's wrath was reserved for ministers whose people died

---

[75] Richard Truman, *A Christian Memorandum, Or Advertisement wherein is handled the Doctrine of Reproofe* (Oxford, 1629), chap. 3, esp. pp. 51-2.
[76] See above, p. 257.
[77] Jones, *Commentary upon … Hebrewes*, pp. 630-1.
[78] Stock, *Doctrine and Use of Repentance*, p. 144; Samuel Gardiner, *Portraitur of the prodigal sonne* (1599), p. 28. See also Henry Smith, "The Art of Hearing," in *Thirteene Sermons* (1592), fol. C4r.

in ignorance due to his negligence. Edward Vaughan expressed this belief with admirable economy when he wrote that "the bloud of every Parishioner that dieth ignorantly in his sinne, shall be required of the Pastor."[79] This was a common theme. Robert Humston, for example, reminded fellow preachers that "it is ... required in the stewards, that they be found faithfull, full of affections, pastoral care and zeale, especially towardes that people and flocke committed to their charge, whose bloud shall be required at their hands."[80] Truman argued, "If we reprove not sin in others, we make our selves guilty of the same sinne…. In Gods Consistory, the not corrector as well as the law-breaker is both guilty of the sinne and subject to the same reward."[81] John Mayer wrote that "ministers ... shall answer for doing the worke of God negligently, and become guilty of the bloud of those, that are committed to their charge, in that they doe not use the best meanes to convert them."[82]

If sermons were the best means to convert the people, and conversion must precede salvation, preaching could be described as virtually essential for salvation – and if preaching was essential then so was the preacher. Bernard wrote in *The Faithfull Shepheard* that people cannot believe what they have not heard, and they cannot hear without a preacher: "It is therefore verie necessary" and "Ministers of the Gospel are called Light, Salt, Saviours, Seers, Chariots of Israel, & Horsemen thereof, Pastours, Planters, Waterers, Builders, and Stewards, Watchmen, Soldiers, [and] Nurses" in the Bible because these were "such things, and callings, as are most common, and also needfull to necessarie uses: that the necessity of them [i.e., the ministers] heereby may be considered of, both for the Church and Commonwealth."[83] George Downame, citing St. Paul's first letter to the Corinthians, told his hearers quite simply that it was through the minister that they came to faith.[84] Samuel Hieron, whose capacity for flogging a metaphor for at least an hour

---

[79] Edward Vaughan, *A Plaine And perfect Method, for the easie understanding of the whole Bible* (1617), p. 56.

[80] Robert Humston, *A Sermon Preached at Reysham* (1589), p. 9.

[81] Truman, *Christian Memorandum*, pp. 118-20.

[82] Mayer, *Praxis Theologica*, p. 183. See also Downame, *Two Sermons*, p. 16; Williams, *Best Religion*, p. 1103.

[83] Bernard, *Faithfull Shepheard*, pp. 1-2.

[84] Downame, *Two Sermons*, p. 28 (citing 1 Corinthians 3: 5).

more than it could endure was truly breathtaking, wrote in *The Spirituall Fishing* "that (ordinarily) there is not more hope of a mans salvation, without any able and industrious Minister, then there is that the fish in the Sea will of itselfe come ashore...." Indeed, even after being caught, the fish would labor mightily to throw itself out of the boat and back into the sea of ignorance, misery and sin.[85] Other metaphors were deployed as well. Jones, describing preachers as "gods Torch-bearers, that carry the flaming Torch of the Word of God before your eyes, to shew you the way to the Kingdome of Heaven," argued that "ordinarily not one man or woman can goe to heaven, unlesse a Preacher carry him on his shoulders" just as "not one sheafe can get into the barne, unlesse a harvest man do carry it."[86]

It is easy when reading such words to imagine that what we are encountering is merely old wine packaged in new wineskins – the clericalism of the Roman church rebaptized in a Reformed rite but essentially unchanged.[87] Certainly, as we shall see, later critics were to accuse preachers of elevating their own words (in the sermon) over those of God (in the unmediated text of the bible), but preachers like Downame, Bernard, Hieron and Jones understood what they were arguing to be solidly grounded in Scripture itself.

Preachers used a number of key biblical texts in making this argument. The text that was used first and most commonly was from St. Paul's letter to the Romans:

> For whosoever shall call upon the name of the Lord shall be saved. How then shall they call on him in whom they have not believed? and how shall they believe in him of whom they have not heard? and how shall they hear without a preacher? And how shall they preach, except they be sent? as it is written, How beautiful are the feet of them that preach the gospel of peace, and bring glad tidings of good things!... So then faith cometh by hearing, and hearing by the word of God.[88]

---

85   Samuel Hieron, *The Workes of M* *Sam. Hieron* (1634), 1:639-46; quotation from 645. For a discussion of the limits Hieron saw in the minister's role, see Ibid., 2:198.

86   Jones, *Commentary upon ... Hebrewes*, p. 633.

87   On this theme generally, see Neal R. Enssle, "Patterns of Godly Life: The Ideal Parish Minister in Sixteenth- and Seventeenth-Century English Thought," *Sixteenth Century Journal* 28 (1997), 3-28. I will address the accusation of clericalism in my forthcoming article (see n. 59 above).

88   Romans 10: 13-15, 17 (King James Version).

This passage had been the basis of the discussion of preaching in *The Bishops' Book*[89] and Latimer also used it in his sermons when he argued that preaching "is the footstep of the ladder of heaven, of our salvation. There must be preachers, if we look to be saved." In later sermons, Latimer described the preaching office as "the office of salvation, and the only means that God hath appointed to salvation."[90] Parr responded to those who believed that "the Ministers office is least necessarie" by arguing from this text "that Faith and the promised good things cannot be attained without preaching. Next to Christ, it is the greatest benefit which God hath given to men."[91] In his 1581 catechism, William Hopkinson wrote that we need Christ in order "to pacifie the fathers wrath" and if God's wrath is not pacified but "be kindled yea a little we shall perish." Citing Romans 10, he argued that we cannot come to Christ without faith, and we cannot come to faith without preaching; therefore, without preaching we cannot escape God's wrath.[92] Vaughan saw in preaching the promise of comfort to the despairing parishioner he created in a dialogue published in 1617. When the parishioner lamented that "as for me, silly soule, … I have no meanes of comfort, I have no place to hide myselfe, nor helpe to flye away," Vaughan countered that preaching was that means of comfort because it was the source of faith but "take away the preacher take away the word, take away the word take away hearing, take away hearing take away Faith, take away Faith take away calling upon God, take away calling upon God take away salvation in Christ."[93] These are just a few examples of the ways in which preachers and writers used Romans 10.[94]

If Romans 10 provided the theoretical statement about the necessity of preaching, Acts 8 provided the illustrative example. In the

---

[89] See above, p. 261. In fairness to the medieval church, it should be noted that Thomas Brinton, bishop of Rochester (1373-1389) also cited it in his sermons obliging those with *cura animarum* to preach regularly: Roy Martin Haines, *Ecclesia Anglicana: Studies in the English Church of the Later Middle Ages* (Toronto: University of Toronto Press, 1989), p. 204.

[90] Latimer, *Sermons and Remains*, 1, pp. 200, 418; see also pp. 291, 306, 349, 358.

[91] Parr, *Workes*, p. 137.

[92] Hopkinson, *Preparation*, fols. B3v-4r.

[93] Vaughan, *Plaine And perfect Method*, pp. 21, 23, 25-6.

[94] Two additional examples have been already been used in this essay: Dent, *Plaine Mans Path-way*, pp. 299, 336-7; Bernard, *Faithfull Shepheard*, p. 2.

final section of that chapter, we read about Philip's encounter with an Ethiopian eunuch, a high official in the Ethiopian queen's court, who was sitting in his chariot reading the prophecy of Isaiah. When Philip asked him if he understood what he was reading, the eunuch replied, "How can I, except some man should guide me?" Philip then began to preach to him about Jesus, after which the eunuch asked to be baptized.[95] John Rogers used this story to demonstrate the problem with "bare reading" of the Word: it was an encounter with the Word but it was "not that which God hath used or doth use to the working of Faith."[96]

This passage was used by some to advocate an almost child-like dependence on preachers by the laity. Greenham, for example, said that as the eunuch "would not interprete the word without a guide," it is necessary "for a time like babes [to] hang at the mouthes of the Ministers, because wee cannot … goe without a leader."[97] Gardiner wrote that "we must repaire to the priests lips" in order to understand the Word "for wee cannot of our selves understand what we read without an interpreter, as the chamberlain of Queene Candace flatly answered Philip [for] a man without a preacher, is as hee that is blinde without a leader, which can never find the way. For our darknes is like the Egyptian darknes, grosse, and palpable."[98]

When William Massie preached in 1586 that "where preaching faileth there the people perisheth," he gave as his reference Proverbs 29:18.[99] Greenham and Robert Some used the text in virtually identical ways. Greenham, for example, said that preaching was "the most principal means to increase and beget faith and repentance in Gods people … and where this ordinary means of salvation faileth, the people for the most part perish."[100] The difficulty here is that this is not what the text literally says. In the Geneva Bible, the translation most familiar to Massie, Greenham, and

---

[95]   Acts 8: 26-38.

[96]   John Rogers, *The Doctrine of Faith*, 5th ed. (1633), p. 55.

[97]   Parker and Carlson, *Practical Divinity*, p. 343.

[98]   Gardiner, *Portraitur of the prodigal sonne*, p. 27. See also Jones, *Commentary upon … Hebrewes*, p. 323; Vaughan, *Plaine and perfect Method*, p. 28.

[99]   William Massie, *A Sermon Preached at Trafford* (1586), fol. A8r.

[100]   Parker and Carlson, *Practical Divinity*, p. 339; Robert Some, *A Godlie Treatise of the Church* (1582), fols. C3r-C3v. See also Bishop Latimer's sermon preached to Edward VI on 29 March 1549: "take away preaching, and take away salvation": *Sermons and Remains*, 1, p. 155.

Some, the passage is given as: "Where there is no vision, the people decay." This faithfully renders the original Hebrew. The Vulgate translated the Hebrew word for vision as *prophetia*, reflecting the sense of the Hebrew text that God's will for the people was communicated through a prophet.[101]

What is striking is that there is no direct warrant for reading this passage as Massie and others did; the word "preaching" does not occur in the Hebrew or in any translation. When Stockwood wrote that "godly King Solomon doth testifie" that where "the worde is not preached, there the people must perish," Hooker was quite right to respond that this "is more then the wordes of Salomon import."[102] However, an equation between prophet and preacher was a common theme. John Reynolds, preaching in 1586 on the prophet Haggai, for example, said "the preacher is a prophet, not because he is able to foretell things to come, but because he speaks the word of the Lord and applies it to his age."[103] According to Hieron, the New Testament meaning of prophesying "is even the very same which we term preaching."[104] (This would explain why the preaching exercises over which Queen Elizabeth I and Archbishop Grindal collided were known commonly as prophesyings.)

These are not, of course, the only scriptural passages that were pressed into service to explain the importance of preaching. They are however those that were most commonly used, and collectively they make clear the stakes as perceived by the preachers: without preaching, people could not come to faith and therefore would perish in eternal damnation. As Mayer wrote, "The preaching of the word is so necessary, that the want of it is set forth a soarer famine, then the want of corporall food."[105]

---

[101] I am very grateful to Dr. Simon P. Sibelman for assisting me with the Hebrew meaning of this passage.

[102] Stockwood, *A very fruiteful Sermon*, A4v; Hooker, *Laws of Ecclesiastical Polity, Book V*, pp. 99-100. For a similar comment, see Downe, *Certaine Treatises*, p. 20.

[103] Quoted in C. M. Dent, *Protestant Reformers in Elizabethan Oxford* (Oxford: Oxford University Press, 1983), p. 203.

[104] Crockett, *Play of Paradox*, p. 9, quoting Samuel Hieron, *The Dignity of Preaching* (1616), p. 3. For other discussions of the preacher as prophet, see Gosson, *The Trumpet of Warre*, pp. 52, 55; William Perkins, *The Art of Prophesying Or A Treatise Concerning the Sacred and Only True manner and Method of Preaching*, in *The Works*, ed. Breward, 333; and Ward, *Sinners Inditement*, pp. 1-15.

[105] Mayer, *Praxis Theologica*, p. 171. Mayer was referring to Amos 8:11-12, a passage also cited in a similar context in Gardiner, *Portraitur of the prodigal sonne*, p. 28.

All of these arguments were subject to criticism from a number of writers and preachers. They did not deny that sermons were important and could bring people to saving faith. However, they argued that the preachers cited above could be seen to be derogating from God's sovereignty and exalting their own words over the Word.[106] Hooker, for example, argued for a definition of preaching that was much broader, because to limit preaching to sermons was to "shut up [the Word] in so close a prison." For Hooker, reading the Bible was just as likely a way to be saved: "Reading doth convey to the minde that truth without addition or diminution, which scripture hath derived from the holie Ghost. And the ende of all Scripture is … faith, and through faith salvation." The example of the eunuch was not relevant to Hooker; he lacked "a key unto knowledge" that people now have so that they can now learn from reading "which he without an interpretor could not." For Hooker, in sum, the Scriptures were clear and accessible to contemporary Christians.[107]

Hooker's argument was a common one. William Covel, for example, agreed that to limit the benefits of the Word to preaching sermons was to bind the Holy Ghost to one form – and that a form of human wisdom. While sermons could drone on and on for two or three hours – "a time too long for most preachers to speake pertinently" – the texts on which they preached were brief, simple and easy to understand, according to Covel, and "sometimes the Word, by being read … preacheth it selfe to the hearer."[108] Martin Fotherby and John Downe also asserted that the Bible was easy to understand, at least in "all fundamentall points and duties necessary to salvation." As Downe put it, "if [these points] were written with a sunbeame they could not be more cleare." For Fotherby, reading Scripture was "not a faint or a feeble kind of Preaching … but it is a mighty and a powerfull kind of preaching; both sufficient, and efficient to beget in our hearts both faith and all other spiritual vertues…."[109]

---

[106]   See, for example, William Covel, *A Just and Temperate Defense of the Five Books of Ecclesiastical Policie* (1603), p. 79; Downe, *Certaine Treatises*, pp. 38-43; Martin Fotherby, *Foure Sermons, Lately Preached* (1608), pp. 45, 53; Hooker, *Laws of Ecclesiastical Polity, Book V*, pp. 87-8.

[107]   Hooker, *Laws of Ecclesiastical Polity, Book V*, pp. 92, 102-3.

[108]   Covel, *Just and Temperate Defense*, pp. 78-80.

[109]   Downe, *Certaine Treatises*, p. 27; Fotherby, *Foure Sermons*, pp. 28-9.

The proof of this for Downe could be found in the many examples of those who were saved by "bare reading", such as Augustine and Anthony the Hermit. As Downe pointed out, John Foxe and others acknowledged that "in the blind times of Poperie," many were saved through reading; but while Foxe considered this extraordinary, Downe did not. This was because Downe understood "hearing" in Romans 10 to be intended analogically. He noted that when people receive a letter, they speak of having *heard* from someone; thus, when St. Paul spoke of the necessity of hearing, he expected his audience to understand that he referred to reading. By this interpretation, reading could be understood as an ordinary means of salvation. It must be, in fact, because "it is a strange point in Divinity that the Ordinary meanes should at any time fayle in the Church" as sermons had during the time of popery.[110]

Charles Sonnibank and Robert Shelford also echoed Hooker's argument about the relevance of the eunuch in their time. Sonnibank noted that the eunuch was puzzled by a prophecy of Christ's passion and death; he could not understand it because "no eye but the eye of faith, can pearce and looke into" passages on such topics. Shelford told his reader that the eunuch "was out of the Church, which is the house of light…"; as a result, "the scripture was to him a mysterie, but to thee it is no mysterie." Sonnibank admitted that there were passages that "bee full of high and heavenly mysteries, which the eye of reason, & naturall understanding cannot pierce" but much of Scripture was quite clear in expressing God's power and wisdom, the duties and reverence owed to God by all creatures, and "such things as invite men to faith, and exhort them to holinesse of life."[111]

The ways in which preachers like Greenham used the story of the eunuch to make expansive claims for the preachers alarmed many. Archbishop John Whitgift anticipated much of this discourse, objecting to making the minister the "only mouth of the people" and fearing a clericalism in which "the people wholly depend upon the minister's words, and as it were hang upon his lips."

---

[110] Downe, *Certaine Treatises*, pp. 18-19, 22, 29. Richard Baxter reported that God chose "to instruct and change" his father "by the bare reading of the Scripture, without either Preaching or godly Company": Patrick Collinson, *The Religion of Protestants: The Church in English Society 1559-1625* (Oxford: Clarendon Press, 1982), p. 250.

[111] Charles Sonnibank, *The Eunuche's Conversion* (1617), pp. 72-3; Robert Shelford, *Five Pious and Learned Discourses* (Cambridge, 1635), p. 64.

This is precisely what happened. John Downame, for example, wrote that "our eyes must be fastened upon the Preacher, as the eyes of our Saviour Christs hearers were upon him; and like them, we must hang upon his lips, as the child upon his mothers brests, to sucke from them the sincere milke of the Word...."[112] For his part, Whitgift argued that a preaching ministry was not necessary; a reading ministry was just as valid because faith came through the Word rather than any individual's interpretation of it. Men like Downame, on the other hand, seemed to make the minister so central that there was real danger that the instrument would usurp the place of the author, God.[113]

Hooker reminded his readers that sermons were not God's Word, but "that which giveth them their verie beinge is the witt of man, and therefore they oftentimes accordinglie tast too much of that over corrupt fountaine from which they come."[114] Fotherby worried that the status being demanded for sermons as the "sole ordinary meanes to beget a true faith in us" implied that the Scriptures themselves were inadequate and imperfect until men "adde unto them [their] vocal and speaking expositions, to make them perfect." Fotherby did not want to set up "word of men" in opposition to "word of God" and thus reject sermons utterly. Rather, he argued that while sermons are the words of men, they should be given credit with their hearers for their agreement with the Scriptures, for "if they dissent from them, no pulpit can sanctifie them, no spirit can make them to bee the word of God...." A true sermon was not God's words literally, but it did not differ from them in substance just as an ambassador's words were his own but were taken from his master's instructions.[115]

In response to these critics, the proponents of the narrower understanding of preaching were careful to remind their audience that it was God who had established preaching in its place. Brinsley wrote that preaching "is the ordinance of God; his power unto salvation: that is his powerfull instrument which he hath in his

---

[112]   Downame, *Guide to Godlynesse*, p. 393; see also above p. 272.

[113]   Sharon L. Arnoult, "John Whitgift, *The Book of Common Prayer* and the Emergence of Anglican Religious Identity," unpub. NACBS paper. See *The Works of John Whitgift, D.D.*, ed. John Ayre, 3 vols. (Cambridge, 1851-3), 1, pp. 206, 539; 3, pp. 28-57, 490-3.

[114]   Hooker, *Laws of Eccleiastical Polity, Book V*, p. 99.

[115]   Fotherby, *Foure Sermons*, pp. 49, 51-3.

wisdome appointed and set apart for the working of the salvation of his people."[116] John Donne preached that sermons are "Gods Ordinance, to beget Faith [and] to take away preaching, were to disarme God … for by that Ordinance, he fights from Heaven."[117] If the Holy Ghost was bound or limited, as critics claimed, it was because, as Vaughan argued, God deliberately "tyed and bound himselfe to the ministery of his word preached" as the means to faith. Vaughan noted, for example, that in Acts 10, God appointed Peter to bring faith in Jesus to the centurion Cornelius, rather than an angel or the Holy Ghost, "because he had sanctified and dedicated his holy word for that purpose, and he would shew throughout all posterities, that the preaching of his word, was the onely outward meanes of faith."[118] Parr observed, "God could have taught the Eunuch without Philip; converted Paul, without Ananias; instructed Cornelius, without Peter; opened Lyda's heart, without Paul: but he used (not the Ministery of Angels, but) the Ministery of men, to teach us…. The Ministery of the Word, is by the wisedome of God, which reverence thou, unlesse thou accountest thy selfe wiser than God."[119]

It is worth looking carefully at the language used to describe the necessity of preaching. George Downame, for example, claimed that "by the preaching of the worde, men are brought to salvation, and … without it ordinarily men cannot attaine to salvation."[120] Archbishop Grindal, in his infamous letter to the queen defying her order to suppress prophesyings, wrote that "public and continual preaching of God's word is the ordinary mean and instrument of the salvation of mankind."[121] Jones asserted that "without [preachers] you cannot be saved … and ordinarily not one man or woman can goe to heaven…."[122] Philips preached that "no man ordinarily can hope or looke for the power of salvation without preaching."[123] In each of these examples – and many more could

---

[116] Brinsley, *The Preachers Charge*, p. 13.
[117] Donne, *Sermons*, 7, p. 320.
[118] Vaughan, *Plaine and perfect Method*, p. 27.
[119] Parr, *Workes*, p. 137. Along these lines, John Donne preached that the Holy Ghost speaks to us but "sends us to the Ministery of man": *Sermons*, 5, p. 40.
[120] Downame, *Two Sermons*, pp. 26-7.
[121] Edmund Grindal to Elizabeth I (1576), quoted in Cressy and Ferrell, eds., *Religion and Society in Early Modern England*, p. 95.
[122] Jones, *Commentary upon … Hebrewes*, p. 633.
[123] Philips, *Certaine Godly and Learned Sermons*, p. 89.

be provided to the same effect – the qualifier "ordinary" or "ordinarily" appears.

This made clear that God's sovereignty was not challenged. As Philips said, God could save "by bare reading, yea and without reading, for he can knocke when he list, and open where he list; he can make corne to grow without sowing, as he did in Hezachiahs time."[124] Downame, Vaughan and Parr readily agreed that there were some whom God had signed for salvation who never heard a sermon because of natural defects or because they dwelled where "the publike ministery and preaching of the Word is wanting." In these cases, God's will was clearly adequate, and circumstances would not "be any let ... in their progresse to faith and salvation." Although Parr argued that the deaf "are barred from Faith and Salvation, to be attained by hearing," they were not barred "absolutely, because God when he pleaseth, can extraordinarily worke faith without the senses." But as Vaughan pointed out, this could not be used to rationalize laziness. Not having a preacher in one's own parish should move one to go elsewhere to hear sermons, something that Vaughan noted was relatively easy to do since "in this his Maiesties religious governement, they may have preaching else where, not farre off." For Downame and Parr, neglecting sermons was like refusing to eat the food that God provided, placing faith in God to save us by extraordinary means.[125] Hieron likened such an attitude to feeling that because God chose to feed the Israelites with manna one may "lie under a hedge in the Sunne, looking till Mannah drop into [one's] mouth."[126]

These men did not disparage reading the Bible, but they did insist that it was usually insufficient in itself. Charles Richardson affirmed that the Word was "perfect to all uses and purposes" but was not effective without preaching; it was a sword in a scabbard, which cannot cut unless "drawne out by application. Now the bare reading of the Word cannot doe this: it is the powerfull preaching of it that worketh this effect."[127] Greenham was one of many who saw reading as only a preparative to preaching, arguing that

---

[124] Ibid., p. 90.
[125] Downame, *Guide to Godlynesse*, p. 482; Parr, *Workes*, pp. 136-7; Vaughan, *Plaine and perfect Method*, pp. 38-40.
[126] Hieron, *Workes*, 1, pp. 581, 578. For a similar image in one of Latimer's sermons, see *Sermons and Remains*, 1, pp. 306.
[127] Charles Richardson, *A Workeman, That Needeth Not To Be Ashamed* (1616), p. 69.

preaching and reading "may not bee severed asunder" in the quest
for salvation because reading Scripture or hearing it read made for
a better hearer of preaching. Dent taught that both public and private reading of Scripture were "necessary and profitable" because
they made a person readier to benefit from sermons.[128] Gervase
Babington argued that the ignorant gained more from sermons
than from Bible reading. Unlike Covel, who criticized preachers for
obscuring meaning by "the paraphrasticall inlarging" of their texts
for two or three hours, Babington found that preachers revealed
"more plainly" what the text meant.[129] But both Babington and
Vaughan stressed that neither reading nor preaching would do any
good unless it was God's will, and that all people should pray for
grace "that what we reade, or heare read or preached unto us out
of [God's] heavenly booke by the ministery of men, may by him
bee made a savour of lyfe unto us."[130]

This was essentially the rebuttal to the charge that preachers promoted human wisdom over the divine Word. They were quite willing to accept the analogy to ambassadors, and many explicitly used
that image to explain how they saw the relationship between their
preaching and God's Word.[131] The words might technically be
theirs, and the fruit of years of painstaking study and prayer, but
they did not expect them to have any life and especially any efficacy
other than what God willed. John Downame cautioned hearers not
to make an idol out of the Word preached because it had no power
to save on its own.[132] Humston, after describing the study and preparation that a preacher should employ before preaching, concluded
that "when wee have done what wee can, except God give winde
to our sayles, wee shall never runne the poynt aright...."[133]

But even if preaching were necessary for salvation, why did that
require an original sermon delivered by its author? Was it not ade-

---

[128]   Parker and Carlson, *Practical Divinity*, pp. 266, 339; Dent, *Plaine Mans Path-way*,
p. 300.
[129]   Covel, *Just and Temperate Defense*, p. 80; Gervase Babington, *A profitable Exposition
of the Lords Prayer* (1588), p. 185.
[130]   Babington, *A profitable Exposition*, p. 195; Vaughan, *Plaine and perfect Method*, p. 38.
[131]   See especially Stoughton, *Five Sermons, On II Cor. V. XX.* (1640). See also
Brinsley, *The Preachers Charge*, pp. 3-5; Downame, *Guide to Godlynesse*, p. 393; *idem, Treatise
of Securitie*, pp. 37-8; Latimer, *Sermons and Remains*, 1, p. 349; Parr, *Workes*, p. 136.
[132]   Downame, *Guide to Godlynesse*, p. 481.
[133]   Humston, *Sermon Preached at Reysham*, p. 10.

quate to *read* a printed sermon from the pulpit? Did this not satisfy the need of the congregation to hear God's word preached? Fotherby argued that it must surely be preferable to have a wise sermon written by someone else to a muddled effort produced by the local minister. Moreover, Fotherby noted that there was a sound biblical precedent for reading sermons, since Jeremiah commanded Baruch to read a sermon that he (i.e., Jeremiah) had written.[134] Hooker criticized the reasoning of those who excluded reading sermons. Why, he wondered, should reading the sermon by which one of the apostles converted thousands not have the same effect now? To claim that it did not now have that power implied that its original force was in its accidents or externals rather than its doctrine, which Hooker dismissed as a feeble argument.[135] The preachers themselves, with their apparent enthusiasm for rushing to publish sermons, seemed to be providing the best evidence to support their opponents' line of attack. As Shelford observed, "assoon *[sic]* as there is any rare sermon preached, by and by it is put to print, and from the presse it is disperst all the land over. There is scarce a house in any town, but one or the other in it by reading can repeat it" to others. That being the case, he concluded that it was impossible to "starve for want of preaching, when the best preachers in the land ... by this means countinually preach unto [us]."[136] But Shelford misunderstood or misrepresented the motives of those who published their sermons. Printed sermons were certainly better than no sermons at all, and necessity (for example, when the minister was unable through ignorance to write his own sermons) might require that they be read from the pulpit,[137] but they were primarily for private study so that "they who never knewe nor heard them may yet reape benefit by their writing."[138]

Late Tudor and early Stuart preachers were "in general agreement that in matters of religious devotion the ear is to be trusted more than the eye."[139] They associated the eye with popery, contrasting that with a reformed religion of the ear. Brinsley, for example, criticized Roman churches for being "built rather for the eye,

---

[134] Fotherby, *Foure Sermons*, pp. 46-7 (citing Jeremiah 36: 7-8).
[135] Hooker, *Laws of Ecclesiastical Polity, Book V*, pp. 107-8.
[136] Shelford, *Five Pious and Learned Discourses*, p. 78.
[137] See, for example, Babington, *A profitable Exposition of the Lords Prayer*, pp. 171-5.
[138] Downe, *Certaine Treatises*, p. 16.
[139] Crockett, *Play of Paradox*, p. 53.

then the eare," and dismissed their religious services as nothing "but eye service."[140] The ear, on the other hand, was the way chosen by God. For example, Hieron stated that "preaching *by a voice* [was] the choice and principal meanes, by which the Lord would bring his people unto the true and saving knowledge of himselfe."[141] John Donne made the most sustained argument in this regard, based on the conversion of Saul/Paul. Saul's conversion could not come through his eyes, since he had been blinded, but came through the Word *spoken*: "Here then is the first step of Sauls cure, and of ours, That there was not onely a word, the Word, Christ himselfe ... but a Voyce, the word uttered, and preached, Christ manifested in his Ordinance." Donne did not dismiss the eye, which he described as a "natural way to come to God," but he asserted that God had "super-induced a supernaturall way, by the eare." Although hearing itself is natural, "yet that faith in God should come by hearing a man preach, is supernatural. God shut up the naturall way, in Saul, Seeing; ... But he opened the supernaturall way, he inabled him to heare, and to heare him. God would have us beholden to grace, and not to nature, and to come for our salvation, to his Ordinances, to the preaching of his Word, and not to any other meanes."[142]

Many preachers were prepared to argue, in spite of Hooker, that it was precisely the accidents or externals – the preacher's voice and movements, for example – that gave sermons their power to save. The *delivered* sermon not only was live, it was life-giving; the printed sermon might teach or provide material for reflection, but it was essentially dead. John King made this perspective clear by apologizing in the preface to the published version of his sermons on Jonah, that he "changed [his] tongue into a pen, and whereas [he] spake before with the gesture and countenance of a living man, have now buried [himself] in a dead letter of less effectual persuasion."[143] Calling the people to repent and be reconciled with God was not

---

[140] John Brinsley, *The Glorie of the Latter temple Greater Then Of The Former* (1631), pp. 17-18. (I owe this reference to Merritt, "Puritans, Laudians, and Church-Building," p. 956.)

[141] Samuel Hieron, *Sixe Sermons* (1608), fol. B1r.

[142] Donne, *Sermons*, 6, pp. 216-17.

[143] John King, *Lectures upon Jonas delivered at Yorke* (Oxford, 1597), *4 (quoted in Keith Thomas, "The Meaning of Literacy in Early Modern England," in *The Written Word: Literacy in Transition*, ed. Gerd Baumann [Oxford: Clarendon Press, 1986], p. 113).

an intellectual undertaking, a matter to be achieved through text alone. Rather, it was the preacher's thundering voice or dramatic gesture that might break through to the sinner. The "plain style" of preaching associated with this period "referred to content not delivery."[144]

John Rogers, the Dedham lecturer from 1605 to 1636, who was well known for this theatrical preaching, shared King's view that the printed sermon was cold in comparison to the original. For Rogers, print could not capture the spontaneous elements of preaching including "those stirring passages that God brought to hand in the heat of preaching"[145] and he ruefully acknowledged that in his printed works he omitted "many things in the Uses and Applications of the Points delivered in Preaching...."[146] Thus, the printed version could not begin to achieve the same effect as the original.

Rogers produced the printed versions of his sermons from memory, because preachers like him did not believe that it was appropriate to read from a formal text even when it was of their own sermons. Although expected to prepare carefully, using all of the scholarly resources at their disposal, ministers were to deliver their sermons either completely extemporaneously or from only the sketchiest of notes. Bernard, for example, made clear that sermons were to be given from memory, but he did encourage the use of written aids so that the preacher would not leave out important points. The "chiefe heads" should be noted on "a little peece of paper, a word or two for every severall thing"; this is perfectly respectable, and "many very learned and woorthy Divines use this helpe" at the university and elsewhere.[147] The true sermon, therefore, was almost exclusively an aural affair. This, the preachers believed, was God's intention and the only sure way in which they could fulfill their vocation.

---

[144] Bremer and Rydell, "Puritans in the Pulpit," p. 51.
[145] Ibid.
[146] Rogers, *Doctrine of Faith*, fol. A5r.
[147] Bernard, *Faithfull Shepheard*, pp. 82-5. See also Perkins, *Art of Prophesying*, in *The Works*, ed. Breward, p. 344. It is beyond the scope of this essay to explore the controversy over whether sermons could or should be delivered from texts, which I am doing in a separate article.

The House of Prayer: Emergence of an Alternative Vision

The vision of preaching and of the relationship between the preacher and his audience described above did not go unchallenged during this period. In addition to those critics already cited, most non-preaching ministers must have rejected it. How numerous these men were is difficult to determine. A number of sources are so blatantly polemical that even when the historian suspects that their figures are roughly correct, they must still be disregarded. For example, Stockwood claimed in 1579 that "scarse the twentieth parishe were provided of his able Teacher." However, he made this statement in a passionate and partisan letter to the godly earl of Huntingdon that prefaced the printed version of his Paul's Cross sermon on preaching and ministry.[148] Even the totals given in relatively systematic surveys of the ministry are not reliable because the men who conducted the surveys often defined preaching in ways that excluded what less biased observers might include. For example, a survey of Herefordshire ministers conducted in 1640, probably for Sir Robert Harley, concluded that there were only twenty "constant and conscionable preachers" in the shire. However, the surveyors excluded Dr Hughes, the rector of Kingsland, because he "hath preached against preaching" and Mr Sherbone of Pembridge for his "very pragmaticall preaching for shipmoney."[149] The content of these two men's sermons did not meet the standard for "conscionable" preaching, and they were not counted as preachers, when it seems clear that their parishioners had what an unbiased observer would consider to be preaching.

Nor are visitation records a reliable guide to the presence of a non-preaching minister. While, as discussed above, churchwardens were far more likely to present non-preachers than they were in the decades before the Reformation, we can not assume that all such ministers were being presented. The presentment process still depended almost entirely on the initiative of either the minister (who was not going to turn himself in) or of the churchwardens elected in any given year. Local priorities and expectations continued to determine whether the bishop or archdeacon was made aware of lapses within his domain.

---

[148]   Stockwood, *A very fruiteful Sermon*, fol. A3r.
[149]   Corpus Christi College, Oxford, MS 206, pp. 13, 14.

Neither those ministers who did not preach nor those already cited in this essay who criticized the high vision of preaching offered an alternative vision. Their criticisms were either passive or essentially reactive and limited. A final line of criticism, which appeared in embryonic form in the late years of Elizabeth's reign and achieved maturity in the 1630s, did offer that missing counter-vision. While often associated with the Laudian regime, it predates it by several decades and it survived it as well. This model, which elevated worship and corporate prayer above preaching, dominates Anglican ecclesiology even to this day.

John Howson, in a Paul's Cross sermon in 1598 and an Oxford sermon in November 1602, bemoaned the neglect of prayer and worship in the English church. While affirming that preaching was "the ordinarie meanes to live well," he criticized a loss of balance in the church: "I complaine not that our Churches are auditories, but that they are not oratories: not that you come to Sermons, but that you refuse or neglect common prayer...."[150] But Howson lived in a country ruled by a monarch "who, if anything, gladly dispensed with sermons, but religiously attended the complete sung service in chapel every Sunday and feast day,"[151] and in which there was, if anything, a paucity of preachers. His complaints might apply in some areas of the country, but they lacked genuine urgency.

That, however, changed with the accession of James I in 1603. As Peter McCullough has observed, "the one thing that could certainly get [James] off his horse was a good sermon." Under James, the amount of court preaching soared and the sermon became "the pre-eminent literary genre" of the court.[152] What was truly alarming to some, however, was the way in which the king's passion for sermons transformed the court worship. James's entrance was the cue for the preacher to make his way to the pulpit, even if that meant curtailing the chapel services in progress—a dramatic "elevation of sermon over service."[153]

---

[150]   John Howson, *A Second Sermon preached at Paules Crosse the 21 of May 1598* (1598); idem., *A Sermon preached at St. Maries in Oxford the 17 day of November 1602* (Oxford, 1602). See Dent, *Protestant Reformers in Elizabethan Oxford*, pp. 208-12.

[151]   Peter E. McCullough, *Sermons at Court: Politics and Religion in Elizabethan and Jacobean Preaching* (Cambridge: Cambridge University Press, 1998), p. 156.

[152]   Ibid., pp. 116-25.

[153]   Ibid., p. 155-6.

Even before the Jacobean style had manifested itself, Richard Bancroft had implored James at the Hampton Court Conference "that there be amongst us a *praying* ministry; it being now come to pass, that men think it the only duty of ministers to spend their time in the pulpit." Bancroft accepted that preaching was necessary in a "church newly to be planted," but not in one such as England's, which was "long established."[154] As the new king's practices became clear, they gave new resonance to Howson's precocious complaint and it was repeated – often in strikingly similar words – by some of James's own court preachers.

The first concentrated assault came from Richard Meredeth, a court preacher since 1599. In a sermon preached in 1606, Meredeth praised prayer at length, concluding with blunt criticism of the "new-fangled, and over-licentious opinion ... that all the chiefe parts, and points of the christian religion consisteth in the reading of scriptures, frequenting of Lectures, and hearing of Sermons." Meredeth argued that sermons could "teach men to live wel & vertuous ... soberly, justly, & godlily," but were of no use to those who had not "prepared and sanctified" their hearts by prayer, comparing them "unto a mariner which would governe his ship without a roudder...." To give sermons precedence over prayer and worship was to make "thy porch bigger then thy house." This metaphor was part of what became a recurring theme, introduced by Meredeth, in such sermons by later preachers: that in the Bible God's house was called a house of prayer, but never a house of preaching. In spite of that, "the heddy, giddy, presize disciplinarian cannot perswade himselfe that hee can be edified by comming to the Church, unlesse there be a Sermon...."[155]

The reference to God's house as a house of prayer was clever and potent. Listeners would have instantly recognized the reference and would have known without prompting that, in driving the moneychangers out of the Temple, Jesus accused them of turning a house of prayer into a den of thieves. Although Meredeth *said*

---

[154] Lori Anne Ferrell, *Government by Polemic: James I, the King's Preachers, and the Rhetorics of Conformity, 1603-1625* (Stanford: Stanford University Press, 1998), p. 142.

[155] Richard Meredeth, *Two Sermons Preached before his Maiestie* (1606), pp. 40-5. The Scriptural references are to Isaiah 56: 7 and Matthew 21: 13. On Meredeth and his sermons, see McCullough, *Sermons at Court*, pp. 156-9.

"house of preaching," who could have failed to *hear* "den of thieves" in their mind and made an equation between the two? Meredeth said something else that was quite subversive. While claiming not to oppose sermons–a standard disclaimer, as we have seen–the most that he would accord them is that they were "great helps ... in the cause of salvation"–a far cry from the orthodox (and Scriptural) assertion that preaching was the "ordinary means" to salvation. Howson had, in fact, done something similar when he called sermons "the ordinarie meanes *to live well.*" This could hardly have been accidental, but was probably a calculated attempt to undermine the single most substantial claim on which their opponents based their vision of vocation. In this sense, Meredeth and Howson also challenged the discourse offered by promoters of "bare reading," who almost always continued to maintain that sermons were at least *one of*–but not the *only*–ordinary means of salvation. Moreover, they were appropriating the word "prayer" in a way that altered its conventional use. In *A Guide to Godlynesse*, Downame listed prayer as first among the means to obtain and increase a "lively faith," but he was referring to *private* prayer, not corporate worship.[156] Downame's usage was in line with traditional writing on the subject, but that deployed by his contemporary Meredeth would push it from the field as the assault on preaching continued.

In 1617, preaching before the king, John Buckeridge echoed Howson by attacking those who "turne oratories into auditories, and temples into scholes, and all adoration and worship into hearing of a sermon."[157] Also in 1617, Lancelot Andrewes complained, "All our holinesse, is in hearing: All our Service, eare-service: that were in effect, as much as to say, all the body were an eare."[158] It is no small irony that the most persistent opponent of the tyranny of sermons was the greatest preacher of the day and James's most favored preacher as well. Obviously, Andrewes was not opposed to preaching. But, as Peter McCullough has explained, Andrewes placed the sermon in a larger liturgical context; it was not com-

---

[156] Downame, *Guide to Godlynesse*, pp. 47, 124.

[157] John Buckeridge, *A Sermon preached before his Maiestie at Whitehall, March 22 1617* (1618), pp. 10-11, quoted in Kenneth Fincham, *Prelate as Pastor: The Episcopate of James I* (Oxford: Clarendon Press, 1990), p. 232.

[158] Peter McCullough, "Making Dead Men Speak: Laudianism, Print, and the Works of Lancelot Andrewes, 1626-1642," *Historical Journal* 41 (1998), 410-11.

plete in itself, but part of a process that was completed by the reception of communion.[159] The king, who seems to have shown little interest in the sacrament, was creating something as monstrous and improbable as a body that was all ear: a service that was all sermon.

These Jacobean anti-sermon sermons were highly court-specific.[160] In other words, they were written to address the king directly and to comment on his sermon-centered piety. Rarely were voices outside of the court known to speak similar words.[161] Moreover, the goal of these preachers was essentially to restore a sort of balance – not to disparage preaching or to displace it from its soteriological status. For example, in his 1617 Paul's Cross sermon on the eunuch's conversion, Sonnibank complained that public reading of Scripture was being shortened or omitted by ministers so that they could begin their sermons "as if preaching were onely necessary, and there were either none, or very small use ... of publique reading ... in the publique Congregation." Sonnibank argued that they should "mince, and curtall, and shorten their Sermons," but at the same time he insisted that preaching was "the ordinary and most effectuall meanes of mans salvation" and "a more excellent way to winne soules to God" than "bare reading," which might "leave a blessing behind it" but was not the surest source "for our new birth, & conversion."[162]

However limited and situational their intentions might be, by publishing these sermons, Meredeth and his fellow-travelers moved the discourse into a wider arena,[163] a development that would reach new levels in the 1630s when Laudian control of printing tended to

---

159 McCullough, *Sermons at Court*, pp. 147-55, 161-2.

160 Ibid., p. 160.

161 Richard Eedes, preaching in Oxford in 1604, condemned "that idle and perfunctory hearing of sermons which too many make only the duty and fruit of ther religion as yf they ought [i.e., owed] nothing but their eares to the Lord." BL, Sloane MS 848, fol. 8r, quoted in Dent, *Protestant Reformers*, pp. 206-7. It is noteworthy that this sermon was not printed. It is possible that there were more anti-sermon sermons preached outside the court that are unknown now because they were not considered worthy of publication, but even that judgment tells us something about the perceived importance of the discourse outside of court circles.

162 Sonnibank, *Eunuche's Conversion*, pp. 75-80.

163 It should be noted that Andrewes did not publish the sermons cited here; they were published posthumously by John Buckeridge and William Laud for polemical purposes: McCullough, "Making Dead Men Speak".

ensure that the print debate was extremely one-sided.[164] Some Caroline preachers reiterated some of arguments made within Jacobean court circles. Henry Valentine, in a 1626 Paul's Cross sermon, said that prayer was superior to preaching because although there was a time to preach, "it is but a time." Prayer, on the other hand, knew no particular time, day, or season: it "is an Ubiquitary." As had earlier preachers, he spoke also of the "monstrous" attitude of those who would "shrink up all religion into preaching [and] make all the bodie an eare...."[165] Visitation sermons by Richard Tedder in 1636 and John Swan in 1639 also repeated this image.[166]

But Richard Tedder, preaching on Luke 19:46 ("My house is a house of prayer."), bluntly rejected any pretense of parity between prayer and preaching: "Prayer is the End, to which Gods house is erected.... Though there may be other religious duties to be exercised in Gods House, yet there is none other mentioned, but Prayer. God sayes, *Domus Precationis*, not *domus Praedicationis*, not excluding preaching by commending Prayer, but preferring Prayer before Preaching." He even felt that little preaching was needed in his own time, except for "weeding out of Schisme."[167] Swan also argued that excessive preaching tended to "detract from the honour of the House of God," and argued that Christ's words in speaking of a house of prayer, and never a house of preaching, were intended "to shew the excellencie of publike Prayer in the Congregation," which should neither be "put downe, or disrespected, to let Preaching have the chiefe preheminence in the holy Temple."[168]

More moderate voices could still be heard even at this point. Downe, a Devon preacher whose works were published posthu-

---

[164]   For a persuasive discussion of this topic, see Anthony Milton, "Licensing, Censorship, and Religious Orthodoxy in Early Stuart England," *Historical Journal* 41 (1998), 625-51.

[165]   Henry Valentine, *Noahs Dove: Or A Prayer For The Peace of Ierusalem* (1627), pp. 24-5, 30.

[166]   Richard Tedder, *A Sermon Preached at Wimondham, In Norfolk, at the Primary Visitation of the Right Honourable and Reverend Father in God, Matthew, Lord Bishop of Norwich, on the third of June, Ann. Dom. 1636.* (1637), p. 12; John Swan, *A Sermon, Pointing out the Chiefe Causes, and Cures, of such unruly Stirres, as are not seldome found in the Church of God* (1639), p. 17.

[167]   Tedder, *Sermon Preached at Wimondham*, p. 11.

[168]   Swan, *Sermon, Pointing out the Chiefe Causes*, pp. 13, 16.

mously in 1633 by George Hakewill,[169] was hardly a Laudian, as is clear from his generally Calvinist views on predestination. On the other hand, Hakewill spoke at length in the funeral sermon that prefaced the volume about Downe's deathbed confession of sins to and absolution by a minister, followed by reception of the Eucharist.[170] This was a practice much favored by John Cosin[171] and Downe is known to have had support within Cosin's circle.[172] Downe occupied a middle ground between preaching and prayer already underpopulated and destined to become even more so after his death.

What Downe tried to do was to build a bridge between supporters of prayer and of preaching by refusing to see the two practices as opposed. He argued that in Christ's ministry, preaching and prayer were joined. Invoking marriage imagery, Downe asserted that what God joined should not be separated, and that "hardly ... can [prayer and preaching] bee divorced without the maiming or mangling thereof." Preaching and prayer were inextricably joined together in the minister's vocation: "As in Preaching we are the mouth of God unto the people; so by Prayer ought we to bee the mouth of the people unto God. ... As we are bound to plant and water by Preaching: so we are by Prayer to mediate unto God for increase." Downe refused to be drawn into expressing an opinion as to which was "more noble" but affirmed that both were "alike in worth and dignitie. ... They are not subordinate one unto the other: but both coordinate unto the same maine end."[173]

Peter Hausted, arguably the most aggressive Laudian foot soldier,[174] preached a sermon at the dedication of a church that is much more typical of the dominant mood of the times. He sums up

---

[169] Downe, *Certaine Treatises.*
[170] Ibid., pp. 51-2.
[171] John Cosin, *The Works of the Right Reverend Father in God John Cosin*, ed. J. Sansom, 5 vols. (Oxford: John Henry Parker, 1843-55), 1, pp. 28-9.
[172] Kenneth Fincham and Peter Lake, "Popularity, Prelacy and Puritanism in the 1630s: Joseph Hall Explains Himself," *English Historical Review* 111 (1996), 865.
[173] Downe, "Concerning the force and efficacy of Reading," pp. 68-70, in *Certaine Treatises.*
[174] In 1632, Hausted's vicious anti-puritan play, *The Rivall Friends*, was performed by a Queens' College students; the offense it caused allegedly contributed to the suicide of the Vice-Chancellor of Cambridge University: Adam Fox, "Religious Satire in English Towns, 1570-1640," in *The Reformation in English Towns 1500-1640*, eds. Patrick Collinson and John Craig (New York: St. Martin's Press, 1998), p. 239.

the Laudian counter-argument so well that he will be quoted at length:

> We doe not reade in any place that [the church] is called the House of Preaching, but the house of Prayer, for that is the cheefe use of these Houses, and we doe then honour God the most when wee pray to him. Preaching is a holy institution of the Lords, but there be degrees in Holinesse. ... [W]e must not then goe up into the Temple (as many doe) onely to preach, or to heare Sermons, with a contempt and scorne of the Common-Prayer. Preaching now adayes is made an Idoll of amongst many, who are growne to be all Eare, no Heart, no Hand, no Lip; whilst Praying ... which is the chiefest part of Gods Worship and Honour, is, if not, altogether, yet too much neglected. In the Name of God although yee will not allow Prayer (as yee ought) the Preheminence, yet at the least let Praying and Preaching (like two Twin-Sisters) lovingly goe hand in hand together.[175]

Hausted's "twin-sisters" were, however, a far cry from Downe's married couple, since Hausted made clear that prayer was superior to preaching and ought to be so recognized.

The Arminians had among them those who held even more aggressive and original views about preaching. The most extreme was the septuagenarian Shelford, erstwhile member of Peterhouse and then Arminian rector of Ringsfield in Suffolk, who published a work in 1635 – described as "rotten stuff" by Archbishop Ussher[176] – in which he mounted a frontal assault not only on "our Puritanes" but on knowledge itself. Some men, according to Shelford, demand a sermon every day for more knowledge, and in pursuit of knowledge "will run from church to church, from preacher to preacher, and from one opinion to another, untill they have lost and confounded themselves in the tower and Babel of their own fancies." But knowledge, he argued, is overrated: "Knowledge threw the angels out of heaven to hell; knowledge threw Adam and Eve out of an earthly Paradise into a wildernesse of miseries...." But still the Puritans lament: "We have no sermons, we want a preacher, we shall die in our sinnes, we know not what to do."[177] Shelford's response is that God provides many types of preachers for us. Parents

---

[175] Peter Hausted, *Ten Sermons* (1636), p. 211.

[176] Nicholas Tyacke, *Anti-Calvinists: The Rise of English Arminianism c.1590-1640* (Oxford: Clarendon Press, 1987), pp. 53-6.

[177] Robert Shelford, "The ten Preachers, Or A Sermon Preferring holy Charitie before Faith, Hope, & Knowledge," in *Five Pious and Learned Discourses*, pp. 58-9, 62.

are preachers for their children and servants, as are all faithful
Christians to their neighbors. Indeed, all creatures are preachers
because (according to Psalm 19) they "declare the glory of God."
Shelford also asserts that the prayer book service itself is preaching.
It contains everything necessary for salvation: true faith (the
Creeds), good life (the Ten Commandments), prayer (the Lord's
Prayer), and grace (the Sacraments). To those who object that it can
not be preaching "because it is not spoken out of the pulpit, nor
delivered out of a text. I reply, Are not the articles of the faith, the
Lords prayer, and the Sacraments exprest in scripture? are not
these texts? But they are not delivered out of the pulpit. If the pulpit make a sermon, then where dost thou reade that Christ and his
Apostles at any time made sermons?"[178] What is striking about this
list is not only that Shelford has defined preaching more broadly
than his predecessors, but that in so doing he has included everything *except* an actual live sermon. In Shelford's polemic, the
Laudian counter-vision is most fully developed and the connection
between the preacher and his audience completely severed.

Conclusion

In fairness to Laud and his associates, it needs to be admitted that
they were not opposed to preaching. Matthew Wren, in his 1636
orders for Norwich diocese noted that sermons were required on
Sunday and holy day mornings and at marriages and were permitted at funerals. Other "preaching or expounding" might occur, but
only with "express allowance from the bishop."[179] Archbishop
Laud himself made clear in a report to King Charles I on the state
of the province of Canterbury that he did not object to regular sermons if the preachers followed the rules and were conformable. For
example, he noted his concern that in the thirty-four churches of
Norwich, there had been only four morning sermons; the others
had been in the afternoon, displacing the catechism. However,
Bishop Wren had attended to that and all sermons took place in the
morning. He also noted his approval of the lecture in Henley-on-

---

[178]   Ibid., pp. 62-77.
[179]   E. Cardwell, *Documentary Annals of the Reformed Church of England*, 2 vols. (Oxford:
The University Press, 1844), 2, p. 257.

Thames, the only one in the diocese of Oxford, since all of the ministers involved were conformable and had the bishop's license.[180]

Both Wren and Laud thus endorsed regular preaching, but they
did so within a vision that was fundamentally different from that of
the mainstream of Elizabethan and Jacobean divines. Conforming
bishops such as Whitgift and Jewel and nonconforming ministers
such as Greenham and Bernard agreed that preaching was the first
duty of the minister and the ordinary means of salvation ordained
by God. For Laud, however, the sermon was markedly inferior to
the sacraments, as the pulpit was to the altar. The altar, according
to Laud, was "greater than the pulpit; [for] there it is 'This is My
Body'; but in the pulpit it is at most but ... 'This is My Word.'"[181]

Victory, if it can be called that, belonged finally to the Laudians.
Anglicanism today is far more renowned for its liturgy than its
preaching. Squabbles within the various national churches that
make up the Anglican Communion are frequently centered on revi-
sions of the prayer book, with the centrality of worship so taken for
granted that it becomes the locus of passionate argument. This
change is also clear in the services associated with ordination and
ministry. For example, in the service for celebrating a new ministry
in the American *Book of Common Prayer*, the new minister prays that
"I may faithfully administer your holy Sacraments, and by my life
and teaching set forth your true and living Word."[182] This could
hardly be in starker contrast with the priorities and vocabulary of
the 1550 Ordinal. The Episcopal Preaching Foundation sponsors
a series of ready-to-preach sermons entitled "Sermons That Work,"
the ninth and tenth volumes of which are currently being prepared
– a sort of *Dormi Secure* for the twenty-first century. That they are
able to do this, and advertise it in the Episcopal Church's national
newspaper,[183] without provoking choruses of outraged protest
shows how far we have traveled since the reign of James I. Al-

---

[180] *The Works of ... William Laud, D.D.*, ed. W. Scott and J. Bliss (7 vols., Oxford:
John Henry Parker, 1847-60), 5, pp. 339, 342. In the same report, Laud noted the
disruptive effects of the Yarmouth lecturers, who had left for New England after being
censured by High Commission. There had been no lectures in Yarmouth since then,
"and very much peace in the town, and all ecclesiastical orders well observed." Ibid.,
5, p. 340.
[181] Ibid., 6, pp. 56-7.
[182] *The Book of Common Prayer* (New York: The Seabury Press, 1979), p. 563.
[183] *Episcopal Life*, vol. 11, no. 3 (March 2000), 6.

though for nearly one hundred years—the crucial century after the break from Rome—the discourse was profoundly different, it is the spiritual successors of Meredeth and Shelford who shape the discourse of modern Anglicanism.

The implications of this change for our understanding of the English church may be profound. It is a commonplace to speak of the Reformation reducing the role of the minister and thereby diminishing his prestige. According to received wisdom, it was Laud and his allies who attempted to restore dignity and respect to the clergy.[184] But in the discourse on the relationship between preacher and audience, it is clear that mainstream Elizabethan and Jacobean divines accorded the highest possible prestige to ministers. Their role was no less important than before the Reformation and they labored to make that clear to congregations, not out of any reactionary urge to retain power slipping away, but out of genuine concern for salvation. It was ministers, wrote Stockwood, "whom it pleaseth God to use as the onely ordinary meanes by preaching of the worde to worke faith in the heartes of the hearers."[185] As the Laudians dismantled this understanding of ministry, might it not be the case that it was in fact they—and not the first generations of Protestant reformers—who reduced the status of ministers? They might restore the title of priest, but was it not a hollow title once stripped of the saving mission assigned to it by Christ Jesus himself? As William Sclater preached at Paul's Cross in 1610, "I cannot yet see, what that great and important businesse of the Ministery should bee, to which it may beseeme Preaching to give place. I am sure not Sacraments. Christ sent me not to baptize (saith the Holy Apostle) but to preach the Gospell. ... Is there any thing, more honourable?"[186]

A preliminary version of part of this essay was presented at the Reformation Studies Colloquium, held at the University of Oxford in

---

[184] See, in particular, Christopher Haigh, "Anticlericalism and the English Reformation," in *The English Reformation Revised*, ed. C. Haigh (Cambridge: Cambridge University Press, 1987), pp. 56-74; Andrew Foster, "The Clerical Estate Revitalised," in *The Early Stuart Church, 1603-1642*, ed. Kenneth Fincham (Basingstoke: Macmillan, 1993), pp. 139-60.

[185] Stockwood, *A very fruiteful Sermon*, fol. A3v.

[186] William Sclater, *A Threefold Preservative against three dangerous diseases of these latter times.* (1610), fol. E4r. He was quoting I Corinthians 1: 17.

March 1998. For their assistance, I am deeply grateful to Kathie Martin, who performed interlibrary loan miracles while I was researching this essay, to Margaret and Peter Spufford, and to Simon Sibelman.

Bibliography

Arnoult, Sharon L., " 'The Face of an English Church': The *Book of Common Prayer* and English Religious Identity, 1549-1662," Ph.D. diss., University of Texas, 1997.

Atkinson, Clarissa, *Mystic and Pilgrim: The* Book *and the World of Margery Kempe* (Ithaca, NY: Cornell University Press, 1983).

Blench, J. W., *Preaching in England in the Late Fifteenth and Sixteenth Centuries. A Study of English Sermons 1450-c.1600* (New York: Barnes & Noble Inc., 1964).

Bremer, Francis and Ellen Rydell, "Puritans in the Pulpit," *History Today* 45, no. 9 (1995), 50-4.

Carlson, Eric Josef, "Auricular Confession and the English Church: A Problem in Pastoral Ministry, " Conference paper, Reformation Studies Colloquium, University of Warwick, Coventry, UK, 2000.

— "Anticlericalism, Social Discipline, and the Parish in Tudor and Early Stuart England," Conference paper, North American Conference on British Studies, Washington, D.C., 1995.

— *Marriage and the English Reformation* (Oxford: Blackwell, 1994).

Carlson, Eric Josef, ed., *Religion and the English People 1500-1640. New Voices/New Perspectives*, Sixteenth Century Essays and Studies, vol. 45. (Kirksville, Missouri: Thomas Jefferson University Press, 1998).

Collinson, Patrick, *The Birthpangs of Protestant England: Religious and Cultural Change in the Sixteenth and Seventeenth Centuries* (Basingstoke: Macmillan, 1988).

— *The Elizabethan Puritan Movement* (London: Jonathan Cape, 1967).

— *The Religion of Protestants: The Church in English Society 1559-1625* (Oxford: Clarendon Press, 1982).

Crockett, Bryan, *The Play of Paradox: Stage and Sermon in Renaissance England* (Philadephia: University of Pennsylvania Press, 1995).

Dent, C. M., *Protestant Reformers in Elizabethan Oxford* (Oxford: Oxford University Press, 1983).

Enssle, Neal R., "Patterns of Godly Life: The Ideal Parish Minister in Sixteenth- and Seventeenth-Century English Thought," *Sixteenth Century Journal* 28 (1997), 3-28.

Ferrell, Lori Anne, *Government by Polemic: James I, the King's Preachers, and the Rhetorics of Conformity, 1603-1625* (Stanford: Stanford University Press, 1998).

Ferrell, Lori Anne and Peter McCullough, eds., *The English Sermon Revised: Religion, Literature and History 1600-1750* (Manchester: Manchester University Press, 2000).

Fincham, Kenneth and Peter Lake, "Popularity, Prelacy and Puritanism in the 1630s: Joseph Hall Explains Himself," *English Historical Review* 111 (1996), 856-81.

Fincham, Kenneth, *Prelate as Pastor: The Episcopate of James I* (Oxford: Clarendon Press, 1990).

Foster, Andrew, "The Clerical Estate Revitalised," in *The Early Stuart Church, 1603-1642*, ed. Kenneth Fincham (Basingstoke: Macmillan, 1993), pp. 139-60.

Gradon, Pamela and Anne Hudson, eds., *English Wycliffite Sermons*, 5 vols. (Oxford: Clarendon Press, 1983-96).

Haigh, Christopher, "Anticlericalism and the English Reformation," in Christopher Haigh, ed., *The English Reformation Revised* (Cambridge: Cambridge University Press, 1987), pp. 56-74.

— *English Reformations: Religion, Politics, and Society under the Tudors* (Oxford: Clarendon Press, 1993).

Herr, Alan Fager, *The Elizabethan Sermon: A Survey and a Bibliography* (New York: Octagon Books, 1969).

Hudson, Anne, *The Premature Reformation: Wycliffite Texts and Lollard History* (Oxford: Clarendon Press, 1988).

Kaufman, Peter Iver, *Prayer, Despair, and Drama: Elizabethan Introspection* (Urbana and Chicago: University of Illinois Press, 1996).

Lake, Peter, "The Laudian Style: Order, Uniformity and the Pursuit of the Beauty of Holiness in the 1630s," in *The Early Stuart Church, 1603-1642*, ed. Kenneth Fincham (Basingstoke: Macmillan, 1993).

Maclure, Millar, *The Paul's Cross Sermons 1534-1642* (Toronto: University of Toronto Press, 1958).

Marshall, Peter, *The Catholic Priesthood and the English Reformation* (Oxford: Clarendon Press, 1994).

McCullough, Peter, "Making Dead Men Speak: Laudianism, Print, and the Works of Lancelot Andrewes, 1626-1642," *Historical Journal* 41 (1998), 401-24.

— *Sermons at Court: Politics and Religion in Elizabethan and Jacobean Preaching* (Cambridge: Cambridge University Press, 1998).

Merritt, J. F., "Puritans, Laudians, and the Phenomenon of Church-Building in Jacobean London," *Historical Journal* 41 (1998), 935-60.

Milton, Anthony, *Catholic and Reformed: The Roman and Protestant Churches in English Protestant Thought, 1600-1640* (Cambridge: Cambridge University Press, 1995).

— "Licensing, Censorship, and Religious Orthodoxy in Early Stuart England" *Historical Journal* 41 (1998), 625-51.

Owst, G. R., *Preaching in Medieval England. An Introduction to Sermon Manuscripts of the Period c.1350-1450* (Cambridge: Cambridge University Press, 1926; repr. New York: Russell & Russell, Inc., 1965).

Parker, Kenneth L. and Eric J. Carlson, *'Practical Divinity': The Works and Life of Revd Richard Greenham* (Aldershot, Hants. and Brookfield, VT: Ashgate, 1998).

Seaver, Paul S., *The Puritan Lectureships: The Politics of Religious Dissent, 1560-1662* (Stanford: Stanford University Press, 1970).

Spencer, H. Leith, *English Preaching in the Late Middle Ages* (Oxford: Clarendon Press, 1993).

Tyacke, Nicholas, *Anti-Calvinists: The Rise of English Arminianism c. 1590-1640* (Oxford: Clarendon Press, 1987).

Wabuda, Susan, "The Provision of Preaching during the Early English Reformation: with Special Reference to Itineration, c.1530 to 1547," Ph.D. diss., University of Cambridge, 1992.

Walsham, Alexandra, *Providence in Early Modern England* (Oxford: Oxford University Press, 1999).

CHAPTER NINE

PREACHER AND AUDIENCE: SCANDINAVIA

Jens Chr. V. Johansen

The propaganda of the Scandinavian reformation tried to paint a picture of a completely new situation regarding the sermon, as something introduced by the Lutheran reformers.[1] But in her *Revelations*, Saint Brigid of Sweden (1303-1373) wrote that the priests should use few and simple words so that the congregation could understand it… "thi hvad den enfoldige almue ej forstår, plejer den mere at studse over end opbygges ved".[2] Sermons given by Swedish mendicant friars are also known.[3] Statutes of synods from the fifteenth and early sixteenth centuries emphasize the duty to preach through the Gospels on Sundays and Holy Days. Thus hardly anything could have been as wrong as the Reformation propaganda; instead, the emphasis should have been put on the difficulties congregations had in hearing a proper sermon, both before and after the Reformation.

---

[1] Martin Schwarz Lausten, *Biskop Peder Palladius og kirken 1537-1560* (Copenhagen: Akademisk Forlag, 1987), p. 64 and Herman Råberg, *Den evangeliska Predikoversamhetens Grundläggning och Utveckling i Finland intill År 1640* (Helsingfors: J.C. Frenckell & Son, 1883), p. 4.

[2] Johanne Skovgaard (ed.), *Den Hellige Birgitta. Kilderne til hendes historie og udvalg af hendes skrifter* (Copenhagen: Det Schønbergske Forlag, 1921), pp. 166f.: "if simple folk do not understand something, they are startled more often than they are edified". The Latin version is in Lennart Hollman (ed.), *Den Heliga Birgittas Reuelaciones extrauagantes* (Uppsala: Almqvist & Wiksell, 1956), Added Revelation 23.

[3] H.B. Hammar, "Reformationstidens predikan i Sverige," in *Reformationen i Norden: Kontinuitet och förnyelse*, ed. Carl-Gustaf Andrén (Lund: C.W.K. Gleerups Bokförlag, 1973), p. 263.

Before the Reformation

Prior to the Reformation, problems in preaching were of a dual
nature. On the one hand, there was a definite lack of priests in the
rural areas;[4] by contrast, the towns were well supplied with preachers. On the other hand, the training of the priests left much to be
desired. Due to the geographical size of Denmark, the problem
may have been less severe there than in the three other Scandinavian countries, where distances are immense. However, we should
remember that the number of towns in Denmark was considerably
higher than in any of the other Scandinavian countries (ninety
towns in Denmark, thirty-six in Sweden, five in Finland and sixteen
in Norway).[5] The opportunity to hear a sermon would therefore
have been higher in Denmark. From 1396 to the end of the Middle
Ages, the Scandinavian countries had been united in the Kalmar
Union.[6] When the Danish king Christian II perpetrated the so-
called Stockholm "Blood-bath" in 1520, Scandinavian union ended
definitively, and the countries went their separate ways: Denmark-
Norway under the kings of the House of Oldenburg, and Sweden-
Finland under the noble Gustavus Vasa, who in 1521 was elected
regent.

The Reformers from all the Scandinavian countries argued that
even if the congregations had the opportunity to hear sermons, they
most certainly would not have been able to understand them, as
they were given in Latin. It is easy to be deceived by the idea that
almost all extant sermons from the period are in Latin. This does
not necessarily mean that they were given in Latin. While the official language of services was Latin, sermons were given in the vernacular in almost all cases. We should keep in mind as well that
many sermons were given in the streets, and these had to be in a
language that people could understand.[7]

---

    4 Anne Riising, *Danmarks middelalderlige prædiken* (Copenhagen: G.E.C. Gads Forlag,
1969), p. 33.
    5 Grethe Authén Blom (ed.), *Middelaldersteder. Urbaniseringsprocessen i Norden 1*. Det
XVII. nordiske historikermøte Trondheim, 1977 (Oslo: Universitetsforlaget, 1977), pp.
12, 130, 156, 191.
    6 Poul Grinder-Hansen et al., eds., *Margrete I – Regent of the North: The Kalmar Union
600 Years*. Essays and Catalogue (Copenhagen: Nordisk Ministerråd & Danmarks
Nationalmuseum, 1997).
    7 Riising, *Prædiken*, p. 9.

In some towns, sermons were mostly delivered by mendicant friars, as priests were often engaged in saying masses. However, we simply do not know how often people could hear sermons, as most sources only relate how often the clergy ought to give one and not how often they actually did.[8]

The poor education of most parish priests may be one reason for the popularity of the mendicants. Apparently, parish priests could have a hard time getting their message across to those in attendance. Several times we hear of congregations being enjoined to remain in church until the service had ended. It could also be difficult for the priests to keep them silent.[9] It is thus not surprising that the most common complaint about priests was that they lacked erudition.[10] However, these complaints together with those of an immoral life led by the clergy, resound all over Europe, usually in harsher terms than what is found in the Scandinavian countries.

A poor education would have made many priests ill suited to the task of writing a sermon themselves, and if they actually delivered sermons, they were probably borrowed. This was not that difficult, as many homiletic guides were written to facilitate the delivery of sermons without the priest having to know very much about either theology or the Scriptures. Commentaries on the Bible – *postils* – were written to serve as sermons for those priests who did not have the ability to write sermons. However, in reality although many were written, a limited number of very popular sermons were used everywhere in Scandinavia, often repeated without modification right up to the dawn of the Reformation.[11]

It was even easier to use a collection of sermons with *exempla* and many of the most widespread collections were written for such use. Nobody objected to this practice as sermons were supposed to convey the faith in an unchanged form.[12] Peter Madsen of St. Peder's Church in the Danish city of Ribe wrote a collection of sermons ca. 1450-1460.[13] Without doubt, Madsen had borrowed from the *Sermones de tempore et de sanctis* written by Peregrinus Polonus in the first half of the fourteenth century. At least twenty sermons were

---

8 Ibid., p. 32.
9 Ibid., p. 386.
10 Ibid., p. 427.
11 Ibid., pp. 44ff.
12 Ibid., pp. 46ff.
13 Apart from Peter Madsen's sermons very few medieval ones have survived.

taken from Polonus although the figure might be higher as he, as well as Madsen, made extensive use of the Dominican Jacobus da Voragine's *Legenda aurea*.[14]

In theory, writers of medieval sermons used a multi-level interpretation based on the *sensus literalis*, the historical intention as it spontaneously emanated from the text, and the *sensus spiritualis* which gave the text a deeper spiritual significance. Danish writers of sermons did not go to such lengths; most of the time they used an allegorical interpretation.[15] Madsen often used interpretations through the use of similarity, and in doing so he not only used Scriptures but the examples from nature as well. Thus he proves the Resurrection by using three proofs of equal nature: the Book of Job states it in Chapter 19, verse 25. "For I know that my Redeemer liveth;" from the characters of the Hebrew Scriptures it can be seen in Ezekiel's vision of the bones that came together,[16] and the Created proves it through the Phoenix that rose from the ashes.[17]

In many sermons, quotations make up almost half the text, without any interpretation of the quotations, as they are being used to support an idea. Madsen wrote that Christ shed his blood in order to break the hard hearts of the congregations and make them repent, and he went on to say that it was metaphorically described in Matthew 27:51 when the earth shook and the rocks cracked on Good Friday. The quotations were thus adapted to an already existing interpretation of the text.[18] The apocryphal gospels were often used on an equal footing with Scriptures and the Lives of the Saints, so they must be regarded as integral to preaching.

Part of preaching is teaching the congregation the true understanding of their position in relation to God, humanity and the universe. That is the reason why many sermons deal with original sin. Yet they do not distinguish between original sin and the sins of the day (actual sin), probably because the authors considered humans to exist in the latter state.

In principle, all preachers strove to relate their teachings to the

---

[14]　Riising, *Praediken*, pp. 56ff.

[15]　Ibid., p. 89.

[16]　*Ezekiel*, Ch. 37.

[17]　Riising, *Prædiken*, p. 101.

[18]　Ibid., p. 108.

daily lives of the audience. This can easily be detected by the fact that the sins most often mentioned in Danish sermons are arrogance and greed.[19]

Danish preachers emphasized that all sin sprang from free will, because otherwise it would not be sin. However, with the help of God all temptations could be resisted. Not many topics are as strongly emphasized by the preachers as this: human will is absolutely free. Doubtless the emphasis stems from the belief that predestination, determinism, and fatalism were considered not only as sinful, but also as heretical.[20] Mortal sin springs from an evil will and can only be obliterated through a renewal of grace by means of the sacrament of penance. Venial sins are more often looked upon as a lack of ability, because humanity is not perfect, and these kinds of sins can be forgiven through prayer, alms, and confession. However, the preachers rarely distinguished between the two types of sin and at least on the surface seemed to regard everything as mortal sin. It is understandable that the most usual sermon was on penance.[21] The lack of sermons on indulgence is conspicuous. As the question of free will is one of the most important issues in late medieval theology, it would be interesting to see if the influence of nominalism can be detected in the sermons. But the keywords that denote nominalism do not appear in the sermons.[22] Tacitly they assume that human beings are capable of doing a great deal through their own free will.

Although all preaching involved the teaching of God and his Law, it is only in Peter Madsen's sermons on the mass that we find an explanation of the sacraments. The church is the Tabernacle of God, where the sacraments are kept and administered. Baptism is given to those who enter, and the Last Rites to those on their way out. Other sacraments are given to those who are in the world; yet others administer the sacraments and take holy orders. Others have to fight to stay afloat morally, but they sink under the burden, and they are given the sacrament of penance. Others who continue the struggle obtain courage through confirmation. Ideally, many are nurtured through the sermon as well as through the Eucharist; in

---

[19] Ibid., p. 136.
[20] Ibid., p. 145.
[21] Ibid., pp. 181f.
[22] Ibid., p. 455.

order to prevent some from stumbling they are helped through the sacrament of marriage.[23]

The sermons represent the average and the respectable; we do not find either polemical sermons or ones dealing with church politics. The suspect sermons of the pardoners are also missing. The so-called "Sermon of Portens" by the canon of the Lund Cathedral, Christiern Pedersen, printed in Paris in 1515,[24] is among the few surviving sermons. The content cannot be described as original, although it contains an independent adaptation of texts apparently by William of Paris.

The topic of sorcery quite naturally emerges in a few of the late medieval sermons.[25] Peter Madsen and Christiern Pedersen both preached about sorcery. The canon was most adamant that those believing in astrology, sorcery, and prophecies did not have firm faith in the Lord and were heretics. To prophesy and to predict the future were sins closely related to devil worship, because it was assumed that the Devil knew the future and that human beings could only predict it with his aid.[26] Peter Madsen mentions many forms of sorcery and magic in his long sermon on the First Commandment; it is a sin to believe that one should not undertake new dealings such as trade agreements and marriage on certain days, popularly known as "ominous days." It is a sin to read auguries in the flight or song of birds, the barking of a dog, or a hare crossing the road. Many kinds of sorcery mentioned by Madsen are connected to misappropriation of the Eucharist, which might be a reason why the late medieval church did little to increase the taking of the Eucharist by lay people and particular looked with suspicion on older women taking frequent communion.[27] Sorcerers were put on the same footing as heretics, although heresy as a conscious deviation from faith is rarely mentioned in the sermons.

Closely connected to the question of sorcery were descriptions of

---

[23]   Ibid., p. 179.

[24]   Ibid., p. 60.

[25]   On Scandinavian witchcraft and sorcery in general see the articles in Bengt Ankarloo and Gustav Henningsen, eds., *Early Modern European Witchcraft. Centres and Peripheries* (Oxford: The Clarendon Press, 1990); see also Jens Chr. V. Johansen, "Faith, Superstition and Witchcraft in Reformation Scandinavia," in Ole Peter Grell, ed., *The Scandinavian Reformation. From Evangelical Movement to Institutionalisation of Reform* (Cambridge: Cambridge University Press, 1995).

[26]   Riising, *Praediken*, pp. 336ff.

[27]   Ibid., pp. 339ff.

Hell. The notion of Hell is dominated by the details of horror and torment; as elsewhere Hell is divided into different parts each corresponding to the nature of the offense. Madsen enumerates seven chambers – with fire, coldness, darkness, stench, worms, mutual strife, and despair.[28] It is especially agonizing to see the devils. However, the authors differ in their opinion of the power of the devils.[29]

After the Reformation

Traditionally the Reformation in Sweden has been dated to the meeting of the Swedish Parliament in Västerås in 1527, but the country did not receive a Church Order until 1571 and then only in a confessionally vague form. It was not until the Uppsala Assembly of 1593 that it finally opted for Lutheranism. In Västerås it was decided that if the bishops could not provide the parishes with a minister who could or would preach the Word of God, the king should remedy the situation. At the church assembly in Örebro in 1529 it was decided that each sermon should contain the Lord's Prayer, Credo, and Hail Mary. From the treatise by the Swedish Reformer Olaus Petri *Förmaning till alla evangelisk predicare* [An Injunction to All Evangelical Preachers] (1535), it is clear that the sermons ought to have a didactic aim, and Gustavus Vasa, the king, wanted to include an injunction to the congregations about obedience towards the authorities, too.[30]

As early as 1528, Petri published *En nyttog postilla* [a useful postil], consisting of twenty-seven sermons translated from Luther's *Church-postil* [a small postil], and in 1530 *En litjen postilla* was published in order to help the ministers who had trouble reaching the congregations with their message. In this book, he describes how they should begin and end each sermon. They should begin with a prayer, proceed to the supplication of the Holy Ghost, and then read the Gospel of the day. They should end with yet another prayer and read aloud the confession of sins.[31] The importance of the Bible was

---

28 Ibid., p. 300.
29 Ibid., p. 210.
30 Yngve Brilioth, *Predikans historia. Olaus Petri-Föreläsningar hållna vid Uppsala Universitet* (Lund: C.W.K. Gleerups Förlag, 1945), pp. 170ff.

stressed, as Petri wrote that the minister could improve the sermon through reading selected chapters of the Bible. Petri did not insist that all ministers write their own sermons, but at least they were to read one from the *postilla*.[32] The Swedish sermons of the Reformation generally derived a clear inspiration from Germany,[33] but were never identical to the German ones. More help was needed, and in 1549 Georg Norman's *Kurtz Ahnleitung* was published, in which he gave ten short and practical rules explaining the best way to deliver a sermon. It should be noted that Norman represented a step forward, as his demands regarding sermons were more far-reaching and precise than had been true immediately after the Reformation. *Kurtz Ahnleitung* was followed in 1555 by a rewriting of Veit Dietrich's *Kinderpostille* [Children's Postils] by Olaus Petri's brother, Archbishop Laurentius Petri. This book served the Swedish clergy for more than a half century, as it was published again in 1630 and 1641. In a pastoral letter, Laurentius explained that a rural minister should deliver a sermon based on the catechism for half an hour, and then spend another half hour explaining the Gospel. The sermons should contain a didactic section on the Law and God's anger at human sin, followed by one on God's grace and mildness. The minister should always remember to finish with an injunction to respect the authorities. In the towns, at evensong, the ministers should use the epistle for the sermon.

At the meeting in Uppsala the Finnish church was represented by Bishop Ericus Erici from Åbo and three other clerics from the same city; the decision to officially acknowledge Lutheranism was later signed by 250 ministers and thus came into force in the whole of Finland.[34] The evangelical sermon was like many other aspects of the Finnish church imported from Sweden. Martin Skytte was appointed bishop of Åbo in 1527 and through his work the sermon became more common in Finland. In the Finnish-speaking areas it took longer than in Swedish regions before the ministers could institute Lutheran teaching, not least because they could not read the Latin and Swedish literature and profit from it.[35] That eventually

---

31 Brilioth, *Predikans historia*, p. 175.
32 Hammar, "Reformationstidens predikan," p. 264.
33 Henrik Ivarsson, *Predikans uppgift. En typologisk undersökning med särskild hänsyn til reformatorisk och pietistisk predikan* (Lund: G.W.K. Gleerups Förlag, 1956), p. 2.
34 Råberg, *Predikoverksamhet*, pp. 25ff.
35 Ibid., pp. 14ff.

happened when Mikael Agricola[36] returned to Finland in 1539.
Several of his unpublished collections of sermons from the decade
from 1542 onwards gave the Finnish clergy an opportunity to hear
sermons in the vernacular and find directions for preparing them.
Paavali Juusten, who was bishop of Åbo from 1563 until his death
in 1575, wrote during his Russian captivity a volume of sermons in
Latin for all Sundays and Holy days, where according to Juusten
sermons should be given in the morning, at noon, and in the evening. He used an analytical method of preaching with an emphasis
on erudition, consolation, and punishment.[37]

Olaus Petri's sermons were made up of two parts: first a retelling
of the text, then the exegesis. In many ways they remind us of the
medieval sermons that still existed, (and the sermons of the Danish
Reformer Hans Tausen mentioned below) but Petri constantly
stressed the importance of the Gospel.[38] There appears to have
been remarkable agreement on doctrine among the leading Swedish and Finnish reformers.

Denmark-Norway witnessed a full Reformation and received a
Protestant Church Order in 1537/1539, written under the supervision of Johannes Bugenhagen. But as early as 1528, the Danish
king[39] Frederick I had introduced Lutheranism in the southernmost
part of Denmark, where his son Christian–later to be Christian III
–ruled. The young prince had ordered ministers to preach and interpret the Holy Gospel in accordance with Martin Luther's books
of sermons.

The Church Order of 1537/1539, which must be seen as the
judicial foundation of the Danish church, ordered that preaching
should concentrate on three main topics: 1) the Holy Gospel with
a call for true penance, improvement, and faith, 2) the sacraments;

---

[36]   Mikael Agricola (1510-1557) was sent to Wittenberg by Martin Skytte, where he
lived from 1536 to 1539. When he returned to Åbo, he was appointed headmaster of
the school, where he worked as a reformer. Before 1554 he was appointed bishop. The
Finnish upper class did not accept Lutheranism as readily as they did in the other Scandinavian countries, but veered towards Reform Catholicism. See the entry by Harry
Lenhammar in Hans J. Hillerbrand, ed., *The Oxford Encyclopedia of the Reformation* (Oxford:
Oxford University Press, 1996).
[37]   Raaberg, *Predikoverksamhet*, p. 21.
[38]   Brilioth, *Predikans historia*, p. 177.
[39]   On the Lutheranism of Frederick I, see Thorkild C. Lyby, *Vi evangeliske. Studier
over samspillet mellem udenrigspolitik og kirkepolitik på Frederik I's tid* (Aarhus: Aarhus
universitetsforlag, 1993).

and 3) teachings during childhood. In order to help the preachers, the Church Order enumerated fifteen subjects that could be used in sermons: the Law and piety, the gospels and faith, penance, the Cross, prayer, good deeds, free will, Christian freedom, God's eternal providence, human ideas, the authorities, marriage, the saints, fasting, and images. However, the king emphasized that the clergy should be careful when approaching subjects such as providence and freedom, because they went beyond human intellectual capacity. The clergy ought as the foundation of theology to own the Bible, The Book of Sermons by Luther, The Augsburg Confession, the *Loci Communes* of Melanchthon, the Visitations Articles of Saxony and the Church Order.[40]

The Church Order contained articles on the timing of sermons; in addition to the Sunday service, sermons should be given on Wednesdays and Fridays in towns and on certain holy days throughout the year. No sermon ought to last longer than an hour. The Church Order specified the method of preaching by quoting Luke 10:16: "He who hears you hears me," saying that the preachers were the representatives of Christ.

Most of the Catholic priests continued in their jobs throughout Scandinavia after the Reformation, largely because very few preachers had been educated in the new evangelical tradition. Both Catholic priests and their new Lutheran colleagues were recruited from the peasantry, which formed the bulk of their congregations. Most of them lacked the basic skills of writing a sermon. Assistance in teaching them to preach in the new, proper manner came mainly from the bishops and the deans during their visitations and at the synods.

The authorities knew that it would take some time for the clergy to accustom themselves to this new situation. They were allowed to read the Sunday sermon from a printed Danish book of sermons, until they got into the habit of writing sermons themselves. The bishop of Scania, Niels Palladius, thought that the *postils* by Johannes Brenz, Johannes Spangenberg, Hans Tausen, along with the translation by Peder Palladius[41] of the one by Anton Corvin

---

[40] Schwarz Lausten, *Biskop*, p. 65.
[41] Peter Palladius (1503-1560) was the first Lutheran bishop of Zeeland; in 1531 he matriculated at the University of Wittenberg, and in 1537 after he had completed

could be used. In the early 1550s, in the course of a visitation, the bishop of Northern Jutland (Vensyssel) inquired about the books owned by the clergy in his diocese,[42] and the most common among the sixty-eight were the *postils*, especially by Corvin; no less than sixty-seven owned a copy. Thirteen had the one by the bishop of Ribe, Hans Tausen, twelve owned Johannes Spangenberg's Latin *postil*, and nine were the owners of those by Melanchthon and Luther. Only a few had the one by Johannes Brenz. Apparently *En nøttelig Bog om S. Peders Skib, det er: om den hellige oc christelige Kircke* [A Useful Book on St. Peter's Boat: On the Holy and Christian Church] by the bishop of Zeeland, Peder Palladius, was a very important homiletic aid as well.[43] Handwritten collections of sermons circulated as well, the most popular[44] being that by Peder Poulsen of Roskilde in 1548. Only around fifteen of the Protestant ministers in Vensyssel owned a Bible.

Three components make up any sermon: the message, the congregation, and the preacher. The emphasis differed from time to time. During the years after the Reformation, the message was the primary component: it was most important to express the Gospels purely so that nobody could doubt their importance. The congregation and the preacher did not have an equal part to play. Looking at the sermons this way we can distinguish three homiletic types:[45] the true Lutheran sermon was seen as a reproduction of an incident in the life of Christ; the Philippistic (named after Melanchthon) in which the preacher explained the teaching of the Gospel; and the orthodox where the subject was considered through a paraphrased reading of the chosen text of the Bible.

---

his final doctoral exams, he was summoned by the Danish king to assume the office of bishop of Zeeland. See the entry by Trygve Skarsten in *The Oxford Encyclopedia.*

[42] Hans Tausen (1494-1561) was accepted as a monk in the monastery of the Order of Saint John of Jerusalem; later he studied at the universities of Rostock, Copenhagen, Louvain and Wittenberg. When he was recalled from Wittenberg to preach and teach in Jutland, his sermons became more and more Lutheran, and he was expelled from his order in 1526. After the reformation in Denmark in 1537, he became lecturer at the University in Copenhagen, and in 1541 he was appointed bishop of Ribe. See the entry by Martin Schwarz Lausten in *The Oxford Encyclopedia.*

[43] Anita Hansen (Engdahl), "Gud til ære og kirken til opbyggelse. Niels Hemmingsens homiletik." The Faculty of Theology, University of Copenhagen, 1994, p. 25.

[44] They were all inspired by the *loci*-method of Melanchthon.

[45] A.F. Nørager Pedersen, *Prædikens idéhistorie* (Copenhagen: Gyldendal, 1980), pp. 173ff.

The sermons of the *Churchpostil* by Tausen from 1539 must be considered as the most important homiletic publication of the Danish Reformation. It was written for publication and not only for preaching from the pulpit. Clearly Tausen's position is that the exegesis should follow the text; what the preacher tells the congregation is closely dictated by the text. He identified the preaching with Christ. The words of the sermon were not only the Word of Christ, they quite simply were Christ.[46] Tausen was convinced that the Savior from the crib in Bethlehem through to the time of the Resurrection was alive in the Church through his Words.

Tausen made use of more topics from Luther's preaching, i.e. faith-love, law-gospel, the kingdom of Christ-the kingdom of the world etc;[47] and he was definitely the Danish reformer most inspired by Luther. Tausen's sermons had a clear social function: he stressed loyalty to rank and vocation and obedience to parents. He warned against gluttony and greed, and urged sacrifice for those in need. He wrote of the importance of marriage, encouraging chastity, mutual love, and sobriety.[48] The job of the ministers was critical, because sermons were of the utmost importance; the only way for the congregation to obtain salvation was by listening to sermons. Very few practical instructions are given on how to lead a Christian way of life; thus the view presented of Christ is that of the Savior, rather than an example to follow.[49] Tausen stressed that the preacher should act courageously in public, without paying attention to other persons or adjusting the sermons to "favors and friendship, intention and honour, benefit and profit."[50]

Shortly after the Reformation the first signs of a more didactic sermon can be seen; such sermons seek to explain certain doctrines of the Christian faith. This kind of sermon peaked during the Philippistic period in the last part of the sixteenth century. The sermon's aim is to allow the gospels to stand out clearly; the text is seen as a treasury of doctrines that the preacher must examine with

---

[46]   Ibid., p. 178.
[47]   Finn Fosdal, "Luthers kirkepostil og Hans Tausens Postil," in Knud E. Bugge, ed., *Tro og tale. Studier over Hans Tausens Postil* (Copenhagen: G.E.C: Gads Forlag, 1963), p. 125.
[48]   Knud E. Bugge, "Opfattelsen af prædikens funktion i Hans Tausens Postil," in *Tro og tale*, p. 136.
[49]   Nørager Pedersen, *Prædikens idéhistorie*, p. 189.
[50]   Ibid., p. 192.

skill and learn to explicate devotionally with the congregation. If previously the preacher offered the forgiveness of sins, now he gave an edifying talk on the same subject.[51]

The bishops thought that the time for sermon writing had passed in 1546. At a synod, they prohibited the reading of books of sermons. However, the decision was premature, because in 1555 the prohibition had to be reiterated in stronger terms. Those ministers who continued reading aloud from the books of sermons were ordered to be punished. The prohibition was reiterated more than once.

In 1553, the first homiletic textbook, *De formandis concionibus sacris de interpretatione Scriptuarum populari*, had been published by a professor from Marburg, Andreas Hyperius. According to him, the purpose of preaching was to communicate the Biblical teaching on salvation. In this context, preaching was synonymous with exegesis.[52] The work by Hyperius was only the first among others of the same kind, of which the one by the Danish professor Niels Hemmingsen[53] *De Methodis*, published in 1555 was the first Danish one. In the following year, Bishop Niels Palladius published *Regulæ quædam utiles ac necessariæ concionatoribus observandæ*, in which he laid down some rules that he thought the evangelical preacher ought to bear in mind. He should teach the congregation the true evangelical doctrines; every sermon must be carefully prepared. In order to do so, the minister must study the Bible carefully (through education), and he himself must lead a life that was an example to his congregation.[54] The preacher should stress one main idea that had to be conveyed unambiguously to the audience; this could be done through frequent reiteration. Centered around the main idea, the preacher could gather a few doctrines – *loci communes* – but not too many, as they might confuse the issue. Niels Palladius emphasizes the fact that the congregations have a very limited world of under-

---

[51] Ibid., p. 194.

[52] Engdahl, "Gud til ære," p. 20.

[53] Niels Hemmingsen (1513-1600) matriculated at the university of Wittenberg in 1537; in 1553, he was appointed professor of theology at the university of Copenhagen. He must be considered as the greatest Scandinavian theologian of the century. In the 1570s, Hemmingsen was accused of veering towards crypto-Calvinism, and the Danish king had to suspend his teaching career. However, he continued living and writing in Roskilde until his death. See the entry by Skarsten in *The Oxford Encyclopedia*.

[54] Nørager Pedersen, *Prædikens idéhistorie*, p. 200.

standing, as they mostly consist of "coarse and uneducated people that cannot easily understand difficult, intricate and complicated matters."[55]

Peder Palladius published two collections of sermons.[56] In 1555, he published the collection of sermons *Den overmaade herlige historie om vor Herres Jesu Kristi aerefulde Forklarelse paa Tabors Bjerg* [The Extremely Wonderful Story of the Honorable Transfiguration of Our Lord Jesus Christ on Mount Tabor]. In those sixteen sermons we find a retelling of the evangelical story, but it was not a genuine sermon that had been given, but a sermon that contained articles. The story was just one feature in the sequence of sermons; the function was to indicate the order in which the many doctrines that the story holds would be treated.[57] Through a particular method, the preacher could explain a special concept to the congregation. After having defined the concept, the preacher was to go into its four causes. In 1554, Palladius wrote *En nøttelig Bog om S. Peders Skib*, where he divided the sermon into the four *causae*: *causa efficiens* (asking for the incentive that gives it life), *causa materalis* (asking for the material from which it is built), *causa formalis* (asking for the structure that arranges it) and *causa finalis* (asking for the purpose for which it exists).[58] *S. Peders Skib* is a history of the world ranging from the Creation to the time of the author and with the Day of Judgment ahead. The course of history is depicted as a voyage across the wind-swept sea of the world, and the boat is the Church. On board are upright, pious Christians, Jesus is the master and "high boatswain," but God is on board as well, and he sees to it that the boat remains afloat. Thus the boat could not sink, although it tilts dangerously from time to time. It is called the Boat of St. Peter after the story in Luke 5 about Jesus boarding the boat of Simon Peter, from which he taught the congregations. Then Palladius writes about the catch of Simon Peter; however, he has written a postscript, in which he stresses that he does not teach that the Church is built and founded on the person of Peter the Apostle. That is just

---

[55] Ibid., p. 202.

[56] In both collections Palladius attacked the Catholics, pointing to the fact that as late as the 1550s he feared a Catholic reaction in Denmark; see Schwarz Lausten, *Biskop*, p. 80.

[57] Nørager Pedersen, *Prædikens idéhistorie*, p. 199.

[58] It is a collection of sermons preached in Copenhagen during the summer of 1552.

a "wax nose" the popish pirates have put upon the words of Christ. It is Christ, who is the true rock and foundation of the Church, and the boat is the boat of the Lord Jesus.[59] The *causa efficiens* is God, Christ and the Holy Spirit, the *causa materialis* is the Holy Scripture, the *causa formalis* is the Law and the Gospel, and the *causa finalis* is the salvation of Man and God's Honor.[60]

The aim of the book is primarily to turn the congregations toward a new way of looking at the world after the Reformation. Consequently it ends by stressing the importance of the last thirty years for that time. Christ now rules the boat through his holy gospel, after the cleansing by Luther, and it ends with a confession to "hvad himmelsk kram, der er indført igen i Sankt Peders skib.[61]

By describing the ideal heavenly conditions as a parallel to the social reality of the existing feudal and patriarchal society, Palladius legitimizes the contrast between the experiences of the rich and powerful and the conditions of the poor and unprivileged, who had to fight for their existence all the time.[62] Palladius stresses the sacrosanct nature of the relationship between master and subject by arguing for the importance of church attendance. The nobles ought to go to church each holy day, just like their subjects, but if there was an urgent necessity the peasants could be coerced into fulfilling their duty of forced labor.[63] It is obvious that children and adults must have felt the strict necessity of obedience to their masters, if the bishop said that a lord of the manor could decide if forced labor was more important than church attendance, thereby hampering the salvation of their souls.

The activities of Palladius and the other Protestant bishops had profound significance for contemporary politics; the notion of strict obedience to the authorities at all levels was solidified in the consciousness of the subjects to such a degree that it was made virtually impossible to transgress it.[64]

---

[59]   Alex Wittendorff, "'Evangelii lyse dag' eller 'hekseprocessernes mørketid?'" Om Peder Palladius' historieopfattelse," in Grethe Christensen et al., eds., *Tradition og kritik. Festskrift til Svend Ellehøj den 8. september 1984* (Copenhagen: Den danske historiske forening, 1984), p. 96.

[60]   Nørager Petersen, *Prædikens idéhistorie*, p. 201.

[61]   "The heavenly 'things' that have been reintroduced into the boat"; Wittendorff, "Evangelii," p. 99.

[62]   Wittendorff, "Evangelii," p. 101.

[63]   Ibid., pp. 103f.

[64]   Ibid., p. 116.

In 1555, Palladius directed himself to the clergy, when he wrote *Den Offuermaade Herlige Historie om vor Herris Jesu Christi ærefulde forklarelse paa Thabor bierg, predicker oc vdlagt aff Docter Petro Palladio* [The Incredibly Beautiful Story of the Honorable Elucidation of Our Lord Jesus Christ, Preached and Interpreted by Dr. Peter Palladius. The clergy should assess the congregations in terms of how frail they were and how well suited they were to comprehending everything they heard.

Palladius organized his sermons in the same way; he began with the reading of the text and proceeded to the explanation of difficult words and ideas. Before the exegesis he gives a short repetition of the content of the preceding sermon. In the course of the exegesis he explains each verse word by word, all the time referring to other texts that might clarify and explain the verse in question. He uses the last part of the sermon to address the question of the relevance of the text to the congregation. Palladius finishes with a personal appeal to those listening and a short reference to the sermon that is to follow.[65]

Niels Hemmingsen developed this special kind of preaching which he and Palladius had started; he moved the scene from congregation to classroom, from pulpit to lectern. The didactic sermon reached a final clarification. In *De Methodis* Hemmingsen conceived the preacher as a shepherd feeding his flock with heavenly nourishment, which was the Word of God. Preachers were only the instrument of God in conveying the Word. They were to know the heavenly teaching (*doctrinæ coelestis*), because this teaching was a path prepared by God, on which humans could go from death to life, from the trouble of this world to immortality. The preacher should possess the will to see the Word of God as the only guiding principle.[66] Hemmingsen differed from his predecessors by giving homiletic particulars; he wanted to teach the clergy how they could find the contents for sermons in the Gospels, molding them didactically – rebuking, consoling, and chastising the congregations on the road to salvation. The ministers could do that through the right dialectic method combined with rhetorical directions for the execution of the sermons.[67]

---

65 Schwarz Lausten, *Biskop*, p. 80.
66 Ibid., p. 56.
67 Ibid., p. 63.

Hemmingsen thought that Scripture itself expressed the will of God; however, that did not mean that exegesis could be dispensed with. It could not be for four reasons: 1) because the laity did not know the meaning of words in foreign languages; 2) in order to assess the right order of things; 3) in order to let the identity of the different parts of Scripture testify to the truth of the words of God; and 4) in order to refute the false ideas of heretics.[68]

One of Hemmingsen's purposes was to have the minister address the congregation without "chattiness," a method that should guarantee that the content of the sermons is presented logically and intelligibly. In order to intensify interest and to facilitate comprehension, Hemmingsen suggested the use of imagery and many examples. He saw the content as a system, which he wanted to substantiate with quotations and rational deductions. In the Biblical texts, the doctrines were hidden, and it was the homiletic aim to find and explain them. Differing from Tausen, where the doctrines appeared spontaneously, Hemmingsen had to detect them laboriously. The character of a lecture is ameliorated by the injunctions given to the congregation. It was one of the reasons why the ministers had to learn their sermons by heart and not just read them aloud.[69]

Faith and works were not two distinct things, and in his homiletics Hemmingsen shows how good works were not a condition for faith and justification. Still, we have to do them as reborn creatures in God's image. In accordance with the situation of the congregations and through the dialectics of Melanchthon, possibly inspired by Erasmus, he developed Melanchthon's homiletics into a detailed but well laid-out system.[70] In 1561, Hemmingsen published a *Postilla*, which was translated into Danish in 1576. Here he wrote that the story comes first, followed by the blessing (which the story relates), and finishing with the right use of the holy day.[71]

In 1562, Hemmingsen published *Pastor sive pastoribus optimus vivendi agendique modus*, in which he presented his idea of how a minister ought to give a sermon. Hemmingsen probably wrote *Pastor* because he was worried about the moral decline of the ministers. The

---

[68] Ibid., p. 64.
[69] Ibid., p. 76.
[70] Ibid., p. 80.
[71] Nørager Pedersen, *Prædikens idéhistorie*, p. 209

Reformation had purified the teaching, but the ministers had not improved.

A reading of the sermon on "The Wedding in Cana" shows how Hemmingsen constructed his sermons. It consists of four parts: the wedding feast, the matrimony, the present miracle, and the rules and examples to be deduced from the story. The four parts were further divided into sections and subsections. After having introduced this composition to the congregation, Hemmingsen discusses who are allowed to enter into holy matrimony, and how it should take place. He continues with the conditions for matrimony, i.e. kinship, religion and natural abilities (the question of impotence takes up a considerable part). Hemmingsen stresses that the consent of both parties has to be obtained in order to make it legally binding. Nobody should be coerced into matrimony. The wedding should take place in church for four reasons: the couple will know that this act belongs to the domain of a church, they will hear the word of God at the ceremony, the congregation shall testify to the marriage, and the couple will have the help of the prayers of the congregation. Hemmingsen stresses three reasons for the institution of marriage: so that the spouses can be of mutual assistance to one another; in order to give birth to children, so that each household can have a Christian group to meet in prayer; and to prevent fornication and debauchery.

Perhaps Hemmingsen did not intend the first two parts to be used in the sermons. They might have been enumerated in order to educate the clergy regarding matrimony, which was a field of interest for Hemmingsen throughout his life. In the third part, he described the miracle performed by Christ at the wedding in Cana, and in the fourth part he drew a lesson from the people in the story. From those attending the wedding, we learn how to celebrate without abundance and madness; from the bride and the bridegroom we learn to welcome Christ at the wedding; from the miracle we learn that Christ will transform sour into sweet and bless the couple; from Christ himself we learn to use our fortune for the edification of the church; from Mary we learn to pray for those in need; from the cook we learn with a pure heart to praise the deeds of Christ; from the servants we learn to be obedient to Christ; and from the examples of Christ, Mary and the disciples we learn to participate in the weddings even of poor people and to help them.

This somewhat stereotypical sermon hints at the fact that Hemmingsen would use allegorical interpretations.[72]

Hemmingsen's homilies represented a development during the initial stages of the consolidation of the Reformation from rhetorical restraint towards a relative homiletic independence without a total liberation from rhetoric. Hemmingsen's sermons can be characterized as sermons of penance; he concentrated on an interpretation of the Law in order to bring about remorse.[73]

A comparison between Tausen and Hemmingsen shows that to Tausen the story in itself was a narrative of a divine blessing, and as it was being related, the blessing was brought to the congregation with a redeeming effect. According to Hemmingsen, men and women had to put this blessing into effect in their own lives through specific actions, while to Tausen it was only a question of living through the blessing, which through the grace of God was brought into life.[74]

The *postil* was partly a homiletic text-book for the use of writing sermons and partly a dogmatic book in order to consolidate Lutheran teaching and lead the clergy in their fight against false doctrines. In all likelihood, the fact that the clergy in the last part of the sixteenth century began writing their own sermons can be credited to Hemmingsen.[75]

The Danish professor of theology P.G. Lindhardt has shown in a study of the late sixteenth-century book of visitations by the bishop of Funen, Jacob Madsen, that the ministers often used Hemmingsen's *De Methodis.* But by using the method they did not diverge from his theology.[76] A fragment from a collection of late sixteenth-century sermons shows the use of Hemmingsen's book by a minister. He had written his sermon on the basis of Hemmingsen, made it popular and relevant by retelling the story and using the rhetorical devices, Hemmingsen had made additions in the margin of the *postil.*[77] The influence of Hemmingsen is obvious in Norway

---

[72]   Engdahl, "Gud til ære," pp. 85ff.

[73]   Ibid., p. 118.

[74]   Nørager Petersen, *Prædikens idéhistorie*, p. 211.

[75]   Engdahl, "Gud til ære," p. 120.

[76]   P.G. Lindhardt, "Til Belysning af Niels Hemmingsens Indflydelse på dansk Prædiken omkring 1600," in *Festskrift til Jens Nørregaard den 16. Maj 1947* (Copenhagen: G.E.C. Gads Forlag , 1947), p. 145.

[77]   Engdahl, "Gud til ære", p. 146.

as well; during his visitations, the bishop of Oslo, Jens Nielsen, noted that ministers often used Hemmingsen's *Postil* as a model. Nielsen was very careful at his visitations to note how ministers managed their sermons. In August 1597, he spent six days in Bohuslen giving and listening to sermons; he heard nine, and a couple of times different ministers used the same text so Nielsen could critique their efforts. He wrote down how well they did; one of the ministers simply could not end his sermon, so Nielsen had to ask him to stop; another one did not do especially well, and the bishop demanded that he study more. However, Nielsen admits that many were very good at giving their sermons.[78] Even Nielsen had Hemmingsen as his model, and he as well as the bishop of Stavanger, Jørgen Erikssøn,[79] borrowed from Hemmingsen. This does not mean that they did not have their own style when they preached. It simply shows how influential Hemmingsen was. It is thus not surprising to find the demand for penance as a general topic in the sermons by Erikssøn.[80]

Both Jens Nielsen and Erikssøn complained that the clergy had insufficient funds to buy the necessary books, and Nielsen could tell that some rural clergymen did not own the Danish translation of the Bible.[81] Two collections of sermons for sailors testify to the pastoral care and preaching in Norwegian seaside towns.[82]

It is interesting to note that in these times of witch persecution, we do not find one single sermon on witchcraft in Denmark. This is especially strange compared to the situation in Germany, where the number is amazingly high.[83] References in the Scandinavian

---

[78] Olav Hagesæther, *Norsk preken fra Reformasjonen til omlag 1820. En undersøkelse av prekenteori og forkynnelse* (Oslo: Universitetsforlaget, 1973), pp. 18ff.

[79] Jørgen Erikssøn (1535-1604) was born in Denmark; after an appointment as *rektor* of the cathedral school in the Norwegian town of Bergen, he left to study in Copenhagen and in Wittenberg. In 1571 he was appointed bishop of Stavanger, where he established the Latin school and made it into an efficient instrument for the education of ministers; through visitations he did a fine job of training the clergy in his diocese. See the entry by John E. Quam in *The Oxford Encyclopedia*.

[80] Hagesæther, *Norsk preken*, p. 45.

[81] Ibid., p. 9.

[82] Ibid., pp. 67ff. The first collection was written around 1580 by Tilemannus Henningius of Marstrand and the other in 1601 by Hans Balthersen Fridag of Bergen. It is quite clear that the one by Fridag had been used by sailors, because in the Public Library in Bergen there is a copy bound together with a book on navigation.

[83] Cf. Stuart Clark, *Thinking with Demons. The Idea of Witchcraft in Early Modern Europe* (Oxford: Oxford University Press, 1997).

countries to the subject are to be found scattered throughout the existing stock of sermons. But even so, sermons played a decisive part in the decline of witchcraft trials in Denmark. Many ministers took as a starting point the views first put forward by Johannes Brenz from Schwäbisch Hall, according to which God was the source of all human suffering, because of humanity's sins, and that old women should not be accused of witchcraft even if they themselves believed in it.[84] Even after the start of the Thirty Years' War when Protestants in Germany began to intensify their persecutions of witches, several Danish stayed with the providential tradition which saw God as allowing all suffering. The minister on the island of Fur, Daniel Dirksen, believed that he had been bewitched by a woman, but according to evidence given by one of his colleagues, Dirksen had followed the example of Job and accepted his pain as coming from the hand of God. Some years later during a trial against a man accused of black magic, the minister in Kirketerp stated "that if you have bewitched me I am sure you will be rewarded in time. I, however, will accept it as coming from God."[85]

If the two ministers had not directly been inspired in their belief in providence by the writings of Brenz, they most certainly had drawn on the sermons by Jørgen Erikssøn and by the canon of Ribe, Anders Sørensen Vedel. In *Jonæ Prophetis skiøne Historia vdi 24 Predicken begreben* [The Beautiful History of Jonah's Prophecy, Explained in 24 Sermons] from 1592, Erikssøn pointed out that adversity should never be attributed to the Devil or sorcerers, because it was God's punishment for sins, and in *Den XC. Psalme, Mose Guds Mands Bøn* [The Sixtieth Psalm, the Prayer of God's Man Moses] from 1593, Vedel wrote in the third sermon that sorcerers should not be given the honor of being thought able to cause death or disease.[86] It is remarkable that sorcery did not re-emerge as a subject in subsequent Danish theological writings, as opposed to the spiritualization of the relationship between sin and adversity which was covered extensively. During the first two decades of the seventeenth century, this aspect was given only moderate attention by

---

[84] H.C. Erik Midelfort, *Witch Hunting in Southwestern Germany 1562-1684. The Social and Intellectual Foundations* (Stanford: Stanford University Press, 1972).

[85] Jens Chr. V. Johansen, *Da Djævelen var ude…Trolddom i det 17. århundredes Danmark* (Odense: Odense Universitetsforlag, 1991), p. 148.

[86] Ibid., pp. 149ff.

theologians, but from the start of the 1620s it became more and more dominant, coinciding with the growth of a Penance (or pre-Pietist) movement.[87]

For generations the piety of penance as formulated by bishop Jesper Brochmand[88] dominated theology in Denmark-Norway. The orthodox sermon was primarily exegesis, and the method of preaching was to serve this purpose. In his *Sabbati Sanctification, det er gudelig Betænklning og kort Forklaring over alle Evangeliger og Epistler* [A Religious Reflection and Short Explanation of All Gospels and Epistles],[89] he gave a meticulous interpretation of both parts, which made a tremendous impact, becoming the devotional book of family homes.

There are indications that the method from the century of the Reformation dominated the ordinary Sunday sermon well into the seventeenth century.[90] Brochmand's thoughts are characterized by a deeply heartfelt piety, but they are also marked by a definite mistrust in humanity's spiritual abilities. He does not possess any of these, and the Christian lives spiritually only on what he is given by God.[91] Collections of sermons from the 1620s to the 1640s demonstrate Brochmand's influence; they are all characterized by a powerful demand for penance and "living faith," fortified through religious scrupulosity and resistance to temptation. However, the climax is not physical suffering and distress, but scrutiny of faith.[92] The sermon does not systematically relate the story, but is an anno-

[87] Johansen, *Djævelen*, pp. 152ff.

[88] Jesper Brochmand (1585-1652) was born in the Danish town of Køge. At the age of sixteen, he matriculated at the University of Copenhagen; later he studied in Leiden. In 1610, he was appointed *professor pædagogicus* at the university and in 1615 professor of theology. In 1633 Brochmand published his principal work on dogmatics *Universæ theologiæ systema*, which was printed abroad. In 1639 he was made bishop of Zeeland. His work in the Danish church was of great importance; he decided that women were allowed to sing psalms, and in order to bring the texts and the melodies in line with one another, he scrutinized the book of hymns.

[89] The *postil* was in two parts; the Winter part was published in 1635 and the Summer part in 1638.

[90] Hagesæther, *Norsk preken*, 123

[91] J. Oskar Andersen, "Dansk Syn paa Fromhed og 'Gudfrygtigheds Øvelse' i ældre luthersk Tid," in A.E. Sibbernsen (ed.), *Thomas Kingos Aandelige Siunge-koor* (Copenhagen: Levin & Munksgaards Forlag, 1931), p. xlii.

[92] Oskar Andersen, "Dansk Syn", p. xl; cf. the sermons by Benth Thorsøn *Aandelige Rustkammer* (1622), Brochmand's own *It Christen Menniskes aandleige Kamp* (1627) and the two sermons by the bishop of Ribe Jens Dinnysøn Jersin, *Vera via vitæ, det er: En rictige Vey, som fører til det evige Liff* (1633) and *Troens Kamp oc Seyr* (1636).

tated reading of the *pericope*. The true meaning of the sermon is not to reproduce the incident in the text, but to display the doctrines or ethics of the same. As a matter of fact the sermon does not intend to bring Christ together with his redemption near to the congregation: the aim is fulfilled by the mere fact that it supports the truth of the Gospel so that they remain unwaveringly firm.[93]

A comparison between the sermons of Hemmingsen and Brochmand shows that Hemmingsen found numerous doctrines in the text using the story itself, the blessings, and the use of these blessings, while Brochmand by and large only extracted one subject, identical with the actual subject of the text. Hemmingsen had a number of ways of approaching the text, whereas Brochmand only had one, which consisted of a reading of the existing text. To Hemmingsen it was a question of a systematic presentation of the doctrines in their totality; this explains why he normally could not find sufficient material in the text, but had to seek elsewhere in order to find supplementary material. Brochmand felt bound by the text; he did not have the audacity or the need to transcend the Gospel of the day. The quotations from the Bible should substantiate the doctrines, making the story clear and preventing misunderstanding, but they should not supplement an insufficient account of the doctrines.[94]

A sermon by Brochmand from the third day of Easter on Luke 24:36 gives a good picture of what he thought a sermon should contain. When the text stresses repentance and forgiveness of sins, Brochmand writes,

> You, servants of the Word of God, should know what you should preach in the congregation, and you, the audience, should know what to expect from learning and teaching. In the congregations you should mourn your sins with heartfelt emotion, you should with constant faith in your heart embrace and understand Christ, who died because of your sins and was resurrected for your righteousness; you will preach that you shall prove your sorrow in your sins and your faith in Christ with holy deeds, which are the fruits of conversion. You shall preach that God for the sake of Jesus Christ will forgive your trespasses and after this life will give you eternal Life.

---

[93] Nørager Pedersen, *Prædikens idéhistorie*, p. 216.
[94] Ibid., p. 217.

The sermon has an educational content, focused on the things humans ought to do and those things that Christ will do.[95]

Well into the seventeenth century, the average clergyman in the countryside in Denmark-Norway received only very modest theological training. In the new constitution, the *Novellæ Constitutiones* of the University of Copenhagen from 1621, it was stated that no one could hold a living without having studied for two or three years in the faculty of theology at the University of Copenhagen, or for at least one year if they had studied at a foreign university.[96] Maybe the clergy had failed in their work with the congregations. Perhaps they had not influenced them effectively through their sermons, because something was definitely wrong. God had turned his back on the king and his people.

The years after the Danish entry into the Thirty Years' War and the subsequent defeat mark a tightening of church policy in Denmark and Norway. Days of public penance, including special services, were prescribed every Friday for the towns, while the rural parishes were allowed to concentrate their activities into one Wednesday a month. The policy reached a peak in the comprehensive penitential ordinance of March 1629. The ordinance in effect introduced a regular church discipline. It stated that although the light of the gospel did not shine as brightly in other countries as in Denmark, people were in fact more pious. Many people in Denmark and Norway lived in the erroneous opinion that outward signs of piety, such as church attendance, the taking of sacraments, the singing of psalms, and praying were adequate. Consequently, a body of elders was to be appointed in every parish. The leading parishioners were to serve as assistants to the ministers. They were to assemble with the ministers at least four times a year in order to discuss parish matters and the behavior of their parishioners. Where impiety was detected, they were to take action first through private admonition, next by official reproof by the minister in the presence of witnesses, then by exclusion from the sacraments, and finally by excommunication and exclusion from the Christian com-

---

[95]   Ibid, p. 219.

[96]   Jens Glebe-Møller, "Det teologiske fakultet 1597-1732," in Svend Ellehøj et al. (eds.), *Copenhagens Universitet 1479-1979*, V (Copenhagen: G.E.C. Gads Forlag, 1980), pp. 130-131.

munity.[97] This situation lasted until 1636 when seminars were instituted on sermons and a homiletic examination was created in order to ensure that congregations received good "servants of the Word": these seminars and examinations were introduced in the Faculty of Theology at the University of Copenhagen.[98]

Orthodox Swedish preaching had a definite aim not only within the parish but also within the realm; a prophetic vocation can be seen in many of the sermons, a demand for bringing sinners to moral reform. Penance was the keyword.[99] This demand was not only aimed at the humble in society, but it reached up to the top as well. It can be seen in the sermon on punishment given by the court preacher Johannes Rudbeckius in 1617 and directed towards the king, Gustavus Adolphus.[100] On the other hand, the Swedish church saw a close connection between the Reformation and the Swedish Crown. Sweden had missed out on the celebrations which took place in most evangelical countries in 1617; instead the choice fell on 21 January 1621, which was the centenary of Gustavus Vasa's election as leader. However, 21 February and 21 March were also to be used as commemorative days. The king himself chose the texts to be preached, all taken from the Old Testament. The bishop of Stängnäs had the sermons which he gave on these days printed. The interesting point in the sermons is the linkage of national patriotism and the Reformation. The texts were used to rationalize events in Swedish history, and through the sermons, the kings received confirmation from the church of Vasa's importance for Sweden in political as well as religious terms. Several other leading members of the Swedish church had their sermons printed as well.[101]

The same development towards penance as in Sweden can be seen in Finland with the appointment of Isak Rothovius as bishop of Åbo in 1627; even though he did not write in Finnish, his influence on the Finnish church must not be underestimated.[102] His call

---

[97]   Thorkild Lyby and Ole Peter Grell, "The Consolidation of Lutheranism in Denmark and Norway," in *The Scandinavian Reformation*, pp. 136-137.

[98]   Oskar Andersen, "Dansk Syn," p. xlv.

[99]   Ivarsson, *Predikans uppgift*, p. 289.

[100]   Brilioth, *Predikans historia*, p. 195.

[101]   Irgun Montgomery, "The Institutionalisation of Lutheranism in Sweden and Finland," in *The Scandinavian Reformation*, pp. 171-172.

[102]   Råberg, *Den evangeliska Predikoverksamhet*, p. 42.

for penance and the punishment of sin did not leave much space for consolation; there was a ruthless streak to his sermons, where the punishment of God is described in the same terms that the prophets of the Old Testament had used.[103]

It should be noted that although Rothovius did not write in Finnish, his predecessor Ericus Erici wrote the first collection of sermons published in the vernacular. It was *Postilla eli ulgostoimitus niinen evengeliumitten pääle cuin ymbäri ajastajan saarnatan jumulan seuracunnas* [Publication of the Gospels which Are Preached in the Congregation of God During the Year] from 1621-1625, which was to become a model for Finnish sermons for many decades. Erici followed the analytical method of preaching, and his *postil* was a work of deep originality, although strictly faithful to the text. However, he did not demand that other ministers follow in his footsteps, but stressed that other *postils* by men of learning could be used.[104]

Even though ministers now wrote their sermons, it seems that just like before the Reformation it could be hard to capture the attention of the congregation. Perhaps their skills had not improved sufficiently. It could also be because they now often gave sermons lasting more than an hour, so the body of elders had to patrol the aisles with a rod in hand to awaken those who had fallen asleep during the service. This happened in spite of the ordinance that specified that sermons should not be too long or long-winded such that the congregations would get bored.[105] However, there are indications that these complaints largely stemmed from listening to funeral sermons. The sermons in Brochmands's *Postil* did not last more than an hour at a normal reading pace, and the sermons for Lent by Anders Kieldsen Tybo could not have been longer than forty to fifty minutes.[106] Bishop Rothovius stressed in a sermon from 1633 that it ought not to last longer than an hour, and that the minister should learn it by heart.[107] The Swedes had their share of problems as well; in the same way as, before the Reformation, congregations were enjoined to remain in church until the reading of the prayers had ended and the Lord's Supper had been given. It

---

[103]   Ibid., pp. 48ff.
[104]   Ibid., pp. 29ff.
[105]   Hagesæther, *Norsk preken*, 74.
[106]   Ibid., p. 125.
[107]   Råberg, *Den evangeliska Predikoverksamhet*, p. 46.

was a disgrace that they ran out of church as soon as the sermon had ended.[108]

Of course the question can be posed, how much do we actually know about the ordinary sermon given in a rural church on a Sunday? The printed sermons that we have do not represent the average preaching. If the minister wanted his sermons to be printed, in all probability he was very conscientious and thorough in his own preaching. In 1618, Eric Suenonis had his Christmas sermon printed, and he wrote that it was the same simple sermon he had given each year for twenty-five years to his congregation.[109]

During the last decades of the seventeenth century, the balance between the three components of the sermon shifted towards the congregation. The audience was the most important and next came the Gospel. This was clearly seen during the so-called "English epoch," when the minister as a civil servant employed by the state took over the educational control of the parish.[110]

Bibliography

Andersen, J. Oskar, "Dansk Syn paa Fromhed og 'Gudfrygtigheds Øvelse' i ældre luthersk Tid", in A.E. Sibbernsen, ed., *Thomas Kingos Aandelige Siunge-Koor* (Copenhagen: Levin & Munksgaards Forlag, 1931).

Ankarloo, Bengt and Gustav Henningsen, eds., *Early Modern European Witchraft. Centres and Peripheries* (Oxford: The Clarendon Press, 1990).

Brilioth, Yngve, *Predikans historia. Olaus Petri-Föreläsningar hållna vid Uppsala Universitet* (Lund: C.W.K. Gleerups Förlag, 1945).

Blom, Grethe Authén, ed., *Middelaldersteder. Urbaniseringsprocessen i Norden 1. Det XVII nordiske historikermøte Trondheim 1977* (Oslo: Universitetsforlaget, 1977).

Bugge, Knud E., "Opfattelsen af prædikenens funktion i Hans Tausens Postil", in *Tro og tale. Studier over Hans Tausens Postil*, ed. Knud E. Bugge (Copenhagen: G.E.C. Gads Forlag, 1963).

Clark, Stuart, *Thinking with Demons. The Idea of Witchcraft in Early Modern Europe* (Oxford: Oxford University Press, 1997).

---

[108] Brilioth, *Predikans historia*, p. 182.
[109] Hammer, "Reformationstidens predikan," p. 280.
[110] Nørager Pedersen, *Prædikens idéhistorie*, p. 229.

Fosdal, Finn, "Luthers kirkepostil og Hans Tausens Postil", in Knud E. Bugge, ed., *Tro og tale. Studier over Hans Tausens Postil* (Copenhagen: G.E.C. Gads Forlag, 1963).

Glebe-Møller, Jens, "Det teologiske fakultet 1597-1732." in Svend Ellehøj et al., eds., *Københavns Universitet 1479-1979*. Bd. V (Copenhagen: G.E.C. Gads Forlag, 1980).

Grinder-Hansen, Poul et al., eds., *Margrete I – Regent of the North: The Kalmar Union 600 Years*. Essays and Catalogue (Copenhagen: Nordisk Minister-råd & Danmarks Nationalmuseum, 1997).

Hagesæther, Olav, *Norsk preken fra Reformasjonen til omlag 1820. En under-søkelse av prekenteori og forkynnelse* (Oslo: Universitetsforlaget, 1973).

Hammar, H.B., "Reformationstidens predikan i Sverige", in Carl-Gustaf Andrén, ed., *Reformationen i Norden: Kontinuitet och förnyelse* (Lund: C.W.K. Gleerups bokförlag, 1973).

Hansen (Engdahl), Anita, "Gud til ære og kirken til opbyggelse. Niels Hemmingsens homiletik", Prisopgave ved Københavns universitets Teologiske fakultet, 1994.

Hillerbrand, Hans J., ed., *The Oxford Encyclopedia of the Reformation* (Oxford: Oxford University Press, 1996).

Hollman, Lennart, ed., *Den Heliga Birgitta Reuelaciones extrauagantes* (Uppsala: Almqvist & Wiksell, 1956).

Ivarsson, Henrik, *Predikans uppgift. En typologisk undersökning med särskild hänsyn till reformatorisk och pietistisk predikan* (Lund: C.W.K. Gleerups förlag, 1956).

Johansen, Jens Chr. V., *Da Djævelen var ude… Trolddom i det 17. århundredes Danmark* (Odense: Odense universitetsforlag, 1991).

—, "Faith, Superstition and Witchcraft in Reformation Scandinavia", in Ole Peter Grell, ed., *The Scandinavian Reformation. From Evangelical Move-ment to Institutionalisation of Reform* (Cambridge: Cambridge University Press, 1995).

Lindhardt, P.G., "Til Belysning af Niels Hemmingsens Indflydelse paa Dansk Prædiken omkring 1600", in *Festskrift til Jens Nørregaard den 16. Maj 1947* (Copenhagen: G.E.C. Gads Forlag, 1947).

Lyby, Thorkild C., *Vi evangeliske. Studier over samspillet mellem udenrigspolitik og kirkepolitik på Frederik I's tid* (Aarhus: Aarhus univeristetsforlag, 1993).

Lyby, Thorkild and Ole Peter Grell, "The Consolidation of Lutheranism in Denmark and Norway", in Ole Peter Grell, ed., *The Scandinavian Ref-ormation. From Evangelical Movement to Institutionalisation of Reform* (Cam-bridge: Cambridge University Press, 1995).

Midelfort, H.C. Erik, *Witch Hunting in Southwestern Germany 1562-1684. The Social and Intellectual Foundations* (Stanford: Stanford University Press, 1972).

Montgomery, Irgun, "The Institutionalisation of Lutheranism in Sweden and Finland", in Ole Peter Grell, ed., *The Scandinavian Reformation. From Evangelical Movement to Institutionalisation of Reform* (Cambridge: Cambridge University Press, 1995).

Nørager Pedersen, A.F., *Prædikenens idéhistorie* (Copenhagen: Gyldendal, 1980).

Riising, Anne, *Danmarks middelalderlige prædiken* (Copenhagen: G.E.C. Gads Forlag, 1969).

Råberg, Herman, *Den evangeliska Predikoverksamhetens Grundläggning och Utveckling i Finland intill År 1640* (Helsingfors: J.C. Frenckell & Son, 1883).

Schwarz Lausten, Martin, *Biskop Peder Palladius og kirken 1537-1560*)Copenhagen: Akademisk Forlag, 1987).

Skovgaard, Johanne, ed., *Den Hellige Birgitta. Kilderne til hendes Historie og Udvalg af hendes Skrifter* (Copenhagen: Det Schønbergske Forlag, 1921).

Wittendorff, Alex, " 'Evangelii lyse dag' eller 'hekseprocessernes mørketid'? Om Peder Palladius' historieopfattelse", in *Tradition og kritik. Festskrift til Svend Ellehøj den 8. september 1984*, eds. Grethe Christensen et al. (Copenhagen: Den danske historiske Forening, 1984).

CHAPTER TEN

PREACHING IN THE LOW COUNTRIES, 1450-1650

Jelle Bosma

Introduction

During the late medieval and early modern times the countries now known as Belgium and the Netherlands underwent enormous changes, not just political, but also in the cultural and especially the religious aspects of life. As a result, the area was split into two separate states: each acquired its own identity and history. The northern part (the Netherlands) became one of the first republics in early modern Europe. It gained independence and freedom from the Habsburg regime through a long battle with the Spanish empire. More by accident than incidentally, the Dutch state was able to form a political experiment unique in early modern Europe. Instead of a monarchy, it became an oligarchy, in other words: a country ruled by its own inhabitants.[1] The Dutch Republic flourished and was to become one of the leading nations in international trade in the seventeenth century. It produced and attracted all kinds of scientists, philosophers, and artists.

By 1650, the Dutch Republic was at the peak of its power, while the southern part (Belgium), still under the Habsburg regime, had less autonomy and fewer outside contacts. The north thus became a more interesting and important state than the south. In late medieval times, however, the situation was completely different. Along with Tuscany in the Mediterranean, Flanders formed one of the

---

[1] A recent, most informative and brilliant study on this subject is: J. Israel, *The Dutch Republic; Its Rise, Greatness, and Fall, 1477-1806* (Oxford, 1995). A general outline is also given in D.E.H. de Boer, ed., *Delta: Nederlands verleden in vogelvlucht, I: De Middeleeuwen 300-1500* (Leiden, Antwerp, 1992); S. Groenveld and G.J. Schutte, *Delta: Nederlands verleden in vogelvlucht, II: De nieuwe tijd 1500-1813* (Leiden, Antwerp, 1992). Much further information can be found in the older reference work: *Algemene geschiedenis der Nederlanden, 4-6: Middeleeuwen and Nieuwe tijd* (Haarlem, 1979-1980).

most vibrant centers of Europe. In those days Antwerp, Bruges, and Ghent were the leading northern towns in trade, art, and industry. How could this enormous change come about? What was the underlying reason for it and what was the role of religion in this process? Before we come to our subject – the social history of preaching in this period – we have to delve a little deeper into the political developments of both countries, in order to broaden the context of our subject. For the role of the sermon in this period can only be explained within this historical and political framework.

In the fourteenth century, the Low Countries became a part of the Burgundian state. A Burgundian duke ruled the area that ran roughly from the northeast of France to the north of Holland. Although the Burgundian rulers brought some modernization along with a more centralized and unified system of government, their influence in the Low Countries was limited, for their administration lasted only one century.[2] In 1482, the last duchess died childless and, as she was married to a Habsburg, the area became a part of a much larger state: the Habsburg empire. The Habsburgs originated in Central Europe (Austria). Now they also ruled the Low Countries, and some years later were to extend their territory even more by purchasing the Spanish crown as well as the title of German emperor. Thus, the fate of the Low Countries fell into the hands of foreign leaders possessing a European empire. The linkage between the Low Countries and Spain, where the Habsburgs normally resided and where their regime was centered, would become an important factor in subsequent developments in the sixteenth and seventeenth centuries. Its central theme in the early modern period was the authority of the Habsburg rulers in the Low Countries, particularly in matters of religion. Most prominent in this conflict was the role of two rulers: Charles V (1500-1558) and his son Philip II (1527-1598). Both of them were confronted with all kinds of new, "heretical" developments in their northern countries, for the Reformation had a deep impact on society in the Low Countries. Charles V and Philip II tried to suppress the new heresies in the same way as they did in other parts of their empire (particularly Spain). They installed new governors, a drastic and effective Inquisition, and eventually led a fierce military campaign

---

[2] See on this period the famous study of J. Huizinga: *The Waning of the Middle Age* (Harmondsworth, 1965).

against their rebellious northern subjects. Still, they were only partly successful. The Low Countries would slowly enter a period of rebellion and finally, as a result of this, split up into southern and northern parts. The importance of religion in the period from 1450-1650 is critical and can hardly be overestimated. However, there is not a great deal of information on the subject of the social history of preaching. The lack of sources, especially about the conduct and beliefs of ordinary people, makes the task at hand more difficult.

Religion in the Fifteenth Century

As in most of Europe, religious expression and visibility was prominent in the Low Countries during the fifteenth century. Churches, monasteries, and convents, along with priests, monks and nuns, were everywhere and formed an important and not to be overlooked element in society. Estimates of the percentage of ecclesiastics lead to a figure of one or two per cent of the total population (one priest for every hundred citizens).[3] Apart from the parish clergy, more or less directly under Roman influence, there were numerous monasteries and convents, containing regulars of several orders. Often large parts of cities had a religious function, and the power of religious institutions could sometimes lead to protests from town councils. Their commercial production led to further problems with laymen who did not have the benefits of cheap workers and tax reduction. The Church had special institutions for the poor as well as hospitals run by friars. Most clergymen, however, were engaged in church services and the numerous liturgical ceremonies. There were numerous masses for the dead, which formed a sort of religious industry outside the normal lay economy.

---

[3] In the Utrecht diocese (the area north of the rivers Lek, Maas, and Waal) the percentage was even higher. In total some 700,000 persons were living here, while the number of ecclesiastics in this area can be estimated at 18,000 (including nuns, monks, etc.). This means that about 2.5 percent of the total population had a religious function; five percent of all adults, or one in every twenty! See R.R. Post, *Kerkelijke verhoudingen in Nederland vóór de Reformatie, van ± 1500 tot ± 1580* (Utrecht, Antwerp, 1954) pp. 39, 148, 165-166.

The Church, however, had its problems.[4] At the beginning of the fifteenth century the so-called Great Schism led to serious quarrels within the Church focusing on the leadership of the Church. Should a pope rule with absolute authority, or should a council? And if the pope was the supreme, God-given leader, which pope should one follow? For in Rome and in Avignon there were a pope and a counter-pope, each with their own followers. Although in 1417 a new, generally accepted pope was chosen and recognized with absolute authority, the specter of competing popes had brought about disillusion and disorder in the Church and a loss of prestige. The undermining of the Church affected the whole of society, for the Church was not just a religious organization. The Church formed a state inside the state, while at the same time it was an international organization, employing an immense number of people in various social positions. The degree of hierarchy was clearly visible in its clergy. Bishops were often noblemen or other members of the elite, usually with little or no religious training. They normally had to pay for their installation or obtained their position through nepotism. A religious career was popular because of the financial benefits, often received without attending to religious obligations. On the other hand, there were many poor clergymen serving small parishes and combining this with other activities in order to survive. Many of these ecclesiastics had almost no education; some were married; and some were not even able to read. The Church thus resembled society in many aspects, and in a way it looked more like a juridical, political, economical, or even an artistic institution than a spiritual one.

In the fifteenth century, all kinds of initiatives were taken to reorganize and renew the Church. Some came from laymen and others from regular clergy who were discontented with the present state of their orders. In the Low Countries they were often influenced by an earlier reform movement called *Devotio Moderna*. Its founder, Geert Groote (1340-1384), son of a merchant in the town of Zwolle, strove for a more strict and pious life both within and outside the

---

[4] Some general information and more recent literature can be found in: De Boer, *Delta: Nederlands verleden in vogelvlucht*, I, 211-222, 291-292; *Algemene geschiedenis der Nederlanden*, IV, pp. 378-438, 486-492; R.R. Post, *Kerkgeschiedenis van Nederland in de Middeleeuwen* 2 vols. (Utrecht, Antwerp 1957).

Church.[5] To this end he gave many sermons and founded a congregation in which lay members and ecclesiastics lived together according to these rules. This congregation was named after the place where it was founded: Windesheim, a small village not far from Zwolle. At the end of the fifteenth century, almost a hundred monasteries were members of the Windesheim congregation. This atmosphere of renewal in the fifteenth century led to the foundation of an impressive number of new monasteries in the Low Countries. Many belonged to the Franciscan or Carthusian orders. The founders of these monasteries also aimed at a more strict and pious life. Furthermore, they wanted to restore the old rules of conduct in existing monasteries that had gradually lost contact with their initial aims. These regulars belonged to the so-called Observant movement (after the Latin *observare*, that is: to observe the monastic rules).[6]

It is not easy to say how these developments within the Church influenced the religious practice of ordinary people in the Low Countries.[7] Some may have become members of one of the new religious initiatives that sometimes also accepted lay members. Many others experienced religion regularly in their everyday life. Sundays and feast days were all linked with important Christian events such as the birthday of a saint or something similar. Religious and semi-religious festivities, processions, and worship of local relics and saints were popular events. Local "miracles" were also widespread, particularly miracles concerning the Eucharist.[8] This often led to pilgrimages, which were extremely popular in the fifteenth and early sixteenth centuries. Liturgical services were often performed at local places of pilgrimage, but some people traveled as far as Jerusalem.

Most prominent in daily religion, however, was the mass, con-

---

[5] See R.R. Post, *The Modern Devotion: Confrontation with Reformation and Humanism* Studies in Medieval and Reformation Thought, no. 3. (Leiden, 1968).

[6] See Post, *Kerkgeschiedenis van Nederland in de Middeleeuwen*, II, pp. 97-175.

[7] Some general information and further literature on this subject can be found in: J. van Herwaarden and R. de Keyser, "Het gelovige volk in de late middeleeuwen," in *Algemene geschiedenis der Nederlanden*, IV, pp. 405-420, 489-490.

[8] In Amsterdam, for instance, in 1345 a sick man accepted the host but had to vomit, and by doing this the host landed in the fireplace, where it was found completely intact sometime later. This "miracle" led to all kinds of worship, including a yearly procession still observed today. See R.B. Evenhuis, *Ook dat was Amsterdam; de kerk der hervorming in de goude eeuw*, 2 vols. (Amsterdam, 1965-1967) I, pp. 13-16.

ducted every Sunday and holiday.[9] In the towns one could attend mass at many places, for besides normal parish churches, masses were conducted in monasteries and convents. Public masses were delivered in Latin, involving choir-singing and other liturgical elements. The most important moment of the mass, however, was the Eucharist which for many people formed the heart of their religion[10].

Last but not least, spiritual care and education was provided by preaching on Sundays and holidays. It was normally a task of the priest and the curates.[11] Some orders like Franciscans and Dominicans also specialized in preaching to ordinary people. They were often quite successful, as they had to extend their churches because of their popularity.[12] Furthermore, Franciscans and Dominicans often preached in parish churches.[13] Interest in these church services was greater during Lent. We do not, however, have any significant information about the practice of preaching, its attendance, and popularity in the Low Countries. The only thing we know is that the sermon formed one element in the numerous religious practices and worship of the Low Countries. We can therefore assume the role of preaching must have been limited in the vast medieval religious complex. Moreover, it is very difficult to get into the mind of the average lay man or woman. How did they participate in the religious activities held by the Church?

---

[9]   See R.R. Post, *Kerkelijke verhoudingen in Nederland vóór de Reformatie*, pp. 409-419.

[10]   A detailed description of a normal mass based on relevant Dutch sources can be found in an older, although still useful work: W. Moll, *Kerkgeschiedenis van Nederland vóór de Reformatie*, 5 vols. (Arnhem, Utrecht, 1864-1871), here vol. II, part 3, pp. 274-335.

[11]   We have hardly any information about the delivery of sermons. The few recent studies about medieval Dutch sermons do not speak about this matter, probably due to lack of sources. See for instance: G.C. Zieleman, *Middelnederlandse epistel- en evangeliepreken* (Leiden, 1978).

[12]   This happened, for instance, in the city of Dordrecht where the church of the Franciscans had to be rebuilt around 1375 in order to accommodate the large audience. See J. van Herwaarden (ed.), *Geschiedenis van Dordrecht I; geschiedenis van Dordrecht tot 1572* (Hilversum, 1996) pp. 326-327.

[13]   See Moll, *Kerkgeschiedenis van Nederland vóór de Reformatie* vol. II, part 3, pp. 335-347.

A Popular Preacher: Johannes Brugman

The lack of sources about public worship in the late medieval period makes it difficult to find more detailed and explanatory information on the practice and popularity of preaching. One of the few exceptions is the legendary mendicant Johannes Brugman, who lived from ca. 1400 till 1473. His name lives on, even today, in the Dutch saying: *praten als Brugman* (talking like Brugman).[14] Brugman was a Franciscan monk, a member of one of the most important groups of mendicants. His splendid reputation as a popular preacher is the result of his extensive travels through the Low Countries and parts of Germany during the years during the years 1455 to 1463. These travels led to all kinds of myths and legendary stories. Many of these can easily be rejected as later inventions, while others can no longer be verified. Brugman nonetheless makes it possible to reconstruct the role of a popular preacher in the late Middle Ages.

Brugman was an early and important member of the Observant movement in the Low Counties. His activity as a popular preacher was closely related to his attempt to renew his order. By preaching all over the country, he hoped to win as many people as possible for the Observantine cause. Brugman must have been quite well educated, for in his later years he served his order as a lecturer, and he is said to have studied in Paris. In his early years, he became a member of one of the first Franciscan monasteries in the Low Countries that practiced the Observant rules. It was located in the town of Mechelen. The Franciscans there did not like the new, stricter mendicants who tried to take over "their" monastery. Such rigid rules did not appeal to them, and they started a campaign against the Observant monks.

Ordinary people helped the "old" Franciscans and began to tease the newcomers, by singing all kinds of ironic and vulgar songs about them.[15] The town council of Mechelen tried to intervene in

---

[14]   See the recently published work: N. Lettinck, *Praten als Brugman; de wereld van een Nederlandse volksprediker aan het einde van de Middeleeuwen* (Hilversum, 1999). More details can be found in: F.A.H. van den Hombergh, *Leven en werk van Jan Brugman O.F.M.; met een uitgave van twee van zijn tractaten* (Groningen, 1967); W. Moll, *Johannes Brugman en het godsdienstig leven onzer vaderen in de vijftiende eeuw*, 2 vols. (Amsterdam, 1854).

[15]   The city council of Mechelen banned a woman named Katheline Goblijns for singing one of these songs. The songs must have been drinking songs, most popular in

these quarrels; they forbade the singing and sentenced one person to leave the town for two years. Later, the conflict escalated and violence occurred between the two types of monks. Brugman, who became leader or *gardiaan* of the monastery, must have played an important role in this conflict. In his travels, he would often meet the same kind of opposition from "traditional" Franciscans, who rejected the Observantine cause. Brugman nevertheless maintained his efforts by traveling repeatedly through the country and spreading his message of conversion.

Extensive research in accounts of Dutch towns makes it possible to reconstruct Brugman's travels fairly exactly. For instance, in the period between 1458 and 1463, we know that he visited 36 places and traveled more than 1200 miles.[16] As a mendicant, he normally went on foot from town to town and preached in churches, monasteries, and convents. Although neither Brugman's career in Mechelen nor his efforts for the Observantine cause were trouble-free, town councils normally appreciated his visit and gave him food and wine (which he liked, calling it "a heavenly pleasure"). Ordinary people came to listen to his sermons, in which he often pleaded for them to lead austere, pious, and just lives, with charity and honesty as important rules of conduct. The worldly and luxurious lives of priests, monks, rulers, and others were fiercely attacked by Brugman. This appealed to many people, for monasteries were often quite wealthy at the time. A truly poor mendicant was unusual and must have been a relief for the audience. In his sermons, Brugman also treated everyone in the same way, whether churchmen or laity, upper or lower class. He criticized their sinful and worldly conduct, such as gambling, lack of piety, vengefulness, etc.[17] Many of these sermons were held in churches or monasteries, though Brugman sometimes preached in the open air (for instance in a churchyard). He was able to keep his audience attentive for a

---

the local pubs. The content was very humiliating and slanderous for the Observants, as the chorus was: "am I still a good observant". See Van den Hombergh, *Leven en werk van Jan Brugman*, p. 14.

[16]   Van den Hombergh, *Leven en werk van Jan Brugman*, pp. 15-42. Van den Hombergh checked all the sources and concluded that Brugman walked in the period mentioned at least 2000 kilometers. This study tries to verify many earlier works on Brugman, such as: Moll, *Johannes Brugman en het godsdienstig leven onzer vaderen in de vijftiende eeuw.*

[17]   See Moll, *Johannes Brugman en het godsdienstig leven onzer vaderen in de vijftiende eeuw*, I, pp. 167-179.

long period, even though he sometimes spoke for as long as five hours.

In 1462, Brugman arrived in Amsterdam. The town council was not pleased and sent secret agents to the place where he preached. Once again, Brugman tried to found an Observantine monastery, and the local rulers feared that it might become a rival of the religious institutions already in town. In their report, the agents carefully described Brugman's gestures during the preaching, as well as his popular tone. Brugman held several pieces of paper with rhetorical questions written on them. He took them one by one and read them aloud.

> Am I, Brugman, here to earn some money?
> Do I want to hire a church?
> Do I send the sick far away from me?

As could be expected, Brugman answered these questions in the way the people liked. He pleaded passionately for the cause of the new monastery and finally raised the crucifix that he always brought with him. At this climactic moment, he asked his audience to raise their hands too, if they supported him. They did so in large numbers and some of the more enthusiastic listeners cried that they were willing to die for the cause. Brugman responded that he was also prepared "to lose his old neck" this time.[18] Scenes like this show us how charismatic, lively, successful and – one might say – demagogic Brugman was as a popular preacher. After this visit to Amsterdam, the town council forbade Brugman to return. The Observantine movement, however, remained popular with the ordinary people. Moreover, the present ruler of the Low Countries, Philip the Good (1396-1467) duke of Burgundy, supported the cause. Brugman thus ignored the town council, returned to Amsterdam the same year, and finally opened the Observant monastery. The saying *praten als Brugman* is the sole result of this affair.[19]

Brugman preached to both lay and clerical audiences. He fre-

---

[18] See Lettinck, *Praten als Brugman*, pp. 4-6; Evenhuis, *Ook dat was Amsterdam*, I, pp. 17-18.

[19] Other stories tell how he made peace in Friesland, where two political factions fought a long and rude battle. It is, however, not certain if this is just a legend, made up in later times.

quently stayed in convents during his travels, especially in those run by tertiary nuns.[20] His preaching was widely appreciated there, because of his pious tone and sincere message. Sometimes the nuns wrote down his sermons (most probably afterwards): so the content of some of them has been preserved.[21] Brugman normally preached in his mother tongue, although some of his sermons and his more theological writings have come down to us in Latin.[22] The sermons show that he followed in many ways the homiletic rules and traditions of his time. He typically allegorized the scriptural passage he was explaining: Jerusalem was not just the capital of Israel; it also stood for the Church of Christ or the Heavenly City.

Brugman also used numbers. He chose, for instance, the four wheels on a coach as the theme for a sermon. These wheels were fear, resignation, patience, and love, that together had to carry the souls of the true Christians into heaven. Christ's suffering was another popular theme in his sermons. Brugman painted it in vivid colors and pointed at Christ as the ultimate example, especially for regulars. Sometimes he combined Christ's suffering in a mystical way with almost erotic language. His insistence on the abandonment of all worldly pleasures and a striving for heavenly salvation come through clearly. Similar themes can be found in many other sermons from this period. Brugman's fame as a popular preacher was undoubtedly the result of his personality and charisma.

---

[20]   On the practice of preaching for nuns, who often used manuscripts with sermons for devotional purposes, See R.D. Schwieger, "Sermons for Nuns of the Dominican Observance Movement"; and V.M. O'Mara, "Preaching to nuns in late medieval England," in Carolyn Muessig, ed., *Medieval Monastic Preaching*, Brill's Studies in Intellectual History, no. 90 (Leiden, Boston, Cologne, 1998), pp. 75-119.

[21]   These sermons or fragments of sermons were published relatively late, in the twentieth century. They were found in Franciscan manuscripts, sometimes in several editions. In total, some forty-four sermons are known. See J. Brugman, *Verspreide sermoenen; uitgegeven met inleiding en toelichtingen door dr. A. van Dijk O.F.M.* (Klassieke Galerij, no. 41. (Antwerp, 1948); *Onuitgegeven sermoenen van Jan Brugman O.F.M. Ingeleid en bezorgd door dr. P. Grootens S.J.*, Studiën en tekstuitgaven van Ons Geestelijk Erf, bezorgd door het Ruusbroec-genootschap te Antwerp no. 8. (Tielt, 1948).

[22]   Most of the sermons printed in the Netherlands before 1500 are in Latin, with only a few published in Dutch. The Latin sermons were probably used in monasteries and convents, for study or reading. Many of these are from well-known medieval authors, such as Bernard of Clairvaux (ca.1090-1153) and Bonaventure (ca. 1221-1274).

The Changing Role of Preaching during the Reformation

Although Luther's *Ninety-Five Theses* of 1517 and his later writings did not cause the troubles in the Church in the Low Countries, they surely influenced and accelerated the process. The Dutch Reformation was a long, intense, and complex process that gradually spread over the country and differed from place to place. In the early sixteenth century it was most intense in the industrial city areas of Flanders: around Bruges, Ghent, and Antwerp. After the iconoclastic revolt that took place in the so-called Wonder Year (1566), its focus shifted to the northern parts of the Low Countries. There, the religious troubles were more political and led in 1572 to the Dutch Revolt.

Probably the most intriguing factor of the Reformation in the Low Countries is the fact that it was not, like in many other European areas, a state-organized affair. In many countries, political leaders chose to back the "new" religion, while in the Low Countries the process swelled up from below and was urged on by the masses.[23] Another striking difference was the influence and popularity of humanism in the Low Countries.[24] From the beginning of the sixteenth century, Erasmus (ca. 1466-1536) and his teachings had a stronghold at the University of Louvain, close to Brussels. All kinds of studies were published there, as well as in Antwerp where famous printers like Christopher Plantin (ca. 1520-1589) lived. The high level of urbanization and the relatively good educational system in the Low Countries further enabled many people to learn about the new religious ideas.

An important effect of the Reformation on church service was its attack on the monopoly of the ecclesiastics in matters of worship. With the idea that any Christian is as close to God as an ordained priest, everyone with some religious education could become a preacher and perform his own ceremonies. The sermon could thus become an effective weapon in the "spiritual war" between the

---

[23]   See Israel, *The Dutch Republic*, pp. 74-105. See also: J. Decavele, "Ontstaan van de evangelische beweging en ontwikkeling van de protestantse kerkverbanden in de Nederlanden tot 1580", in *Ketters en papen onder Filips II; het godsdienstig leven in de tweede helft van de 16e eeuw* 3th impr. (Utrecht, 1986), pp. 41-57. Also informative is A. Duke, *Reformation and Revolt in the Low Countries* (London, Ronceverte, 1990).

[24]   See Israel, *The Dutch Republic*, pp. 41-54; Duke, *Reformation and Revolt*, pp. 1-28.

"old" and the "new" religion.[25] It would be used extensively by both Catholics and Protestants in order to promote their ways of thinking. For the reformers, it was probably the most valuable mass medium of communication, apart from their many illegal publications.[26] Initially, some Catholic priests preached in favor of the new religious ideas; more often, however, they would oppose the heretics.[27]

In October, 1520 Nikolaas Baechem (†1526), a Louvain professor, fiercely attacked Luther in a sermon held at the university. In his fulmination, he warned the audience not just against the fallacies of the German monk, but also against Erasmus who at that time had published a critical edition of the New Testament.[28] Such outspoken sermons could lead to fierce reactions. In the town of Dordrecht, a Dominican doctor preached in a similar way and was attacked by an angry crowd.[29] The Catholic clergy was at this time still viewed as the sole possessor of the Word of God, as delivered from the pulpit. They soon had to compete with several rivals who had to deliver their sermons in secret, for the "new" religion had to stay underground during the first decades of the Reformation. In this stage of the religious revolt, the risk was simply too high for the "heretic" preachers and their followers to express their opinions publicly.[30]

---

[25] See C. Augustijn, "Godsdienst in de zestiende eeuw", in *Ketters en papen onder Filips II*, pp. 26-40; here pp. 26-28.

[26] Some of these publications were sermons. Promptly–in 1520–several sermons of Luther were translated into Dutch and printed in the Low Countries. Often these publications were published secretly; sometimes this could be done more openly outside the country. See for instance Andrew Pettegree, *Emden and the Dutch Revolt; Exile and the Development of Reformed Protestantism* (Oxford, 1992), pp. 87-108.

[27] Jacob Praepostius was prior of the Augustinians at Antwerp and a student of Luther. In his sermons, he criticized the church in a similar manner to Luther. However, he had to retract his opinions. In the city of Amsterdam, a heretic priest, who had a great many listeners, was caught and sentenced to death by the Inquisition. See Evenhuis, *Ook dat was Amsterdam*, pp. 20-21. Many other examples of Catholic clergy preaching in favor of the new religious ideas are given in Duke, *Reformation and Revolt*, pp. 36, 52-53.

[28] See Augustijn, "Godsdienst in de zestiende eeuw", p. 28. Augustijn quotes Erasmus, who wrote about this incident in one of his letters.

[29] There were many more incidents all over the country, especially against mendicants and Grey Friars. See Duke, *Reformation and Revolt*, pp. 34-35, 75.

[30] Secret meetings and conventicles reportedly arose around 1524. Normally people gathered for reading and discussing the Bible. Sometimes lay preachers presided at these meetings. See Duke, *Reformation and Revolt*, pp. 36-38.

In 1520, Emperor Charles V took drastic measures against the new heretics in the Low Countries. Their books were burned; two years later an Inquisition was installed that in many aspects conformed to the organization already active in Spain. The first victims of this soon very unpopular Inquisition were two Augustinian friars at 's-Hertogenbosch who were sentenced within a year and burnt to death in Brussels. The impact of these executions on public opinion was immense. The reform movement was forced to go underground, and many followers went abroad, where they founded refugee churches, for instance in London and in the north German town of Emden.[31] There they were able to work freely on their theology, to build up an organization and to experiment openly with new types of worship.

The Catholic mass was rejected by the new theologians as an all-too-magical ceremony, as were many other sacraments. Instead of the traditional sacraments, the reformers returned to the true Word of God as they saw it: in other words the explanation of the Scriptures. Preaching thus became more important than ever in the newly-founded churches.[32] All kinds of people in the Low Countries, including quite a few members of the elite, sympathized with the new developments. Gradually they had lost confidence in the Catholic Church, not least because of its fierce persecution, and many shifted towards new ways of religious thinking. These people formed a network of undercover crypto-Protestants in the country, who used other types of gathering such as the Chambers of Rhetoric to express their opinions.[33]

It was in this atmosphere of repression and clandestine gathering that new religious groups appeared, the first of which were the Anabaptists. In some parts of the country, where the Habsburg regime was only installed in 1536 (like Groningen), they could gather more or less freely and listen at night in the countryside to self-appointed chiliast prophets.[34] In these rather peculiar meet-

---

[31]   See Andrew Pettegree, *Foreign Protestant Communities in Sixteenth-Century London* (Oxford, 1986); and by the same author: *Emden and the Dutch Revolt*.

[32]   See Pettegree, *Foreign Protestant Communities*, pp. 63-67.

[33]   See, for instance, G. Marnef, *Antwerp in the Age of Reformation: Underground Protestantism in a Commercial Metropolis 1550-1577*, trans. J.C. Grayson (Baltimore and London: Johns Hopkins University Press, 1996), pp. 29-33.

[34]   Some thousand people attended these meetings. The prophets preached that Christ was not the Messiah and therefore the Old Testament religion was still in order.

ings, the prophets predicted the end of times, tried to heal sick people and even led some of their listeners to circumcision. Their message was utterly violent. "Kill, kill the monks and the papacy! Kill
the governments all over the world and particularly our government! Convert yourselves, convert yourselves: their salvation is at
hand now and here, their salvation is at hand…"

In 1534, many of these radical Protestants, full of apocalyptic
dreams, came out into the open and acted as their prophets had
instructed them.[35] They captured the German town of Münster,
turned it into a theocracy and drove away the bishop. Their dream
did not last long, for within a year they were besieged and their
movement was fiercely persecuted. More than 2000 Anabaptists
were executed – some two-thirds of all Inquisition victims in the
Low Countries (an extremely high number in comparison to other
European countries).[36] The Anabaptists recovered under new leadership, as Menno Simons (1496-1561) gave the remainder a more
peaceful aspect and a new organization. They gathered in secret
congregations, on ships or in houses, where they read the Scriptures, sang religious songs and occasionally delivered sermons.

In these chaotic times the Anabaptists were not the only religious
group that practiced clandestinely. All kinds of libertine preachers
and sects were active in the Low Countries, often working on their
own initiative and completely isolated.[37] Others, mostly members
of the elite, had similar intentions and followed spiritual leaders
such as David Joris (1501-1556) and Hendrick Niclaes (1502-ca.
1580), who claimed to be empowered prophets. Their followers had
their own, more hidden network, as they were often quite well-to-
do and well educated. Apart from these particular groups, they

---

See A.F. Mellink, *De wederdopers in de noordelijke Nederlanden, 1531-1544* (Leeuwarden,
1981) repr. of the 1954 Groningen edition, pp. 254-269.

[35]   Many of these came from Holland, where some similar incidents occurred. In
Amsterdam, some people walked naked in the streets and prophesied the end of times.
See Mellink, *De wederdopers in de noordelijk Nederlanden, 1531-1544* ; see by the same au-
thor: *Amsterdam en de wederdopers in de zestiende eeuw* (Nijmegen, 1978), pp. 27-76.

[36]   See Groenveld, *Delta: Nederlands verleden in vogelvlucht*, II, p. 55. Jonathan Israel
mentions a total of about 2,500 victims. See Israel, *The Dutch Republic*, p. 100. More
detailed information on the Inquisition and its victims can be found in Duke, *Reformation
and Revolt*, pp. 71-100, 152-174.

[37]   P.M. Crew, *Calvinist Preaching and Iconoclasm in the Netherlands, 1544-1569*, Cambridge Studies in Early Modern History (Cambridge, 1978), pp. 58-63. For the case of
some preachers active around the city of Maastricht, see W. Bax, *Het protestantisme in het
bisdom Luik en vooral te Maastricht, 1505-1557* ('s-Gravenhage 1937), pp. 42-75.

were seldom organized and never intended to build new congregations.

In the refugee churches at Emden and London, as well as in areas around these churches, several types of Protestants came together openly. Many debates were held in these circles, where some
refugees studied theology and became learned preachers. As a result of these discussions as well as foreign influences, the churches
developed around 1550 a better type of organization and more
doctrinal coherence.[38] The foreign influence came mainly from
German and Franco-Swiss Protestants, especially from those living
in Geneva under the leadership of the French reformer John Calvin
(1509-1564). Churches organized in this way were built up from
below – around the local congregation that formed a more or less
independent institution. All congregations were linked together in
synods and shared a generally accepted confession of faith. This
new – Calvinist – type of Protestantism appealed to many people in
the Low Countries, who were looking for some kind of unity in the
existing religious chaos. Calvinism soon became popular and gradually spread throughout the region. In several places it led to the
founding of secret congregations (churches "under the cross"),
linked together in a tight network.[39] From time to time, Protestant
ministers traveled through the Low Countries and visited the newly
founded underground groups, mostly just small conventicles.[40]
These ministers could not, however, be too open, and thus their
role as preachers was limited.

Hedge Preaching and Iconoclasm in the Year 1566

The Protestant ministers did not stay underground all the time.
Sometimes they gathered their people secretly every Sunday and
occasionally they even disturbed Catholic ceremonies.[41] It would

---

[38]   See Pettegree, *Emden and the Dutch Revolt*, pp. 57-86.
[39]   For the situation in Antwerp, the biggest city in this period, which had a substantial underground religion, Marnef, *Antwerp in the age of Reformation*, pp. 133-152.
[40]   Crew, *Calvinist Preaching and Iconoclasm in the Netherlands*, pp. 51-64.
[41]   The Calvinist minister of Antwerp, Adriaan van Haemstede, set up weekly
religious meetings around 1550. In 1558, he preached openly on a street corner during
a religious procession. See Crew, *Calvinist Preaching and Iconoclasm in the Netherlands*, pp. 66-

however take until 1560 before the ministers started to work more openly. During the iconoclastic revolt of 1566 (the so-called *beeldenstorm*), this process would increase and bring the clandestine preachers to the peak of their power. This sudden rise of Protestant preaching was the result of the "Moderation" of April 1566, a decision taken by Margaret of Parma (1522-1586), at that time regent of the Low Countries, to suspend the edicts concerning the Inquisition and other measures against the heretics. A soon as this decision was taken, Calvinist ministers, coming from refugee churches abroad, entered the country and started to preach publicly outside the towns. These religious meetings were held in the open air and were therefore called hedge-preachings or *prêches.* They would soon become immensely popular and would deeply influence the course of the religious revolt, not least as they resulted in iconoclasm.

In 1562, a Calvinist preacher from London was the first to deliver a sermon publicly in a little village in West Flanders. Leaflets were distributed to inform the people of this occasion. The service started at nine o'clock in the morning, was held in a churchyard and lasted two hours. Meanwhile – it was Sunday – a priest was conducting mass inside the church next to the cemetery. The Calvinist minister was obviously eager for a confrontation. He stood on a bench, surrounded by a crowd that was armed with knives and sticks. Some two hundred people attended this meeting, which included psalm-singing and public prayers. In 1562, such a public service was still a dangerous act, as ninety-three of the listeners were prosecuted for their attendance and at least nine of them were executed.[42] Despite these dangers hedge-preaching became steadily more popular, particularly in the summer of 1566 when people expected toleration to be the new official line. Initially these meetings were only attended by small numbers of people who often belonged to the lower classes. But rapidly this changed and the hedge-preachings became a mass movement, as we learn from the reports of eye-witnesses.

> As on Saturday last, [there] was a proclamation… that no man should go to the sermons upon pain of hanging; whereupon on Sunday…

67; Marnef, *Antwerp in the Age of Reformation*, p. 67; Augustijn, "Godsdienst in de zestiende eeuw", p. 32.

[42] See Crew, *Calvinist Preaching and Iconoclasm in the Netherlands*, pp. 67-68; Augustijn, "Godsdienst in de zestiende eeuw", pp. 28, 32.

[there] went out of the town... above sixteen thousand persons, all with their weapons in battle array; and so, after the sermon [they] returned to the town, and went to the high bailiff's house (who had taken one preacher prisoner two or three days before) and commanded him to deliver the prisoner; which he refused. Whereupon they went to the prison and broke it, and delivered the preacher; and so, everyone departed.[43]

The report makes clear how the hedge-preachings formed a signal for many Protestant sympathizers to come out into the open. It further shows how this soon led to radicalism and violence. Initially, however, the open-air meetings were peaceful and rather improvised gatherings. At Ghent for instance the preacher stood on the ladder of a mill, using it as a pulpit. He spoke in a Flemish dialect, was bareheaded and dressed in grey. Occasionally, he read a text from the book he was holding, admonishing sinners and praying for the enlightenment of the king and the pope. The congregation sat in rows, divided into three groups of about thirty each, with each holding a booklet of psalms that sold for a *denier*.[44] Contemporaries were most astonished by the increasing popularity of the meetings, for they soon attracted not just thousands of people but also many respectable citizens. Estimates of the attendance run from 7000 to 14,000 listeners and even numbers like 25,000 are mentioned.[45] Many of these listeners came armed to the illegal meetings, just in case some danger should occur during their gathering. Among them were men sitting on horseback, gentlemen, city notables, etc. The hedge-preachings thus attracted a wide range of people from all classes of society. Outside the town of Ghent there were at a certain time as many as three places where the meetings were held.[46]

As the hedge-preachings gained popularity all over the Low

---

[43]   The report is from Richard Clough, an Englishman living in Antwerp in 1566. Quoted in Crew, *Calvinist Preaching and Iconoclasm in the Netherlands*, p. 9.

[44]   See Crew, *Calvinist Preaching and Iconoclasm in the Netherlands*, p. 8.

[45]   The hedge preachings were most popular in Flanders, but later they spread throughout the country. In Antwerp, the hedge preachings attracted some 4000-5000 listeners in May and June. By July, the attendance grew to 25,000. See Pettegree, *Emden and the Dutch Revolt*, pp. 114-115; Marnef, *Antwerp in the Age of Reformation*, pp. 57, 88-105. In Holland, where the scale of the hedge preachings was never this large, the first meeting was held outside the city of Hoorn in July. Later there were also meetings in the direct surroundings of Amsterdam with circa 5000 listeners. See Evenhuis, *Ook dat was Amsterdam*, I, pp. 51-56.

[46]   See Decavele, "Ontstaan van de evangelische beweging", p. 53.

Countries the people who organized them increasingly demanded freedom of worship. The eyewitness report quoted earlier already showed how this sometimes led to openly aggressive actions. Protestants resisted the local government and tried to free preachers or other sympathizers from jail. Although these actions differed in intention and aggression, they formed a clear sign of the enormous change of mind that had taken place.[47] Sometimes Protestants started to demand the use of churches for their services; and on some occasions they even captured a church violently.[48] In August, 1566 these activities would culminate and evolve in genuinely violent actions against church property: the so-called *beeldenstorm*.[49] During these iconoclastic actions, churches were attacked and images and paintings inside were smashed or destroyed. The actions originated in West Flanders and were to become the most violent in the southern provinces of Flanders and Brabant, particularly in Antwerp.[50] Later, they also spread to the north of the Low Countries, where small groups of Protestants attacked church interiors.

In some places, Catholics resisted the Protestant challenge, but far more often there was no response at all, and many local officials condoned or sometimes even supported the stripping of the churches.[51] Historians ever since have debated the significance of these actions – whether they were just public riots in connection with economic decay, a Calvinist plot, or maybe an act of magic – however they always underline the religious background of this strange sudden outbreak of violence.[52] Iconoclasm turned out to be

---

[47]   See Crew, *Calvinist Preaching and Iconoclasm in the Netherlands*, pp. 5-20.

[48]   The first occurred in some places in Holland, especially in autumn when the weather became too bad for outdoor services. See Duke, *Reformation and Revolt*, pp. 137-139. The last occurred in the city of Maastricht, where armed Calvinists captured two churches in the center of town. See W. Bax, *Het protestantisme in het bisdom Luik en vooral te Maastricht, 1557-1612* ('s-Gravenhage, 1941), pp. 101-137.

[49]   See Israel, *The Dutch Republic*, pp. 147-152. See also Duke, *Reformation and Revolt*, pp. 125-151.

[50]   See Marnef, *Antwerp in the Age of Reformation*, pp. 88-105.

[51]   See Israel, *The Dutch Republic*, pp. 150-151.

[52]   See ibid., 148-149; Crew, *Calvinist Preaching and Iconoclasm in the Netherlands*, pp. 20-38. Israel is certain that the *beeldenstorm* was "purely and simply an attack on the Church and not anything else." Crew carefully describes all the arguments to call it something else. She shows how the actions were often undertaken by small groups of men at night, describing how they normally did not steal anything and often only cut off the hands and the faces of the images. See also Pettegree, *Emden and the Dutch Revolt*, pp. 109-133. Pettegree agrees with Israel about the religious meaning of the iconoclasm.

the beginning of the Dutch Revolt; they occurred, however, against the backdrop of the expected reaction.

Shortly after the image breaking, King Philip II sent a new, strong, and severe leader to the Low Countries, the duke of Alva (1507-1582), who entered the country with a large military force and an even more severe Inquisition.[53] The resulting repression, the military troops, and Alva's many privileges led to the escalation of the conflict. From this point on the religious revolt turned into a civil war, for some of the towns openly declared themselves in favor of a more tolerant religious policy, while others stayed loyal to the king's hard line in matters of religion. It is not possible to describe the complex later developments here in detail, but the outcome was the independence of the northern provinces of the Low Countries.[54] Initially Alva's troops captured many towns that openly supported the Revolt. Their inhabitants were punished severely, Protestants were executed or driven out of town, and Catholicism was reinstated as the official religion. At this moment, the rebellion seemed in great danger and some 60,000 people saw no other option than to emigrate. They went to Germany and England where they settled around the refugee churches in Emden and London.[55] Alva's strategy appeared highly effective.

In 1572, however a rebel fleet of so-called Sea Beggars (*Gueux*) took by surprise the small but strategically important Dutch town of Brielle. This victory was to become a turning point and the beginning of the freedom of the northern provinces, as the defeat of Alva's troops at Brill encouraged many northern towns to declare themselves independent of the Habsburg regime. Under the leadership of William of Orange (1533-1584) they joined forces and were transformed into a political union that accepted Calvinism as its official religion. During the ongoing battle, the southern parts of the Low Countries remained most firmly in the hands of the king, while the north steadily fought its way into freedom. In the south

---

[53]   See Israel, *The Dutch Republic*, pp. 155-168.

[54]   A detailed report of the conflict and the later developments is given in Israel, *The Dutch Republic*, pp. 169-546.

[55]   See Pettegree, *Emden and the Dutch Revolt*, pp. 147-170. Abel Eppen, a farmer living in the north of the Low Countries, was one of the many fugitives. He wrote a detailed report about his adventures during these years. See W. Bergsma, *De wereld volgens Abel Eppen; een ommelander boer uit de zestiende eeuw*, Fryske Histoaryske Rige no. 3. (Groningen, Leeuwarden, 1988).

the revolt led to a short upsurge of Protestantism in 1577, when Calvinists took over the town of Ghent. Gradually they would take over most of the towns in Flanders, but this was only temporary, for in 1585–with the siege of Antwerp–their last stronghold was lost.[56] Thus in Brabant, Flanders, and the other southern areas, the Habsburg regime was installed for the next several centuries and Catholicism remained the official religion. The north, on the other hand, became a predominantly Protestant country that gradually evolved into the successful Republic of the Seven United Provinces, later called the Netherlands. For 150,000 Protestants in the south, there was no alternative but to move elsewhere: to the north.

The New Status Quo after 1572

One of the principal consequences of the developments in 1572 was the disappearance of the Catholic Church from the north of the Low Countries, where it became illegal, or at least had to go underground. William of Orange favored religious tolerance, but public emotions had risen so high during the civil war that this no longer seemed an option.[57] Thus the mass was forbidden and the Catholic clergy were driven out of the towns. Monasteries and convents were closed, monks and nuns expelled, and traditional ways of worship (pilgrimages, devotion of relics, etc.) abolished.[58] Church property was seized by the town councils and used for secular aims. From now on Calvinism was the prevailing religion in the rebellious state and therefore the church buildings were handed over to its congregations. The churches were stripped – this time

---

[56]   The Reformation in Flanders was in some aspects more radical than in the north of the Low Countries. In the years 1578 and 1579, Flemish Protestantism became the dominant religion of the country, while Catholicism was completely abolished, not just in towns but also in villages in the countryside. In Antwerp circa 50 percent of the population was Protestant; in Ghent the percentage was about 30 percent. See Decavele, "Ontstaan van de evangelische beweging", p. 55.

[57]   From the beginning of the troubles, the Prince of Orange pleaded for religious tolerance and the condoning of both Catholic and Protestant worship. Some years later (in 1578) he proclaimed a "Religious Peace" in Brussels. Disapproval of this peace program by the king as well as by many of the Protestants led to the end of it. See Israel, *The Dutch Republic*, pp. 195, 202-213.

[58]   See J.J. Woltjer, "De religieuze situatie in de eerste jaren van de Republiek", in *Ketters en papen onder Filips II*, pp. 94-106, here pp. 94-95.

officially–and rearranged for the new type of worship that centered around the preaching of the Word of God. Paintings from this early period show the radical nature of the change. Churches had been highly decorated places of worship, full of colors and altars, paintings, relics, and all kinds of devotional objects. Now they were painted white and completely emptied, except for the pulpit, a dozen chairs, a font, and some benches.[59]

The Calvinists not only stripped the churches, but also tried to alter many religious traditions. They wanted for instance to abolish all holidays linked with important Christian events, such as the birthday of a saint or similar occasions. Nevertheless, it took some time before these changes became generally accepted and approved, since the traditions were firmly rooted in society. The first decades of the new state thus formed a transition period in which religious practice gradually changed, while it took a rather long time before things stabilized and a new tradition was established. This gradual change in matters of religion, in contrast to the fast political developments of these years, is one of the characteristics of the Dutch Revolt. The society of the new state could hardly keep up with the speed of the developments and changes.[60] When the "old" religion was forbidden in 1572, Dutch society lost at once its former public church, along with its institutions and staff. The Calvinist public church was still under construction. However, it lacked a learned ministry and did not appeal to all of the population. The chaotic religious situation that emerged from these developments influenced people within and outside the newly installed public church, for the Reformed ministers had to face the frustrating paradox that their church services did not attract great numbers, while Catholicism was fairly nonexistent or led a secret, hidden life. Not surprisingly the religious situation after 1572 has been characterised as an "ecclesiastical vacuum".[61]

---

[59]   See, for instance, the reproduction of a painting of a church interior (opposite the title page) in W. Bergsma, *Tussen Gideonsbende en publieke kerk; een studie over het gereformeerd protestantisme in Friesland, 1580-1650*, Fryske Histoaryske Rige, no. 17 (Hilversum, Leeuwarden, 1999). See also G.D.J Schotel and H.C. Rogge, *De openbare eeredienst der Nederl. Hervormde kerk in de zestiende, zeventiende en achttiende eeuw*, 2nd enl. impr. (Leiden, 1906).

[60]   See Duke, *Reformation and Revolt*, pp. 199-226; Bergsma, *Tussen Gideonsbende en publieke kerk*, pp. 405-436; Woltjer, "De religieuze situatie in de eerste jaren van de Republiek", p. 104.

[61]   See Israel, *The Dutch Republic*, p. 363.

In the first decades of the new state, only a small minority of the population belonged to the Calvinist Church. Many people were neither Catholic nor Protestant but adhered to the so-called floating middle group. These people for all intents and purposes lacked any organized religion and thus public worship in fact suffered a severe loss by the Revolt. Preaching had become more important than ever, but–paradoxically–few people attended the services. Often churches stood empty in the towns, with hardly any Calvinist worshippers, nor ministers to conduct the church services. Many towns had but one or two ministers (only a fraction of the former huge numbers of the Catholic clergy).[62] This early group of Protestant ministers formed a very diverse group: many of them lacked a university background, some were former Catholic clergymen, and others self-taught or self-appointed ecclesiastics. This could lead to all kinds of troubles.[63] Only in 1575 was a university founded–in Leiden, where the new ecclesiastical staff of the public Church could be properly trained.[64] Paintings from this early period of the Republic show how chaotic a church service could be in those days. Churches were only partly filled with an audience that was grouped around the pulpit. Some of the audience were sitting, others standing or walking through the church building in which dogs could also be seen. It seems that most of those present were listening, while others talked, fed a child, or slept. Young people sometimes gathered in special areas and the noise they made could disturb the service.[65]

---

[62]   In the town of Dordrecht, two ministers arrived from abroad shortly after the entrance of rebellious troops. Some of the Catholic clergy were either expelled or taken hostage. See F. van Lieburg, "Geloven op vele manieren", in: W. Frijhoff, ed., *Geschiedenis van Dordrecht II; geschiedenis van Dordrecht van 1572 tot 1813* (Hilversum, 1998) pp. 271-304, here pp. 271, 275. The lack of ministers was even worse in the countryside, for instance, in Friesland: see Bergsma, *Tussen Gideonsbende en publieke kerk*, pp. 181-184.

[63]   See Bergsma, *Tussen Gideonsbende en publieke kerk*, pp. 212-215. The first generation of ministers was often in trouble, frequently because of drinking, fighting, and other types of misbehavior. In the province of Friesland, one could become a minister even in 1620 without a university background. See also: A. Th. van Deursen, *Bavianen en slijkgeuzen; kerk en kerkvolk ten tijde van Maurits en Oldenbarnevelt*, 3th impr. (Franeker 1998), pp. 36-37.

[64]   In 1585 a second university was founded in the Friesian town of Franeker. Groningen followed in 1614, later Utrecht as well as Harderwijk. Not surprisingly it took some time before these institutions met the demand for educated ministers.

[65]   See Evenhuis, *Ook dat was Amsterdam*, II, pp. 45-46.

The estimations of the percentage of Church members around 1600 run from five to ten per cent of the total population of the Republic.[66] It took approximately half a century before this percentage increased significantly and people belonging to the floating middle group made up their minds, choosing either the public Church or one of the other denominations. In the town of Dordrecht, for instance, the large majority of the population in 1620 still belonged to no religious denomination.[67] In other towns the situation was similar.[68] We do not know whether these undecided people completely lacked religious organization. Catholicism may no longer have appealed to them as the result of the severe Spanish action during the earlier years of the Revolt. Moreover, there was often no place of worship where the "old religion" could be practiced, depending more or less on the region in which one lived. For many undecided people, however, Calvinism was hardly an alternative, due to its strict doctrine, ethics, and organization. Nevertheless some of these people must have been in contact with the new public Church, where they were baptized and occasionally went to the church services, although they refused to become official members.[69] These people were called *liefhebbers van de gereformeerde religie* ("favorers of the Reformed religion") by the Calvinists.[70] It would take several generations before the majority of them became a member of the public Church.

The process of confessionalization took place mainly in the first half of the seventeenth century, a period of stabilization after the exciting initial years of the Republic. In this period the different religious groups started to profile themselves in order to "win the

---

[66] See Bergsma, *Tussen Gideonsbende en publieke kerk*, pp. 13-18. More detailed information on this subject is available in: J.J. Woltjer, *Friesland in hervormingstijd* Leidse historische reeks, no. 7 (Leiden, 1962). Woltjer states that even in 1620 no more than only one-fifth of the population was a member of the Calvinist Church.

[67] In 1573 the Calvinist Church had only 463 members. One year later there were 536 members, while the total population must have been about 12,000 people. The Catholic Church had some 500 members around 1600, and about 2000 in 1656. See F. van Lieburg, "Geloven op vele manieren", pp. 272-273.

[68] In the city of Haarlem in 1620, half of the population was not a member of any denomination. Only 20 percent belonged to the Calvinist Church, 12.5 percent was Catholic, circa 14 percent was Anabaptist, 1 percent Lutheran and 1 percent belonged to the French-speaking Calvinist Church. See J. Spaans, *Haarlem na de Reformatie; stedelijke cultuur en kerkelijk leven, 1577-1620* ('s-Gravenhage, 1989), p. 104.

[69] See Bergsma, *Tussen Gideonsbende en publieke kerk*, pp. 103-137.

[70] See Van Deursen, *Bavianen en slijkgeuzen*, pp. 128-160.

souls" of the many undecided people.[71] Despite Alva's severe repression, several Protestant groups had survived the later Spanish
period, including the Anabaptists and the Lutherans who formed
important rivals to the public Church. Catholicism on the other
hand – though illegal – was twenty years after the beginning of the
Revolt still present in the Republic. At that time, many people lost
their former aversion against the "old religion," leading to a revival
of Catholicism and the increase of its popularity. All these non-
official religious denominations (the Anabaptists, Lutherans, and
Catholics) were only condoned in the Republic and therefore not
as successful as the official public Church in the process of
confessionalization. Moreover, they had to deliver their church
services in private and in secret or at least in hidden places. Soon,
however, they were allowed to build their own meeting places, secret churches or *schuilkerken*. Public worship was thus delivered at
several places; and sermons in those days could include strong polemical elements, as the ministers stressed the doctrinal differences
between the denominations in order to strengthen the identity of
their congregation.[72]

The relatively peaceful coexistence of all these religious groups
in the Republic led to a colorful practice of worship. Depending on
the region in which one was living it was normally possible to attend several church services. The public Church worshipped not
just on Sundays but also during the rest of the week. On Sunday
there was sometimes an early service, held at six or seven o'clock in
the morning. The regular service started at nine o'clock and an extra service was held in the afternoon. Finally, during the week, one
could attend a service on Wednesday or sometimes on each day of
the week.[73] Was there much attendance at public worship and what
did a Sunday look like in the early seventeenth century? Since the
new public Church acted in cooperation with the authorities, it
could ask them to protect their services, enabling the believers to
worship undisturbed. According to English travelers, the authorities
acted without any zeal. The Netherlands, in those days, was far

---

[71] See W. Nijenhuijs, "De publieke kerk veelkleurig en verdeeld, bevoorrecht en
onvrij" and "Religiegeschiedenis 1621-1648: kerk in meervoud," in *Algemene geschiedenis
der Nederlanden*, VI, pp. 325-343, 397-411, 450-451.

[72] See J. Hartog, *Geschiedenis van de predikkunde en de evangelieprediking* (Amsterdam
1865), pp. 14-88; Evenhuis, *Ook dat was Amsterdam*, II, pp. 30-34.

[73] See Van Deursen, *Bavianen en slijkgeuzen*, pp. 168-171.

from a puritanical country.[74] Around 1600, for instance, attempts to prohibit traveling and sailing on Sundays did not stand a chance. The measurements taken lasted only for the time of the church service. If people had to work on Sundays – in times of harvest or for other special reasons – this was normally no problem. Fishermen were allowed to sail and to sell their products on Sundays. Shops were open, enabling the workers who earned their salary on Saturday evening to do their shopping[75].

The enforcement of the Sunday laws did, however, differ from place to place. On some occasions, an ambitious bailiff arrested someone for a small offense, such as the grazing of an animal, while a more tolerant approach could also be found. Moreover, relaxation formed an even greater threat to church services than working. Pubs were especially popular rivals to the Church. It was forbidden to sell drinks during the time of worship, but this rule was easily bypassed since foreigners were normally permitted to have a "reasonable" drink. Apart from that there were a variety of sports played on Sundays, such as cockfighting, ball games, and not least golf or *kolf* as it was called (one of the most popular sports in the Republic). When the synod of Dordrecht introduced an afternoon service in 1618, it suffered largely from the competition of public recreation. Many laborers had no other day off but Sunday; and since the Sunday laws differed from place to place, town dwellers could go out of town and visit pubs in the countryside.

For the many Dutchmen who sailed abroad, there were other means and methods of worship. Often the captain of a ship possessed a few religious books, such as Bullinger's *Huysboeck*, containing fifty sermons.[76] On Sunday he could improvise a church service by reading one of the sermons and singing a Psalm with the sailors. Sometimes there was even a pastor on the vessel who was able to do this more officially. Usually, these pastors did not have a very good reputation, which is understandable since their job was even less popular and less well paid than that of a simple minister in a little village in the homeland. Nevertheless, travel journals tell us

---

[74] Ibid., pp. 26-33, 169.

[75] See Evenhuis, *Ook dat was Amsterdam*, II, pp. 42-45.

[76] Johann Heinrich Bullinger (1504-1577) was an important theologian during the Reformation. His *Sermones decades* or *Huysboeck. Vijf decades, dat is, Vijftich sermoonen van de voorneemste hoofdstucken der christelijcker religie* was printed nine times in the period 1563 to 1612; it was one of the most popular sermon books in the Protestant Republic.

how seriously they sometimes took their duties.[77] In 1598, a ship sailing to the East Indies (the present state of Indonesia) anchored on a Sunday in a little bay off an island. The reverent Philips Pietersen of Delft, a sound and pious man, held two sermons that day on the beach. In the morning he preached the first part to the sailors, and in the afternoon he did it for the rest of the men. Pietersen preached *seer straffelijk, niemand ontsiende* (severely, and not sparing anyone) according to the journal. In the afternoon, he baptized a local resident as well as two of the sailors.

In the Dutch colonies, normally the same traditions were maintained as in the motherland. Thus, in New Amsterdam, the small Dutch stronghold on Manhattan (with no more than just a few hundred inhabitants), church services were held in exactly the same way as in the Netherlands. Here we see how the close links between the government and the public Church could lead to conflicts, for the minister of this small community came into conflict with the director of the colony. The minister, Everhardus Bogardus (1607-1647) fiercely attacked and criticized the director Willem Kieft (†1647) in his sermons. Their dispute was about leadership in the colony and about a brutal war against the native population. Bogardus used his influence in the community to oppose the director by fulminating against him in his sermons. When he excommunicated Kieft from the Lord's Supper, their conflict was complete. Kieft, in his turn, tried to disturb the church services, in order to isolate the minister from his audience. The church in the little Manhattan colony was located near the fortress, the center of military power. Everyone coming to church was looked at and teased by the soldiers. Kieft further ordered his troops to make as much noise as possible during the services conducted by his enemy.[78] Thus soldiers were beating drums and shooting guns, playing skittles, stumping, dancing, singing, and jumping. Without any doubt, this was an extreme situation. It would later come to an end when both Kieft and Bogardus went to the Netherlands to bring their dispute to court. When their ship was shipwrecked off the English coast, both men drowned.

---

[77] See *Begin ende voortgangh, van de Vereenighde Nederlantsche Geoctroyeerde Oost-Indische Compagnie* (Amsterdam, 1646), p. 5.

[78] See W. Frijhoff, *Wegen van Evert Willemsz: Een Hollands weeskind op zoek naar zichzelf, 1607-1647* (Sun Memoria III) (Nijmegen, 1995), pp. 564-794; here p. 745.

Conclusion

As we have seen, enormous changes took place in the Low Countries during the period from 1450 to 1650, and religion played an important role in this process. Changing ideas about religion led to a civil war that resulted in the birth and the rise of a new nation: the Dutch Republic. Preaching was an aspect of worship both in the early period—when the Low Countries were still united—as well as later in the newly-founded Dutch state (and in the southern part of the Low Countries). Nevertheless, the role of the sermon changed dramatically in the period described here. Initially preaching was just an element in the colorful and diverse medieval religious practice; later it was to become the center of worship. The mendicant Brugman was in a way a unique phenomenon with only a short, temporary effect on the religious practice of his times. Likewise, the hedge preachings formed just an incident and an important element in the Dutch Revolt, having both a political and a religious function. These preliminary "incidents" (both Brugman and the hedge-preachings) were to be followed up by a more broadly accepted religious practice: the preaching by the Protestant ministers who served their country as its sole religious staff (and conscience). In the seventeenth century and afterwards, public worship became steadily more and more installed as a stable national tradition, involving large parts of society. Churches were re-furnished with benches and other signs that symbolized society's hierarchy. This development made the church service an increasingly organized moment of worship, that lost its improvised and rather chaotic character of the late sixteenth century. In the second half of the seventeenth century, Church membership would increase till finally every citizen was absorbed by the new religious order.[79]

Bibliography

Algemene geschiedenis der Nederlanden, 4: Middeleeuwen (Haarlem, 1980).
Algemene geschiedenis der Nederlanden, 5-6: Nieuwe tijd (Haarlem, 1979-1980).

---

[79] The public Church contained at last some 60 per cent of the population as members. More than 30 percent were Catholic and the rest of the population belonged to the smaller religious denominations.

Bax, W., *Het protestantisme in het bisdom Luik en vooral te Maastricht, 1505-1557* ('s-Gravenhage, 1937).

— *Het protestantisme in het bisdom Luik en vooral te Maastricht, 1557-1612* ('s-Gravenhage, 1941).

Begin ende voortgangh, van de Vereenighde Nederlantsche Geoctroyeerde Oost-Indische Compagnie (Amsterdam, 1646).

Bergsma, W., *De wereld volgens Abel Eppens; een ommelander boer uit de zestiende eeuw* (Fryske Histoaryske Rige III) (Groningen, Leeuwarden, 1988).

— *Tussen Gideonsbende en publieke kerk; een studie over het gereformeerd protestantisme in Friesland, 1580-1650* (Fryske Histoaryske Rige XVII) (Hilversum, Leeuwarden, 1999).

Boer, D.E.H. de (ed.), *Delta: Nederlands verleden in vogelvlucht, I: De Middeleeuwen 300-1500* (Leiden, Antwerpen, 1992).

Brugman, J., *Onuitgegeven sermoenen van Jan Brugman O.F.M. Ingeleid en bezorgd door dr. P. Grootens S.J.* (Studiën en tekstuitgaven van Ons Geestelijk Erf, bezorgd door het Ruusbroec-genootschap te Antwerpen VIII) (Tielt, 1948).

— *Verspreide sermoenen; uitgegeven met inleiding en toelichtingen door dr. A. van Dijk O.F.M.* (Klassieke galerij 41) (Antwerpen, 1948).

Crew, P.M., *Calvinist Preaching and Iconoclasm in the Netherlands, 1544-1569* (Cambridge Studies in Early Modern History) (Cambridge, 1978).

Deursen, A.Th. van, *Bavianen en slijkgeuzen; kerk en kerkvolk ten tijde van Maurits en Oldenbarnevelt*, 3rd impr. (Franeker, 1998).

Duke, A., *Reformation and Revolt in the Low Countries* (London, Ronceverte, 1990).

Evenhuis, R.B., *Ook dat was Amsterdam; de kerk der hervorming in de goude eeuw*, 2 vols. (Amsterdam, 1965-1967).

Frijhoff, W., *Wegen van Evert Willemsz.: Een Hollands weeskind op zoek naar zichzelf, 1607-1647* (Sun Memoria III) (Nijmegen, 1995).

— (ed.), *Geschiedenis van Dordrecht II; geschiedenis van Dordrecht van 1572 tot 1813* (Hilversum, 1998).

Groenveld, S. and Schutte, G.J., *Delta: Nederlands verleden in vogelvlucht, II: De nieuwe tijd 1500-1813* (Leiden, Antwerpen, 1992).

Hartog, J., *Geschiedenis van de predikkunde en de evangelieprediking* (Amsterdam, 1865).

Herwaarden, J. van (ed.), *Geschiedenis van Dordrecht I; geschiedenis van Dordrecht tot 1572* (Hilversum, 1996).

Hombergh, F.A.H. van den, *Leven en werk van Jan Brugman O.F.M.; met een uitgave van twee van zijn tractaten* (Groningen, 1967).

Huizinga, J., *The Waning of the Middle Ages* (Harmondsworth, 1965) [transl. of *Herfstij der Middeleeuwen* (Haarlem, 1919)].

Israel, J., *The Dutch Republic; Its Rise, Greatness, and Fall, 1477-1806* (Oxford, 1995).

Ketters en papen onder Filips II; het godsdienstig leven in de tweede helft van de 16e eeuw, 3rd impr. (Utrecht, 1986).

Lettinck, N., *Praten als Brugman; de wereld van een Nederlandse volksprediker aan het einde van de Middeleeuwen* (Hilversum, 1999).

Marnef, G., *Antwerp in the Age of Reformation; Underground Protestantism in a Commercial Metropolis 1550-1577*, trans. by J.C. Crayson (Baltimore and London: Johns Hopkins University Press, 114th ser., I, 1996).

Mellink, A.F., *De wederdopers in de noordelijke Nederlanden, 1531-1544* (Leeuwarden, 1981) reprint of the Groningen, 1954, edition.

— *Amsterdam en de wederdopers in de zestiende eeuw* (Nijmegen, 1978).

Moll, W., *Johannes Brugman en het godsdienstig leven onzer vaderen in de vijftiende eeuw* 2 vols. (Amsterdam, 1854).

— *Kerkgeschiedenis van Nederland vóór de Reformatie*, 5 vols. (Arnhem, Utrecht, 1864-1871).

Muessig, C., *Medieval Monastic Preaching* (Brill's Studies in Intellectual History, vol. 90) (Leiden, Boston, Köln, 1998).

Pettegree, A., *Foreign Protestant Communities in Sixteenth-Century London* (Oxford, 1986).

— *Emden and the Dutch Revolt; Exile and the Development of Reformed Protestantism* (Oxford, 1992).

— *Kerkelijke verhoudingen in Nederland vóór de Reformatie, van ± 1500 tot ± 1580* (Utrecht, Antwerpen, 1954).

— *Kerkgeschiedenis van Nederland in de Middeleeuwen* 2 vols. (Utrecht, Antwerpen, 1957).

— *The Modern Devotion: Confrontation with Reformation and Humanism* (Studies in Medieval and Reformation Thought, 3) (Leiden, 1968).

Schotel, G.D.J. & Rogge, H.C., *De openbare eeredienst der Nederl. Hervormde kerk in de zestiende, zeventiende en achttiende eeuw*, 2nd enl. impr. (Leiden, [1906]).

Spaans, J., *Haarlem na de Reformatie; stedelijke cultuur en kerkelijk leven, 1577-1620* ('s-Gravenhage, 1989).

Woltjer, J.J., *Friesland in hervormingstijd* (Leidse historische reeks VII) (Leiden, 1962).

Wouters, A.Ph.F. and Abels, P.H.A.M., *Nieuw en ongezien; kerk en samenleving in de classis Delft en Delfland 1572-1621*, 2 vols. (Delft, 1994).

Zieleman, G.C., *Middelnederlandse epistel- en evangeliepreken* (Leiden, 1978).

PART THREE

PREACHING AND THE GEOGRAPHY OF
THE REFORMATIONS

CHAPTER ELEVEN

RAMIFICATIONS OF LATE MEDIEVAL PREACHING: VARIED RECEPTIVITY TO THE PROTESTANT REFORMATION

Anne T. Thayer
(Lancaster Theological Seminary)

What difference does preaching make? Do people attend to what their preachers say and shape their beliefs and behaviors as a result? If so, can we as historians recognize the ramifications of preaching? For instance, in that great cluster of changes known as the Reformation, can we discern people acting on the religious understandings inculcated by preachers in previous decades? In this chapter, I will argue that this is indeed the case. Specifically, I offer evidence that the varied penitential teachings of late medieval preachers contributed to the diverse religious outcomes of the Reformation, encouraging its establishment in some areas, fostering its repudiation in others.[1]

Penitence commends itself as a fruitful locus for the investigation of the influence of preaching in these patterns of religious change. Annual confession, followed by communion, was the major ecclesiastical obligation for late medieval lay people. Preachers devoted themselves to moving their listeners to take up the penitential process of contrition, confession, and satisfaction to gain forgiveness of their sins. Although particularly stressed in Lent, the sacrament of penance was seen as an appropriate topic for preaching at any time during the liturgical year. More widely, penitence was a vital feature of late medieval religious culture as evinced by the many institutions, materials, and practices that were infused with a penitential spirit, including ecclesiastical legislation, books for clergy and laity,

---

[1] An earlier version of this paper was presented at the Sixteenth Century Studies Conference, St. Louis, Missouri, October, 1996.

visitation reports, catechetical instruction, pilgrimages, endowed masses, indulgences, new church construction, various forms of piety on behalf of the dead, and the cult of the saints.

Penitence was also a major focus of attention in the Reformation, drawing the ire of reformers and their followers, while serving as a test of Catholic orthodoxy. Luther detested the late medieval sacrament of penance and attacked it on both pastoral and theological grounds. Protestant pamphleteers assaulted confession as a tool of unwarranted clerical domination. Protestant city councils labored to eradicate Catholic penitential practices, even as they sought to put evangelical alternatives in place. Catholics, in turn, reasserted the validity and necessity of the sacrament of penance and succeeded in reinvigorating many traditional penitential forms. Frequent recourse to confession came to be a mark of piety and a favored tool of spiritual growth. For both Catholics and Protestants, penitential issues played a leading role in self-definition and communal identity.[2]

In order to learn how penitence was preached to the laity prior to the Reformation, we might examine the sermons of famous penitential preachers, such as Vincent Ferrer or Bernardino of Siena, whose preaching missions were notable public events in the fifteenth century. Travelling with an entourage of confessors, such preachers sought to bring about immediate repentance and confession. However, more typical and more influential in shaping lay understanding was the ongoing Sunday, and occasional weekday, preaching provided by both the secular clergy and the mendicants in these years. As David d'Avray writes,

> The long term impact on the mind of at least a significant proportion of the listeners was probably much greater than that of the revivalist sermons. It might be described as the drip-drip method of inculcating beliefs. The same or similar *topoi* would be greatly repeated year in, year out, and eventually they would become assumptions.[3]

---

[2] This is a major thesis of Katharine Jackson Lualdi and Anne T. Thayer, eds., *Penitence in the Age of Reformations* (Aldershot: Ashgate, 2000).

[3] Nicole Bériou and David L. d'Avray, *Modern Questions about Medieval Sermons, Essays on Marriage, Death, History and Sanctity*, Società internazionale per lo studio del medioevo latino: Biblioteca di medioevo latino 11 (Spoleto: Centro Italiano di Studi Sull'alto Medioevo, 1994), p. 9.

The ideas taught in regular preaching provided the religious and mental equipment with which people made sense of their lives and evaluated, and sometimes adopted, new understandings.

Model sermon collections give us access to these ideas. These books of sermons for the Sundays and major celebrations of the liturgical year (*sermones de tempore*) and for the feasts of the saints (*sermones de sanctis*) were in widespread use on the eve of the Reformation. While written for the clergy, and indeed often providing their users with a basic theological and ecclesiastical education, their content was largely intended for dissemination to the laity. They convey the essence of what was considered worth preaching in a very usable form. These books could be employed in a variety of ways. A preacher could translate a given sermon from Latin into the vernacular and preach it largely as written. He could read sermons in the collection to help inspire his own sermon writing. He could mine the collection for scriptural interpretations and illustrative anecdotes; the printed collections often came with extensive finding aids to facilitate such usage. Model sermon collections do not enable us to know exactly what was preached when, where, by whom, or to whom, but they do give us excellent access to the ideas in circulation from which many preachers were regularly drawing inspiration. This is particularly true of cities and towns (where, importantly, the Reformation's fate was largely determined).

The advent of printing greatly increased the availability of model sermon collections to preachers. The numbers of editions of individual collections printed indicate which ones were in greatest demand, while their printing locations provide a guide to the geographical range of their popularity. Printers printed what they thought they could sell and reprinted what actually did sell. While some collections were in print all over Europe, others were printed predominantly in one region, suggesting a more localized demand. Here works of local authors and works congenial to regional religious traditions were often reprinted and these, in turn, reinforced local preferences.

In order to study "typical" preaching on penitence and test for its subsequent influence in the era of the Reformation, I have selected a group of ten model sermon collections that were frequently reprinted between 1450 and 1520. (See Table.) Three of these were in print across Europe while the others were printed more region-

Table: Selected Popular Model Sermon Collections

Number of Printed Editions, 1450-1520

Rigorist Collections:	Total	Empire	Italy	France	Switzerland	Netherlands	England	Unknown
*Johannes Herolt, OP *Sermones discipuli de tempore et de sanctis*	84	44	1	30	2	2	1	4
*Johannes of Werden, OFM *Sermones dormi secure, de tempore et de sanctis*	31	12	0	15	1	1	0	2
"Paratus" *Sermones parati de tempore et de sanctis*	29	21	0	2	0	2	0	4
Michael of Hungary, OFM *Sermones praedicabiles per totum annum*	33	13	0	4	0	11	1	4

Moderate Collections:	Total	Empire	Italy	France	Switzerland	Netherlands	England	Unknown
John Mirk, OSA *Liber Festivalis*	20	0	0	3	0	0	16	1
Gabriel Barletta, OP *Sermones quadragesimales et de sanctis*	19	2	4	12	0	0	0	1
"Meffreth" (Petrus Meffordis of Leipzig?), secular? *Ortulus reginae (de tempore et de sanctis)*	15	5	1	0	7	0	0	2

Absolutionist Collections:	Total	Empire	Italy	France	Switzerland	Netherlands	England	Unknown
*Roberto Caracciolo, OFM *Quadragesimale de poenitentia*	28	7	13	4	4	0	0	0
Olivier Maillard, OFM *Sermones dominicales*	11	3	0	8	0	0	0	0
Gregorius Britannicus, OP *Sermones funebres et nuptiales*	10	0	9	0	0	0	0	1

*Collections with international popularity

ally, making it possible to assess what was commonly taught and what was distinctive to particular regions. These sources lead me to the conclusion that the preaching of penitence had discernibly different characters in various parts of Europe in the decades prior to the Reformation, and that these differences had real historical ramifications in subsequent years.

The Consensus

Although this study focuses on differences among the sermon collections, all across Europe preachers shared important basic understandings of the penitential process and conveyed important common expectations for penitents. When baptized Christians commit mortal sin, that is, deliberate and serious sin, it is understood that they incur both guilt (*culpa*), resulting in eternal damnation, and penalty (*pena*), requiring temporal satisfaction. Forgiveness of these sins requires participation in the sacrament of penance, a penitential process involving a combination of divine grace and human effort.[4]

Sinners are to feel sorrow (contrition) over having sinned and resolve to leave their sins behind. Preachers often teach the definition put forward by Aquinas, "Contrition is sorrow voluntarily assumed for sins with the intention to confess and to satisfy."[5] Next, sinners are to make an explicit confession of all their sins to a priest. The Fourth Lateran Council in 1215 made annual confession obligatory for all Christians, a message faithfully passed on in the sermons. The preachers are unanimous in teaching that a good confession is preceded by careful self-examination, omits no sin or pertinent detail, makes an honest self-accusation, and is made with contrition.[6] At the end of the confession, the penitent receives the

---

[4]   Venial sins, less serious sins which did not remove one from a state of grace, were more easily discharged through ordinary pious practices such as worthy reception of the eucharist, sprinkling with holy water, fasting and generous alms, recitation of the Lord's prayer, devout personal confession of the sinner, and the general confession made in church. See for instance, Roberto Caracciolo, O.F.M., *Quadragesimale de poenitentia* (Venice: Bartolomeo de Cremona, 1472), Sermon 28.

[5]   E.g., Johannes of Werden, O.F.M., *Sermones dormi secure de tempore* (Nuremberg: Anton Koberger, 1498), Sermon 39.

[6]   E.g., Johannes Herolt, O.P., *Sermones discipuli de tempore et de sanctis unacum promptuario exemplorum* (Strasbourg: Martin Flach, 1492); used in conjunction with *Sermones*

priest's pronouncement of absolution and reconciliation with the Church. By this stage, eternal guilt is believed to be forgiven. Penitents are then to perform works of satisfaction to pay any remaining temporal penalties for their sin and encourage their progress in virtue. Confessors have a great deal of flexibility in what they may assign to penitents for satisfaction; prayer, fasting, and almsgiving are commonly enjoined. God, in turn, forgives sinners by his mercy and empowers them with spiritual grace to live new lives. No stage in the process was separable from the others; the process as a whole issues in full forgiveness. Even when a preacher stresses one particular aspect of the process over the others, it is as part of the whole that it makes its special contribution to the sinner's reconciliation with God, Church, and neighbor.

Diversity Of Emphasis

Despite the common understanding that penitents proceed from contrition through confession to satisfaction and that this process restores the sinner to grace, divergences in the preachers' theological understandings and rhetorical emphases variously shape the overall character of the penitential message across the sermon collections. Because forgiveness of sins is the crux of the matter, the fundamental differentiating question is, "Where (and how) in the penitential process does the preacher understand forgiveness to take place?" The answer to this question usually corresponds with the part of the process that is most accentuated by the preacher and contributes significantly to the overall penitential tenor of a collection. The teaching given on related issues, such as the amount of spiritual help available to the penitent and the role(s) of the confessor, generally flows from the position taken on this initial question. Based on their characteristic emphases, the ten sermon collections surveyed here cluster into three groups, "absolutionist," "moderate," and "rigorist."

A note of caution is in order – none of the sermon collections considered here offers a rigorously consistent point of view. The authors drew heavily from other sources, with the result that within

---

discipuli de tempore et de sanctis unacum promptuario exemplorum (Reutlingen: Michel Greyff, c. 1479-82); *de tempore*, Sermons 43 and 44.

a given collection, there is a range of teachings and exhortations. Nevertheless, the "drip-drip" method works on even the contemporary reader, and the characteristic thrust of the penitential sermons of each collection emerges.

In their preaching on the penitential process, "absolutionist" sermon collections emphasize confession to such an extent that their direct treatment of contrition and satisfaction becomes minimal. While maintaining the commonly held expectations for the penitent, these sermons are characterized by their high view of the priest's absolving power. This group is led by Roberto Caracciolo, whose *Quadragesimale de poenitentia* was popular in print all over Europe. Also included are the *Sermones dominicales* of Olivier Maillard, popular in France, and the *Sermones funebres et nuptiales* of Gregorius Britannicus, popular in Italy. The overall penitential message of these absolutionist collections is encouraging and helpful. The mercy of God, available in the penitential process, is highlighted to promote the sinner's confidence in forgiveness. This is particularly clear in Caracciolo. A sermon entitled "Concerning the infinite mercy of God by which the Father, most pious and sweet, calls the soul to penitence, even freely promising to all the worst sinners forgiveness and remission," begins, "God, the most pious Father of all, offers sinners the opportunity to return to him, to the everflowing, unfailing, and inexhaustible fountain of his mercy. . ." In the voice of Christ, the preacher urges his audience to listen "so that you may hear me exhorting you to repent and receive forgiveness and release from your sins by my abundant mercy."[7]

Confession is the cornerstone of the penitential process for these preachers. Maillard says,

> Concerning confession, it is to be noted here first of all that it is most necessary that we confess well, because on this hangs our salvation. For it is said in John 20, "Those whose sins you forgive will be forgiven." And this is done in confession. And 1 John 1, "If we confess our sins, God is faithful so that he remits us our sins…".[8]

Confession is crucial because it brings the sin of the penitent into contact with the absolution of the priest. Following Duns Scotus, Maillard teaches that the essence of the sacrament of penance is the

---

[7] Caracciolo, Sermon 4.
[8] Olivier Maillard, O.F.M., *Sermones dominicales* (Paris: Jean Petit, 1511), Sermon 39.

absolution itself.[9] The power of the sacrament of penance, like that of all the sacraments, comes from the passion of Christ. Maillard likens Christ to a doctor who gives a medicine to one who is frequently sick to take whenever he needs to be made well. The medicine with which Christ heals is his blood. In the sacrament of penance, it is applied through the words of absolution of the priest.[10]

Using another curative image, Caracciolo teaches that as the sick had to get into the pool of Siloam by human means in order to obtain divine healing, so the priest delivers the sinner to God by his ministry of absolution. Although God is the efficient cause of the healing of sins, it is to be obtained through the ministry of priests. "Indeed, by the authority conceded to them, they help penitent sinners through absolution so that they might be saved."[11] As is typical among the absolutionists, Caracciolo stresses the establishment of the absolving authority of priests through the power of the keys.

> [Christ] gave them power to judge in the forum of the conscience, not just to the apostles whose successors are the bishops, but also to the other disciples whose successors are the lesser priests. And he gave that power himself directly when after his resurrection he said to them, "The sin of those whom you remit will be remitted to them."[12]

Caracciolo teaches that priests should give the benefit of absolution generously through sacramental penance.[13] The penitent can count on this readily available spiritual power. Indeed, Caracciolo cites peace of mind from the knowledge of forgiveness received as one of the many benefits of confession.[14]

The sacramental absolving power of the priest can make up for the deficiencies of the penitent in the teaching of Maillard and

---

[9]   Maillard, Sermon 2 on penitence. The essence of the sacrament "is the absolution of a penitent made with certain words said with the right intention by a priest having jurisdiction effectively signifying, by divine institution, the absolution of the soul from sin."

[10]   Ibid., Sermon 1 on penitence.

[11]   Caracciolo, Sermon 28, introduction.

[12]   Ibid., Sermon 27, chapter 2.

[13]   Ibid, Sermon 27.

[14]   Ibid, Sermon 28, chapter 1. Caracciolo reiterates Pope Alexander V's list of nine things that confession gives the penitent: knowledge of sin, satisfaction, peace of mind, diminution of penalty, multiplication of intercession, augmentation of grace, remission of guilt, avoidance of further sin, and glorification of God. See also, Gabriel Barletta, O.P., *Sermones (quadragesimales et de sanctis)* (Lyons: Etienne Gueynard, 1507), Sermon 24.

Caracciolo. Although this is not a major point in their sermons, its presence indicates the power they understand to reside in the absolution. A sinner's attrition (inadequate sorrow over sin) is said to be "formed" into contrition by the power of the keys.[15] As Caracciolo says, "Sometimes a man is not contrite before confession and by confessing his sins is made contrite and they are forgiven him."[16] Similarly, Maillard expects penitents to have "some displeasure" over their sins when they come to confession.[17] The standards for such displeasure are not spelled out, but it is clear that it is not the thoroughgoing, heart-rending kind of contrition for which rigorist preachers such as Werden and Herolt will call. Here the penitent is encouraged to trust in the power of Christ mediated by the priest, rather than in his or her own efforts. Forgiveness is the sure consequence of the absolution.[18] This contributes to the overall tone of reassurance of the absolutionist penitential message.

The priority placed on confession and absolution leaves little room for explicit exhortation to contrition or satisfaction. Caracciolo's collection contains three sermons devoted to confession, but none devoted specifically to contrition or satisfaction in the present life.[19] Maillard's requirements for perfect penitence touch on contrition and satisfaction, but focus on confession: repair the damage done to others, stop sinning, fully recollect sins before going to confession, confess with discretion, confess completely.[20] Even so, these preachers do value these other parts of the penitential process. Maillard teaches that the sinner should have true contrition. He quotes Augustine, "Sorrow should be urged to the degree that the love of sin clings to the sinner."[21] Ultimately sorrow over sin will lead to rejoicing. According to Caracciolo, contrition is the appropriate response on the part of penitents to the recogni-

---

[15] The formation of attrition into contrition is a distinctively Franciscan doctrine and does not appear in the sermons of the Dominican absolutionist, Britannicus. To date I have not found it in the sermons of the Franciscans falling into the rigorist or moderate categories.

[16] Caracciolo, Sermon 28, chapter 1.

[17] Maillard, Sermon 2 on penitence.

[18] This is in line with Scotist theology and includes the expectation that true contrition is very rare.

[19] These are Sermons 27-29. Satisfaction in hell and purgatory have their own sermons.

[20] Maillard, Sermon 2 on penitence.

[21] Ibid., Sermon 19.

tion of their own sins. Caracciolo tries to elicit this response by
stressing the goodness and mercy of God and by evoking the pains
of hell.[22] Humbling oneself in light of the greatness of the power of
God is a good start on the penitential process, and tears are a sign
of good repentance.[23]

The acceptance of satisfaction is part of the humility of a proper
confession. But these preachers characteristically deliver their exhortations to satisfaction along with encouraging reminders of the
divine help available to lighten the load. Britannicus praises the
effort virtuous persons put into penitential disciplines. Sermon 22,
for example, is a funeral sermon for one who occupied himself with
works, vigils, abstinences, fastings, and infirmities; went to church
willingly and with alacrity; and gave alms. But most importantly,
this person knew that he was invited to heaven and tried to live his
life with this goal in mind.[24] Although Maillard acknowledges that
Christ set an example of penitence and suffering for Christians to
follow,[25] he still maintains that, despite the reluctance of many,
penitence is easy.

> If they fear the penalty, why then don't they fear that other one which
> is truly bitter and eternal? Why not rather embrace that which is an
> easy, brief, and light labor, even penitence assumed here? I say it is easy,
> then, on account of the gathering of grace which God is ready to infuse,
> which makes it light and sweet.[26]

Similarly, Caracciolo notes that some people are discouraged from
repenting because it includes doing good works, something they
imagine to be onerous or impossible. He does not want them to be
paralyzed by such thinking and asserts that people have free will to
do such works as well as divine aid to help them.[27]

The relatively light demands for contrition and satisfaction have
the effect of downplaying the responsibilities of the penitent and
raising the expectation of ecclesiastical or divine help, thus promoting confidence in sacramental forgiveness. These absolutionist
preachers teach that the Church, especially through its sacraments,

---

22   Caracciolo, Sermon 59; Sermon 13, introduction.
23   Ibid., Sermon 15; Sermon 1.
24   Gregorius Britannicus, O.P. *Sermones funebres vulgares litteraliterque pronunciandi, Itam
sermones nuptiales pulcherimi* (Venice: Petrus Bergomensus, 1505), Sermon 22.
25   Maillard, Sermon 1 on penitence.
26   Ibid., Sermon 3 on penitence.
27   Caracciolo, Sermon 1.

has much to offer to help the sinner. Absolutionist sermon collections were most popular in Italy and France, countries whose Catholicism would ultimately endure.

The second group of sermon collections are those whose penitential exhortations also center around confession, but which call more strenuously for contrition as well. They teach that sins are forgiven in the conjunction of the absolution given by the priest with the contrition brought to confession by the penitent. These are labeled as "moderate" because their penitential teachings offer spiritual help to sinners, while holding out substantial expectations for the penitent. This group is represented here by John Mirk's *Liber festivalis* (popular in England), Meffreth's *Ortulus reginae* (most popular in South Germany and Switzerland), and Gabriel Barletta's *Sermones quadragesimales et de sanctis* (interestingly, more popular in France than in the author's native Italy).

The major emphasis in the penitential preaching of the moderate preachers is confession. All three are strongly oriented toward ecclesiastical institutions and practices, and regularly remind their listeners of their obligation to make an annual confession. Mirk is seeking to promote orthodox Christian faith in the face of Lollardy; here the necessity of oral confession to a priest and respect for the clergy become litmus tests.[28] Both Meffreth and Barletta find it useful to reiterate arguments for the necessity of confession.[29] Barletta even teaches that those who have committed only venial sins are obligated to confess, "because the Church so orders it, and the sinner ought to confess himself to be a sinner *in potentia* not *in actu.*"[30]

Even so, these preachers present confession as a wonderful opportunity which their hearers should not miss. They enthuse about the spiritual benefits of confession, all of which are closely connected to the power of the priest to absolve sins. Mirk promotes confession as a cleansing of the soul. The only one of the preachers to write in the vernacular, Mirk generally does not talk about "absolution" or even about "confession." His word is "shrift," an all-

---

[28]   H. Leith Spencer, *English Preaching in the Late Middle Ages* (Oxford: Clarendon Press, 1993), p. 188.

[29]   Meffreth [pseud. (Petrus Meffordis of Leipzig?)], *Sermones de tempore et de sanctis, sive hortulus reginae, de tempore pars estiualis* (Basel: Nicolaus Kesler, [before 11 July, 1486]), Sermon 70; Barletta, Sermon 25.

[30]   Barletta, Sermon 25, part 1. This is an interesting application of Thomistic categories to practical religiosity.

encompassing word with sacramental force that incorporates confession, absolution, and the satisfaction imposed in confession,
which was itself seen as a sign of absolution.[31] "Shrift" brings one
back to baptism.[32] Phrases like "going to God and Holy Church"
pepper the collection and give the impression that Mirk himself
does not make much distinction between coming to Church and
coming to God. Mirk often exhorts sinners to "shrive themselves
clean," or refers to penitents who were "shriven clean" of their sins.
Barletta says that "the priest can open heaven to the penitent sinner." This comes through the power of the keys, which in turn provides the clergy with their dignity.[33] Like the absolutionist Caracciolo, Barletta teaches that "confession is good for a certain security
of mind from the knowledge of forgiveness received." By the power
of the keys, confession also diminishes the penalty for sin. It multi-
plies the penitent's intercessors and augments grace. Confession
washes the soul. Considering the blessings of confession, Barletta is
moved to exclaim, "O glorious confession! O holy thing!"[34]

To illustrate that reliable and helpful spiritual assistance is available within the Church to help sinners attain forgiveness of sins,
Meffreth compares the priest to a mid-wife. Women conceive children without sorrow or pain, but, with the exception of the Virgin
Mary, they give birth with pain. Similarly, a soul conceives sin in
delight. "But it is born when the sinner confesses and produces his
sin in the light to the priest, and this cannot be done except with
sorrow and the contrition of penitence." When it is time for a baby
to be born, the woman, regardless of her social station or desire for
privacy, needs to show herself to a midwife. Thus there is no one,
still pregnant with sin, who does not need another person to whom
to confess. But after confession, the penitent will feel joyfully liberated of the weight of sin.[35]

---

[31] According to the *Oxford English Dictionary*, by the fifteenth century, "shrift"
means: 1.) penance imposed after confession; 2.) absolution (which the imposition of the
penance implies); 3.) a confessor; 4.) to go to confession; 5.) confession to a priest, sacrament of penance (with Mirk's *Festial* cited as an example here). The verb "to shrive"
means to impose penance on a person, hence to administer absolution to, to hear the
confession of.
[32] John Mirk, O.S.A., *Mirk's Festial: A Collection of Homilies*, ed. Theodor Erbe, Early
English Text Society, Extra Series, 96 (London, 1905), Sermon 23.
[33] Barletta, Sermon 25, introduction.
[34] Ibid., Sermon 24, part 2.
[35] Meffreth, Sermon 94.

As this discussion from Meffreth suggests, contrition as a necessary corollary to confession is the strong secondary emphasis in the
penitential preaching of these moderate collections. Barletta urges
sorrowful consideration of sin and mental confession to God as vital
preparation for oral confession.[36] While Mirk occasionally tells
exempla in which sins are forgiven directly by God in contrition,
more typical of his penitential teachings are stories in which contrition is firmly tied with confession to a priest. For example, Mirk
recounts that a certain man lived a very wicked life, but spent the
last week of his life crying in contrition. He kept a priest nearby so
that he could confess any sins that came to mind. A monk from a
nearby monastery died the same day as this man, and reported
back to his abbot that the sorrowful neighbor had gone to joy without further pain. "Thus," Mirk concludes, "the great contrition
that this man had before he died quenched the great pain that was
ordained for him."[37] The sincerity of his contrition was demonstrated in his determination to confess his sins.

Contrition leads to confession for Barletta and Meffreth too. Indeed, Barletta's most powerful messages concerning contrition
come in the context of preaching on preparation for confession. For
example, in order to urge people to prepare for confession by considering sorrowfully the things they have done and making mental
confession to God, he tells an *exemplum* showing the salvific power
of contrition. A meretricious woman killed her mother and buried
her secretly. But one day at preaching, she was struck with compunction, dropped dead and went to heaven.[38] Meffreth, too, con-
tends that true contrition is contrition that sees the penitential process through to the end.[39] He is also quite willing to draw on the
contritionist tradition of Peter Lombard which sets high standards
for the contrite penitent. In a sermon on the publican praying in
the temple, growth in contrition on the part of the penitent leads to
forgiveness.[40]

---

[36]　Barletta, Sermon 24, part 1.
[37]　Mirk, Sermon 17.
[38]　Barletta, Sermon 24.
[39]　Meffreth, Sermon 6. The metaphor he uses here is that of fetal development.
Complete development yields a male child (true contrition); defective development
(hypocritical contrition) yields a female child.
[40]　Ibid., Sermon 70. Meffreth is particularly prone to citing contradictory authorities as they suit his rhetorical purposes. He quotes both Lombard and Duns Scotus on

These moderate preachers urge satisfaction on their listeners more vigorously than do the absolutionists. In keeping with their ecclesiastical orientation, Lent figures prominently in such exhortation. Barletta describes Lent as the time of lay penitence, the time when it is especially fitting for folk to confess and satisfy.[41] Mirk views Lent as a satisfactory tithe for the year; sinners fast to satisfy for the year's guilt. During Lent, penitents cultivate the contraries of the major sinful tendencies of humankind, the sins to which Eve succumbed and the temptations that Christ resisted in the desert: gluttony, vainglory, and covetousness. These sins are defeated by means of abstinence from meat and food, meekness in thinking lowly thoughts, and generosity in serving the poor.[42]

Even so, confessors ought not to impose heavy penances, according to Meffreth, for the more willingly the penance is done, the more it avails for internal purgation. Meffreth warns the confessor (the user of his sermon collection), "The man on whom you impose a heavy burden of penitence either rejects the penitence, or accepting it, since he is unable to bear it, stumbles and sins more."[43] Barletta also urges priests to act graciously toward penitents, comforting them rather than scolding bitterly, keeping in mind their own vulnerability to sin. Indeed, God permitted Peter to fall and deny Christ "so that in his guilt he might learn how he ought to have mercy on others."[44] Satisfactions imposed under the mercy of God should be taken up willingly.

These moderate authors, especially popular in France, Switzerland, and England, place their penitential accents first on confession as providing forgiveness and consolation, and secondly on the penitent's contrition as an important contribution to forgiveness. Strong proponents of the institutional Church and the spiritual help it offered, they still expect penitents to assume more responsibility than the absolutionists do. The sixteenth-century religious outcomes of the regions trained on such preaching would be prolonged and mixed.

---

the locus of forgiveness (contrition and absolution respectively). He is placed among the moderates because the net effect is to encourage sinners to come to confession while encouraging them to take significant penitential responsibilities.

[41]   Barletta, Sermon 25.
[42]   Mirk, Sermon 19.
[43]   Meffreth, Sermon 6.
[44]   Barletta, Sermon 24, part 3.

The final group of sermon collections, the rigorists, stress contrition and/or satisfaction over confession in their penitential preaching. The leading collection in this group is that of Johannes Herolt; his *Sermones discipuli* constituted *the* best selling sermon collection in northern Europe in the fifty or so years before the Reformation. Also included in this group are Johannes of Werden's *Sermones dormi secure*, widely popular in northern Europe; the anonymous *Sermones parati*, popular in Germany; and Michael of Hungary's *Sermones praedicabiles per totum annum sive sermones tredecim*, popular in the Netherlands and Northern Germany. In terms of numbers of printed editions, this group outweighs the other two groups combined; it was a very potent force in late medieval preaching. These sermons place the greatest stress on the penitential obligations of the individual and offer relatively little ecclesiastical or divine help to the penitent.

For all four of these rigorist preachers, there is no salvation without contrition. As Herolt says, "It is to be known that when someone is truly contrite and has the intention to confess and do satisfaction, then God in that true contrition forgives him all his sins."[45] Michael of Hungary affirms that forgiveness results from contrition and illustrates this with the example of three resurrections performed by Christ. He raised the daughter of the synagogue leader from death in her room; she is the sinner with hidden sin whom Christ resuscitates by contrition of heart and easily forgives. Christ raised the widow's son at the city gate; he represents the public sinner who is raised through contrition but with greater difficulty. Finally Christ raised Lazarus, the habitual sinner, with the greatest difficulty. He too is forgiven in contrition of heart, but has significant temporal penalties to pay. These are to be assigned by the clergy, here represented by the apostles.[46] For the rigorist preachers, true contrition, including the consequent intention to sin no more, constitutes the critical transaction between the sinner and God.

Not surprisingly, the preachers in this group have high standards for contrition. Werden teaches that contrition ought to be not only bitter and based on one's own sins, but also continual and all inclu-

---

[45] Herolt, Sermon 13.
[46] Michael of Hungary, O.F.M., *Sermones praedicabiles per totum annum, licet breves, s. Sermones tredecim* (Strasbourg: Georgius Husner, 1494), Sermon 13.

sive. He exhorts his listeners to see themselves as great sinners, just as David did. He sinned only once, yet said that he had sinned more than the sands of the sea and that his sins were more numerous than the multitude of the stars.[47] According to Herolt, the interior sorrow of contrition ought to be the sinner's greatest sorrow, exceeding the sorrow that would arise from the loss of all one's temporal goods and the loss of parents, spouse, or children.[48] The stakes are high; this is a rigorous calling for the laity.

In light of the importance of contrition, these preachers urge their audiences to take the initiative and exercise individual responsibility for their contrition. Hungary says that when the sinner remains in sin, it is as if Christ were sleeping and not keeping watch. He exhorts the sinner to wake Christ up "through contrition of heart and devout prayer, and thus to arise from sin."[49] Using horticultural images inspired by the parable of the workers in the vineyard, Werden asserts that the Christian needs to plough up his heart. As the iron of the plough cuts the ground, so contrition for sin ought to rend the heart. Making oneself into a fruitful vineyard is hard work, but penitence changes it from a thorn-producing desert to a vineyard that produces the good fruit of good works.[50] The anonymous author of the *Sermones parati* warns, "Nothing is more useful to the sinner than his conversion. For nothing will be as useful to him as penitence, even if he has as many masses sung for him as there are stars in the sky, and even the intercession of the blessed Virgin and all the saints do not avail like penitence."[51]

Yet, alongside exhortation to individual responsibility for contrition, several of the rigorist preachers also teach that contrition is the work of God. The *Sermones parati* teach that just as a fish cannot escape a trap without outside help, so no one can be liberated from

---

[47] Werden, *de tempore*, Sermon 17.

[48] Herolt gives four signs by which true contrition may be identified. First, the contrite person sorrows over sins committed and would rather submit to any penalty than knowingly mortally sin again. Second, he is ready to satisfy for his sins by means of loss or injury as well as by restoration of goods taken. Third, the contrite penitent forgives others for injuries done to him. And finally, the contrite are willing to resign from any office or business that cannot be conducted without mortal sin. Herolt, *de tempore*, Sermon 43.

[49] Hungary, Sermon 13.

[50] Werden, *de tempore*, Sermon 11.

[51] Paratus [pseud.], *Sermones parati de tempore et de sanctis.* (Speyer: Peter Drach, c. 1492), *de tempore*, Sermon 5.

servitude to sin without divine help.[52] Werden states explicitly, "true contrition is not infused except by God. A person can confess and weep but never have true contrition unless God infuses it. As it says in Jeremiah 31[:19], 'After you converted me, I repented.'"[53] Hungary's preaching regularly portrays God calling, even impelling, the sinner to contrition through divine inspiration.[54] Such teaching provides a note of reassurance along with the call to contrition.

Contrition and satisfaction had a close and often reciprocal theological relationship in the later Middle Ages, and so the rigorists give more stress to satisfaction than the other groups of sermon collections do, viewing it as the appropriate continuation of contrition.[55] They exhort penitents to exert themselves in satisfaction. "For," as Hungary says, "as you labored in guilt, so you ought to labor in penitence."[56] The call to satisfaction is especially strong in Herolt who tends to treat all aspects of the penitential process in terms of their satisfaction value. It is his fundamental conviction that sinners must satisfy for their sins through suffering. He encourages his listeners to take up works of satisfaction on their own initiative, and, especially in the case of grievous sins, to do more satisfaction than the priest assigns.[57]

Indeed for the rigorists, the most important role for the confessor is to assign appropriate satisfactions. Although Werden occasionally teaches that the priest's words of absolution grant forgiveness,[58] in general, these preachers follow the theological tradition of Peter Lombard in which the confessor announces the forgiveness of eter-

---

[52]   E.g., Paratus, *de sanctis*, Sermon 47.
[53]   Werden, *de tempore*, Sermon 12.
[54]   Hungary, Sermons 5, 7.
[55]   Up through the early Middle Ages, satisfaction had been the centerpiece of the sacrament of penance. One performed rigorous penitential activities to demonstrate one's sincerity and desire for reconciliation while expiating one's sins. By the twelfth century, increased stress was placed on contrition as satisfactions tended to become lighter. This came out of a recognition that satisfaction could not be demanded in cases of death bed confession. It also reflected the increased participation in the sacrament of penance by lay persons who could not undertake the rigorous satisfactions performed largely in monasteries in earlier centuries. Thus many preachers and theologians saw contrition as a type of satisfaction. The repentant sinner needed a solid combination of contrition and satisfaction.
[56]   Hungary, Sermon 12.
[57]   Herolt, *de tempore*, Sermon 85.
[58]   Johannes of Werden, O.F.M., *Sermones dormi secure de sanctis* (Nurnberg: Anton Koberger, 1494), Sermon 25.

nal guilt already granted by God in contrition. Herolt warns confessors not to absolve those who clearly intend to go on sinning; it is a grave sin to absolve someone who is probably not absolved before God.[59] The confessor does, however, have an important judging role when it comes to assigning the temporal penalties for sin. Herolt calls for a full confession, "because a greater penance is to be assigned if it was done twenty times than if it was done once or twice."[60] While teaching on the resurrection of Lazarus, Hungary claims, "The fact that Christ handed him bound to his disciples to be released was to show that although man is forgiven his guilt in contrition of heart, yet he remains bound to a penal debt, concerning which penalty, the power was given to Peter and his successors to absolve and remit in the debt of oral confession and works of satisfaction."[61]

As a group, the rigorists promote demanding satisfactions. Herolt relates an *exemplum* of two monks in a monastery. One was very nice and received sparing treatment from his confessor. The other was not so nice and routinely received punishments for his sins. After their deaths it became known that the nice brother was suffering in purgatory, completing his satisfactions, while the other was enjoying the peace of heaven.[62] Herolt thereby urges his hearers to satisfy and, in the process, teaches the laity to expect rigor from their confessors and to view it as salutary. Indeed, the rigorists often present satisfaction as a life-long process. The anonymous author of the *Sermones parati* commends the perseverance of Mary Magdalene's penitence. "Hence it is read of her that after the ascension of the Lord, she lived in the roughest hermitage and did penitence for thirty years."[63] He conveys the message that those who are truly contrite will not be satisfied to do some limited amount of satisfaction, but their whole lives will take on a penitential cast. The anonymous author particularly warns against wasted time, teaching that one of the greatest tortures in hell will be the knowledge that one wasted the time when one could have done satisfaction.[64]

---

[59] Ibid., Sermon 145.
[60] Ibid., Sermon 43.
[61] Hungary, Sermon 13.
[62] Herolt, *de tempore*, Sermon 63.
[63] Paratus, *de sanctis*, Sermon 47.
[64] Ibid., Sermon 2.

Along with their stress on contrition and satisfaction, the rigorists also teach the necessity of confession. But, they generally do not dwell on the benefits of confession as the moderate, and especially the absolutionist, preachers do. Their emphasis remains on the responsibilities of the penitent. Confessions ought to be premeditated, complete, self-accusing, tearful, and made in hope and humility.[65] Concern for contrition and satisfaction often colors their treatment of confession. Hungary teaches that Hezekiah did it right. He was close to death, but wept and cried to God, put on sackcloth and ashes and was granted another fifteen years. The weeping is contrition, the crying is confession, the sackcloth and ashes are works of satisfaction.[66] Herolt teaches that the confession itself has satisfaction value from the shame it arouses in the penitent, "for shame is a great part of satisfaction." Indeed one can satisfy, one can pay one's temporal debt, with the coin of shame by confessing the same sin to a number of priests.[67]

In sum, the penitential preaching of this group of sermon collections may be described as rigorous in terms of the expectations placed on penitents, especially in contrition and satisfaction. As Herolt avers, those who wear themselves out and do penitence are made heirs of the heavenly king.[68] Popular all across northern Europe, these collections had their largest base of popular support in Germany where soon the Protestants would be reacting against the responsibility of the penitent for successful forgiveness of sins.

Historical Ramifications

It seems clear that late medieval lay people understood and appropriated the penitential consensus of the preachers. There is plenty of evidence to suggest that many people in late medieval Europe were confessing their sins at least once a year. Multiple heuristic schemes were in circulation to help sinners recall and evaluate their

---

[65] E.g., Herolt, *de tempore*, Sermon 43; Werden, *de tempore*, Sermon 17.
[66] Hungary, Sermon 5.
[67] Herolt, *de tempore*, Sermon 14. The notion that shame is an important part of satisfaction is common in the sermon collections, but Herolt seems to take it especially to heart. Herolt makes it clear that the satisfaction value of confession comes from the shame of the penitent, not from the power of the keys held by the priest.
[68] Herolt, *de tempore*, Sermon 159.

sins. In addition, the mindset fostered by the penitential process bore fruit in a variety of religious activities from pilgrimages to endowed masses. When Martin Luther came on the scene vigorously denouncing penitential practices and responsibilities, people all across Europe understood what he was reacting against. But, did the differences in emphasis among the sermon collections come across to the laity in the various regions of Europe? The responses of both preachers and lay people in the early years of the Reformation, whether clamoring for or denouncing evangelical change, suggest that they did.

The pulpit was a key mode of dissemination for the new teaching that salvation came by grace through faith, rather than via the combination of human effort and divine grace that characterized the late medieval penitential process. Reformers placed a great deal of emphasis on preaching because they were convinced that hearing the word of God was vital to proper theological understanding as well as to the evocation of saving faith. Because many early Protestant clergy had been preachers prior to their move away from the Catholic church, they were particularly well-placed to explain the new religious understandings to the laity in terms with which the laity were already familiar. They and their hearers shared similar conversions from old assumptions to new convictions. Where clergy remained Catholic, they were able to reassert traditional teachings and practices, convincing their audiences that the new ideas were novel and heretical, a danger to the sacrament which provided assurance of salvation.

Printing was another vital vehicle for the transmission of Protestant ideas. Not only did Protestants print in far greater numbers than their Catholic counterparts, but they also dominated the market in vernacular religious writings, gaining an early and important audience for their teachings. Printing patterns of sermons were influential here as well. In the decades prior to the Reformation, Italy had tended to rely on its own preachers' model sermons, only occasionally reprinting a northern collection. This trend continued into the Reformation period. Lutheran and northern evangelical ideas entered Italy slowly and in a limited way. Italy continued to prefer its own sources of inspiration. The movement known as Italian Evangelism had largely indigenous roots, as Roberto Rusconi has argued.[69] Some strongly Protestant-minded Italians chose to leave Italy and set up expatriate religious communities,[70] confirming the power of the established religious ethos. And, as in the late medieval period when the Italian preacher Caracciolo was also popular in the north, Italian ideas continued to be exported and find followers north of the Alps. Indeed, Italy led the effort to define and consolidate Catholicism in the sixteenth century.

There is a striking geographical correspondence between the printing locations of the different groups of late medieval model sermon collections and sixteenth-century religious divisions. The places in which rigorist preaching was most popular tended to adopt the Reformation. Regions where absolutionist preaching was more prominent tended to remain Catholic. This is not simple coincidence. Reflecting and reinforcing local religious sensibilities, the way in which penitence was taught in a particular region provided the basic religious assumptions by which the new ideas were understood and evaluated. Although the deeply-held religious convictions and private devotional practices of individuals are often beyond the historian's reach, we know what confessional norms were established and publicly promoted in various regions.[71] At the very least, enough key individuals, quite often laypeople, were convinced of the value of a particular religious option to work for its establishment. While religious motives were almost never the only ones at work, they were conspicuous, vigorously vocalized, and of notable consequence. The way in which penitence was taught in a particular region shaped and prepared the way many would respond to Protestant ideas.

In Germany, approximately 85% of the sermon collections printed were rigorist in penitential emphasis. Although other types of penitential teaching were also available, Germans were quite likely to have been preached a rigorist message of personal respon-

---

[69] Roberto Rusconi, *Predicazione e vita religiosa nella società italiana* (Turin: Loescher Editore), 1981, p. 205.

[70] Cameron cites such communities in Geneva, Zürich, and the south-eastern corners of Switzerland near Milan. Euan Cameron, *The European Reformation* (Oxford: Clarendon Press), 1991.

[71] There is a good deal of current interest in exploring the diversity of religious belief and practice in communities that were officially Catholic, Lutheran, or Reformed. Several papers given at the Sixteenth Century Studies Conference in St. Louis in October, 1999 addressed this issue. Yet even where diversity flourished, the official religion set important standards of public discourse and practice.

sibility for the forgiveness of sins, with special attention given to
contrition and satisfaction. Herolt's *Sermones discipuli*, which originated in Germany and constituted the dominant voice informing
northern European preaching, was the epitome of rigor in tone,
stressing the need for sinners to assume penitential responsibility
and suffer for their sins.

This was the preaching on which Luther was raised and the understanding of the penitential process which he rejected. He found
the penitential process torturing rather than consoling, leaving him
uncertain about the depth and reliability of his repentance and
hence unsure of his forgiveness. Ultimately, Luther comes to repu-
diate anything that smacks of satisfaction in a broad sense, that is,
anything that requires a sinner to contribute to his own justification. Luther takes particular aim at the call to deep contrition, the
critical element for forgiveness in rigorist preaching. Luther claims
that it is impossible to know more than a small fraction of one's
sins, let alone to have deep contrition for each one. And because
the sinner can't know his sins or the quality of his contrition, neither can his confessor who is to assign appropriate works of satisfaction. Forgiveness does not depend on the inherently uncertain
quality or completeness of the penitent's contrition, according to
Luther; it is rather a gracious gift of God to be received in faith.
Luther writes, "forgiveness of guilt, the heavenly indulgence, is
granted to no one on account of the worthiness of his contrition
over his sins, nor on account of his works of satisfaction, but only
on account of his faith in the promise of God."[72] It makes sense
that such a strong reaction should come from one reared on
preaching that was most stringent on this point.

Because Luther is adamant that forgiveness is to be declared, not
earned, he brings absolution to the forefront of his teaching on
penitence. While this emphasis is parallel to that of the absolutionist
preachers, Luther's theology at this point is actually closer to that
of the rigorists Herolt, Hungary, and the anonymous author of the
Sermones parati who taught that the confessor simply announces to
the penitent sinner that God has already forgiven her. Luther
teaches that the absolution is a declaration of God's promise of

---

[72] Martin Luther, *Luther's Works*, ed. Jaroslav Pelikan et al., 55 Vols. (Saint Louis:
Concordia Publishing House and Philadelphia: Muhlenberg Press and Fortress Press,
1955-1986), "The Sacrament of Penance," vol. 35, p. 12.

forgiveness. Confidence in forgiveness arises from the absolution coming directly from Christ, and thus being fully trustworthy. Christ's sacrifice provides an objective forgiveness that becomes subjectively certain when personally appropriated in faith. The faith to make such an appropriation is itself a gift of God.

Some European Christians, concentrated in the areas where rigorist preaching had dominated, found the freedom from satisfaction, contrition, and full confession taught by Luther joyfully liberating. They were able to accept the absolution as a free declaration of forgiveness on a personal level, satisfying a longing for certainty in the mercy of God. As the Lutheran Augsburg Confession would affirm, this new teaching "reveals a certain and firm consolation of consciences, for before, the whole strength of the absolution was the oppressive doctrine of works, since the learned ones and the monks taught nothing about faith and free remission."[73] A sense of relief, and of retrospective anger at the perceived oppression of late medieval penitential obligations, runs through much early Protestant literature. Many in Germany and the Netherlands, raised on rigorist preaching, proved receptive to Protestant ideas, and embraced religious change.

However, for other Christians whose previous penitential teaching had stressed the mercy of God and the effectiveness of the absolution given by the priest, the new ideas held less appeal. This situation is clearest in Italy. Nearly 80% of the collections printed in Italy were absolutionist in tone, with a few moderate ones, and just a single edition of Herolt. Thus confession, including an emphasis on the absolving power of the priest, was the primary emphasis in Italian penitential preaching. Italy's lack of interest in Herolt and other extremely popular northern sermon collections may well stem from the incompatibility of their theological approach with that prominent in Italy.

Although there were small groups of individuals receptive to evangelical ideas in sixteenth-century Italy, Italy as a whole remained quite impervious to Reformation changes. Luther's message did not have the liberating force that it had in many northern regions, as it addressed issues raised more acutely by preachers popular in the North. To those raised on absolutionist preaching, Lu-

---

[73] Augsburg Confession XI, 2; as cited in Ernst Kinder, "Beichte und Absolution nach den lutherischen Bekenntnisschriften" in *Theologische Literaturzeitung* 9 (1952): 545.

ther's critique of the sacrament of penance as individually burden-
some seemed misplaced. For instance, the Italian Dominican
Cajetan, one of Luther's most vociferous Catholic critics, rejects
Luther's claim that deep contrition for each mortal sin is impossible. He avers, "The argument is wrong in stating that contrition is
never adequate, as we know from the many people who come to
confession with contrition which–although to themselves uncertain–is still genuine and adequate."[74] In the tradition of the
absolutionist preachers, Cajetan urges trust in the sacramental process over individual effort. Indeed he saw the Lutheran call for faith
in personal forgiveness as an additional requirement, making forgiveness, not more certain, but more difficult to obtain. "One must
first grasp that a novel idea has been introduced," he writes,
"namely requiring this kind of faith to such an extent that it is more
necessary than contrition." [75] While the faith conveyed in baptism
enables one to believe that "absolution rightly given by the
Church's minister is efficacious in granting grace to a worthy recipient," one cannot know for certain whether or not one is a worthy
recipient.[76] Thus Cajetan feels that Luther is adding a new and impossible requirement, while Luther sees himself as ridding the
church of impossible requirements and unnecessary and intolerable
uncertainty. Confidence in the trustworthy and divine nature of the
absolution was already familiar in Italy. The removal of the necessary mediation of the priest, who was central to their understanding
of forgiveness, was very threatening. Clerical dignity, based on sacramental authority, would endure. Italy's absolutionist strain of
popular preaching on penitence left it resistant to the Lutheran calls
for penitential change.

France presents a particularly interesting case. Preachers repre-
senting the whole spectrum of penitential emphases were popular
here. Rigorists dominate the field (65% of editions printed), but not
as decisively as they do in Germany. France veered strongly toward
Protestantism before ending up firmly in the Catholic camp. In the
mixture of preparations people received for evaluating the new

---

[74]   Thomas de Vio, Cardinal Cajetan, *Cajetan Responds: A Reader in Reformation Controversy*, trans. and ed. Jared Wicks, S. J. (Washington D.C.: The Catholic University of
America Press, 1978), p. 54.
[75]   Cajetan, *Cajetan Responds*, p. 49.
[76]   Ibid., pp. 51-52.

ideas, we may perhaps see the seeds of religious conflict. The center of Protestant strength was in the south. It had been a center for heresy in the thirteenth century and its religious distinctiveness continues into the present. Here, at Lyons, a great number of rigorist sermons were printed. Here too the sermons of the moderate preacher Barletta found a more congenial reception than in his native Italy. Maillard, the most popular local author in France, strongly absolutionist in tone, was most often printed at Paris, center of theological orthodoxy and the monarchy. The fact that the vigorous printing of rigorist collections did not finally lead to Protestantism is a salutary reminder of the importance of additional factors, such as political considerations. Yet the move toward Protestantism in the first generation of the Reformation, especially in southern France, confirms the significance of such preaching in shaping lay convictions.

What happened in areas where moderate preaching dominated? Here we note a range of outcomes. For Switzerland and southern Germany, where the collection of Meffreth was particularly popular, and sermon collections from across the penitential spectrum were printed, there is a mixture of religious allegiances in the mid-sixteenth century. The Calvinist stronghold of Geneva is quite close to Lyons, where many rigorist collections were printed.

In England Mirk's *Festial* was very popular. Several rigorist collections were also printed here which would have reinforced the contritionist side of Mirk's teaching. Although the Elizabethan Settlement was Protestant, a number of historians have testified to the continuing mixture of religious commitments in England well into the Reformation. Even under Elizabeth, there were those who longed to make the Church of England a middle way between Protestantism and Catholicism.[77] The moderate preachers' orientation toward the institutional Church seems to be reflected in the continuing institutional importance of the Church of England.

****

---

[77] Much of the contemporary Anglican self-conciousness as a *via media*, however, stems from the Oxford Movement and the writings of Newman. I thank Kenneth Parker for his insights into this question.

On the level of regional contexts, a general pattern, simple but
clear, has emerged. The different emphases of the penitential
preaching people were likely to have heard in the years preceding
the Reformation broadly corresponds with their receptivity to evangelical ideas. Such correlation highlights the formative importance
of preaching and its theological messages in shaping religious
mindsets. While it does not answer the question of why a particular
penitential emphasis was dominant in a given geographical region,
it is a clear indication that regional characters in the penitential
teaching for the laity are indeed identifiable and have visible historical ramifications. Arguing for the important contribution of late
medieval penitential preaching to the varied success of the Reformation in the sixteenth century does not discount the contributions
of political, economic, or social motivations. Local studies are
needed to elucidate the interaction of specific factors contributing
to the establishment of the Reformation in particular places. It
does, however, recognize the pastoral efforts of the late medieval
Church and argues for their widespread effectiveness. These findings credit the laity of both the fifteenth and sixteenth centuries
with listening to sermons and allowing their religious understandings to be shaped in ways that made sense to them and make sense
to historians seeking to understand their choices. Preaching helped
to mold and reinforce the convictions against which Reformation
ideas were heard and subsequently accepted or rejected. Preaching
matters.[78]

Bibliography

Barletta, Gabriel, O.P., *Sermones (quadragesimales et de sanctis)* (Lyons:
    Etienne Gueynard, 1507 [BN Rés. D. 24997]).
Bataillon, Louis J., "Approaches to the Study of Medieval Sermons,"
    Leeds Studies in English 11 (1980), 19-35.
Bozzolo, Carla, Dominique Coq, and Ezio Ornato, "La production du
    livre en quelques pays d'Europe occidentale aux XIVe et XVe siècles,"
    Scrittura e civiltà (1984), 129-76.

---

[78] For further discussion of these issues, see my *Penitence, Preaching and the Coming of
the Reformation* (Aldershot: Ashgate, forthcoming).

Britannicus, Gregorius, O.P., *Sermones funebres vulgares litteraliterque pronun-ciandi, Itam sermones nuptiales pulcherimi* (Venice: Petrus Bergomensus, 1505 [BLC D-4426.de.10]).

Caracciolo, Roberto, O.F.M., *Quadragesimale de poenitentia* (Venice: Francis-cus de Hailbron, 1472 [GW 6062]). Used in conjunction with *Quadra-gesimale de poenitentia* (Venice: Bartolomeo de Cremona, 1472 [GW 6064]).

Chrisman, Miriam Usher, *Lay Culture, Learned Culture: Books and Social Change in Strasbourg, 1480-1599* (New Haven and London: Yale Univer-sity Press, 1982).

d'Avray, David L., *The Preaching of the Friars: Sermons Diffused from Paris before 1300* (Oxford: Clarendon Press, 1985).

Edwards, Mark U., Jr., *Printing, Propaganda, and Martin Luther* (Berkeley: University of California Press, 1994).

Herolt, Johannes, O.P., *Sermones discipuli de tempore et de sanctis unacum promptuario exemplorum* (Strasbourg [Martin Flach], 1492 [Hain 8503]). Used in conjunction with *Sermones discipuli de tempore et de sanctis unacum promptuario exemplorum* (Reutlingen: Michel Greyff, ca. 1479-82 [Hain 8476]).

Hirsch, Rudolf, *The Printed Word: Its Impact and Diffusion* (London: Variorum Reprints, 1978).

— *Printing, Selling and Reading, 1450-1550,* second printing (Wiesbaden: Otto Harrassowitz, 1974).

Hungary, Michael of, O.F.M., *Sermones praedicabiles per totum annum, licet breves, s. Sermones tredecim* (Strasbourg: Georgius Husner, 1494 [Hain 9049]).

Kienzle, Beverly Mayne, *Le Sermon: Typologie des Sources du Moyen Age* (Turn-hout, Belgium: Brepols, 2000).

Lualdi, Katharine Jackson and Anne T. Thayer, eds., *Penitence in the Age of Reformations*, St. Andrews Studies in Reformation History (Aldershot: Ashgate, forthcoming in 2000).

Maillard, Olivier, O.F.M., *Sermones dominicales* (Paris: Jean Petit, 1511 [STC 3833.aaa.14]).

Meffreth [pseud. (Petrus Meffordis of Leipzig?)], *Sermones de tempore et de sanctis, sive hortulus reginae, de tempore pars estiualis* (Basel: Nicolaus Kesler [before 11 July, 1486] [Hain 11000; Goff M-446]).

Mirk, John, O.S.A., *Liber Festiualis, Quattor Sermones* (Rouen: James Revy-nell, 1495 [British Museum I.A. 43992]). Used in conjunction with *Mirk's Festial: A Collection of Homilies*, ed. Theodor Erbe, Early English Text Society, Extra Series, 96 (London, 1905).

Paratus [pseud.], *Sermones parati de tempore et de sanctis* (Speyer: Peter Drach, ca. 1492 [Hain 12399]).

Tentler, Thomas N., *Sin and Confession on the Eve of the Reformation* (Princeton: Princeton University Press, 1977).

Thayer, Anne T., *Penitence, Preaching and the Coming of the Reformation* (Aldershot: Ashgate, forthcoming).

Werden, Johannes of, O.F.M., *Sermones dormi secure de tempore* (Nurnberg: Anton Koberger, 1498 [Hain 15977]); *Sermones dormi secure de sanctis* (Nuremberg: Anton Koberger, 1494 [Hain 15979]).

INDEX